The Formation of a Colonial Society

Johns Hopkins Studies in Atlantic History and Culture
Richard Price and Franklin W. Knight, General Editors

The Formation of a Colonial Society
Belize, from Conquest to Crown Colony

O. Nigel Bolland

The Johns Hopkins University Press • Baltimore and London

This book has been brought to publication with the generous assistance of the Andrew W. Mellon Foundation.

Copyright © 1977 by The Johns Hopkins University Press

All rights reserved. No part of this book may be reproduced or transmitted in any form or by any means, electronic or mechanical, including photocopying, recording, xerography, or any information storage and retrieval system, without permission in writing from the publisher.

Manufactured in the United States of America

The Johns Hopkins University Press, Baltimore, Maryland 21218
The Johns Hopkins Press Ltd., London

Library of Congress Catalog Card Number 76-47377

Library of Congress Cataloging in Publication Data

Bolland, O Nigel.
    The formation of a colonial society.

    (Johns Hopkins studies in Atlantic history and culture)
    Bibliography: p. 225
    Includes index.
    1. Belize—Economic conditions. 2. Belize—Social conditions. 3. Belize—History. I. Title.
II. Series.
HC142.B65   309.1′7282   76-47377
ISBN 0-8018-1887-7

Contents

Preface	x
Acknowledgments	xiii

Chapter 1.
Belize: A Brief Guide to an Emerging Nation

Topography and Climate	1
Growth of Population	2
Economic Development	6
Political Development	9

Chapter 2.
Early European Incursions upon the Maya

The Origins of the Maya	14
Ancient Maya Settlements in the Belize River Valley	15
Spanish Expeditions and Their Effects upon the Maya	17
British Woodcutters Encounter the Maya	20
Conclusion	23

Chapter 3.
The Establishment of the British Settlement in the Bay of Honduras in the Eighteenth Century

The Settlement's Raison d'Être: The Logwood and Mahogany Trades	25
The Establishment of the Settler Society	28
Conflicts among the Settlers	32
The Problem of the Location of Executive Authority	36
The Social Structure of the Settlement in the Late Eighteenth Century	40

Chapter 4.
The Institution of Slavery

The Establishment of Slavery	49
The Organization and Occupations of Slavery	53
Slavery and the Law	62

Chapter 5.
The Slaves as Objects and as Subjects
The Conditions and Treatment of Slaves	68
Social Relations between Masters and Slaves	72

Chapter 6.
The Laborers, Free and Enslaved, in the Early Nineteenth Century
The Freedmen during Slavery	86
The Culture of the Slaves and Freedmen	95

Chapter 7.
Apprenticeship and Emancipation
The Laborers during the Apprenticeship Period	106
Inhibitions on the Development of a Peasantry after Emancipation	118

Chapter 8.
Post-Emancipation Society—1
The Return of the Maya to Western Belize	125
Caribs and Creoles	132

Chapter 9.
Post-Emancipation Society—2
Agriculture	136
Immigration	142
Labor Conditions in the Colony	146

Chapter 10.
The Political Economy: The Dominance of the Settlers, 1765–1830
The Problem of the Colonial Settlers	156
The Settler Oligarchy	157

Chapter 11.
The Political Economy: The Decline of the Settlers, 1830–1871
The Dependent Economy	174
Changes in the Political-Administrative Apparatus	178
The Consolidation of Metropolitan Ownership	182
The Creation of a Crown Colony	188

Chapter 12.
Conclusions 194

Appendixes
A. Laws and Customs Relating to Slavery	198
B. Family of Mary France belonging to Alexander France, 1834	201
C. Family of Quashie Cunningham belonging to Sarah Keefe, 1834	202
D. Family of Jane and Sam Burn belonging to William D. Burn, 1834	203
E. Family of Nancy Gambqunil belonging to Ann Smith, 1834	204

Contents

F. Family of Mary Anne and Murphy Anderson belonging to Richard
   John and Anne Anderson, 1834   205
G. Family of Sammy Goff belonging to Estate of Sarah Goff (d.), 1834   205
Notes   206
Bibliography   225
Index   235

List of Tables

1.1	Total Population of Belize, 1790–1970	3
1.2	Population of Belize City and the Six Next Largest Towns, 1881–1970	6
1.3	Distribution of Freehold Land, by Size of Holdings, 1971	7
3.1	Population of the Bay Settlement, by Legal Status and Sex, 1790	42
3.2	Population of the Bay Settlement, by Property, Occupation, and Color, 1790	47
4.1	Slave Population of the Bay Settlement, 1745–1835	51
4.2	Slave Population of the Bay Settlement, by Age, 1816–23	52
6.1	Free Colored and Black Population of the Bay Settlement, 1790–1835	87
6.2	Manumissions in the Bay Settlement, by Sex, 1808–30	88
6.3	Baptisms of Whites, Free Colored, Free Blacks, and Slaves by the Anglican Chaplain in Belize, 1812–29	104
7.1	Slave Population of Belize, by Age and Sex, 1834	107
7.2	Occupations of the Slave Population of Belize, by Age and Sex, 1834	108
9.1	Exports of Sugar from Belize, in Pounds, 1862–68	140
10.1	Exports of Mahogany and Logwood from Belize, 1798–1830	159
10.2	Value of Exports from the United Kingdom to Belize, 1806, 1823, 1829	166
11.1	Exports of Mahogany and Logwood from Belize, 1832–68	175
11.2	Value of the Produce of Belize Exported in 1868	176
11.3	Value of Imports and Exports from Belize, 1857–70	177

Abbreviations

AB Archives of Belize, Belmopan
CO Colonial Office Records, Public Records Office, London
GRB General Registry, Belize City

Preface

It is apparent from even a cursory examination of the problems of development facing the emerging nation of Belize that these problems have their roots in a history of underdevelopment. The history of the entire Caribbean area is a history of extended colonial domination and exploitation. Caribbean colonial territories took the form of vast agrarian factories, producing raw materials such as sugar, cotton, coffee, tobacco, and timber for export to the metropolitan markets. They were in turn dependent upon these metropolises for the importing of all processed and manufactured goods, and frequently for most foodstuffs, in metropolis-controlled shipping. The metropolis-satellite relationship was epitomized by the plantations, which were developed solely to produce commodities for export to the European markets. As Sydney Mintz has expressed it: "The establishment of the plantation system meant a rooted overseas capitalism based on conquest, slavery and coercion, investment and entrepreneurship.... The growth of slave-based economies in the New World was an integral part of the rise of European commerce and industry."[1]

These Caribbean colonial territories were typically stratified into two hostile camps, perpetually confronting each other: the dominant elite, chiefly white, which owned or managed the vast estates and controlled the import-export trade, and a dominated, dispossessed mass, initially composed chiefly of African slaves, whose free descendants constituted one of the first great agrarian proletariats.

The Caribbean's history of colonial domination and dependence has been a factor that has deeply affected the area's social, economic, political, cultural, and even psychological existence. Plantation economies and slavery have long been major characteristics of the Caribbean. These factors and the "black diaspora" that was their complement, provide those common features that enable us to consider the Caribbean as a socio-cultural area.[2] However, although parallel historical factors have produced similarities in Caribbean societies, the colonial experiences of these societies include many variations, and the result is a highly heterogeneous area.

Preface

The associated problems of dependence, decolonization, and development are too frequently discussed in terms of generalizations that amount to little more than platitudes. While their development is clearly important, generalizations should not be allowed to obscure significant differences that exist in the socio-historical experience of particular societies. Moreover, the general problems exist only in particular situations, and it is only through the detailed study of socio-historical particularities that such generalizations may be proposed, examined, and evaluated. It is to such a study of one part of the Caribbean area that this work is oriented.

Previous studies of Belize have not been focused on the same subject as the present one. First, there are some studies that are popular and unacademic in nature, lacking accuracy and scholarly qualities.[3] Other studies consist of more scholarly but very general historical surveys that examine, in a necessarily superficial manner, all aspects of Belizean history from the ancient Maya to the present.[4] Thirdly, there are those studies that have examined particular historical periods, such as the late nineteenth century, or topics, such as diplomatic history, in a more specialized and detailed manner, but these scarcely overlap the subject of the present study.[5] Finally, there are those scholarly examinations of socio-economic aspects of Belize that have a more narrow anthropological or economic focus and an emphasis on the recent past.[6]

The purpose of the present study is to provide a detailed examination of the socio-economic development of Belize in that formative period from its settlement to the establishment of crown colony rule in 1871. In so doing it examines a number of topics that are of interest from the point of view of comparisons with other Caribbean societies. For example, throughout the Caribbean, slavery has been closely associated with the plantation production of sugar (and, elsewhere in the New World, with other plantation crops such as cotton). In Belize, however, the organization of slavery was oriented toward the extraction of timber—first logwood and then mahogany. A question therefore arises concerning the differences in the organization, conditions, and treatment of slaves resulting from their different economic function.

Primarily, however, this study seeks to examine some of the relations between the political economy and the social structure of Belize. The political economy of a dependent colonial society changes in response to the demands of the dominant metropolitan political economy. A change in demands in the metropolitan markets or a change in Colonial Office policy resulting from fresh considerations of international relations is capable of producing dramatic changes in the political economy of the colony. In turn, these changes in the colonial political economy affect the relations of the various social formations and change the colony's social structure. For example, when "An Act for the Abolition of Slavery throughout the British Colonies" was passed by the British Parliament in 1833, it resulted in changed social relations within Belizean society. Emancipation occurred not through the dialectical development of Belizean society, which is not an autonomous social reality, but as a result of an imperial act.

The political economy of a colonial society is not an autonomous reality, but is subject to the fluctuating demands and interests of the metropolis. This is not to say, however, as some simplistic conceptions of imperialism imply, that the colonial settlers are mere instruments of metropolitan interests. On the contrary, the interests of the settlers are frequently antagonistic to those of their mother country, such contradictions often being resolved only after prolonged political and economic, and sometimes even military, struggle. There are therefore three major forces or moments to be considered in an examination of the ways in which colonial political economies evolve and operate in relation to colonial social structures: the forces of the metropolis, the colonial settlers, and the colonized people. One of the major goals of this study is to examine the interaction of these forces, because the evaluation of their outcome is crucial for reaching an understanding of the contemporary problems of decolonization and development that face Belize. Moreover, a clear comprehension of the socio-historical particularities of the colonial experience of Belize is required for that country to be able to attain true decolonization and development.

The first chapter, which outlines the physical setting, the demographic history, and the evolution of contemporary problems of economics and political development, is followed by a brief examination of early Maya settlements and European incursions upon the Maya. Chapter 3 studies the nature of the British settlement established in the Bay of Honduras during the late-seventeenth and eighteenth centuries. Chapters 4 and 5 examine the nature of slavery in Belize, both as an institution and as a pattern of social relations between masters and slaves. Chapters 6 and 7 evaluate the situation of the freedmen during slavery, the culture of the Afro-Belizeans, and the nature of the laborers' experience during the "apprenticeship" period. Particular attention is paid to the reasons for the lack of development of a peasantry after emancipation in 1838. Chapters 8 and 9 examine various aspects of post-emancipation society, particularly the changing composition and growth of the population resulting from immigration, the attempts to develop agriculture, and the conditions of labor in the colony. Finally, chapters 10 and 11 focus on the question of the relation between changes in the colonial political economy and the developing social structure of Belize, particular attention being paid to the rise and fall of the settler oligarchy prior to the establishment of the Crown Colony in 1871.

Acknowledgments

The production of ideas is necessarily a social enterprise, and those people who have influenced my thinking are too numerous to mention individually. A particular acknowledgment must be made to all those who, as colleagues, students, and friends at the University of the West Indies between 1968 and 1972, helped me toward an understanding of West Indian affairs. I owe a special debt of gratitude to Ivar Oxaal who, ten years ago, introduced me to the works of C. L. R. James and Eric Williams, M. G. Smith, and Lloyd Braithwaite, and who, from 1971 to 1975, advised and encouraged the production of my doctoral thesis at the University of Hull. Special mention must also be made of three people who have influenced my theoretical perspectives and my approach to scholarly work: Peter Worsley, Ken Post, and Arnold Sio. Above all, I am indebted to Assad Shoman for informing me in 1963 of the existence of the emerging nation of Belize and for demonstrating, through his social praxis, how people can make their own history, even in circumstances not of their choice. Many of the ideas expressed in this book had their origin in discussions with him, and its content would be unimaginably different without his contribution. Nevertheless, I must accept responsibility for any distortions or errors that remain. To all these people, some of whom may be quite unhappy to be associated in any way with this work, I nonetheless offer my sincere thanks.

The research on which this book is based was begun in 1970 when I was a Research Fellow at the Institute of Social and Economic Research of the University of the West Indies in Jamaica. Alister McIntyre, then the director of the Institute, encouraged my work by enabling me to study in London and Belize from 1971 to 1972. For the Institute's support and for the assistance of the officials of the Public Record Office, the British Museum, and the Royal Commonwealth Society Library in London, and of the General Registry, Archives and National Collection in Belize City, I extend my gratitude. I am also grateful to the Research Council of Colgate University for financing my further research in London in the summers of 1973 and 1974 and for supporting the final preparation of the manuscript.

Acknowledgments

Portions of this book have appeared in the *Journal of Caribbean History* 6 (May 1973); in the *Journal of Belizean Affairs* 3 (June 1974); in *Anthropology and History in Yucatán,* edited by Grant D. Jones (Austin: University of Texas Press, 1976; copyright © 1976 by the University of Texas Press); and in *Land in Belize, 1765–1871: The Origins of Land Tenure, Use, and Distribution in a Dependent Economy,* by O. Nigel Bolland and Assad Shoman (Kingston: Institute of Social and Economic Research, University of the West Indies, 1975). The author gratefully acknowledges the permission of the publishers and journals to adapt materials from these publications for use herein.

I wish to extend a special word of thanks to Mrs. Doris Vaughn, who typed my manuscript with such great skill and patience. For the professional production of the map, Dean Wise receives my gratitude.

Above all, I thank my family—Ellie, Kate, and Monica—for the support that only love can provide.

O.N.B.

The Formation of a Colonial Society

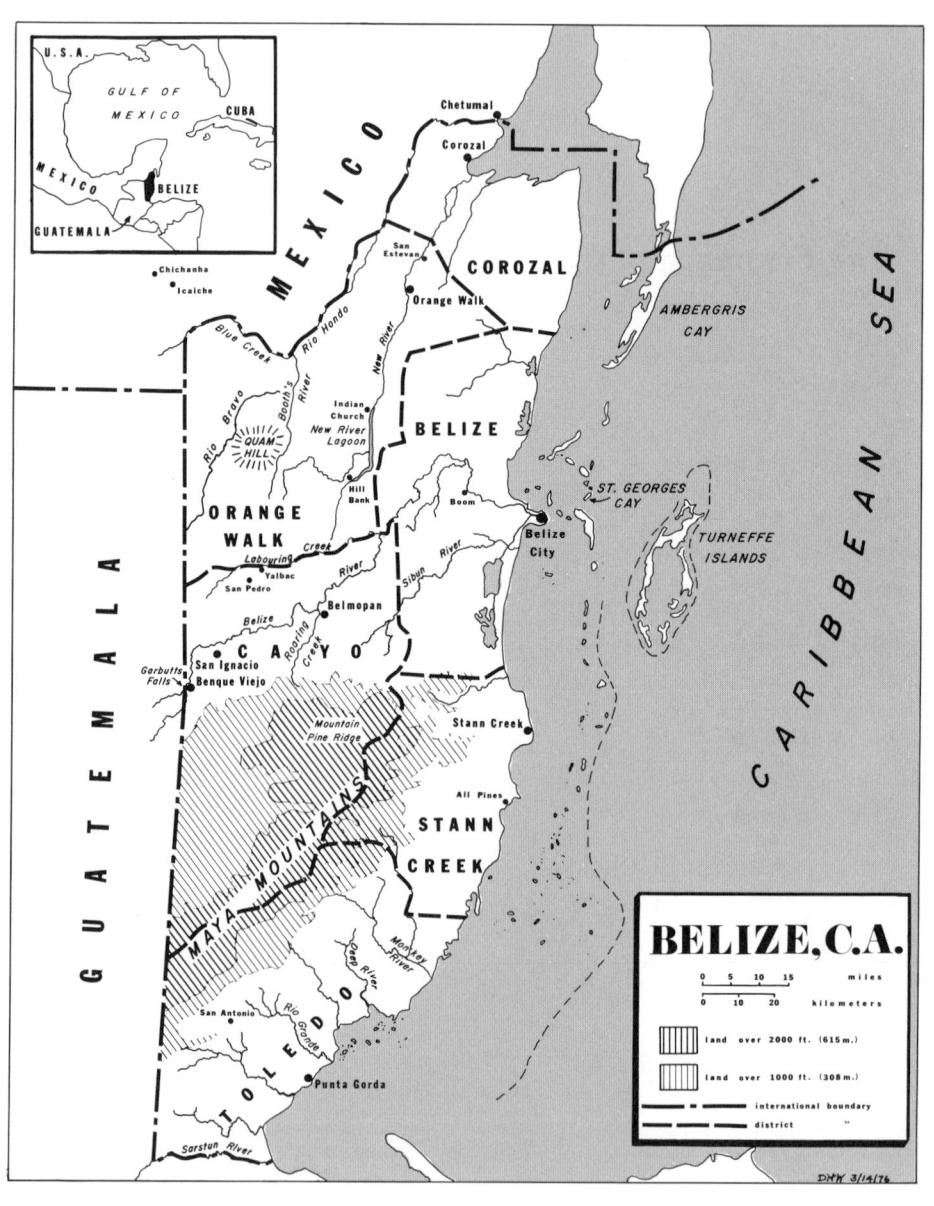

1
Belize: A Brief Guide to an Emerging Nation

TOPOGRAPHY AND CLIMATE

The emerging nation of Belize is situated on the eastern coast of Central America, bordering Mexico to the north and Guatemala to the west and south, and facing the Caribbean Sea to the east. About 174 miles long and 70 miles broad at its widest point, Belize is a coastal strip containing about 8,866 square miles of land, including 266 square miles of island.

The long coastline of Belize is mostly swampy, with thick mangroves, and is punctuated by frequent rivers, the most significant of which are the Belize, New, and Sibun rivers, and the Rio Hondo, which forms the northern boundary. Beyond the low and swampy coastal belt, the land in the north, drained by these rivers and by numerous creeks and lagoons, is chiefly flat and dry, while in the southwest the Maya Mountains rise to over three thousand feet. A major feature of the topography of Belize is the barrier reef, a succession of coral atolls and small islands called cays, that extends almost the entire length of the country and is the second largest reef in the world.

The climate of Belize is tropical, temperatures on the coast ranging from an absolute minimum of 10 degrees Centigrade (50° F) to a maximum of 35 degrees Centigrade (96° F), with a mean monthly average of 24 degrees Centigrade (75° F) in January and 27 degrees Centigrade (81° F) in July. In the interior the temperature sometimes exceeds 38 degrees Centigrade (100° F), except for the mountains, where the mean annual temperature is about 22 degrees Centigrade (72° F).[1] Humidity in Belize City, which averages 88 percent, is uncomfortably high. Rainfall shows considerable regional variation, from an annual average of 40 or 50 inches in the north and west to 160 inches in the south. Punta Gorda, in the south, may sometimes get as much rain in a month as Corozal, in the north, gets in an entire year. Most of the rain falls in the summer months (May to October), which is also the time when Belize is threatened by hurricanes. Hurricanes have been a frequent and violent feature of the climate of Belize: three major storms, in 1931, 1955, and 1961, and many less destructive, have damaged the coastal regions in this century.

The topography and climate of Belize have been very important in the country's social and economic history. The long swampy coastline, humid and infested with insects, was unattractive to European settlers. Though the maze of cays and channels on the reef occasionally provided refuge for pirates and buccaneers, it was not until the development of the logwood trade and the discovery of large stands of logwood in Belize that the country's natural resources became significant to international markets. In the seventeenth and early eighteenth centuries the exploitation of logwood was the basis of a British settlement that consisted of small, more or less temporary camps confined to the northern coastal strip. It was only later in the eighteenth century that these settlers, spurred by a declining logwood trade and a rising demand for mahogany, penetrated the forests of the interior in search of the giant trees. Even then, the expansion was not supported by any extensive rural settlement, and the shifting mahogany works marked a "hollow" frontier. The numerous rivers, creeks, and lagoons of the northern area provided the logwood and mahogany cutters easy access to their timber, and the great seasonal variation in rainfall meant that the dry period used for cutting and "trucking out" was followed by a rise in the rivers that enabled the cutters to transport their timber to the coast. In fact, the very facility with which the timber interests could use the natural waterways discouraged the development of any alternative means of communication. Not until the 1930s were any roads constructed to link the country's major towns, and even now large parts of the country remain remote from road transport or are serviced only by inferior fair-weather tracks.

The intensive exploitation of the rich forest resources of Belize was accompanied by almost complete neglect of agriculture. In part, the absence of agricultural settlement may be explained by the dominance of the timber interests, but topographical and climatic factors were also influential. Since the settlers confined themselves primarily to the coastal regions, the only soil suitable for agriculture that they encountered was on occasional riverbanks. The richer alluvial loam soils were further upstream or in more inaccessible regions, and it was not until the mid-nineteenth century that any serious agricultural development was attempted in the interior. Great variations in rainfall also tended to discourage agriculture, because crops frequently suffered from drought or flooding. (Rainfall in Punta Gorda, for example, has varied from 91 inches in one year to 209 in another.) This climatic uncertainty made agriculture unusually risky, and the inaccessibility of suitable soils combined with the remoteness of markets made it unprofitable until quite recently.

GROWTH OF POPULATION

Though Belize is slightly larger than El Salvador and is about twice the size of Jamaica, its population is considerably smaller than that of its neighbors. The great population density of Jamaica and El Salvador—two million and four million people, respectively—does not exist in Belize, which, with about 125,000 people, has a population density of only about fifteen persons per square mile.

The demographic history of Belize over the past three hundred years may be conveniently divided into three distinct periods. First, from the initial British settlement in the seventeenth century to the middle of the nineteenth century, there was a small and fluctuating population that had reached about ten thousand by 1845. In the second period, as a result of the disruption of the *Guerra de las Castas* in Yucatán, thousands of Maya and *mestizos* sought refuge in Belize in the middle of the nineteenth century, and many of them stayed. The population of Belize, having more than doubled as a result of this immigration, began a century of sustained growth and reached almost sixty thousand by the end of the Second World War. The third period, comprising the last thirty years, has been characterized by an accelerated growth rate that has doubled the population.

The population of Belize, like that of much of the Caribbean, had its origins largely in immigration. At the time of the arrival of Europeans the area was inhabited by Maya, but the number of Maya decreased rapidly as a result of the

TABLE 1.1 Total Population of Belize, 1790–1970

Date	Total Population
1790	2,656
1803	3,959
1806	3,526
1816	3,824
1823	4,107
1826	4,163
1829	3,883
1832	3,794
1835	2,543
1839	2,946
1841	8,235
1845	9,809
1861	25,635
1871	24,710
1881	27,452
1891	31,471
1901	37,479
1911	40,458
1921	45,317
1931	51,347
1946	59,220
1960	90,505
1970	119,645

SOURCES: 1790, "General Return of the Inhabitants in the Bay of Honduras... ," 22 Oct. 1790, CO 123/9; 1803, "A Short Sketch of the present situation of the Settlement of Honduras... ," by Supt. Barrow, 31 March 1803, CO 123/15; 1806, Br. Gen. Montresor to Gov. Coote, 22 Oct. 1806, CO 123/17; 1816–39, Censuses, GRB; 1841, Narda Dobson, *A History of Belize* (London, 1973), p. 338; 1845, E. G. Squier, *The States of Central America*... (New York, 1858), p. 588; 1861–1946, *West Indian Census 1946*, part E... (Belize, 1948), p. viii; 1960, *West Indies Population Census, Census of British Honduras*... (Kingston, n.d.), vol. 1, p. 179; 1970, provisional census figures, unpublished.

conquest and subsequent social dislocation, famine, and epidemics. The British logwood cutters who settled in the late seventeenth century started importing black slaves early in the eighteenth century, and the blacks soon outnumbered the whites in the settlement. Other blacks were brought to Belize as freemen when they were disbanded from West India regiments early in the nineteenth century, and Africans from Spanish slave ships were brought to Belize at the time of emancipation in 1838.

Another group that came to Belize early in the nineteenth century (but, like the Maya, was not enumerated in the first censuses) was the Black Caribs. Mostly escaped slaves from the Windward Islands, they had mingled with Carib Indians, assimilating their culture, and after an uprising in St. Vincent, they were deported to the island of Ruatan off the coast of Honduras in 1797. Spreading through the Golfo Dulce, they were first noticed in Belize in 1802,[2] and the 1861 census reported a population of 1,825 Caribs.

Between 1848 and 1858 thousands of refugees from the *Guerra de las Castas* in Yucatán made their way into the north of the British settlement. In this largely Spanish-speaking group there were white descendants of the Spanish-Mexican colonists, Maya Indians, and *mestizos,* all seeking relief from the disturbances north of the Rio Hondo. By 1861, over half the population resided in the Northern District, and the Spanish-speaking town of Corozal rivaled the English-speaking town of Belize in size. The 1861 census also revealed that 57 percent of the population had not been born in Belize, 85 percent of these foreign-born persons having come from the neighboring republics, chiefly Mexico.[3] While the number of Mexican-born residents declined after 1861, the number from Honduras and Guatemala reached a peak about the turn of the century. Persons born in Africa and the British Caribbean each constituted about 6 percent of the foreign-born population in 1861, but while the former declined, the latter increased; hundreds of Jamaicans, in particular, came to Belize in the late nineteenth century. Some Chinese and Indian indentured laborers were also brought to Belize in the nineteenth century to provide labor in the expanding plantations, but as plantation agriculture declined, the demand for and the immigration of such labor ceased.

During the last century the proportion of the population that is foreign-born has declined steadily, until in 1960 it amounted to only about 8 percent.[4] During the twentieth century, in fact, there has been a net outward migration; population growth has been a result chiefly of natural increase. Between 1891 and 1901, when the total population increased by 6,008 persons, there was a natural increase of only 2,289, so it is estimated that there was a net immigration of almost four thousand persons in that decade. Between 1901 and 1946, however, when the total population increased by 21,741, natural increase accounted for 28,815, showing that there was a net emigration in that period of over seven thousand persons.[5] Since the Second World War, both immigration and emigration have continued, the latter being chiefly to the United States and the former being chiefly from Guatemala, with the addition of about one thousand Mennonites from Mexico in 1958.

In spite of this net emigration, the population has tripled since the beginning of the century and doubled since the Second World War. The birth rate has remained high, and the death rate, particularly the infant mortality rate, has declined. During the last three decades the average annual rate of population growth in Belize has been about 3 percent, a rate more comparable to the Central American neighbors of Belize than to the Commonwealth Caribbean.

One of the results of the declining infant mortality rate and the high birth rate is a very young population: over half the population is under twenty years of age. This fact, combined with a lengthened life expectancy and the emigration of many Belizeans in their potentially productive middle years, has led to a dramatic increase in the dependency ratio. If the persons aged less than fifteen years and those aged sixty-five years or older are classified as "dependents" and the rest of the population as "potential contributors," then the increase in the dependency ratio has been from 72.5 in 1946 to 95.3 in 1960.[6] The working population of Belize is therefore experiencing a rapidly increasing social burden.

The racial/ethnic composition of the population is difficult to ascertain with any accuracy. With the arrival of the Yucatecan refugees in the middle of the nineteenth century, the basic racial/ethnic dichotomy of the country was established. The two largest "communities" were the mostly English-speaking, Protestant, black population, located chiefly in the Belize District, and the mostly Spanish-speaking, Catholic, Maya, and *mestizo* population, who live chiefly in the north and west. Most of the immigration in the last century, with the exception of the Mennonites, who are white and German-speaking, seems to have reinforced these two main communities. The 1946 census stated that 38.4 percent of the population was black, 65.4 percent of whom were urban dwellers, while 17 percent of the population was "American Indian," 87.1 percent of whom were rural dwellers. Seven percent of the population was Carib (most of whom lived in and around Stann Creek Town), 3.9 percent was white, and 2.3 percent East Indian. Of the remainder, 31.1 percent was classified as "Mixed or coloured," a residual category consisting chiefly of Afro-European and Amerindian-European mixtures, and 0.3 percent was Arab and Chinese.[7]

Though Belize has a very low population density, it has a high degree of urban concentration. (In this respect it resembles Guyana rather than the islands of the Commonwealth Caribbean.) Belize City has grown greatly over the last century, changing from a small town of 5,767 persons in 1881, containing about 21 percent of the country's population, to a city of 21,886 in 1946, when it accounted for 37 percent of the population.[8] In 1970 the 39,257 people living in Belize City constituted 33 percent of the total population.[9] Other towns, while following a very individual pattern of development, have also grown rapidly since 1881. Stann Creek Town, now called Dangriga, has long been second only to Belize and now has a population of about seven thousand persons. It is closely followed in size by Orange Walk, Corozal, and San Ignacio. Benque Viejo and Punta Gorda, which were mere villages with five or six hundred people at the beginning of this century, are now substantial towns. Together these seven towns contained 64,639 persons, or 54 percent of the total population, in 1970.[10]

Until the middle of the nineteenth century the British settlement at Belize resembled little more than a trading post attached to a massive timber reserve. Though the picture has changed considerably with the settlement of the interior and the development of towns and internal communications, Belize still suffers from a colonial heritage that focused almost exclusive attention on a port and its connections with the metropolitan markets, to the detriment of the hinterland. Between 1967 and 1970 a new capital, Belmopan, was constructed in the middle of the country, and as the seat of government, it symbolizes an intention to develop the interior. Meanwhile, however, Belize City remains dominant as the country's commercial and urban center.

ECONOMIC DEVELOPMENT

For three centuries the economy of Belize was dominated by the export of timber: first, logwood and then, after the 1770s, mahogany. The mahogany trade, which reached its peak in the boom of railway-coach building in the 1840s, entered a more or less permanent depression in the middle of the nineteenth century. Since then, two forms of agriculture, peasant and plantation production, have competed for control over the country's land. Initial attempts to organize plantations to produce tropical crops like sugar and bananas for export were a failure, and with the depression in the world market in the 1930s, more Belizeans depended upon the small-scale production of chiefly subsistence foodstuffs.

After the Second World War, the export of forest products, largely chicle and mahogany, continued to decline, while plantation agriculture moved ahead.

TABLE 1.2 Population of Belize City and the Six Next Largest Towns, 1881–1970

Date	Belize City	Six Next Largest Towns, Total	Urban Total	Percentage of Belizean Population
1881	5,767	4,930	10,697	39.0
1891	6,972	4,948	11,920	37.9
1901	9,113	6,627	15,740	42.0
1911	10,478	7,862	18,340	45.3
1921	12,423	9,077	21,500	47.4
1931	16,687	9,730	26,417	51.4
1946	21,886	11,186	33,072	55.8
1960	32,867	15,901	48,768	53.9
1970	39,257	25,382	64,639	54.0

SOURCE: Censuses of 1946, 1960, and 1970.
NOTE: The six next largest towns are Dangriga (Stann Creek Town), Orange Walk, Corozal, San Ignacio, Punta Gorda, and Benque Viejo.

Citrus orchards were developed in the Stann Creek District, and Tate and Lyle invested in sugar production in the north. Since 1959 both sugar and citrus exports have exceeded export of forest products. In 1970 the sugar exported from Belize was worth 11.9 million Belizean dollars, or about 39 percent of the total value of exports. Citrus products (fruit segments, juices, and concentrates) were worth 4 million Belizean dollars, and timber exports were valued at 1.8 million.[11] The rapid expansion of sugar and citrus production was dependent upon the establishment of foreign-owned processing plants, local tax relief measures (such as the Development Incentives Ordinance of 1960), and the protected and guaranteed markets offered by Great Britain, Canada, and the United States for these commodities. These capital-intensive agricultural enterprises have expanded at the expense of the small-scale peasant farmers.

The competition between peasant and plantation is most evident in the area of control of land: the structure of land ownership in Belize exhibits gross inequalities. As can be seen in table 1.3, in 1971 only 3 percent of the landowners held 95 percent of the freehold land, while 91 percent of the landowners held a mere 2 percent. Moreover, all but one of the *latifundistas*, who own estates of ten thousand acres or more, were foreigners. In fact, foreigners owned 93.4 percent of all private land-holdings of over one hundred acres in 1971 and over 90 percent of *all* freehold land in the country.[12] One company, the Belize Estate and Produce Company, owned almost a million acres, or about 42 percent of all the freehold land. On the other hand, a large proportion of the small holdings, or *minifundia*, may be judged quite insufficient to provide an adequate livelihood for an average family, and at best they provide a supplement to low wages.

Although about 38 percent of the land area of Belize is suitable for agriculture, and there is a very attractive cultivable-land/population ratio, very little of the land is actually cultivated. In 1888 almost fifty thousand acres were cultivated,[13] at a time when the population was about thirty thousand. The amount of land presently under cultivation is officially estimated at about 250,000 acres, or

TABLE 1.3 Distribution of Freehold Land, by Size of Holdings, 1971

Size of Holdings (in Acres)	Number of Owners	Percentage of Total	Amount of Acreage	Percentage of Total
0–20	2,702	75	23,871	2
21–100	586	16	28,260	
101–1,000	215	6	82,615	3
1,001–10,000	75	2	228,746	10
10,001–25,000	32		459,724	19
25,001–50,000	4	1	139,894	6
50,001–100,000	4		293,567	12
Over 100,000	2		1,133,144	47
Total	3,620	100	2,389,821	99

SOURCE: Land tax rolls, Lands Department, Belmopan.

just above 10 percent of the potential.[14] During the last century, therefore, while the population has quadrupled, the amount of land under cultivation has increased five times. The monopolization of land ownership does not lead to the utilization of land but is, on the contrary, a factor in its underutilization. From the perspective of the *latifundistas* there is a shortage of labor to work on their plantations, and one of their solutions to this problem is to monopolize the land in order to inhibit the development of an independent and self-sufficient peasantry. In other words, the Belize Estate and Produce Company and other monopolistic landowners hold their vast estates not in order to use the land but, by denying its use to others, to keep the population dependent upon them, thereby securing a supply of wage laborers.

Though oil has been sought, it has not yet been found, and Belize, unlike Jamaica or Guyana, has no bauxite resources. Tourism offers many possibilities (accompanied by its usual hazards), but it is still in the early stages of development. Tourism earnings for 1970 have been estimated at 2.3 million U.S. dollars.[15] Manufacturing, consisting chiefly of light industries oriented toward providing import substitutes for the domestic market (clothing, cigarettes, drinks, construction materials, furniture, and fertilizers), represents about 14 percent of the GDP. The major industrial activity, building construction, accounts for about 15 percent of the GDP.[16] One of the recent successes of the Belizean economy has been in fishing (lobsters, conch, and scale fish) both for domestic consumption and for export. Primarily organized on a cooperative basis, the fishing industry earned some two and one-half million Belizean dollars in exports in 1970, pushing timber into fourth place.[17]

Agriculture and fishing account for about 16 percent of the GDP, but contribute almost three-quarters of domestic exports by value. The four principal export commodities, sugar, citrus, fish, and timber, together earned 20.2 million Belizean dollars, or about one-third of the total export figure, in 1970.[18] The Belizean economy is now, as always, highly dependent upon international trade and exhibits a continually deteriorating balance of trade: in 1970 exports were estimated at U.S. $20.84 million, while imports were valued at U.S. $34.74 million.[19] In 1971 Belize joined the Caribbean Free Trade Association, now called Caricom, a block comprising some twelve countries and five million people; its major trading partners, however, are likely to remain the United States, Great Britain, and Canada, who together accounted for 82.5 percent of its exports and 74.1 percent of its imports in 1965.[20]

In summary, though the Belizean economy is no longer so completely dominated by the export of forest products, it remains oriented primarily toward the production of tropical crops for export to metropolitan markets. It is, therefore, highly dependent on and susceptible to fluctuations in the state of international trade. Moreover, the primary resource of the country, its land, remains in the control of large foreign companies that leave much of their land idle and make Belizeans into dependent wage laborers on the remainder.

Since 1960, when the elected members first constituted a majority of the Executive Council, the Belizean government has made a number of attempts to encourage agricultural development. In addition to the incentives it has offered to the export-oriented plantation system, it has encouraged the production of many items for domestic consumption, such as corn, rice, vegetables, beans, and beef, in an attempt to diversify production and reduce the traditional dependence upon imported food. However, the attempt to encourage agricultural development through the use of legislation and taxation must, so far, be considered a failure.

The Rural Land Utilization Ordinance of 1966 was intended to induce the owners of large undeveloped estates to develop their land, pay a tax, or surrender the land in lieu of taxes. The big landowners, who have always opposed land taxes, lobbied for support while refusing to pay the rural land utilization tax on their undeveloped estates in 1967 and 1968. By 1969 a total of 1.23 million acres was exempted from the tax, the Belize Estate and Produce Company alone having succeeded in obtaining exemptions for about 95 percent of its lands. The exemptions effectively subverted the purposes of the law, which was intended to have been "an act of economic emancipation marking a watershed in our history."[21] In 1971 only $128 was collected from this virtually defunct tax, and the combined land taxes made up only 2.4 percent of the total current national revenue.[22]

The big landowners' meager contribution to the national revenue results from the power they exercise in the *latifundia*-dominated political economy of Belize. It is particularly significant that the government's major attempt to promote a program of land reform through a progressive tax on idle land has been frustrated and subverted by these big landowners, who have failed either to develop their land or to make a contribution to the national revenue commensurate with their wealth. Their vast estates remain largely idle, agricultural development remains stagnant, and the people of Belize remain poor dependents. A recent study of *Land in Belize* concluded: "While the Government, on the eve of political independence, is attempting to break the vicious circle of underdevelopment, which can be achieved only with a breakthrough in agricultural development, *the absentee landlords constitute perhaps the biggest single obstacle to the economic emancipation of Belize.*"[23]

POLITICAL DEVELOPMENT

The political development of Belize has always been characterized by a combination of internal and external factors. Not only has Belize been a colonial dependency, but it has also been profoundly affected in its political and constitutional development by international relations, particularly those between Great Britain and Spain. During the first century of their presence in Belize the British were continually harassed by the Spaniards from neighboring provinces, and it was not until 1763 that an Anglo-Spanish treaty gave the British settlement some recognized status. The treaty permitted the "Occupation of Cutting, Loading, and Carrying away Logwood,"[24] but asserted Spanish sovereignty over the area. The assertion of Spanish sovereignty was repeated in subsequent treaties of 1783 and 1786, thereby inhibiting the development of a colonial constitution. After their defeat at the Battle of St. George's Cay in 1798, however, the Spaniards made no further attempt to control the territory.

During the eighteenth century and the first half of the nineteenth century, the British settlers managed their own affairs with a Public Meeting and an elected magistracy that exercised both judicial and executive functions. The first Superintendent appointed by the British government arrived in 1786, but his powers were inadequately defined, and the ambiguity of the location of executive authority gave rise to frequent conflict in the settlement. In the 1820s and 1830s the growing "free colored" population pressed the white settler oligarchy for an extension of civil rights, at the same time that Britain, no longer so inhibited by Spain, which had ceased to be a mainland power, began to press for greater colonial control over the territory. The British Parliament established a Supreme Court in Belize in 1819, and in 1831 the Colonial Office successfully pressured the Public Meeting to grant "all His Majesty's Coloured Subjects of Free Condition... the same Rights and Privileges with British subjects born of White Parents."[25] In 1832 the settler oligarchy lost control over the magistracy, which was thereafter appointed by the Superintendent, and it was soon made clear that the act abolishing slavery was to be applied in Belize as though it were a colony. In 1840 the laws of England were proclaimed to be in force in the settlement, and an Executive Council was appointed to assist the Superintendent.[26] With the international situation becoming more favorable, it became possible for the British government to establish a more unambiguous constitution, and in 1854 the Public Meeting, clearly feeling threatened by a rising tide of democratization, disbanded itself.

The first real constitution of Belize was applied in 1854, and its chief feature was establishment of a Legislative Assembly consisting of eighteen elected and three appointed members.[27] The lifespan of this Assembly was only seventeen years, however, as a number of other factors produced a further constitutional change. During the 1850s the Belizean economy entered a profound and more or less permanent depression, one of the effects of which was the centralization and consolidation of economic enterprises with a more pronounced element of metropolitan ownership. These economic changes undermined the settler elite of Belize, which, when threatened by the Maya in the 1860s, proved unable to raise revenue to meet military expenses. Belize, which had not been declared a colony until 1862, became a Crown Colony in 1871.

The thrust of British colonial policy was toward developing more direct control over its territories, so the threat of the Maya became the occasion for the confirmation of this control and for the political dispossession of a settler elite that had already lost most of its economic power. Under the Crown Colony system, Belize was administered by the Governor-in-Council, the council being an entirely nominated body. The last century of Belizean history can be seen as a succession of attempts by the colonized to erode this imperial control and to gain progressive degrees of political independence.

In 1890 an attempt to introduce elected members into the Council was denied on the grounds that only about four hundred of the colony's thirty thousand inhabitants were white.[28] In 1932 a further rebuff was delivered to the political aspirations of the Belizean people. Exploiting the chronic economic dislocation produced by the world depression and the 1931 hurricane, the British government made it a condition of providing grants and loans that the Governor be granted reserve powers, and the constitution was duly amended.[29] Pressure for a return of the elective principle persisted, however, and in 1936 a new constitution, allowing for five of the thirteen members of the Legislative Council to be elected, was inaugurated, though the Governor's reserve powers remained.[30]

The constitutional history of Belize from 1936 to the present may be divided into four periods. During the first period, from 1936 to 1954, the elected members of the Legislative Council were not only in a minority but were elected by a tiny minority of the population, because the franchise was restricted by property qualifications. In 1936, for example, there were 1,035 registered voters, and in 1945 there were only 822 registered voters in a total population of about sixty thousand.[31] But during the 1930s and 1940s, in Belize as elsewhere in the West Indies, a mass movement that demanded civil rights, trade union representation, and popular political participation was developing. The Belize City Council, election to which was subject to a more liberal franchise than was election to the Legislative Council, became the locus of this discontent. Socioeconomic conditions had deteriorated during the 1930s, there was widespread poverty and unemployment, and no economic development appeared to be forthcoming.

The spark that set off the smoldering discontent was provided in 1949 by the devaluation of the dollar. On the night the devaluation was announced, after weeks of denials that there would be any devaluation, a People's Committee was formed. During 1950 this Committee grew into the first coherent anticolonial political party in Belize, the People's United Party. George Price, who was one of the leaders of the People's Committee, became the leader of the party in 1956, first minister in 1961, and Premier of Belize in 1964.

One of the chief demands of the People's United Party[32] was for universal adult suffrage, and with popular support, this goal was achieved in 1954. The 1954 constitution[33] ushered in the second period of the contemporary constitutional history of Belize. The Legislative Assembly consisted of nine members elected by universal adult suffrage, three official members, and three nominated unofficial members. Though the legislature for the first time contained a majority of members elected by the majority of the people, the Executive Council consisted of the Governor and the three official members of the Assembly, two of the nominated and unofficial members, and only four of the elected members. The latter, therefore, were in the minority. Moreover, as the Governor retained his reserve powers, it was apparent that the struggle for self-government, though enhanced by the achievement of 1954, had not yet been won.

The third period, from 1960 to 1963, saw continuation of the advance toward self-government. In 1960 a further constitutional amendment[34] expanded the Legislative Assembly from fifteen to twenty-five members, eighteen of whom were elected, and a majority of the Executive Council were elected members. The Governor remained on the Council as chairman, but without a vote.

The fourth and present period was inaugurated in 1964. The constitution provides a bicameral legislature, the National Assembly, consisting of a House of Representatives of eighteen elected members and a Senate of eight nominated members. After a general election, the Governor appoints as Premier the member of the House of Representatives who is best able to command majority support. The Premier, in turn, appoints his Cabinet, the chief policy-making body, which is collectively responsible to the National Assembly. Since 1964, therefore, under the leadership of George Price, Belize has had full internal self-government, with only foreign affairs, defense, internal security, and the terms and conditions of appointment of the civil service remaining in control of a Governor appointed by the British government. The People's United Party has dominated the political process in Belize, no lasting coherent opposition having emerged. In 1965 the P.U.P. won sixteen seats in the House of Representatives, and in 1969 it won seventeen seats to opposition's one. Most recently, in October 1974, the P.U.P. lost some seats but retained its control, with twelve out of the eighteen representatives.

The history of the political development of Belize may be divided into three broad stages. In the first of these, lasting until the middle of the nineteenth century, the white settler oligarchy was dominant. Challenged by both the disenfranchised masses and the British Colonial Office, this settler elite relinquished much of its political and administrative control to the latter. By 1854 the British government was willing to assert unequivocally its control of the settlement, which it pronounced a colony in 1862. During this time the settler elite's economic base was undermined by economic depression, with the result that the Colonial Office was able to gain complete control over the political-administrative apparatus of the colony. The second stage, then, beginning in the middle of the nineteenth century, was one in which the British government, through the Colonial Office, exercised control over Belize. The third stage may be said to have begun in the 1930s and 1940s, but it became full-fledged in 1950 with the founding of the People's United Party and the organization of a coherent movement toward self-government and independence. This stage, characterized by a struggle between the colonized masses and the forces of the metropolis, has not yet been resolved.

The fact that Belize is not yet an independent nation may be explained in part by the threat of recolonization by Guatemala.[35] The dispute between Britain and Guatemala over the territory of Belize turns upon differing interpretations of the significance of the eighteenth-century Anglo-Spanish treaties. In the two centuries since those treaties were written, however, a nation has been emerging, which though still reliant upon British defense, seeks self-determination. The other major problem that inhibits Belizean achievement of independence is economic in nature. The economic history of Belize has been aptly described as "a classic of colonial exploitation, of taking away and not giving back.... Of all the wealth taken from the country practically nothing was put back in the way of permanent improvements and capital development."[36] The handful of British grants and loans that have appeared in the last three decades have made a belated contribution to the development of an adequate economic infrastructure, but the Belizean government, which has had some degree of control over its own affairs for only a few years, faces an enormous task in overcoming centuries of exploitation and stagnation. Moreover, there remain major structural problems to be overcome. It is arguable that when over 90 percent of a country's freehold land is owned by foreign companies, it needs more than a constitutional change in order to achieve a meaningful independence.

In 1961 Ian Macleod, then British Secretary of State for the Colonies, stated that Belize could become constitutionally independent whenever it desired.[37] However, even if Belize could become constitutionally independent from Great Britain without being promptly recolonized by Guatemala, such an independence would not be sufficient to negate the socioeconomic consequences of centuries of colonial dependency.

2
Early European Incursions upon the Maya

THE ORIGINS OF THE MAYA

The earliest inhabitants of the area now called Belize about whom anything is known were the Maya. Their ancestors crossed the Bering Straits over twenty-five thousand years ago, and following the game that was their source of food, spread to the southern tip of the Americas within about twenty thousand years. Archaeological research has established the presence of men in Mesoamerica during the late Pleistocene period.

Around 7,500 B.C. the food supply of the big-game hunters began to diminish, and environmental conditions favored the survival of seed gatherers and small-game hunters. The next stage of development was a transition from seed-gathering to planting, and the first primitive farmers appeared around 1,500 B.C. Certainly by 1,400 B.C. cultivation, based upon the dietary trinity of maize, squash, and beans, had become a major aspect of human existence in Mesoamerica. Tools used in farming included the wooden digging stick, its point hardened in fire, the stone axe, and fire, which was used for clearing ground. Simple pottery was made, and houses were constructed of sticks, wattle daubed with mud, and probably a thatch of reeds or straw. Many of these features of early sedentary life in Mesoamerica exist to this day, including the grinding of maize and the baking of maize-meal cakes, or *tortillas,* on a circular griddle.

The major mode of cultivation utilized by these primitive farmers was swidden, or slash-and-burn, agriculture, a form of which is still practiced in many areas of Mesoamerica. While this method requires a large amount of land to maintain productivity, a modification of it, known as the two-field system, enables the cultivator to maintain a more or less permanent residence and kitchen garden, possibly on a fertile valley floor, while farming the more extensive hillsides with the swidden system. As the early Mesoamericans developed the two-field system, clusters of houses were established in the more fertile spots, and villages and communities began to take shape. Religious ideas also developed, involving some projection of the female generative principle into the realm of the sacred and a complex of customs concerning the growing of maize and its preparation as food.

Until around 900 B.C. the population of Mesoamerica appears to have lived either in isolated homesteads or in autonomous communities comprised of individual households. It has been argued that "the community was the autonomous unit of social life. . . . in Middle America it was never obliterated. The simple inventory of farm tools and kitchen equipment, the tasks of farming, the religious concepts geared to the cycle of planting and harvesting, the style of life centered upon the community of one's birth—these have remained basic and stable until today."[1] In the first millenium B.C., however, surpluses increased and became more dependable, and production of the caloric minimum required for subsistence and of the yield required for replacement became more assured, possibly as a result of an increase in the range of plants being used. At any rate, it became possible for some men to utilize the surplus for ends other than subsistence.

Primitive religion in Mesoamerica undoubtedly lacked a priesthood at first; distinctions between the priest type and the layman, and hierarchical distinctions among the priests themselves, came later. In about 900 B.C. a division of labor emerged in Mesoamerica: the peasants began building the ceremonial platforms that were the stages upon which the new religious specialists propounded their ideologies and enacted their roles. The development of this division of labor led, variously in different parts of Mesoamerica, to distinctive styles of art and architecture, to advanced methods of astronomy and systems of calendrics, and to the development of politico-military specialists. The old egalitarian, primitive farming communities became subordinate to centers of power and control as a new type of society developed in Mesoamerica. The society in one of these emergent states, which occupied an area comprising modern Chiapas, Yucatán, Quintana Roo, Guatemala, northwestern Honduras, and Belize, has become known as Maya civilization.

ANCIENT MAYA SETTLEMENTS IN THE BELIZE RIVER VALLEY

Maya civilization, based upon the cultivation of maize, produced great achievements in the arts and sciences. Maya mathematics, astronomy, and calendrics were remarkable and, like their visual arts, were developed primarily in connection with their complex religion. The Maya "cities," too, were not so much urban concentrations of population as elaborate religious ceremonial centers, the magnificent sculpture and architecture of which can still be seen (and discovered) throughout the area. A number of major sites of these ceremonial centers exist in the Belize area: Lubaantún in the Toledo District, Caracol and Xunantunich in the Cayo District, and Altun Ha in the Belize District.

In the Barton Ramie area of the Belize River valley, excavations have revealed the presence of settlers in the Preclassic period of Mesoamerican cultural history (ending about A.D. 300).² Although it is unclear whether these pioneers subscribed to the religious ideas then developing through a larger area, including Tabasco and the Guatemalan highlands, they probably spoke a Maya language and participated in the ancient Mesoamerican cultural traditions concerning the cultivation and preparation of maize.

A century or two before Christ, the population of the Barton Ramie area suddenly doubled, from about seven hundred fifty to one thousand five hundred people. The immigrants who produced this increase invigorated the conservative farming life of the valley, introducing new pottery styles and transforming what had been a series of small hamlets dotted along the river banks into a strip settlement with some unoccupied spaces. At this stage of development, which was probably typical of the process taking place throughout Mesoamerica, these hamlets would have been quite egalitarian, autonomous communities of primitive farmers and their households.

In the early Classic period that followed, the Belize River valley and its settlements became closely linked to other Maya areas, particularly the Petén. The river itself was almost certainly a trade route, linking the important Maya centers of the Petén with commercial centers, such as Altun Ha, near the east coast. While the valley of Mexico was blessed with saline lakes, the Maya of the Petén had to acquire salt from the coast, so this essential dietary ingredient, along with other marine materials, would be supplied by coastal Maya to the inland settlements. The Maya of the Belize River valley built their own ceremonial centers, the major one of which is Xunantunich near Benque Viejo del Carmen, and certainly had close religious connections with the great ceremonial centers of Tikal and Uaxactun. Whether they had close political as well as commercial and religious connections with the Petén area seems likely but has not been confirmed.

About the middle of the sixth century there was a brief hiatus in ceremonial activity in the Petén, and in that period the people of the Belize River valley, still increasing in numbers, exhibited great activity in building house platforms and complexes of houses around little plazas. In addition, they erected and enlarged minor ceremonial centers and manufactured huge quantities of pottery in locally developed styles. By this time the population had grown until the river valley was one continuous strip settlement. Willey et al. estimated that in the strip including Baking Pot, Spanish Lookout, and Barton Ramie, there was a population of about six thousand at this period, supporting one major ceremonial center at Baking Pot and at least three minor ones. At the peak of inhabitation there were probably almost twenty-five thousand people living in the Belize River valley to the southwest of Cocos Bank, or about one-fifth of the entire population of present-day Belize.

Before the end of the late Classic period, however, the Maya of the upper Belize River valley experienced some difficulties, exhibited first at Xunantunich and later at Barton Ramie, where the ceremonial center was not enlarged and may not even have been so widely used as before. "The general effect," according to Willey et al., "is . . . what we might expect of a society that had lost its political and religious direction."[3]

The beginning of the decline of Maya civilization has been dated at 790 A.D., and by the middle of the tenth century the ceremonial centers had been abandoned. The cause of this decline in the southern lowlands has not yet been definitively identified, but it seems that a number of problems internal to Maya society were exacerbated by external factors that hastened a collapse. A recent summary of the problem states: "Classic Maya exposure to, contacts with, and pressures from non-Classic Maya groups at its western frontier set in motion a series of events that resulted in the collapse and eventual extinction of the old Maya way of life."[4] Demographic factors were both a cause and an effect of this collapse. A decline in the population led to a critical inability of the Maya to sustain themselves and to compete with other groups in the changing Mesoamerican context. The collapse then accelerated the demographic decline: "There was a truly massive population loss in the Maya southern lowlands . . . not long after the close of the Classic Period . . . [which] was not followed by a substantial recovery."[5]

The Maya settlements in the upper Belize River valley, linked as they were with the major centers in the Petén, followed a similar pattern of decline and collapse. Though we do not know how long the Maya continued to occupy the area, Barton Ramie was inhabited after the abandonment of the ceremonial centers, and there may have been continual or intermittent occupation of villages in the Belize River valley until the arrival of Europeans in that area early in the seventeenth century.

SPANISH EXPEDITIONS AND THEIR EFFECTS UPON THE MAYA

On his fourth voyage to the west, in 1502, Christopher Columbus entered the southeastern Gulf of Honduras but then turned to the south, toward Panama. A few years later Pinzón and Solís sailed west along the coast of what is now Honduras, turned north in the Golfo Dulce, and passed the coast of Belize. In 1511 some Spanish sailors were shipwrecked on the Yucatán coast, but it was not until Francisco Hernández de Córdoba's voyage to Yucatán in 1517 that the major expeditions occurred, leading eventually to the European conquest and colonization of Mesoamerica.

The expedition of 1519, led by Cortéz, resulted in the conquest of the Aztec empire in Mexico. From that base, expeditions were sent to conquer Guatemala and Honduras. When Cristobal de Olid revolted in Honduras, Cortéz himself undertook an astonishing march from Mexico, through the unexplored interior of Central America to the Golfo Dulce. In 1525, during the course of this march, Cortéz visited Tayasal, the capital of the independent Itzá, now covered by the Guatemalan town of Flores in the Petén. He also passed through the southwest corner of the Toledo District in the south of Belize, at a time when that area was populated by scattered settlements of Mopan and Chol Maya.

The late Sir J. Eric S. Thompson characterized the Chol Maya as worshippers of mountain and river deities and as lacking towns or "a regular whole-time priesthood."[6] The Chol Maya were devastated by Spanish incursions, beginning in 1603, when Fathers Esguerra and Cipriano persuaded them to become Christians. Thirty years later, however, they revolted, burned all the churches, and abandoned the towns into which they had been herded. "For thirty-eight years the Chols retained their independence,"[7] until a series of missionary expeditions between 1671 and 1677 led to their repacification. But in 1678, "the Chols, irked by town life and the restrictions of Christianity, once more fled into the forests,"[8] burning the church of San Lucas Tzalac, which may have been near the Gracias à Dios Falls on the River Sarstoon. In 1685 Father Cano and other priests rebuilt the church and again tried to control the Chols. That time the "pacification" lasted only four years, and the Chols once more burned the church in revolt. At that point the Spaniards changed their tactics. In 1689, 1690, and subsequent years they sent punitive expeditions to round up the Chols and transport them to the Guatemalan highlands, leaving the Manche area, which may once have contained as many as ten thousand people, a virtually uninhabited forest. The Chols were eventually absorbed by the expanding Kekchi Maya, some of whom returned to the area in the late nineteenth century and settled around San Antonio in the Toledo District. The south of Belize, which had been inhabited by Maya in the seventeenth century (a Dominican priest, Father Delgado, encountered many small Maya settlements when he crossed the area in 1677[9]) was thus depopulated by Spanish action and remained practically deserted for a century, until the arrival of the Caribs.

In the north, the Spaniards had undertaken the conquest of the Yucatán peninsula in 1527. The following year the first Governor of Yucatán, Francisco de Montejo, sailed south down the coast of Belize, and in 1531 he sent his lieutenant, Alonso Dávila, to establish a base at Chetumal. According to Thompson, Chetumal was the capital of a Maya province that "stretched southward from the eastern shore of Lake Bakhalal (now Bacalar) to New River Lagoon, and possibly to the Belize River." It was located "not far west of the present town of Corozal... [and] may well have been Santa Rita."[10] The Spaniards were unable to hold Chetumal in the face of Maya counterattacks, so Dávila journeyed south along the swamps and lagoons of present-day Belize, raiding inland Maya villages for food.[11] Dávila's forays during this enforced exploration suggest that, at that time, there was a considerable Maya population near the coast. Though Chetumal was the center of a major province, other Maya settlements to the south and west may have reverted to a pattern closer to that of a thousand years before, consisting of a series of relatively isolated, scattered, and autonomous villages. One substantial village of this type, Tipu, was in existence in the early seventeenth century when the first visit by Spaniards is recorded.

In 1618 Father Bartolomé de Fuensalida and Father Juan de Orbita traveled from Mérida to Bacalar, then up the New River past numerous small villages, and continued overland on their way to the Itzá capital of Tayasal.[12] Only about five days' journey from Tayasal they stopped at a Maya town called Tipu, on a river of the same name. Tipu is a Maya name for the Belize River, and the town may have been located close to present-day Benque Viejo del Carmen and the old ceremonial center of Xunantunich. Tipu had a population of about one hundred families, or about five hundred people, and its headman was then Cristobal Ná. Both his name and the presence of a church in the village indicate some previous Spanish influence from Bacalar. But such influence appears to have been insubstantial, and subsequent Spanish attempts at control proved ineffective.

The trip to Tayasal having been unsuccessful, Fuensalida returned to Mérida, leaving Orbita to officiate at Tipu. Orbita found that the apparent Christianity of the Tipu Maya quickly evaporated, and they soon ceased even to show respect for the priest. When Fuensalida returned, the priests found a large number of Maya idols and discovered that these were still being worshipped with Maya dances and rituals. An opportune reinforcement by the Alcalde of Bacalar and several other Spaniards enabled the missionaries to hold an enquiry, seize and flog the offending Maya, and burn the idols in a large fire in the town square. Threatened with death if they should again lapse from Christian practice, the Maya of Tipu demonstrated the sincerity of their conversion with an apparently convincing display of earnest obedience. Satisfied that they had checked Tipu's apostasy, the missionaries turned again to Tayasal, but when they were driven from Tayasal and retreated to Mérida, the people of Tipu once more abandoned any pretense of Christian practice and burned their church. Shortly after, a Franciscan, Diego Delgado, passed through Tipu, taking Cristobal Ná and eighty other Maya with him to Tayasal. They were all put to death by the Itzá.

According to Villagutierre, the Spanish colonial historian, the Maya of Tipu blocked the paths to the village and erected statues in them, "like ridiculous figures of Spaniards, and in front of them other formidable figures of idols, saying that they were the Gods of the roads, who kept them closed to the Spaniards, to prevent them from entering into their country."[13] Whether or not this symbolism was supported by a more practical resistance, Tipu remained out of Spanish control for about seventy years, until 1695, when Captain Francisco de Hariza from Bacalar escorted a priest to Tipu to reestablish a mission there. Hariza's chief interest, however, was to open negotiations with the Itzá. Tipu was said to be friendly with the Itzá at that time, and Hariza sent a messenger from Tipu, named Matéo Bichab, to Tayasal.[14] The following year Hariza left Mérida with thirty soldiers and eleven priests, seven of the latter intended for the Itzá and four for Tipu, but news of disturbances at Tayasal led them all to retreat.[15] The Spaniards did not succeed in defeating and dispersing the Itzá until 1697, at which time the people of Tipu disappear from our sources.

Though some refugees may have arrived in the upper Belize River valley from Chetumal province and even farther afield in Yucatán, following the brutal Spanish suppression of Maya revolts in the mid-sixteenth century, the people of Tipu seem to have been culturally distinct from those of Yucatán. Thompson refers to a matricula of the town, dated 1655, that "lists men and women with Maya day names, a custom quite unknown in Yucatán at any time."[16] Nor were the Tipu Maya integrated into the Itzá province. Villagutierre stated that the area of the Itzá "and other unconverted tribes" extended for more than one hundred and fifty leagues from the west to the east, where it was bounded by the sea. The "unconverted tribe" at Tipu may have been only one of several communities maintaining their autonomy in the Belize River valley. Villagutierre also mentioned the villages of Lucu and Zaccuc, near Tipu, and a tribe called the Mucules, living somewhere in what is now central Belize, who "were savages and lived barbarously."[17]

The effects of Spanish incursions upon the Maya in the area that is now Belize are hard to evaluate. The priests and soldiers who penetrated the area certainly affected the Maya, though not to the catastrophic extent that they affected the neighboring regions of the Petén and Yucatán. Though the Spaniards never settled within Belize, their *entradas* may have reduced the indigenous population and certainly resulted in some social disorganization, particularly in the south.

Throughout Mesoamerica the indigenous population was decimated by European-borne diseases. In Mexico, for example, it has been estimated that the Indian population was reduced from eleven million at the time of the conquest in 1519 to only one and one-half million in 1650.[18] Some of this reduction occurred as a result of epidemics, some as a result of death in battle, and some from the social disorganization following the conquest. Epidemics did not recognize the limits of Spanish jurisdiction and administration, and many people became victims of European-introduced diseases even before they were overcome militarily by the Europeans, so there is no reason to believe that Belize was spared. The proximity of Cortéz' and Dávila's expeditions to such major communication routes as the Belize River may have introduced diseases that subsequently spread through the Maya of the area in the seventeenth and eighteenth centuries. Though there must have been considerable numbers of Maya near the coast at the time of Dávila's forays, the British, who arrived there a hundred years later, do not mention encountering Maya on the coast at all, and only late in the eighteenth century did they leave records of contacts with Maya inland.

BRITISH WOODCUTTERS ENCOUNTER THE MAYA

The first British settlers who arrived on the coast of Belize in about the middle of the seventeenth century left no record of any contact with the Maya for the first century of their occupation, though we know from the Spanish records that Maya did inhabit the interior in that period. The Maya who had lived near the coast during Dávila's forays in 1531 may have succumbed to epidemics in the interim, or they may have withdrawn to less vulnerable sites. Alternately, or in addition, they may have retreated at the sight of more white men, keeping out of the way of the British logwood cutters as the latter worked up the various rivers, creeks, and lagoons.

There is such a paucity of early British records that evidence of contact between the early settlers and the Maya is unlikely to be discovered. The first British settlers were pirates and adventurers, probably mostly illiterate, who, unlike the Spanish missionaries, would not be inclined to keep accounts of their encounters with the indigenous people. Moreover, if there were any accounts, they are unlikely to have survived, as the continual Spanish harassment of the early settlement was not conducive to the security of historical records. For example, when St. George's Cay, the British settlers' principal residence, was captured by Spaniards from Bacalar on 15 September 1779, it was recorded that all the "Books and Papers of the Merchants and principal Inhabitants should be put into Chests... and delivered to... Merida."[19] Just prior to this attack, however, a description of the state of the settlement had mentioned the presence of small numbers of Maya in the area: "The Indians who live near the English are so inconsiderable that it is unnecessary to take any notice of them."[20]

Up to this time there would have been little occasion for contact, since the British obtained most of their logwood near the coast, where it could be easily loaded on their ships, and the Maya probably preferred to keep out of their way. As the more accessible timber was exhausted, however, the British penetrated farther inland, and in the 1770s the demand for mahogany created by the English luxury furniture industry enticed the British woodcutters into the Maya forests of what is now central and northwest Belize. As the frontier of British exploitation moved inland, contacts between the two peoples increased, the Maya forcing the British to "take notice" of them.

From maps of the late eighteenth and early nineteenth centuries it can be ascertained that the frontier of the British exploitation of timber stretched from the Rio Hondo south through New River Lagoon and Roaring Creek (near present-day Belmopan) to the Sibun River.[21] The Maya who lived to the west of this line responded to British encroachments upon their territory with vigorous military action. In 1788 an "attack of the Wild Indians" was reported as having occurred on the New River,[22] and in 1802 a detachment of troops was requested to "be sent up river to punish the Indians who are committing depredations upon the Mahogany works."[23] Unfortunately, the name of the river was not recorded, but a request made in 1807 for "arms and ammunition for gangs working up the River at Hogstye Bank, who have been attacked by Indians"[24] is more helpful in locating the frontier, for Hogstye Bank was a little above Orange Walk on the Belize River, probably close to Roaring Creek.

Though they ultimately failed to check the expansionism of the British, the Maya were certainly perceived by the latter as a serious threat to the settlement.

Captain George Henderson, who was stationed in Belize with the Fifth West India Regiment at the beginning of the nineteenth century, stated:

> not many years past, numerous tribes of hostile Indians often left their recesses in the woods for the purpose of plunder. This they often accomplished; and if resistance were offered, not infrequently committed the most sanguinary murders. The habitations of these people have never been traced. Their dispositions are peculiarly ferocious. . . . the dread of the military, whom it has been found expedient frequently to dispatch in pursuit of these fugitives, has latterly operated as a very effectual check.[25]

Contrary to Henderson's optimistic assurances, the Maya continued to fight back despite the employment of regular troops against them. As late as 1817, "the exposed and unprotected state of the settlers, surrounded by vast hordes of Indians who are all in the constant habit of breaking in upon their works" was seen as placing the British settlers "entirely at the mercy of the Slave Population."[26] Superintendent George Arthur also reported in 1817 that "we are surrounded by Tribes of Indians who occasionally commit great depredations upon the Cutters."[27] Though "vast hordes" can be assumed to be an exaggeration resulting from fear, there can be no doubt that the number of Maya encountered by the British was no longer as "inconsiderable" as it had been in 1779.

The identity of these Maya is in doubt, however. Thompson has suggested that "British logwood cutters working on the Belize River in the eighteenth century employed Indians . . . [who] were probably the descendants of the Maya of Tipu culture."[28] This is incorrect, for the Indians to whom Thompson refers, who were enslaved rather than "employed" by the British, were not indigenous to the area but had been brought from the Mosquito Shore in 1787.[29] Nevertheless, the Maya whom the British encountered may have included some descendants of the Maya of Tipu and possibly also some refugees from Spanish oppression in the Petén and Yucatán. (The Maya revolt at Quisteil under Jacinto Canek had been savagely suppressed by the Spaniards in 1761.)

Though we cannot be sure of the origin or cultural identity of these Maya, they were probably living in small towns, such as Tipu, and little villages and homesteads scattered around the upper Belize River valley and in the bush and forest to the north. Their political decentralization meant that they were unable to mount a massive attack, but it also meant that they could not be decisively beaten. The number of Maya in the Belize area early in the nineteenth century cannot be estimated, and no attempt was made to enumerate them in the early censuses.

The fears that British settlers had expressed in 1817 of a link between the Maya and the African slaves proved groundless; no mention was made of the Maya when a slave uprising occurred on the Belize River in 1820. By that time, in fact, the Mayan presence seems to have been on the wane, and by 1830, unable to overcome the woodcutters' invasion, the Maya had retired deeper into the forests and rarely appeared to the British settlers.[30] Walker and Caddy, on their expedition to Palenque in 1839, described Duck Run (near San Ignacio el Cayo) as "the highest inhabited spot" on the Belize River and mentioned "wild Indians in the vicinity, who ... at various times emerge from the secret recesses of the Forest for the purpose of plundering."[31] Maya settlements had by that time, it seems, been pushed back to the limits of present-day Belize by the expansionist activity of the British settlers.

CONCLUSION

It has been stated that "there is no record of any indigenous population and no reason to believe that any such existed except far in the interior [of Belize]. There are traces of extensive Maya Indian population ... all over the Colony ... but this occupation was long before British Settlement."[32] Burdon, who knew the records better than anyone else at the time, was a Governor of British Honduras, and the view that the area was uninhabited at the time of British settlement was convenient because it removed some of the stigma attached to its colonization. Stephen Caiger, an apologist for colonialism during the time of emerging nationalism in Belize, wrote of the Maya as "aboriginals" but asserted that they "had abandoned the Belize district long before the seventeenth century. Afterwards, however, hearing of the mild rule of the logwood-cutters as contrasted with Spanish arrogance and cruelty, they percolated over the frontiers from Mexico and Guatemala, in such large numbers that today these Indians compose more than one sixth of the total population, with a culture, industrial life, and a Reservation of their own."[33] Though the reasons why the Maya have "a Reservation of their own" must be left for a later chapter, it is clear that Caiger was arguing, first, that British settlement in Belize did not *displace* any indigenous population, and second, that the Maya *chose* "the mild rule" of the British. The facts of the historical record expose the myth in this account.

The historian Waddell, more guarded in his estimation than Burdon or Caiger, states that it is "not impossible that some remote parts of the country were occupied continuously from the fall of the Maya Civilization to the nineteenth century."[34] While there is not yet sufficient evidence to document a continuous Maya occupation, there is certainly evidence of their presence in the sixteenth and seventeenth centuries and in the late eighteenth and early nineteenth centuries. Moreover, the evidence shows that the Maya settlements were not always so remote that there was no contact between them and the European colonizers.

The Maya of Belize were adversely affected by the Spanish expeditions of the sixteenth and seventeenth centuries, but these *entradas* were so sporadic, the Spaniards showing no interest in settling in the area, that they were much less socially disruptive than was the case in, say, Yucatán. The Spaniards passed through the Belize area simply because it was on their route to Tayasal, and after making a few vain attempts at converting the Maya of Tipu, they left them to their isolated independence. The effect of the British colonizers was to prove far more serious.

For the first century after the arrival of the British, there was little or no contact between them and the Maya. We can assume that during most of the eighteenth century the Maya in the west of present-day Belize were relatively unaffected by the British woodcutting operations near the coast and that they continued to live in small villages or isolated homesteads throughout the area. Only when the British penetrated farther inland in search of mahogany late in the eighteenth and early in the nineteenth centuries were these Maya settlements seriously affected. The British, whose sole concern was then the extraction of timber, perceived the swidden agriculture of the Maya as a threat to the forest reserves, while the Maya viewed British expansionism as a threat to their territory and their independence.

The fresh evidence presented here proves not only that the British displaced the Maya in the territory of Belize but also that the Maya resisted the rule of the British, fighting frequent skirmishes along the frontier of British occupation. Despite their spirited resistance, the Maya were forced back into the forests of the interior. When they reemerged later in the nineteenth century from "the secret recesses of the Forest" into which they had been driven, they were decisively beaten by the British, who then incorporated them into the social structure of the colony as a dominated and dispossessed people.

3

The Establishment of the British Settlement in the Bay of Honduras in the Eighteenth Century

THE SETTLEMENT'S RAISON D'ÊTRE: THE LOGWOOD AND MAHOGANY TRADES

The origins of the British settlement in the Bay of Honduras are obscure. Some historians suggest that a settlement was founded on the Cockscombe Coast in the south during the early 1630s;[1] others claim it was founded about 1638 or 1640 by a Captain Wallice or Willis at the mouth of the Belize River.[2] The latter idea dates back at least to the Honduras Almanacks of 1827 and 1839,[3] though the 1829 Almanack states that the first British settlers came from Jamaica in 1638. Since Jamaica did not become British until 1655, that hypothesis has as little credibility as the others. Whatever the details, which will probably remain in doubt because of the paucity of early records, the purpose of British settlement was to export logwood, a tree from which a dye valued by the woolen industry was obtained.[4]

By the middle of the seventeenth century, British buccaneers, who had previously plundered Spanish logwood ships, were engaged in cutting the tree themselves in various parts of the Yucatán peninsula, particularly in Campeche in the Gulf of Mexico. The suppression of privateering that occurred after the Treaty of Madrid in 1667 encouraged the shift from buccaneering and raiding to logwood cutting and settlement. In 1670, Governor Modyford of Jamaica informed Lord Arlington that there were "about a dozen logwood vessels formerly privateers, selling the wood at £25 and £50 a ton and making a great profit; and that they go to places uninhabited or inhabited only by Indians." Modyford remarked that "if encouraged, the whole logwood trade will be English and be very considerable to His Majesty, paying £5 per ton custom."[5] In 1672, Governor Lynch of Jamaica stated that England might become "the store house of the logwood for all Europe which may be worth £100,000 per annum to the trade and customs,"[6] but by 1682 Lynch was trying to stop the cutting of logwood in the bays of Campeche and Honduras on the grounds that the territory was Spanish. He sent Captain Coxen to the Bay of Honduras to remove the logwood cutters, but the crews mutinied and Coxen himself joined the cutters. The logwood cutters' claim that their business was legitimate, and even that their rights were confirmed by the 1670 Treaty of Madrid, which acknowledged Britain's title to its de facto possessions in the Americas, was not accepted by Spain. The fact that the British cutters were the objects of continual Spanish harassment may have encouraged them to shift southward, away from the more vulnerable Bay of Campeche to the long, desolate, and reef-guarded coasts of what is now Belize. In 1705 a report to the Council of Trade mentioned "the River of Bullys, where the English for the most part now load their logwood."[7]

Early in the eighteenth century, an anonymous writer noted that for the previous twenty-five years the logwood cutters had "supplied a sufficient quantity of logwood (in exchange for British produce) for all the European markets."[8] A Board of Trade report in 1717, emphasizing the importance of the logwood trade, calculated that fifteen thousand tons of logwood had been imported in the previous four years, and, "tho' the Price is at present reduced from £40 to £16 the Tun," its value could not be figured at "less than £60,000 per annum."[9] Spain, which continued to complain of the British logwood cutters' activities, expelled them from the Bay of Campeche in 1717, thereby enhancing the significance of the small but growing settlement in the Bay of Honduras. Despite frequent Spanish attacks (1724, 1733, 1747, and 1751, among others), the British settlers maintained their presence on the mainland and expanded their trade.

By 1751 it was reported that "there was cut last year in the Bay of Honduras above 8,000 Tun of Logwood Sold at an Average in England and elsewhere for at least £20 per Tun, Total £160,000 available Sum."[10] But the once-profitable logwood trade had begun to encounter difficulties. The demand for logwood in Europe was now only about four thousand tons per year, so as production rose above the demand, the London merchants stocked up and reduced the price they paid to the cutters. Robert White, the London agent of the Bay settlers, stated the importance, and the difficulties, of their trade in a memorial in 1783:

> Logwood is chiefly used in dying Colours, Such as Blacks, Blues and purples; Wherefore its Consumption is very great in all the Woollen, Linen, Cotton and Hatt Manufactories.... We not only Supplied all our home Manufactories, but exported large quantities of it to Italy Portugal France Holland Germany and Russia.
>
> Prior to the Settlement of His Majesty's Subjects in the Bay of Honduras, the price of Log-wood in this Kingdom was from £50 to £60 per Ton. From that time the price continued decreasing untill 1749, when it was reduced to £25 per Ton. From 1749 the quantity continued increasing, and the price of course diminishing untill 1756, when they exported from Honduras 18,000 Tons per Annum at £11 per Ton. Lastly from their Reestablishment in the Bay in 1763, their Exportations of this

Article became immense, in so much that there were from 40 to 75 Sail of Ships loading continually in the Bay all the year round, untill about the year 1770; during which time the price continued lowering, till it came to about £6 and £5 per Ton.... the Supplies so far exceeded the home Consumption and all the Demands from abroad, and the Dealers and Speculators were so Overstocked with it, that from 1770 to 1772 there were not above 5 or 6 Sail of Ships loaded at a time, and the whole exportation did not exceed from 5000 to 6000 Tons. For the Market Price here about 1772 became so low, as not to pay the freights and Expenses incurred in Sending it home.[11]

To the economic difficulties of the logwood trade was added the problem of frequent harassment by the Spaniards. However, even when the Spaniards were successful in their attacks, they did not attempt any settlement, so the British would return and resume operations after they had left. This occurred when the Bay was taken in 1754 but reoccupied by the British the following year "without any opposition, the Spaniards having entirely forsaken it."[12]

Not until the Treaty of Paris in 1763 did the British settlement in the Bay of Honduras achieve any recognized status. The treaty emphasized that Spain retained sovereignty over the land, the British being given merely usufructory rights in connection with the "Occupation of Cutting, Loading, and Carrying away Logwood."[13] Though the British rights were strictly limited to logwood extraction, the settlers felt encouraged to systematize their customs and practices to some extent, and Vice-Admiral Sir William Burnaby, in consultation with some settlers, codified a set of rudimentary regulations in 1765. The fact that no British fortifications were allowed in the Bay enabled the Spaniards to capture with ease St. George's Cay, on which many of the principal settlers resided, on 15 September 1779, soon after a new war had been declared. The Bay was deserted until after the peace of 1783.

The 1763 treaty had, for the first time, conceded the right of the British to cut logwood, but it did so at a time when logwood production was actually of marginal profitability. Despite this decline in the logwood trade, however, the British were eager to reestablish their Bay settlement after 1783 because it had acquired a new raison d'être. Even before it was permitted, the settlers had begun to cut mahogany, and with the growth of the English luxury furniture industry, mahogany soon became the most important export of the Bay. It was reported in 1765 that between 25 March and 25 September there were loaded in the Bay "7,449 Tons of Logwood, and 401,231 feet of Mahogany which at £7.10 per Ton for Logwood and ten pence per foot for Mahogany, the Current prices those commoditys bear at present in London, amount to near Seventy three Thousand pounds Sterling."[14] These figures indicate that as early as 1765, mahogany accounted for about a quarter of the total value of exports, and certainly by the 1770s it was by far the most important export, though cutting was not officially permitted until the Convention of London in 1786.

Robert White stated in 1783 that "the Mahogany consumed in Great Britain alone, is estimated at ten times the quantity of all the Log-wood consumed in Europe."[15] Between 1787 and 1802 the average annual export of logwood was 1,750 tons, while that of mahogany was 3,615,000 feet. The Bay settlement, then, survived the economic crisis of the late 1760s and early 1770s when the price of logwood became so depressed. In the last quarter of the eighteenth century, and indeed until quite recently, mahogany was the major export of Belize.

THE ESTABLISHMENT OF THE SETTLER SOCIETY

The first settlers, who came to be known as the Baymen, were ex-buccaneers and adventurers who lived a rough life, relieved only by the occasional visits of ships from Jamaica bringing rum for their carousing. Captain Nathaniel Uring, who sailed from Jamaica in 1720 to get a logwood cargo in Belize, was shipwrecked and lived for four or five months with the logwood cutters on "the River of Bellese." He left the following description of the early settlers:

> In the dry Time of the Year the Logwood-Cutters search for a Work; that is, where there are a good Number of Logwood Trees; and then build a Hut near 'em, where they live during the Time they are cutting. When they have cut down the Tree, they Log it, and Chip it, which is cutting off the Bark and Sap, and then lay it in Heaps, cutting away the Under-wood, and making Paths to each Heap, that when the Rains come in which overflows the Ground, it serves as so many Creeks or Channels, where they go with small Canows or Dories and load 'em, which they bring to a Creek-side and they lade their Canows, and carry it to the *Barcadares,* which they sometimes fetch Thirty Miles, from whence the People who buy it fetch it; but if it so happens that the Wood stands upon a Ridge, or on such high Ground that the Water does not flow to it, they cut it into Logs proper for Backing, and back it out, as they call it.... The Wood-Cutters are generally a rude drunken Crew, some of which have been Pirates, and most of them Sailors; their chief Delight is in Drinking; and when they broach a Quarter Cask or a Hogshead of Wine, they seldom stir from it while there is a Drop left: It is the same thing when they open a Hogshead of Bottle Ale or Cyder, keeping at it sometimes a Week together, drinking till they fall asleep; and as soon as they awake, at it again, without stirring off the Place. Rum Punch is their general Drink, which they'll sometimes sit several Days at also; they do most Work when they have no strong Drink, for while the Liquor is moving they don't care to leave it. I had a very unpleasant Time living among these People....
>
> The Logwood Cutters, during the Floods, dwell at the Barcadares, which is Forty Two Miles up the River, where they have built their Huts upon pretty high Banks, which just keep 'em out of the Water in the Time of the Floods. As soon as they have Notice of any Ship or Vessel's Arrival at the River's Mouth, they flock down on Board in order to purchase such Things as they want, and are sure to provide good Store of strong Liquor.... I had but little Comfort living among these Crew of ungovernable Wretches, where was little else to be heard but Blasphemy, Cursing and Swearing.[16]

The process of timber extraction in the seventeenth and early eighteenth centuries must have been very simple: it merely involved setting up temporary shelters for a camp, cutting the most easily available trees, and rolling them down the river bank to be floated to the ships during flood time. The logwood trees were easy to handle; the average tree was only about two feet in girth and about twenty feet high and could be cut into small pieces without affecting the value. As Gibbs, a nineteenth-century historian of Belize, explained, "Its production for shipment requires less capital than mahogany, and is frequently undertaken by small capitalists employing small gangs.... It is generally brought down the rivers and along the coast in dories, and down the rivers in 'bark logs,' or floating cradles made of Cabbage-palm."[17] The trees grow in stands, almost exclusively in brackish water or in soft spongy soils, near rivers or the coast. These characteristics of the logwood tree meant that a small area of otherwise valueless land yielded large quantities of easily extractable timber.

Since, through the first century or so of the settlement, the number of settlers remained small, and profits in the logwood trade remained lucrative, there was little need to regulate the occupation and disposal of land. A settler could claim a limited area of land for use, such a claim being known as a "location" or "logwood works," and when the timber in that area was exhausted, he could move on to fresh territory. By the 1760s, however, the increase in the number of settlers, and in the competition between them, had induced the British government to bring some law and order into the settlement in the form of "Burnaby's Code." Although the assertion of Spanish sovereignty in the Treaty of Paris precluded the establishment of an unequivocal system of freehold tenure, the fact that the settlement was given some recognized status encouraged the settlers to introduce a system for regulating the boundaries of their logwood works.

On 10 April 1765 the settlers agreed to the following resolutions, which defined their method of staking a claim:

> First—When a person finds a spot of Logwood unoccupied, and builds his hutt, that spot shall be deemed his property; and no person shall presume to cutt or fall a tree, or grub a stump, within less than one thousand paces or yards of his Hutt, to be continued on each side of said hutt, with the course of the river or creek on both sides; and whatever person shall presume, after the limits are ascertained, to enter within those limits, shall, on proof thereof, on oath before one Justice, forfeit double the value of the wood cut, and be obliged to ship it on board of such ship or vessel as the proprietor of the wood shall appoint to receive it.
>
> Second—That no Inhabitant whatever shall occupy two works at any one time in any one River.
>
> Third—That no inhabitant shall claim a double portion of logwood works, under pretence of a partner, except that partner is, and deemed to be, an inhabitant of the Bay.[18]

These rules were clarified in a further resolution made the following year:

> The method of measuring logwood works shall be a straight line of two thousand yards or paces, to be begun and ended at the rivers side, and that the division line be run parallel to the general course of the River; and that no logwood work shall be deemed to be evacuated, as long as the owner lives in the Bay, except he occupy some other work in the same river.[19]

The logwood-cutting operations were frequently extended beyond the official but ill-defined limits of the settlement as laid down in the 1763 treaty. From the Rio Hondo south to the River Sibun, but not west of Roaring Creek (an area one-third the size of present-day Belize), the rivers, creeks, and lagoons were dotted with small timber works, some occupied and some unoccupied. The intervening country remained untouched bush. The character of the Bay settlement was described in 1779, a few days before St. George's Cay was captured by the Spaniards:

> The English Settlers, with their Wives Children and Domesticks, live on St. George's Key, where there is an exceeding good Harbour, at present defenceless.... although this Key is the general place of residence of the Settlers, yet they have Plantations which they visit occasionally, where they employ their Slaves in raising Provisions and cutting Logwood—these Plantations extend along the banks of several Rivers, such as Rio-Honde, New-River, Rowley's-Bight, Northern River, Belize-River, Chaboon River and Manatee Lagoon, for 100 Miles and upwards;—the Banks of the Belize in particular are settled above 200 Miles. The number of English on the Bay may amount to five hundred, 200 of which are able to bear arms; their Slaves of different Ages and Sexes to three thousand, of these there may be 500 to be depended on. The Indians who live near the English are so inconsiderable that it is unnecessary to take any notice of them.[20]

The settlement, therefore, consisted of a number of more or less temporary logwood works and small provision grounds (which are still referred to in Belize as "plantations") and St. George's Cay, a small island a few miles off the Belize River mouth, which was preferred to the mainland as the principal residence of the settlers because of its healthier prospects.

On 15 September 1779, the day the cay was captured by the Spaniards, "there were 101 White people on the Key, when it was taken & 40 of mixed Colour... about 200 or 250 negroes, men, women and children, mostly House-negroes... the principal part that carry on the Logwood & Mahogany cutting business were then up the River."[21] The settlers and their slaves who were captured on the cay were marched to Merida, and some were sent on to Cuba,[22] while fifty white men and two hundred and fifty slaves were reported as having arrived at the islands of Ruatan and Bonacca early in October.[23] The latter were presumably among those men who had been up the various rivers at the time the cay was captured, but what happened to the other twenty-five hundred slaves who were unaccounted for is unknown. They may well have taken this opportunity to flee, as the settlement appears to have been deserted until after peace was attained in 1783.

In the Treaty of Versailles, signed on 3 September 1783, the logwood concessions were defined more precisely than they had been twenty years before, but the permitted area was confined to that between the Hondo and Belize rivers, with the New River as the western boundary. As this area had already been logged for some time it contained little accessible timber, and, by this time, the logwood trade was unprofitable. The settlers petitioned the British government to secure further concessions from the Spanish, and in 1786 an extension of the treaty was signed in London. The Convention of London recognized the de facto situation prior to 1779 and permitted the extraction of both logwood and mahogany as far south as the Sibun River, the area between the Belize and Sibun rivers being referred to as the New Limits. At the same time, the Convention expressly forbade any fortifications, formal government, and agricultural or other productive economic activities apart from woodcutting. The settlers were to be allowed to gather "all the Fruits, or Produce of the Earth, purely natural and uncultivated," but were expressly forbidden to establish "any Plantation of Sugar, Coffee, Cacao, or other like Articles."[24]

The Convention of London, which provided for Spanish commissioners to examine the settlement twice yearly, was as emphatic as the previous treaties had been in maintaining Spain's sovereignty. But while the British government was reluctant to take any action that might be construed as an assertion of its own sovereignty over the territory, the settlers themselves were not so inhibited, and they frequently evaded the effects of Spanish sovereignty, both in their growing assumption of freehold rights and in the extent of the land they actually occupied. The settlers, who had been cutting south of the Sibun River long before the Convention, had gone as far south as Deep River by 1799, and early in the nineteenth century "Stand Creek" was an important settlement "from whence considerable quantities of wood has been shipped, and His Majesty's Ships that come to Honduras generally water there."[25] By 1806 the Rio Grande, just north of present-day Punta Gorda, had been reached,[26] and by 1814 there were settlers at the Moho River south of Punta Gorda.[27] Before the next decade had passed, the present southern boundary of Belize, the Sarstoon River, was occupied.[28] In this crucial matter of actual occupation, therefore, the settlers soon completely ignored the territorial restrictions imposed upon the settlement by the Convention.

The Convention of London also specified that in return for the concessions made by Spain, Britain should give up all its other settlements in the area, notably the Mosquito Shore and Ruatan. The evacuation of the Mosquito Shore settlers and their slaves to Belize was one of the most important events in the social history of the Bay settlement in the late eighteenth century. After the peace of 1783, between five and seven hundred people, including "several loyalists from the American States," had settled in the Bay,[29] but when 2,650 people were evacuated from the Mosquito Shore in 1787, 2,214 of them were removed to the Bay of Honduras. These newcomers were said to outnumber the original residents of the Bay by five to one.[30] Though over three-quarters of the evacuees were slaves, among the free were men who would come into competition with the recently resettled old Baymen over locations.

The population of the Bay settlement fluctuated a good deal in the eighteenth century. There were about five hundred "Merchants and Slaves"[31] in 1735, but a decade later the population had been "reduced to a small quantity of people, not exceeding above Fifty white Men, and about a hundred and twenty Negroes."[32] In 1779, just before the Spanish attack on the settlement, there were said to be 3,500 residents, three thousand of whom were slaves.[33] After the resettlement and the immigration from the Mosquito Shore in 1787, there appear to have been somewhat fewer than three thousand people in the Bay settlement.

A number of groups can be preliminarily identified in the social structure of the settlement in this period. First, there were the slaves, who constituted about three quarters of the population, most of whom had been brought from the Mosquito Shore as the property of a few rich settlers. Second, there were a few hundred free blacks or "colored," most of whom possessed little property and few slaves.* The same can be said for many of the third group, the poorer white settlers. Most of the people in the two latter groups had arrived from the Mosquito Shore in 1787 and were consequently seeking a livelihood in the Bay in competition with the fourth group, which consisted of the established Baymen and the richest of the evacuees, some of whom had previous connections in the Belize area. This fourth group, with its large number of slaves, extensive locations, and political influence, was the dominant group in the society.

CONFLICTS AMONG THE SETTLERS

In 1784 an Irish colonel, Edward Marcus Despard, was appointed the first Superintendent of the Bay settlement at Belize, and soon after his arrival in 1786 he found himself embroiled in difficulties. While his chief responsibility was to enforce the terms of the Convention of London, Lord Sydney had instructed Despard to give priority to accommodating the recently dispossessed Mosquito Shore settlers when distributing the newly conceded land between the Belize and Sibun rivers.[34] These directions, which Despard tried faithfully to execute, did not take into account the fact that the Baymen had been working those lands for years, albeit illegally. The old settlers soon informed Despard, at a time when barely five hundred people had arrived from the Mosquito Shore, that "every logwood and Mahogany tree therein are private property." Despard reported that some thirty settlers had

---

*The term *free colored* is used to refer to freedmen of mixed African and European ancestry, as distinct from *black,* which denotes African descent exclusively. The expression *free people of color,* however, was generally used to include both these categories.

divided the whole of the old District among them and will suffer no interlopers there.... Until the late Convention, the Cutting Mahogany, was always held even by the Old Baymen to be contraband, and, therefore, they cut it where ever they could find it; and they now claim all the wood which they can find in or near the Places which they formerly held in this illegal manner.... Messrs. Hoare, O'Briens, McAuley, Bartlett, Potts, Meighan, Armstrong, Davis, Tucker, and Sullivan and Garbutt... alone possess at least nine Parts in twelve of the present augmented District.[35]

(Some of the people coming from the Mosquito Shore must have been in the Bay previously, as they already held "extensive possessions" in the Old Limits, but they claimed parts of the New Limits because they were evacuees. Among these people were "Messrs. McAuley, O'Brien, Bartlett, Tucker, Meighan, and Davis.")[36]

By 4 August 1787, as the last evacuees were arriving at the settlement, a resolution was passed at a meeting of the Bay settlers at the courthouse on Belize Point:

Resolved that no person who is not actually possessed of four able Negro men Slaves shall be entitled to a mahogany work in any of the rivers without leave first had and obtained of a majority of the Magistrates... Provided always that nothing herein shall in any wise affect persons who formerly resided or now possess or occupy works in Honduras, and that every Freeholder agreeable to the usage of Honduras be entitled to a Logwood work.[37]

When it is noted that the magistrates who had been elected the previous year were Messrs. Hoare, Armstrong, Sullivan, Bartlet, and Potts, it is apparent that the wealthier settlers were legislating to protect their own claims against the poorer of the newcomers from the Mosquito Shore. This interpretation was adopted by Superintendent Despard, who, on 17 August, wrote to Lord Sydney, concerning this resolution, that he had observed

how hard it would be upon many of the Inhabitants who have arrived from the Mosquito Shore, numbers of whom are very poor, but who with one or two Negroes, together with their own labour might support themselves and their families, with some degree of comfort, by cutting Mahogany. Besides the partiality of this law to rich people, I must observe that whatever it may have been formerly, the cutting of Logwood is at present very far from being anywise profitable; and that several very opulent Inhabitants, both of this Country and the musquito Shore, began cutting Mahogany with a single Negro, some without one.... the resolution respecting the distribution of Mahogany grounds... would most effectively exclude the new settlers from any participation of the advantage arising from Mahogany cutting.[38]

This resolution prevented at least two-thirds of the heads of families so recently arrived from the Mosquito Shore from engaging in the territory's principal economic activity. This situation was exacerbated by the fact that agriculture had been specifically forbidden by the 1786 Convention. Despard, though he seemed sympathetic to the problems of the poorer evacuees and at first tried to find provision grounds for them,[39] later carried out the terms of the treaty to the letter, even using Spanish troops to enforce his orders.[40] Given the destitution the poorer evacuees must then have been experiencing, such destruction of their humblest means of subsistence proved highly unpopular.

Despard's problem was to settle the poorer evacuees within the terms of the Convention and of his instructions, both of which he was interpreting very strictly. He planned a new settlement, called Convention Town, to be built on the south point of the Belize River, which was within the New Limits. The settlement was to consist of lots fifty feet wide and one hundred feet deep, and contain small mahogany works, each comprising forty yards of riverbank, which were to be drawn for in a lottery. This plan of Despard's angered the Magistrates and other well-established settlers. In the first place, it emphasized the priority of the claims of the evacuees within the New Limits south of the Belize River. Secondly, the lottery method for distributing the land gave no advantages to those in the community with wealth, prestige, and privilege. A letter from the Committee of Honduras Settlers, signed by Bartlet, O'Brien, Teeling, Davis, Hoare, Young, and Potts, complained of Despard's method of

> dividing the newly ceded district... after the manner of a Lottery, without preference to those who had formerly clear'd ground or built houses, or without any distinction of Age, Sex, Character, Respectability, Property, or *Colour,* the lowest Mulatto or free Negro, had an equal chance with the Honble Col. James Lawrie, lately His Majestys Superintendent & President of His Council on the Mosquito Shore and the Honourable the Members of that same Council, with the Chief Judge of the Colony, were reduc'd in one instant to the same footing with Negroes and indented Servants & in fact Col. Despard has said & continues to say that they are on an equal footing & that he cannot & will not know any distinction between these very different classes of Men.[41]

Of course, it was not true that the rich and privileged were being reduced to an equal footing with the poor and deprived. The former would keep their riches and privileges, while the poor were merely being given a chance "to get the means of subsistence by their labour and industry."[42] Those who were already distinguished by their "Property, or *Colour*" were arguing that they should be free to utilize such distinctions to further their own wealth and privileges by discriminating against the other, "very different," classes. Some of the tensions that existed between the various groups in the settlement, particularly between the poor free colored and the richer white settlers, came to a head on the weekend of 18 and 19 August 1787.

On 18 August, Aaron Young, a Magistrate, complained to his fellow Magistrates that Joshua Jones, "a free man of Colour," had knocked down Young's cookhouse, which was built apart from his dwelling on the South Point of the Belize River mouth. Having obtained a warrant, Young secured Jones's arrest that evening, and the prisoner was held in the courthouse. During the night, the

Magistrates and their friends seem to have been apprehensive that the free colored would attempt to release Jones, so they mounted an armed guard. The "Principal Inhabitants and Merchants" (as they had styled themselves), either through panic or a decision to make a show of force, armed themselves and assembled at the courthouse the following morning. They claimed that "a Scene of the most alarming nature appear'd, a few white people of the very lowest class, a number of Mustees, Mulattoes, and free Negroes running about the Streets and assembling under Arms to the infinite terror of the more respectable & peaceable part of the Community."[43] The "Principal Inhabitants" seem to have exaggerated the activities of their opponents, but their description exposes their fears of the "Commotions rais'd by the People of mix'd Colour and Negroes, who they asserted would soon rule them with a Rod of Iron if not immediately disarmed."[44] It was also reported that "the magistrates and people of property were much alarmed and even terrified; a few went up the river Belize, to be out of the way of the impending evils, others flew to the court-house with what arms time or chance put in their way."[45]

The situation appears to have polarized, the "Principal Inhabitants" collecting at the courthouse, and the "free people of colour" assembling at the store of Mr. Bogle, commissary of provisions. When Despard arrived at Bogle's store, "the people then assembled told him that if he thought it proper they would rescue Jones by force, which they were confident they were very able to do."[46] Despard quieted the crowd and proceeded to the courthouse, where he demanded to know why Jones was being held a prisoner. On being informed of the reason, he replied that Jones had acted on his authority and by his order in pulling down Young's kitchen. There followed a lengthy discussion concerning the extent, limitations, and source of the Superintendent's authority in relation to Burnaby's Code, the "Principal Inhabitants" stating that they "could not in their humble opinion justify the steps which he had taken & said he would take to settle & accomodate a set of men of Colour calling themselves the People of the Mosquito Shore, and who they contended were not so, almost every person of property particularly the WoodCutters of that Country being then present & fully satisfied with the Provision made for them by their representatives in joint Committee with the old Setlers of Honduras."[47] Despard then declared the prisoner free and attempted to release him, but the Magistrates restrained Jones, and Despard was forced to leave him in their power.

On the following day, 20 August, Despard met with a deputation consisting of Messrs. Hoare, O'Brien, Young, Usher, and Bartlet. Despard represented the views and forwarded the complaints of the "new Settlers, particularly the people of colour,"[48] while the deputation expressed their concern over the assembling of these people the previous morning. The outcome of the meeting was inconclusive, and the sources of tension in the Bay settlement remained.

There were two major sources of this tension and conflict among the free population of the settlement. The first of these lay in the socially ambiguous position of the free black and colored: they were not slaves, yet they were not accepted as the equals of the whites. In the incident of 18 and 19 August 1787, this group, joined by some dissatisfied poor whites, were objecting to the way in which the richer, established white settlers discriminated against them. Stopping short of a revolt, they allowed the Superintendent to represent them, but Despard, unwilling to back his judgement with force, was unable to resolve the dispute. In fact, the other major source of tension within the free population lay precisely in the problem of the location of executive authority. The ambiguity of the Crown's authority vis-à-vis the settlers' primitive legislative and judicial institutions encouraged continual struggle within the settlement.

THE PROBLEM OF THE LOCATION OF EXECUTIVE AUTHORITY

From quite early in the nineteenth century the settlers in the Bay of Honduras were in the habit of holding meetings to conduct and comment upon affairs of common interest, and to elect Magistrates. It was the Magistrates' business to administer and enforce the simple rules of conduct that became known as the "Customs of the Bay," thereby combining executive and judicial functions. By treaty with Spain after the Seven Years' War, Britain was not allowed to create any formal government in the Bay, but at the time of Burnaby's visit in 1765, the magistracy was accorded some vague official recognition without the scope of its authority being clearly defined.

The importance of Burnaby's Code has been greatly exaggerated. It hardly established a constitution, except in the most rudimentary fashion, and it is certainly untrue that "the close of the 18th Century saw the confirmation of this native born constitution by Royal Authority."[49] James Stephen, a senior Colonial Office official, emphatically stated in 1839 that the institutions of the Bay settlement had "never been acknowledged by the Government here as lawful."[50] The chief concern of Burnaby's Code, a list of a dozen simple rules, was the maintenance of law and order among the unruly Baymen. That Burnaby's rudimentary constitution was defective and insufficient to maintain law and order is demonstrated by his proviso that the commanding officer of any ship of war would have "full power... to enforce and put in execution all such Laws and Regulations."[51] Though an elementary system of administration existed, whereby settlers gathered together in a Public Meeting to pass resolutions that were deemed to have the force of law and they annually elected Magistrates who acted in a semi-judicial and semi-executive capacity, the defect in the system was the absence of any clear executive power.

During the economic crisis of the 1760s and early 1770s, the absence of such power became apparent, as the Baymen's behavior reflected the tensions engendered by their insecurity. The Lords of the Admiralty received a letter from Rear Admiral Parry informing them that in 1768 "the Bay-men at Honduras have shook off all subjection to the Magistrates, have resisted their power, and that all is riot and confusion in those parts," and later the same year Parry reported that dissension among the Baymen was on the increase. He described the settlers as "a most notorious lawless set of Miscreants [who] pursue their licentious conduct with impunity."[52] In 1771, a petition from "the principal subjects" of the Bay was sent to Admiral Rodney, complaining that they were

> in a State of the utmost disorder and Confusion. The Annual Election of Magistrates has been stopped by the proceeding of a Mob, and an Election carried by force wherein some persons are invested with a power to Administer Justice who have on many Occasions done their utmost to subvert it; the Houses of some have been threatened with fire and one in particular broke open and Effects destroyed; peaceable and orderly men have been knocked down in the Street, insulted and abused when attending their necessary business.[53]

Although warships occasionally visited the Bay from Jamaica, the lack of any permanent police or clear authority meant that Burnaby's Code was unenforceable.

With the appointment of a Superintendent in 1784, the location of executive authority became more ambiguous than ever, although Lord Sydney had stated that the Superintendent's authority overrode that of the settlers and their regulations.[54] Since Despard's chief responsibility was to enforce the terms of the Convention, he soon found himself cooperating with the visiting Spanish commissioners in restricting the settlers to the treaty limits and in destroying the forbidden provision grounds. The settlers, who had been accustomed to ignoring the terms of treaties with Spain and to regulating their own affairs without interference, soon opposed the Crown's representative.

The Public Meeting of the Baymen has been characterized as an example of popular democracy, likened to the New England model,[55] and described as "the nearest approach to true democracy since the days of the Greek city state."[56] In fact, it was not unlike Greek democracy, in that it was the privilege of a free minority in a society divided between the free few and the enslaved many—but that is hardly a "true" or "popular" democracy. Moreover, the assertion that the Public Meeting "comprised all the free Inhabitants of the Settlement"[57] is also inaccurate, restrictions being imposed upon most of the free settlers.

The Public Meetings were actually gatherings of a tiny elite that were dominated by ten or twenty of the richest inhabitants, and any suggestion that they constituted even an incipient democracy is a misrepresentation. The slaves, who made up about three-quarters of the population, were not, of course, involved at all in the Public Meetings. A property qualification of £65 (Jamaica currency) that existed in 1789[58] was raised the following year, when it was reported that "any person entitled to vote at elections for Magistrates for this Settlement... must be possessed of a fixed Habitation or a Negro Slave or a Mahogany or Logwood work or visible property to the amount of Eighty Pounds Current money of Jamaica and that no person of colour was allowed to vote."[59] Elections, the chief business of the Meetings, were therefore the privilege of a mere handful of the richer white settlers. At a Meeting in June 1784, five Magistrates were elected by seven electors, and on 27 June 1786, five Magistrates were elected by sixteen persons. No poll was opened on either occasion. In 1787, although a poll was open for a month and there were many persons recently arrived from the Mosquito Shore in addition to former electors, there were only thirty-nine voters; and in 1788 and 1789, under the same conditions, the number of voters was twenty and forty, respectively.[60] This little white oligarchy struggled to protect and expand its power and privileges at the expence of the poor white settlers, the free colored, and the office of the Superintendent.

The white oligarchy finally succeeded in getting Despard suspended from office in November 1789, and a new election was held on 3 May 1790. Despard offered himself as a candidate and topped the poll with an unprecedented 203 of 250 votes.[61] Four of the defeated Magistrates complained about Despard's canvassing techniques, the number of ineligible voters, and the breadth of the franchise. They grumbled about "ignorant turtlers . . . men of colour, possessing no species of property or an fixed residence" voting for ex-Superintendent Despard. "There are not above 76 wood cutters of all descriptions in the Bay of Honduras, of whom, at least, Twenty hardly deserve that name, and about 40 White housekeepers, being traders and tradesmen, so that, in our opinion, there cannot be above 110 good voters in the Settlement; and on this principle . . . few of Colonel Despard's friends, or even himself, would have been returned as Magistrates."[62] It is equally clear that few, if any, of the people usually returned as Magistrates would have been elected previously if a comparable number of people had voted; but by their own admission, these men wanted to keep the electorate to a mere 5 percent of the total adult population, or about 20 percent of the free adults. The election was an empty victory for Despard, however. Shortly afterward, he sailed for England where he was subsequently arrested for assisting the Irish uprising in 1798 and was held in jail for more than two years without a trial. He was finally hanged in 1803 for involvement in a plot to assassinate George III, seize the Tower of London and the Bank of England, and proclaim a republic.[63]

It has been charged that Despard was attempting to replace the magistracy and the Public Meeting "by direct administration by himself and his nominees."[64] Though it would be hard to substantiate such a charge, Despard certainly had no liking for the Magistrates. He described them, with their handful of associates, as "a very arbitrary aristocracy,"[65] who attempted to monopolize the mahogany business and to make the rest of the population dependent upon them. Despard, in trying to carry out his instructions with regard to the resettlement of the poorer refugees from the Mosquito Shore, for whom he seemed to have considerable sympathy, came in direct conflict with the monopolists and their representatives in the magistracy. He wrote to Lord Sydney:

> The Magistrates have been at great pains to give out that the people who wish to support my authority, are people of the lowest rank, and most infamous Charac-

ters.... [on] the Contrary they are a remarkably quiet and inoffensive sett of people, well attached to his Majesty's Government.... Many of them, it is true, are poor, but on the other hand there are numbers of them possessed of very considerable properties in Slaves, who at present are rather a Burden upon them than any advantage, from the total monopoly exercised by the old Inhabitants.[66]

The "old Inhabitants," however, argued that Despard's approach would have repercussions that would undermine the social fabric they were so eager to preserve. Their London agent argued their case against Despard's lottery plan, saying that it would ruin the settlement:

> It breaks in pieces all the Links of Society, and destroys all Order Rank and Government. The Mulattoes and Free Negroes make good Servants: that they are happy, and well taken Care of in that Station; and rise in Circumstances, according to their Industry Frugality and Ability, preserving still their proper Rank & Station in the Community. But upon this wild and Levelling principle of Universal Equality, they would become intitled not only to elect Magistrates, but themselves to be elected; and what kind of Government must thence ensue, is submitted to Your Lordship. But this is not all. For the Negroes in Servitude, observing the Now exalted Station of their Brethren of Yesterday, would be thence induced to revolt, or to desert to the Spaniards; unless they themselves were likewise made Free. Whichever of these Events took place, the Settlement must be ruined; especially if of good slaves & Servants, they should become Turbulent Seditious & Bad Citizans.[67]

The view of the elite was that good slaves and servants were those who accepted "their proper Rank & Station in the Community," as defined for them by the elite. In making their case, they appealed to principles of conservatism, law and order, and racialism, and they greatly exaggerated Despard's very limited egalitarianism, which really only amounted to a request that the poor and the free colored be given a chance in their new surroundings. The wealthy landowners also raised the familiar specter of slave revolts, a specter that continually haunted the white settlers of the Caribbean even before the massive revolution of Saint Domingue broke out in 1791. Their emotional appeal won the debate. Lord Sydney's instructions to Despard made it clear that the free colored and blacks should be kept in a position dependent upon and subservient to the affluent settlers:

> I will do you the Justice to believe that in the distribution of those Lands you were actuated by the best motives, though at the same time it could have been wished that you had made some Distinction in the Extent of Lots so to be disposed of, between affluent Settlers and Persons of a different description, particularly people of Colour, or Free Negroes, who, from the natural Prejudices of the Inhabitants of the Colonies, are not, however valuable in point of character, considered upon an equal footing with People of a different Complexion.... some measures should be taken to find Employment for the people who have lately arrived in the District, particularly those of small property, and people of Colour, to prevent their becoming a Public Burthen.... I would recommend your calling to your assistance

some of the most respectable of the Inhabitants, and having the benefit of their advice, endeavour to fix the people above mentioned in some employment, from whence they may be likely to obtain subsistence.[68]

Not even the immediate problem of the resettlement of the Mosquito Shore evacuees was resolved to everyone's satisfaction, as can be seen from the fact that fourteen of them petitioned in 1793 that they, together with their families and slaves, should be permitted to return to the Mosquito Shore. They stated that they were unable to support themselves by cutting wood or growing provisions and did not wish to be "half British Subjects as we are at present."[69]

Though Despard's successor, Superintendent Hunter, proposed a "Plan of Police" for the settlement in 1790,[70] the problem of the absence of a clear and unequivocal definition of the location of executive authority remained, and the conflicts resulting from this ambiguity persisted well into the nineteenth century. When Superintendent Hunter arrived he declared that the "Ancient System of Regulations [was] to be restored,"[71] and after 1791, when he left, the settlers managed themselves. When war broke out again in 1796, Lieutenant Colonel Barrow was appointed Superintendent, but largely for military reasons. Subsequent Superintendents frequently found themselves in conflict with the Magistrates over the question of the location of authority in the Settlement. Thus Superintendent Hamilton wrote in 1807 that "the powers of His Majesty's Superintendent are not defined and the Magistrates would wish to insist that he has no Civil power over them whatsoever. This is a point I will not give up. I consider myself as Chief Magistrate."[72] Hamilton's successor, Lieutenant Colonel Smyth, was told by the Magistrates that they did not know "how far they were amenable to the Laws of Great Britain," which Smyth protested was "an extraordinary assertion" from Magistrates of a British settlement.[73]

Superintendent George Arthur summed up the problems of his position in 1819 by saying, "The Office is, and ever has been, so very undefined as to deprive the Representative of the Crown of the Authority necessary for the administration of Public Business."[74] It appears that the Superintendents' actions frequently offended the vested interests of the settlement's elite, and although the Superintendent's powers were gradually extended, he was not given clear control over the Magistrates or the Public Meeting that represented that elite. The oligarchy continued to make and execute the laws, and until 1854 the anomalies of the constitution of the Bay settlement remained unresolved, the Colonial Office avoiding a decision on the problem because the settlement was not recognized as British territory.

THE SOCIAL STRUCTURE OF THE SETTLEMENT IN THE LATE EIGHTEENTH CENTURY

When the Mosquito Shore was evacuated in 1787, 2,214 people were removed to the Bay of Honduras. Over three-quarters of these evacuees were slaves, but the

1,677 slaves were distributed very unequally among the 537 free people.[75] A list was compiled by Superintendent Despard of 1,420 people from the Mosquito Shore who required a supply of provisions; 903 of those listed were slaves and 517 were free.[76] Of the free people, 215 were described as "Heads of Families"; over half these heads of families (112) possessed no slaves at all and another 42 of them possessed a total of 102 slaves. However, almost half of all the slaves on this list (445) were in the possession of just nineteen heads of families, and a mere eight of the latter owned 259 slaves. That it was generally the poorest of the evacuees who required provisions is indicated by the fact that the remaining twenty freemen unaccounted for in the list (all of whom may not have been heads of households) must have possessed the remaining 774 slaves between them. It is clear, then, that while most of the Mosquito Shore settlers owned no slaves, or very few, some of them owned large numbers. (This view is supported by a letter from the Mosquito Shore some years earlier, stating that one William Pitt was on his deathbed, and that "his Possessions are much the largest of any here among them are about four hundred high spirited Negroes from whom an immediate danger more than threatens.")[77]

From this estimation, it appears that fewer than forty of the Mosquito Shore settlers were bringing to the Bay over 1,200 slaves, or almost three-quarters of the total. Although this list cannot be considered a representative sample of the total population, other data reinforce this picture of the very unequal distribution of slave ownership in the Bay settlement.

The composition of the settlement's population can be more fully ascertained through the study of two early censuses: "List of the Inhabitants of Honduras, taken by His Majesty's Superintendent, in January and February 1790, in consequence of His Catholick Majesty's Concession of 30th May 1789, permitting them to cultivate gardens,"[78] and "General Return of the Inhabitants in the Bay of Honduras, Free people of every description and Slaves, returned 22nd October, 1790."[79] The latter census lists the inhabitants by name and distinguishes between men, women, and children, white, free, and slave, while the former names heads of families (in three districts: Sibun, Belize, and the Northern District), and enumerates the men, women, and children, both free and slave, in each household. From these two documents a fairly clear picture of the social structure emerges, though the figures are not, of course, wholly reliable.

When Despard enumerated the population in January and February 1790, the total was 2,915 (738 free and 2,177 slaves), though he said there were "besides fifty or sixty more (mostly persons employed in fishing and piloting) who did not give in their names for garden grounds," nor did the census attempt to enumerate the Maya, who were outside the bounds of the settlement. The census divided the territory into three areas, and enumerated 58 percent of the population in the "River Belize, its branches and creeks," 8 percent in the "River Sibun and its branches," and the remaining 34 percent in "Salt Creek, Northern River, Rowley's Bight and New River." Though the numbers would fluctuate with the seasonal nature of woodcutting, in 1790 almost all the inhabitants worked in the Belize River valley and the hundreds of smaller rivers, creeks, and lagoons to the north. The census also differentiates between those people who were living in Convention Town, the settlement created by Despard on the south point of the Belize River mouth for the poorer evacuees from the Mosquito Shore, and the remainder of the population. In 1790 this town held 470 people, or about 16 percent of the total population. The town that was developing on both banks of the Belize River mouth, now known as Belize City, had replaced St. George's Cay as the principal residence of the settlement by the late eighteenth century.

The census of 22 October 1790, a summary of which is given in table 3.1, provides more details on the composition of the population. Toward the end of the eighteenth century the slaves constituted about three-quarters of the population, the whites amounted to about one-tenth, and the remainder were "free people of color," both black and mixed. There was a marked sexual imbalance in the population, with a 2:1 ratio between men and women. This imbalance was particularly acute among the whites, where there were almost four times as many men as women. Among the "free people of color" however there were actually more women than men. These figures suggest that the white men established relationships with slaves, some of whom they manumitted along with the resultant offspring. Consequently there were more white men than free men of color, but there were almost three times as many free colored women and children as there were white women and children.

Since there was no regular system of freehold tenure in the Bay settlement (registration of land ownership was not instituted until 1858), the only available measure of the wealth of a free settler was in the number of slaves he possessed. By this measure it is apparent that the "estates" of the Bay settlers were small compared to those of, say, Jamaica, where one or two hundred slaves per estate was not uncommon, and some had over five hundred.[80] In the Bay settlement only one owner possessed over one hundred slaves at this time; James Pitt Lawrie was listed in the first census as the head of a family with 126 slaves. The

TABLE 3.1 Population of the Bay Settlement, by Legal Status and Sex, 1790

	White		"Free People of Color"		Slaves		Total
	N	Percentage	N	Percentage	N	Percentage	
Men	174	13	120	9	1,091	79	1,385
Women	46	7	132	19	515	74	693
Children	41	7	119	21	418	72	578
Total	261	10	371	14	2,024	76	2,656

SOURCE: "General Return of the Inhabitants in the Bay of Honduras, Free people of every description and Slaves, returned 22nd October, 1790," CO 123/9.

disparity in slave ownership that was indicated by the list of Mosquito Shore evacuees requiring provisions in 1787 is confirmed by the censuses of 1790. The twenty estates that had at least thirty slaves possessed a total of 1,085 slaves, or about half of all the slaves in the settlement. At the other end of the spectrum, 35 of the 159 free heads of families listed possessed no slaves at all, and another eighteen owned only one, two, or three slaves each—that is, less than the minimum required by the regulation of 1787 for a new settler to be allowed to cut mahogany. At least one-third of these free heads of families were thereby deprived of engaging in the principal economic activity of the settlement.

The domination of the economy by a few settlers was encouraged by the shift from logwood to mahogany cutting as the basis of the settlement's economy. While the extraction of logwood was a small-scale operation in terms of the number of slaves and the area of land required, the extraction of mahogany necessitated a considerable change. The mahogany tree is very large; the average commercial tree is about seven feet in girth but trees range from six to seventeen feet, and they rise to between seventy and one hundred feet in height. Mahogany grows in a more scattered manner than logwood, and in areas farther from the coast, and whereas logwood can be cut into chunks for shipment, mahogany must be shipped in large logs. It was therefore considerably more difficult and expensive to cut and transport mahogany; the process required more capital, more slaves, and more land, than logwood cutting. The shift from logwood to mahogany cutting, therefore, encouraged the evolution of a small group of wealthy cutters and made it increasingly difficult for the poorer settlers to establish themselves independently in the settlement's economy. Though according to the resolutions of 1787 every freeholder was entitled to a logwood work, it was pointed out at the time that "the cutting of Logwood is at present very far from being anywise profitable."[81]

The Public Meetings at which these resolutions were passed were controlled, as has been indicated, by a handful of wealthy cutters and their representatives in the magistracy. Through this legislation, enforced by the Magistrates, twelve of these cutters claimed four-fifths of the entire area encompassed by the treaties, or about two thousand square miles. It is obvious that, despite their ownership of several hundred slaves, these few men could not possibly work all this land, so the question arises as to why they were determined to hold so much more land than they could use. The answer, it would appear, lies in the way in which they used this monopolization: not only to exploit the timber resources, but also to wield power over the other inhabitants of the settlement.

The very limited size of the population encouraged the propensity of the wealthiest and longest-established settlers to fulfill several roles simultaneously. At this period in the history of the settlement there was little or no specialization within the elite. The men who had succeeded in establishing themselves as the wealthiest and most influential cutters in the early logwood trade were the best equipped for expanding their operations to exploit the demand for mahogany.

These same men, who had established connections with London merchants for exporting their timber, were also able to develop the import trade, so vital since the local cultivation of provisions was prohibited, and consequently to control retailing. The economic crisis engendered by the decline of the logwood trade in the late 1760s and early 1770s had led some of the settlers to fall into debt with London merchants and with the wealthier cutters and traders of the Bay.[82] The latter fixed the price of logwood and mahogany, which was used as currency within the settlement, and as Magistrates, they had control over taxation. The economic interests of the wealthy cutters did not lie exclusively in timber extraction, therefore, and their determination to claim all the available land must be seen in this total context. Despard described the Magistrates as "almost our sole importers, exporters, and retailers, too; and they had the equity to import, just what served themselves; and their private purposes of keeping the people poor and totally dependent upon them; for they not only set their own price upon their goods, but also upon the logwood and mahogany which they received in payment for them."[83]

Within the political structure of the settlement the wealthy cutters controlled the legislature and judiciary and succeeded in retaining their executive powers even when these were challenged by the Crown's representative. By using their political power to enforce and maintain their monopoly of land ownership, the wealthy settlers were able to limit access to the primary economic resource of the settlement and were thus able to restrict competition in timber exporting. Seen within the context of their almost total control of the settlement's political economy, their monopoly of land ownership was simply one way, albeit a fundamental one, by which the elite exercised their power to force the poor settlers into dependence upon them.

The extent of the power of the Magistrates, and the manner in which they exercised it, is illustrated by their treatment of some of the Mosquito Shore evacuees who were denied access to mahogany and who attempted to defy the Magistrates' authority to dispose of land. The following is from a petition to the Superintendent from three white Mosquito Shore settlers who, it can be ascertained from the censuses, owned between twelve and twenty slaves each and were therefore not among the poorer refugees:

> A combination hath been formed against us by the former English Inhabitants of the Bay of Honduras and some few people from the Musquito Shore, who raising themselves into a kind of legislative body, form laws and regulations, and make Magistrates to enforce these Laws and endeavour to cause every Individual of the Community to sign those Laws. . . .
>
> As these Laws or regulations seem also (to us) to be partial and in favor of one sett of people, and palpably calculated to enslave another, we openly gave such opinion of them and absolutely refused to sign them, declaring we knew of no legal authority as yet in this country (especially to distribute Lands) but what lay with his Majestys Superintendent. Many of us were then told, that if we continued of that

opinion, we should be looked upon as men who had devested themselves of the rights and privileges of British Subjects, in withdrawing ourselves from the protection of the Magistrates and that therefore whatever injury may be done us we could not expect redress. That we would soon find ourselves in a very dissagreeable situation, As we would not be able to furnish ourselves with any kind of necessary or articles as we might be in want of, although we had money to pay for them for none would be sold or disposed of to those who did not conform So that we must either conform or leave the Country. These maxims they have actually put in practice....

The Mahogany works in the new limits we have found all possessed by the former Bay people who claim every Spot, where Mahogany is to be cut, under various pretences. Some of us have looked but found every place claimed, some of us have cut wood, our Negroes have been turned away and ordered to cut no more, some of the Mahogany we have cut hath been attached as the property of old Baymen.

Thus persecuted and daily depreciated the prospect before us being a most melancholy aspect....[84]

With such political and economic pressure being exerted upon the white property owners, it seems likely that a similar effort was being made by the oligarchy to ensure the dependence of poor whites and the "free people of color." In a situation where there was insufficient labor to work all the vast lands held by the elite, the latter perceived all but the richest Mosquito Shore evacuees not just as potential competitors for the settlement's resources but also as potential laborers. The wealthier settlers therefore obstructed all the other freemen from acquiring lands in order to deny them an independent means of livelihood and force them into a position of dependence. Despard noted, in a letter written just after the "Principal Inhabitants" had made their restrictive regulations, that the Magistrates had forbidden ownership of mahogany or logwood works by the free colored unless the latter were naturalized by consent of all the Magistrates, "by which law not less than eighty people... who have come from the Mosquito Shore are entirely excluded from any means of gaining a Subsistence, unless they will become the Servants of these Legislators, which really seems to be the principle intention of this partial rule."[85]

Despite this discrimination against the free colored, a number of them possessed a good many slaves and held positions of authority within the settlement's militia. Thus, James Pitt Lawrie, who, with 126 slaves, was the largest slave owner in the settlement at the end of the eighteenth century, was named in a "List of Free people of Colour in Honduras employed in or contributing to the defence of the Settlement" as the commander of the right wing of the First South Side Battalion. Jonathan Card and Stephen Winter, both described as "coloured men," possessed over thirty slaves each and were thus among the top twenty slave owners. John Neal and George Crawford, described by Despard as "people of colour, very intelligent... and both possessed of very considerable properties in slaves,"[86] owned twenty-three and fifteen slaves respectively. James Hewm, another "coloured man" who, like Jonathan Card, commanded a division of the militia, possessed twenty-two slaves, and Joshua Jones, the "free man of Colour" who was arrested on 18 August 1787, owned seventeen slaves.

Superintendent Hunter reported in 1790 that "there are a great number of people of mixed colours in this Settlement, principally natives of the Mosquito Shore.... Some of these People possess considerable properties, and are Men of fair Character." Hunter went on to say that, as was West Indian custom, they were deprived of many privileges, but he recommended that

> His Majesty's Superintendent and the Committee shall have the power of granting or allowing to Free People of mixed colour, Inhabitants of this Settlement, such privileges and immunities, as may to them appear proper, according to the behaviour, character, property or station of such person of colour, who may make application to His Majesty's Superintendent and the Committee for such privileges, which shall be enrolled in a Book, kept for that purpose, Three months prior to their taking upon them, or exercising such privileges; provided always, that nothing in this article shall extend to the privilege of acting as Jurors, or being elected to any public Offices.[87]

These members of the free colored group, though denied political privileges, were, in their possession of slaves and their participation in the militia, demonstrably trying to join the system that had been created and dominated by the white elite. The majority of the free blacks and colored, however, did not acquire economic wealth any more than they acquired political power; instead they became the employees of rich cutters and traders or drifted away from logging to become subsistence farmers or fishermen. Much the same is true of the poorer whites, who were small tradesmen, turtlers, or fishermen, or were the employees of their more powerful neighbors. These poor whites probably amounted to fewer than one hundred and fifty people, possessing few slaves and little influence in the settlement.

Table 3.2 is a contemporary effort to classify the population of the Bay settlement using the criteria of property, occupation, and color. It would appear that while the settlement was dominated by a small group of white men who managed to withhold privileges and rights from other settlers, the ownership of slaves and participation in the economy and militia was not an exclusive prerogative of white men. The social structure did not consist simply of white masters and black slaves, though this was the fundamental distinction that affected the social position of the more ambiguously placed people—poor white men and slave-owning black men. Between the tiny elite and the mass of slaves there were a few hundred people who were either employees, dependent upon the elite, or were self-employed at the subsistence level, gardening and fishing for their livelihood. This intermediate social stratum did not constitute an integrated "middle class," however, because racial factors intervened to divide it. There is no doubt that the "natural Prejudices" mentioned by Lord Sydney continually operated, as they did during the resettlement of the Mosquito Shore evacuees, in favor of the white group and to the disadvantage of the black group within this stratum.

TABLE 3.2 Population of the Bay Settlement, by Property, Occupation, and Color, 1790

"His Majesty's Subjects who occupy the district allotted for cutting wood in the Bay of Honduras by the Definitive Treaty of 1783 and the Convention of 1786, may be classed in the following manner viz.

Description	Number
1. Cutters and Exporters of wood possessed of considerable property	13
2. Cutters of wood possessed of less property	34
3. Cutters of wood possessed of small property	24
4. Traders and Housekeepers	24
5. Tradesmen and Housekeepers	18
6. People of small property in the service of Wood Cutters, and employed as Clerks, Overseers, and Masters of Droggers	12
7. People of no property, and employed by Wood Cutters and others as Clerks, Masters of Droggers, Tradesmen, and Labourers	37
8. Housekeepers of very little property, principally Refugees from America, who support themselves and families by raising Vegetables, hunting and fishing	14
9. Turtlers residing in the district, possessed of Boats and Nets fit for carrying on the business, and who employ Servants	8
10. Turtlers of no property, of no fixed place of Residence and employed by the Master Turtlers among the Keys and Reefs along the Coast	63
11. People of mixed Colour possessed of property, and of whom, about one third are Wood Cutters of the 2nd class, but not enumerated there	16
12. People of mixed Colour, possessed of no property, and employed by Wood Cutters and others, as Tradesmen, Fishermen, and Labourers	24
Total:	287

It is believed there may be about Fifty British Subjects in Honduras not enumerated in the above Statement, consisting of Turtlers, Fishermen and free Negroes, many of whom have no place of fixed Residence, and are possessed of no property.

The number of Slaves in Honduras, may be estimated at Two Thousand, and are principally in the possession of the 1st, 2nd, 3rd, 4th and 11th Classes and are indeed their most valuable property."

SOURCE: CO 123/9.

The free colored, many of whom may once have been slaves, were not concerned with eliminating the fundamental social distinctions in the society. They were, instead, eager to extend their own rights and privileges within the existing social order; but they possessed no power with which to gain concessions from the oligarchy. Had the free colored appealed to and roused the slaves, the distinction between themselves and the slaves, which was a differentiation they wanted to preserve and extend, might well have been swept away in a hurricane of social change. So, during the confrontation of 18 and 19 August 1787, these men chose not to involve the slaves on their behalf, but to rely instead upon the ineffective representation of the Superintendent. Unwilling to risk their existing status, the free colored remained in an ambiguous social position, denying any affinity with the slaves, yet themselves denied identity with the whites.

The social structure established during the eighteenth century remained essentially unchanged, therefore, while the handful of white settlers and merchants became more firmly entrenched in their economic and political power. However, while the white oligarchy maintained its power, it remained uneasy.

Though the threat from the Spaniards was checked at the battle of St. George's Cay in 1798, the legal and constitutional status of the territory remained undefined and provided little security for the settlers. But more important, because it could not be settled by periodic peace treaties, was the continual and pervasive apprehension on the part of the elite about the behavior of the majority of the population. Throughout the eighteenth and well into the nineteenth centuries, the free settlers, white and black, were haunted by the specter of revolts among the slaves.

4
The Institution of Slavery

THE ESTABLISHMENT OF SLAVERY

The first settlers in the Bay of Honduras cut their own logwood. Early in the eighteenth century, however, as their business became more established and profits remained high, these settlers strove to expand their enterprises. Shortage of land posed no problem, and there were plentiful supplies of accessible logwood available. The problem for those settlers who wished to expand their woodcutting operations was to secure adequate supplies of labor. The same problem had previously faced settlers on the Caribbean islands in connection with the production of sugar. In Barbados, for example, in the seventeenth century, as the cultivation of tobacco gave way to that of sugar, the planters sought adequate supplies of labor for their plantations. Amerindian and European labor proved unsatisfactory, and the planters turned to the population of Africa, which, raped by the slave trade, provided slave labor for the vast estates of the Caribbean. The settlers in the Bay of Honduras relied upon the same source to provide the labor for cutting logwood in the early eighteenth century.

The earliest reference to the presence of Africans in the Bay of Honduras is dated 1724. In that year a Spanish missionary reported that the British settlement consisted of "about three hundred English, besides Mosquito Indians and negro slaves, these latter having been introduced but a short time before from Jamaica and Bermuda."[1] Another nineteenth-century historian quoted from a Guatemalan gazette of 1730 that reported Spaniards crossing New River and making "prisoners sixteen Englishmen and an Englishwoman with her daughter, sixteen negroes and four negresses."[2] Whatever the date at which Africans first appeared in the Bay, before the middle of the eighteenth century they outnumbered the white settlers. An appeal for military assistance in the face of Spanish threats in 1745 stated that the settlement was "reduced to a small quantity of People, not exceeding above Fifty white Men, and about a hundred and twenty Negroes."[3]

The African slaves who were imported to cut logwood were brought through the West Indian islands. One early-nineteenth-century account stated that "these have mostly been imported from Africa by the intercourse with Jamaica, no direct importation having ever taken place; but many of these people are creoles of the different West Indian Islands, and several have been brought into the Settlement, by their owners, from the United States."[4] Later it was stated that "the Blacks . . . have been . . . imported from Africa, either direct or through the West India Islands."[5]

Though many of the slaves brought to the Bay may have been "Creoles" born in the Caribbean, others must have been brought from Africa via the Jamaican slave markets, or following a period of that socialization to slavery known as "seasoning." In 1769, a complaint that the Spaniards granted escaping slaves asylum in Yucatán on the grounds of their supposed conversion to Catholicism informs us that "many of them are New Negros, that can't speak a single word of any European language, and Consequently not very solicitous about any religion."[6] These "New Negros" would appear to have been Africans who, coming more or less directly from Africa, would retain many aspects of their national cultures. The names of many of the slaves recorded in a 1790 census[7] also indicate African birth, though this cannot be relied upon as an accurate indication of their national origin (these include such names as Congo Will, Angola Will, Guinea Sam, Eboe Jack, Mongola Sam, Mundingo Pope, and Corromontee Tom). Unfortunately, the eighteenth-century records do not provide any indication of the proportion of imported slaves who were West Indian "Creoles" or African born; however, from the names of some of the slaves it would seem that, among those of African birth, most were Ibo, or were from farther south, in the Congo or Angola. Given the fact that most of the slaves were brought to the Bay settlement in the second half of the eighteenth century, this indication of the origin of the African-born slaves is supported by estimates of the principal sources of British slaves during this period, namely, the Niger and Cross deltas in the Bight of Benin (mostly Ibos) from 1730 to 1790, and Southwestern Africa, particularly the Congo and Angola, from 1790 to 1807.[8]

Next to be considered is the number of slaves, the proportions of men, women, and children in the slave population, and the ratio of the slaves to the rest of the population of the settlement. Table 4.1 provides those statistics that are available on the slave population from 1745 to emancipation. Though these figures must be treated with caution (even the censuses were incomplete enumerations), they do indicate certain broad demographic characteristics of the slave population, its numerical relation to the rest of the population, and changes in these features over a period of about one century.

The most obvious feature is that from an early date, the slaves were the numerical majority of the population. At the time the Spaniards captured the settlement in 1779, it was estimated that there were three thousand slaves in the Bay, or about 86 percent of the total population. After the resettlement following the peace of 1783, the population was much smaller, and even after the settlement of the Mosquito Shore evacuees in 1787 the slave population was only a little over two thousand. With the development of the demand for mahogany

TABLE 4.1 Slave Population of the Bay Settlement, 1745–1835

Date	Number of Slaves				Slaves as Percentage of Total Population
	Male	Female	Children	Total	
1745	....	....	....	120	71
1779	....	....	....	3,000	86
1790a	1,216	550	411	2,177	75
1790b	1,091	515	418	2,024	76
1803	1,700	675	584	2,959	75
1806	1,489	588	450	2,527	72
1809	....	....	....	3,000	73
1816	....	....	....	2,742	72
1820	1,537	600	426	2,563	....
1823	1,440	628	400	2,468	60
1826	1,373	577	460	2,410	46
1829	1,113	486	428	2,027	52
1832	895	435	453	1,783	42
1835	686	318	180	1,184	47

SOURCES: 1745, Inhabitants of the Bay of Honduras to Major Caulfield, 8 June 1745, CO 137/48; 1779, unsigned letter to Gov. Dalling, 3 Sept. 1779, CO 137/75; 1790a, "List of the Inhabitants of Honduras... January and February 1790...," CO 123/11; 1790b, "General Return of the Inhabitants in the Bay of Honduras... 22nd October, 1790," CO 123/9; 1803, "A Short Sketch of the present situation of the Settlement of Honduras..." from Supt. Thomas Barrow, 31 March 1803, CO 123/15; 1806, Br. Gen. H. T. Montresor to Gov. Sir Eyre Coote, 22 Oct. 1806, CO 123/17; 1809, "Remarks upon the Situation Trade etc...." by Barrow, 1 May 1809, CO 123/18; 1816, Census of the Population, GRB; 1820, Census of the Slave Population, 31 Dec. 1820, GRB; 1823, 1826, 1829, 1832, 1835, Censuses of the Population, GRB.

(permission to extract that timber was granted in 1786) the settlement began to grow again. Hundreds more slaves were imported in the last years of the eighteenth century and until the abolition of the slave trade in 1807. (The apparent decline in the population of the settlement in 1806 may be accounted for by incomplete enumeration; the source states that "as there exists several, who from their remote situation, have not given in their Returns, the real Total may be calculated at about 4000,"[9] of which the slaves probably amounted to nearly three thousand.) In 1809 it was again estimated that there were three thousand slaves in the settlement. Throughout this period, beginning with the resettlement in 1783, the slaves amounted to about three-quarters of the total population in the Bay settlement.

Following the abolition of the slave trade, the number of slaves in the settlement decreased; it dropped from about three thousand in 1809 to a little over one thousand at the time of emancipation. During these two decades the proportion of the slaves in the total population also declined dramatically, from about three-quarters to less than half of the population. The slaves in the settlement seem to have been unable to reproduce themselves. There was probably a high rate of mortality resulting from such factors as disease, malnutrition, ill-treatment, and overwork. Suicide, sometimes brought on by eating dirt, was also known among the slaves in Belize.[10] Additionally, the rate of reproduction was very low; only in 1832 were there more slave children than slave women. These two aspects are, of course, intimately related; as Roberts has shown in the case of Jamaica, "the failure of reproduction as a means of assuring population growth among the slaves was to a large extent rooted in the prevailing levels of mortality."[11] Another feature of the slave population that affected slaves' ability to reproduce themselves was the severe imbalance of the sexes. The men always greatly outnumbered the women, generally at the ratio of two or three to one. As there were very few white women in the settlement, the male slaves were frequently competing, on most unequal terms, with white men for the sexual favors of the slave women. The consequence of this unusually high demand upon the bodies of the slave women was probably extreme promiscuity, which, in turn, would be associated with widespread abortion and the spread of venereal diseases that would reduce fecundity. Additionally there was probably a strong reluctance on the part of the slave women to give birth to children who would inherit their despised social status. Certainly the practice of abortion was said to be "extremely common" among the slave women and had "its avowed professors."[12]

The three censuses that provide data on the age distribution of the slave population, in 1816, 1820, and 1823 (see table 4.2) show that the proportion of children remained at about 17 percent, while the proportion of slaves who were over forty years of age increased from 17 to 23 percent, reemphasizing the inability of the slaves to reproduce themselves.

In conclusion, it can be stated that as long as slaves could be imported into the Bay settlement, their numbers increased, but with the abolition of the slave trade in 1807 the numbers of slaves, and their proportion to the rest of the population, declined dramatically. This decline was due, in part, to high mortality rates, but a variety of factors made it impossible for the slave population to increase naturally. In addition, one must consider the rate of manumission, which reduced the number of slaves and expanded the growing group of free blacks and free colored in the settlement. The censuses of 1816 and 1820,[13] for example, state that between 1 January 1807 and 31 December 1820 a total of 228 slaves were manumitted; this was about 8 percent of the total slave population in that period. The rate of manumissions increased in the 1820s, however,

TABLE 4.2 Slave Population of the Bay Settlement, by Age, 1816–23

	Age in Years								
	9 and under		10 to 20		21 to 40		41 and above		Total
Date	N	Percentage	N	Percentage	N	Percentage	N	Percentage	
1816	458	17	448	16	1,361	50	475	17	2,742
1820	426	17	341	13	1,252	49	544	21	2,563
1823	400	16	411	17	1,078	44	549	23	2,438

SOURCE: Censuses of 1816, 1820, and 1823, GRB.

310 manumissions being reported between 1 January 1821 and 31 December 1830.[14] Finally, while the importation of slaves had diminished, their emigration continued; large numbers of slaves escaped from the settlement during slavery and even during the four-year period of "apprenticeship" that followed abolition in 1834.

THE ORGANIZATION AND OCCUPATIONS OF SLAVERY

Unlike the situation in the rest of the Caribbean, "cultivation" formed "no part of the leading pursuits of the British Settlers at Honduras. The cutting of mahogany and logwood is, therefore, almost their sole occupation."[15] Throughout the Caribbean, the institution of slavery was developed to answer the needs of European settlers who required large numbers of laborers for the cultivation of tropical crops, particularly sugar cane. Whether developed in the seventeenth century in Barbados or in the eighteenth century in Jamaica, whether for the cultivation of sugar cane in Brazil or cotton in the United States, slavery has been primarily associated with the large-scale production of tropical crops on plantations, to the extent that the organization of slavery in the New World from the Deep South in America to northeast Brazil has been virtually synonymous with the plantation system of production. Where cultivation was unimportant and timber cutting was the primary occupation, however, it may be expected that the organization of slavery would differ in certain respects from that required on a plantation.

Sugar plantations were frequently large estates on which slaves would generally live a fairly settled existence as long as they remained the property of the same master. Most slaves on such estates were organized into large work gangs, chiefly according to their physical strength; and though some slaves occupied positions requiring great skill, such as that of boilerman, the majority were unskilled field laborers, shifted from task to task according to the master's needs. Although there was a division of labor among the slaves, chiefly between skilled workers, field laborers, and domestics, there was a degree of interchangeability in the different occupations, particularly in relation to the preparation, planting, cultivation, and harvesting requirements of the seasonal cycle.

In addition to these differentiations according to production functions, there were also differentiations in terms of power. Just as the economic roles of slaves were defined by the masters, so, too, was the hierarchy of control that was so characteristic of the social system of the plantation. The white hierarchy consisted of the planter or his attorney, the managing overseer, and the supervising "bookkeepers," while the highest position among the field slaves, that of the driver of a gang, was the lowest position in this hierarchy of control. The driver's task was to urge other slaves to work, and to punish them if they failed to work, and there were frequent abuses of this delegated authority. Nevertheless, the drivers of the various gangs constituted a kind of slave elite within the plantation society; their superior status was recognized by the whites, not simply in the authority delegated to them but also through various material rewards. Other distinctions in status arose from color and place of birth, but these criteria, as well as those based on skill and power, were defined by the masters according to the latter's prejudices and the requirements of organization for plantation production.

The organizational requirements of timber extraction in Belize differed somewhat from those of plantation production, with consequent differences in the experiences of the slaves. First, the extraction of timber entailed the continual shifting of the production units from location to location as the timber resources became exhausted in a particular area and required the settler to lay a claim to new areas. This led to the establishment of a large number of small timber works, some occupied and some unoccupied, dotted along the rivers, creeks, and lagoons of the Bay area, the vast intervening area remaining untouched bush. The slaves worked, therefore, in small, more or less temporary and isolated camps in the middle of an uncultivated and essentially uninhabited terrain.

The second difference between the experience of slaves in Belize and those on plantations results from the actual process of cutting and extracting the timber. The extraction of logwood, as has been indicated previously, was a very small-scale operation, so that initially a white settler could undertake it "with a single Negro, some without one."[16] With the shift toward mahogany extraction in the second half of the eighteenth century, however, there was an increase in the amounts of capital, land, and labor required.

The most complete description of mahogany extraction during the period of slavery is by Captain George Henderson, who was stationed in Belize with the Fifth West India Regiment at the beginning of the nineteenth century:

> There are two seasons in the year for the cutting of mahogany: the first commencing shortly after Christmas, or at the conclusion of what is termed the wet season, the other about the middle of the year. At such periods all is activity, and the falling of trees, or the trucking out those that have been fallen, form the chief employments. Some of the wood is rough-squared on the spot, but this part of the labour is generally suspended until the logs are rafted to the different rivers' mouths. These rafts often consist of more than two hundred logs, and are floated as many hundred miles....
>
> The gangs of negroes employed in this work consist of from ten to fifty each; few exceed the latter number. The large bodies are commonly divided into several small ones, a plan which it is supposed greatly facilitates labour....
>
> The mahogany tree is commonly cut about twelve feet from the ground, and a stage is erected for the axe-man employed in levelling it. This to an observer would appear a labour of much danger, but an accident rarely happens to the person engaged in it....
>
> The logs of mahogany are generally brought out by cattle and trucks to the water side, or to the Barquadier, as it is termed in this country, which has been previously prepared by the foreman of the work for their reception. When the

distance is great, this is a labour of infinite and tedious difficulty. As soon as a sufficient number to form a raft is collected, and the waters have gained the necessary height, they are singly thrown from the banks, and require no other aid or guidance than the force of the current to float them to the booms, which are large cables placed across the rivers at the different eddies or falls. Here they are once more collected, each party claiming his own from the general mass, and formed into separate rafts for their final destination. Sometimes more than a thousand logs together are supported by the booms....

Labour here, and that with a small share of occasional relaxation, almost exclusively occupies the attention of whites and blacks; and, engaged in pursuits that lead to distant and in widely different directions, it seldom happens, perhaps not more than once in many months, that the settlers of Honduras have any kind of intercourse with each other, or for the same interval with their homes or families. The setting out on a mahogany cutting expedition resembles in some degree that of departing on a long voyage, the preparations for both being nearly similar; and the dreary time that must be passed in the woods, in this employment, may not unaptly be compared to what is felt by many in a long confinement on shipboard.[17]

In summary, the extraction of mahogany was a seasonal occupation, each season of cutting and trucking requiring the laborers to spend long periods of time in the isolation of the camps. The mahogany trees, once found, cut, and trimmed, were trucked (that is, drawn by teams of cattle) through temporary paths in the bush to the nearest riverside, at the place called the "barquadier," from whence the gangs would fan out to cut the mahogany, bringing the trees to the river to be formed into rafts. From the various barquadiers the rafts would float down river, usually in the rainy season, to a boom, such as Burrell Boom on the Belize River, where they were re-sorted and reformed for the final trip to the river's mouth. At the river's mouth the logs were finally squared and readied for shipment.

A number of distinct occupations were clearly required for mahogany extraction. First, there was the dangerous and highly skilled job of the axmen, who felled the trees by swinging a heavy ax on a springy platform about twelve feet above the ground. These axmen worked singly or in pairs, rather than in a gang. Their work was certainly very arduous, but given the fact that it required great physical strength and a technique that would take a long time to acquire, the axmen may have developed some satisfaction in their work and achieved some pride in and status from their occupation. Certainly they could be differentiated by skill from others in the gang whose task was to trim the tree after it had been felled, to clear the rough track down which it was to be drawn to the riverside, and to roughly square the trunks at the river's mouth. Another important occupation was that of the cattlemen, whose job it was to feed and work the cattle used in trucking the huge trunks. Finally, there were the people, probably women or youths, who prepared the food and looked after the provisions of the laborers. It is this division of labor to which Henderson refers when he says that the large gangs of slaves were divided into several smaller ones to facilitate labor. One major difference is apparent here between the work experience of slaves in Belize compared to those on sugar plantations: while most plantation slaves worked in large gangs, sometimes numbering a hundred or more, the slaves involved in mahogany extraction worked in small groups of ten or twelve, and in the extraction of logwood these groups could be even smaller.

The much smaller size of the gangs involved in timber extraction, and the isolation in which the gangs worked, may have inhibited the spread of solidarity among large numbers of slaves, but it probably increased the solidarity within the gang, whose members would soon come to know and depend on each other closely. The smaller size of gangs also limited the necessity for controlling the slaves. The foreman, whose job was chiefly that of integrating the productive activities of the gangs at the mahogany works, probably had some authority, but the drivers, ubiquitous on the plantations, were "not known to any Gang"[18] in Belize.

Though there was little or no differentiation among the slaves in terms of power, there was differentiation in terms of skill. More skilled even than the axmen were the huntsmen, upon whom the success of the whole enterprise depended and whose job involved great prestige and status. The best description of the occupation of huntsman, its skills, and the opportunities it provided for the huntsman's advantage is Henderson's account at the beginning of the nineteenth century:

> Each gang of slaves has one belonging to it, who is styled the huntsman. He is generally selected from the most intelligent of his fellows, and his chief occupation is to search the woods, or as in this country it is termed, the bush, to find labour for the whole. A negro of this description is often valued at more than five hundred pounds.
>
> About the beginning of August, the huntsman is dispatched on his errand.... He cuts his way through the thickest of the woods to the highest spots, and climbs the tallest tree he finds, from which he surveys the surrounding country. At this season, the leaves of the mahogany tree are invariably of a yellow reddish hue, and an eye accustomed to this kind of exercise can discover, at a great distance, the places where the wood is most abundant; and without compass or other guide than what observation has imprinted on his recollection, he never fails to reach the exact point to which he aims.
>
> It not unfrequently happens, when the huntsman has been particularly successful in finding a large body of wood, that it becomes a contest with his conscience, whether he shall disclose the matter to his master, or sell it to his neighbour: a liberal equivalent for this breach of fidelity being always punctually discharged. Those, however, who afford encouragement to such practices, by such impolitic temptation, are perhaps not more mindful of the old adage than of their interest, as it cannot but indirectly sanction their own slaves to take equal advantage whenever the opportunity presents itself.
>
> On some occasions no ordinary strategem is necessary to be resorted to by the huntsman to prevent others from availing themselves of the advantage of his discov-

eries; for if his steps be traced by those engaged in the same pursuit, which is a very common thing, all his ingenuity must be exerted to beguile them from the true scent. In this, however, he is not always successful, being followed by those who are entirely aware of all the arts he may use, and whose eyes are so quick, that the lightest turn of a leaf, or the faintest impression of his foot, is unerringly perceived.... Patents for discovery having never been contemplated by the Honduras wood-cutters, any invasion of the right appertaining to it has therefore seldom been very scrupulously regarded by them. And it consequently happens, that persons so engaged must frequently undergo the disappointment of finding an advantage, they had promised to themselves, seized on by others.[19]

The absence of any system of land registration, or even of a legal system of freehold tenure, made a settler's claim to a mahogany works very tenuous, despite the attempts made in the Public Meetings to regulate such claims. The result was a great deal of competition between settlers for the valuable mahogany trees growing in the poorly charted interior of the bush, and a consequent dependence upon both the skills of the huntsman in finding the mahogany and his sense of duty in reporting it. Somewhat like the boilerman on the sugar plantation, therefore, the huntsman had the skills upon which the success of the entire enterprise depended. The fact that a failure or a false move could practically ruin a settler gave the huntsman considerable independence and advantages that he could exploit if he so chose, and made him the most valued slave of all. The occupation of huntsman must have had considerable status among the slaves and must have been much sought after, not least because of the great freedom it entailed.

Apart from the occupations directly connected with the extraction of timber, slaves were engaged in two other activities: domestic work and the cultivation of provisions. In 1779 it was stated that there were "about 200 or 250 negroes, men, women and children, mostly House-negroes"[20] on St. George's Cay, these domestics being in the ratio of about two to every white resident. At the beginning of the nineteenth century the town of Belize consisted of about two hundred houses, many of which, particularly those owned by the "opulent merchants," were "spacious, commodious, and well finished."[21] These houses, while not comparable in ostentatious splendor to some of the West Indian planters' great houses, were maintained by domestic slaves. Though the masters of Belize did not possess the armies of domestics that Jamaican planters owned, they had slaves whose job it was to clean the house, sew, wash and iron clothes, cook and serve food, and even to tend their children. Sometimes the women were required to perform sexual as well as domestic roles, such activity occasionally being an avenue to their freedom or that of the children of such unions. Given the fact that white men outnumbered white women by three or four to one, many of the masters took black or colored concubines who became the mistresses of their houses, supervising the activities of domestics. These "housekeepers" had a rather insecure position in the home and an ambiguous social position in the community, so it is not surprising that there is evidence of their harsh treatment of domestic slaves, such treatment being the housekeepers' way of emphasizing social distance from the slaves despite their physical proximity.

The third occupation engaged in by slaves was the cultivation of provisions for consumption in the settlement. From the eighteenth century on, slaves were occupied in "making plantations," an expression used to this day in Belize to refer to the cultivation of small plots of vegetables, corn, and other subsistence crops. A description of the settlement in 1779 referred to the settlers' "Plantations which they visit occasionally, where they employ their Slaves in raising Provisions and cutting Logwood—these Plantations extend along the banks of several Rivers."[22] Attempts to cultivate even these small plots for subsistence were systematically discouraged by Spanish officials who visited the settlement to enforce Article III of the 1786 Convention, which limited the settlers to gathering the uncultivated "Produce of the Earth." The settlers complained in 1787 when Superintendent Despard "went in his own Person and made our Negroes at our Upper Works dig up by the Roots everything that grew in a very large plantation which was on the North Side of Belize River before the War, and had been cleared and replanted at great Expense since the Peace."[23] Other complaints followed concerning the actions of the Spanish commissioners who, in destroying every cultivated spot they could find, diminished the availability of provisions and encouraged discontent among the slaves:

> The Spaniards have very lately cut down the Plantain Walks and Provision Grounds of the Settlers, particularly in the New River, upon which the individuals residing there have at all times had their Chief, or Sole dependence. This has greatly injured the Owners and given great disgust to the Negroes employed in that River, whose subsistence depends upon their little Plantations; And the Negroes disgust in that Country being a prelude to their desertion, will, in proportion as it extends, enrich the Spaniards, and ruin the English Settlers.[24]

An improvement occurred in this situation in 1789 when Spain permitted the cultivation of small plots for garden produce,[25] but after 1796 the Spaniards were unable to effect any restriction upon the plantation grounds. Plantation grounds, therefore, had been established before the 1779 evacuation, were continued after the resettlement of 1784, despite the treaties forbidding cultivation, and then flourished unmolested after 1796.

Although the masters frequently employed their slaves in growing provisions, the plantation grounds were, to a large extent, cultivated on the slaves' initiative. A settler described in 1788 how the slaves were "ever accustomed to make Plantation as they term it, by which means they support their Wives and Children, raise a little Stock and so furnish themselves with necessaries etc. To deprive them of this Privileges would be attended with the worst of Consequences and they have already signified they will not set still and suffer the Spaniards to destroy their Grounds."[26] In the following year a similar concern was voiced: the destruction of provision grounds would "occasion very great Disturbances from the resentment of the Negroes; whose Food very essentially depends upon the production of these Provision Grounds."[27]

That the masters encouraged the slaves to grow provisions in order to cut the costs of maintaining their labor force is supported by an observation made in 1806 concerning one kind of arrangement under which these grounds were cultivated: "The Slaves have pieces of ground allotted them for cultivation, which enables the most industrious, to make an agreement with their Masters in lieu of Provision."[28] These arrangements would be more necessary in times of war, when there would be a tendency for the price of imported food to rise and for the reliability of regular supplies to decrease. Though it is not possible to obtain a clear picture of the extent of the plantation grounds, Henderson wrote: "Every Settlement at Honduras has its plantain walk; and many of these comprehend an extent of, at least, an hundred acres... the pine-apple and melon, being very commonly interspersed between the rows of plantains." He also mentioned that the banks of the Sibun River, which today is one of the chief areas of small farms producing for the Belize City market, were "thickly studded with plantations."[29] It must be emphasized, however, that these plantations were for subsistence products only, no cultivation of export crops being undertaken in this period.

Though the principal tasks allocated to male slaves were concerned with timber extraction, and female slaves were primarily domestics, some men and women were also engaged in cultivating subsistence crops. Sometimes they were required by the masters to engage in cultivation, producing crops for the consumption of the masters' other slaves, but sometimes they worked more for themselves, despite many obstacles in their way. One significant obstacle was the very nature of the logging operations. The work was arduous—most of the day was occupied with cutting and much of the night in trucking—so the slave would generally be exhausted and have little time or energy left to devote to his plantation. In addition, the fact that logging camps were temporary, and masters could shift their slaves from one camp to another, meant that a slave would not be sure whether what he sowed in one season would be available for harvesting in another. Despite these obstacles, many slaves did make plantations, the custom being widespread among them even when visiting Spanish officials could destroy the crop before it could be harvested.

There were three possible types of plantation in which the slaves could be involved: those on which they worked for the masters to feed other slaves, those on which they grew provisions purely for their own and their families' subsistence, and those on which they produced food for sale. The slaves probably engaged at various times in a combination of these activities.

Though it can be assumed that most of the produce grown by slaves on their own account was for the consumption of their families, it appears that they also participated in a rudimentary marketing system, whereby some of the produce was taken into the town of Belize for sale. In 1803 a Magistrates' meeting accepted a tender for building a market house on each side of the Belize River.[30] Two years later a meeting "resolved unanimously that all Higlers such as carry Trays, Baskets, Bowls or any other Vessel to sell Goods in the Streets, save and except Bread, Plantains, Yams, or other articles the produce of this Settlement"[31] should pay a license, thereby inplying that there were some vendors, not required to take out a license, who marketed agricultural produce of the settlement. That this resolution was intended to apply to free farmers rather than slaves is made apparent by another resolution made the same year forbidding a "Slave or Slaves to hire himself to himself with a view to pursue Trade."[32] The practice of slaves engaging in marketing their produce obviously continued, however, as a committee investigating the hiring of slaves to themselves in 1810 reported "a continuation of such Evil Practices.... pursued, by various Slaves in open violation of said Law," and recommended "that Slaves of either Sex shall not be permitted to hire themselves to themselves *for any purpose whatever*."[33] The reason given for deeming such activities "Evil Practices" was that "such Slave being under no control of his Master, becomes subject to no authority, but what results from his own Will, which naturally tends to create Insubordination thereby diminishing respect to his proprietors."[34] A penalty of £500 was therefore imposed to deter such independent activity on the part of the slaves.

It is unlikely that the slaves' agricultural produce was sold within the mahogany camps, since the number of workers in any one camp was quite small. The masters appear to have required some of their slaves to cultivate provisions with which to feed the rest. Unlike the organization of labor in the sugar plantations of the Caribbean, where there were various jobs of varying difficulty associated with sugar production, so that jobs could be allotted to women, children, and the infirm within the plantation, the tasks involved in logging were uniformly arduous. In order not to lose the labor of those slaves who were unfit for the more demanding jobs of cutting and hauling logs, the masters sometimes put them to work growing provisions. A report of 1809 supports this notion:

> The effective men can only find employment in cutting and obtaining Mahogany and Dye Woods Women, Children and Aged Men are of course unequal to the labour required in this business, there are a great number of Coloured free persons and slaves of the latter description that would be very advantageously employed in the pursuits arising from agricultural improvement.... the labour of two infirm men has been known to furnish Rice and Indian Corn sufficient to feed Thirty negroes through the year.[35]

The author was here making a plea for allowing the cultivation of commercial crops for export, but his account makes it clear that there was some arrangement by which a few slaves were given the task of growing provisions to feed the others. The 1834 slave register gives additional evidence in support of the view that the masters allotted the task of growing provisions to those slaves who were physically unable to do the heavier work of timber extraction. In the register there are forty-eight slaves (about 2.5 percent of all the slaves) listed as plantation laborers, eleven of these being women. Of the thirty-seven "plantation men," three were between the ages of nine and fifteen years, four were between forty and forty-nine, and thirty were fifty years or older. None of the plantation men were in the most physically mature age range of sixteen to thirty-nine years (see table 7.2).

The principal tasks allocated to the African slaves by their masters were connected with the cutting of logwood and mahogany. The arduous nature of such tasks meant that only mature and physically fit slaves could be so employed, while women, children, and the aged or infirm were engaged in domestic work or the cultivation of provisions. The emphasis placed on the slaves' ability to cut timber became associated with the assumption that they were in some way incapable of, or averse to, agricultural pursuits, and this assumption has been used to attempt to explain the relative lack of interest of contemporary Afro-Belizeans in farming. In the late nineteenth century, for example, Gibbs referred to the "invincible distaste of the mass of native coloured labourers to the avocations connected with the cultivation of the soil, and their inherent preference for the life of the mahogany or logwood works."[36] Such an explanation ignores the historical facts, however. In the first place, the enslaved Africans were a people with a tradition of agriculture, their employment in timber extraction having been secured not by choice, tradition, or inherent aptitude, but by force. Secondly, as will subsequently be demonstrated, there were structural constraints imposed upon the ex-slaves at the time of emancipation to ensure that they remained in the employ of the mahogany houses. And thirdly, to the extent that a "distaste" did develop, it may be seen as a cultural change resulting from the impositions of the masters during the period of slavery.

While the masters repeatedly praised the slaves' performance at logging, they simultaneously stressed their ineptitude and aversion to agriculture. Though it may be true that some slaves could gain a degree of satisfaction from their proficiency at some of the specific skills of logging, they nevertheless repeatedly demonstrated a strong inclination to cultivate the soil. The masters were probably ambivalent about their slaves "making plantation." On the one hand, such moonlighting could save the masters' funds by providing food, but on the other hand, the masters were afraid they might lose their sources of labor through the desertions of slaves who became accustomed to acquiring an independent livelihood. A tension existed, therefore, between the slaves, who may have associated farming with independence and freedom, and the masters, who sought to keep them in an economically dependent position. In this situation, the masters' reiteration of the theme that the blacks would never be any good at agriculture and had therefore better keep to logging can be seen as a self-serving way of instilling self-doubt in the minds of the slaves. To the extent that the masters succeeded in propagating the myth of the slaves' ineptitude at agriculture, then, they could keep the slaves, and the freedmen, dependent upon them. Moreover, the longer the masters could maintain the myth, the more likely it was to appear fulfilled, as old traditions were abandoned and new ones adopted.

SLAVERY AND THE LAW

The earliest statement concerning the slaves' status in law is an assertion, made in 1803, that "the Consolidated Slave Law of Jamaica is adopted in this Settlement, so far as the local situation thereof will admit."[37] Given the fact that the consolidated slave laws of Jamaica, passed in 1800, were "largely a codification of what was already prevalent in custom,"[38] it is hard to evaluate to what extent these laws, the product of a plantocracy, could be adopted in Belize. Only a decade later, a slave was tried for the murder of his master "by a Court Martial composed of the Officers of Militia... there being no criminal Code in force here by which so atrocious an offender could be tried & adequately punished."[39] Though a slave court had apparently been established in about 1787, it was only "for the trial of Slaves for offences not amounting to felony,"[40] the laws failing to make provision for dealing with other offences by slaves until the establishment of the Supreme Court in 1819. This indicates that there was a very incomplete codification of slave laws, or of application of the Jamaican laws, in Belize, and that individual cases were frequently treated on an ad hoc basis. If the prosecution of slaves for serious offences remained on such a casual basis until 1819, it may be assumed that any protection of slaves that may have been provided by the law was applied as casually.

In 1821, Superintendent Arthur considered it necessary, in view of the fact that doubts had arisen "in the minds of several of our Subjects settled in Honduras, whether an Act of the Legislature of our island of Jamaica, commonly called 'the Consolidated Slave Law,' is considered in force in our Settlement of Honduras: And whereas there are no other laws whatever for the protection of the Slave Population Known or promulgated in our said Settlement," to proclaim the Jamaican slave laws to be in force in Belize.[41] Bathurst's legal advisers, however, gave the opinion that Arthur's proclamation could have no legal validity, as Arthur possessed "no authority to form or introduce laws for the Government of the Settlement."[42] Nevertheless, Bathurst, fearing "the unbounded oppression to which the Slave Population would be exposed, if it were imagined that there existed no legal restraint for their protection,"[43] authorized Arthur to enforce the Jamaican slave laws in the settlement.

The most complete account of laws relating to slavery in Belize is provided by the report of the "Commissioners of Inquiry into the Administration of Criminal and Civil Justice," following their visit to the "Settlement of Honduras" in 1825.[44] The generally favorable account of these commissioners should be treated with caution, however, as the chief source of their information, "the principal merchants and inhabitants,"[45] were also the chief slave owners, who had a vested interest in supplying a picture of content and well-being.

Beginning with a statement that "the Jamaica Consolidated Slave Act is said to be 'in use, in this settlement, as far as local circumstances will permit it to apply,' "[46] the report continues with a series of brief summaries of laws and customs relating to slavery. (See Appendix A.)

One of the most interesting features that emerges from the commission's report on these laws and customs is the relative ease with which the slaves could obtain their freedom. Among the ways slaves could be manumitted were self-purchase, purchase by others, bequest by will and testament of the owner, or gift by the owner. Of 169 slaves who obtained their freedom between 1 January 1826 and 31 December 1830, 11 percent purchased their own freedom, 18 percent had their manumission purchased by others, 29 percent obtained manumission by bequest, and 38 percent were freed by gift.[47] Since the most common forms of manumission were by means of gift and by bequest of the owner, it can be assumed that many of these manumissions were to secure the freedom of slave mistresses and the children borne by such women of the masters. On the other hand, the fact that there was no tax on manumission and no obligation for the owner to pay any security to the settlement would encourage unscrupulous masters to make a gift of freedom to those of their slaves who, as a result of age, sickness, or other infirmity, had become a burden to them. A surprising number of slaves in Belize were able to purchase their own freedom, sometimes at little cost, but often at considerable expense; for example, one slave, a veritable "Napoleon of finance,"[48] paid £450 to obtain his freedom in 1829.[49]

One noteworthy feature of the law in Belize is expressed in the first paragraph of the commissioners' report, stating that someone in actual possession of liberty did not require written evidence of manumission but would be assumed to be free unless he could be proved a slave. The examinees stated to the commissioners that in cases of disputed freedom, the *onus probandi* would lie with the person objecting, that the courts were guided by "the principle of general law and equity," and that if a future case were to be brought against the same person of color by a second objecting person, then "the court would receive the evidence of the former action."[50] Moreover, it was stated that once a free person received value for the purchase of a slave's freedom, whether or not he signed a manumission, he would lose his right to the slave, "although it might require the decision of the court."[51]

An interesting case, which illustrates the unusual precedence placed upon freedom in Belize, came before the Supreme Court in 1823.[52] A slave called Priscilla Meighan had been manumitted by her master, Edward Meighan, who died insolvent in 1816. His widow, Anna, from whom he had been legally separated for five years prior to his death, claimed ownership of Priscilla on the grounds that her husband's insolvency made the manumission invalid. Priscilla had her manumission paper, in which Edward Meighan acknowledged receipt of £50 in cash in return for her manumission, but Anna's attorney argued that Meighan "could not, according to the custom and usage of this settlement, dispose of his property by deed of gift, and more particularly by the manumission of his slaves, except to the material injury of his creditors,"[53] and Priscilla's manumission had therefore been illegal. The court, however, considered Anna's case "altogether insufficient to deprive the plantiff of freedom" on the principle that, "by the custom of this court, the question of freedom has ever taken precedence over matters of debt, where no objection was made at the time such deed was executed, or within a reasonable time after."[54]

Little is said in the commissioners' report concerning the types of punishments inflicted upon slaves, though it was stated that the owner might, legally and simply on his authority, inflict corporal punishment to the extent of thirty-nine lashes on his slave for misconduct or ill behavior, and that owners had the power to imprison their slaves at their own expense, though the duration of such imprisonment would be at the "discretion of the court."[55] If slaves were found guilty of giving false evidence in court they were subject to imprisonment.

On the question of possible differentials in punishment for the same offence committed by a free person or a slave, the examinants stated that "free black persons and slaves are liable to the same punishment,"[56] which indicates that different punishments would be considered suitable for free colored persons or whites. On some occasions it appears that slaves were even favored against free blacks, on the grounds that discretion should be exercised "in favour of the slave from the low state of his intellectual cultivation."[57] One such case occurred in 1827 when mercy was recommended for a slave found guilty of assaulting a free black on the ground that he had been provoked by the taunt that he was "a damned negro slave." Marshall Bennett, the presiding Magistrate (and also the biggest slave owner in the settlement), felt that the slave should have sought redress by resorting to legal action but gave the opinion that "the Magistrates would never allow even in the most remote degree, abusive and contemptuous language to be used towards slaves, particularly by a class of persons who differed from them only in having the good fortune to obtain their manumission. It was quite misfortune enough for a person to be a slave without being taunted with it, or it being made a term of reproach, particularly by one of their own class."[58] This indicates that blacks, irrespective of whether they were free or enslaved, were beginning to be considered members of the same class of society, differing in status from the colored and whites. Certainly the evidence does not bear out the assertion, apparently based on a misunderstanding of the commissioners' report, that "there was no difference between the treatment of slaves and free persons."[59] There are indications, rather, that, with the increased numerical parity between the free and the enslaved population in the 1820s, distinctions were increasingly made in terms of color, the free blacks being unable to rid themselves of the social stigma of their real or assumed former slave status.

There are many indications of inequalities in punishments administered by the law—examples of severe, even savage, treatment of blacks and of lenient treatment of whites. In the case, previously mentioned, of a slave tried by court martial in 1813 for the murder of his master, the slave was tried, convicted, sentenced, and publicly executed, all within the space of two days, in order to make a stern example "for the safety and even the very existence of the Settlement."[60] The swiftness and severity of the justice meted out in this case does not seem warranted by the fact that the slave killed his master in rivalry for a free colored woman,[61] such a crime passionel usually being treated with greater leniency when occurring between men of equal status.

Many of the punishments imposed upon slaves were explicitly intended to set an example to other slaves, as in the case of a slave who was sentenced to be hanged on the very spot where he had "set fire to the dwelling House of his Mistress." It was argued that, "in order to preserve Tranquillity in the settlement . . . [the] wretch who has committed so wanton, so wicked, and so attrocious a crime, should receive the sentence so justly awarded." Any lesser sentence, such as transportation, "would stimulate other abandoned wretches to make similar attempts on the lives and properties of the Inhabitants and their is every reason to apprehend, that in a little time, Assisinations, Murders, Burning of Houses, and other Acts of outrage & Injustice would be perpetrated, in short every species of Cruelty resulting from a dreaded Spirit of Commotion and Insurrection might justly be Expected."[62]

It would seem that the severe punishment of offending slaves had been considered a useful deterrent to other slaves for as long as slavery had existed. In the eighteenth century it was reported that a number of supposed ringleaders of a rebellion were put to death "by burning, gibbeting & other methods of torture at St. George's Key."[63] Another case, explicitly advocating that an example was required, occurred in 1787:

> A Negroe man named Joe the property of Mr. Henry Jones was yesterday tried for the murder of a white man & found guilty. . . . He was therefore according to the former usage & Custom of Honduras condemned to be hanged this day & his body afterwards to be hung up in Chains. Necessity & Custom can only justify these proceedings. . . . Example is certainly wanting among the Negroes, who have of late acted as if they thought it impossible for this Country to punish them.[64]

While a slave who merely injured his owner could be hanged for such an offense, the owner receiving £60 Jamaican currency as compensation for the loss of his slave,[65] a master who subjected his slave to cruel and unusual punishment far beyond the customary limit of thirty-nine lashes was treated leniently by his peers—supposing such a case would ever reach a court. John Armstrong, who was the settlement's chaplain from 1812 to 1824, stated that "the necessary means of protecting slaves from oppression and cruelty are withheld, and every attempt to shield them from barbarous usage is considered an invasion of the rights of the owner; and, to such an extent is this carried, that even in cases of the most flagrant abuse and injustice, it is almost impossible to convict a master of cruelty, or to recover for the injured slave either right or remuneration."[66]

An example of the lenient sentencing of an owner actually brought to trial and convicted for cruel treatment of a slave occurred in 1816. One Michael Carty was convicted

> of having caused a poor young Negro Female, his property, to be stripped naked, and her hands being tied to her feet with tight Cords, a stick was passed under her Knees, and above the Elbow-bend of her Arms, a large Cattle Chain was fastened round her kneck with a Padlock, and in this agonizing posture, exposed to the burning heat of the Sun, was this wretched Female tortured from Morning until night, constantly, during that time, flogged with a severe cat by her inhuman Master and Servant in the most wanton and barbarous manner—sometimes on her buttocks, at other times, being turned over on the stick, on her face and breast. . . . her wounds festered to such a degree that her life was considered in the greatest danger.[67]

Far from considering this a suitable case by which to set an example as far as the masters' behavior was concerned, the white jury merely sentenced Carty to a fine of £50 Jamaica currency, or about £35 sterling, and "the poor female was doomed to remain the Slave of this cruel wretch, still more exasperated against her then ever."[68] Superintendent Arthur, moved by the evidence that "characters like Carty, who having rapidly accumulated property, and acquired thereby dominion over their fellow creatures, exercise their Authority with such wanton cruelty,"[69] went so far as to order the Magistrates to withhold from Carty his license to sell liquor.

By way of emphasizing the contrasts between the punishments administered to slaves and to masters, two further cases of the punishment of slaves in this period may be referred to. In 1817, a slave woman was found guilty by a Summary Court of "insolence and bad conduct" to her mistress and was sentenced to one hundred lashes on her bare back, then to be led round the town "at the cart's tail." Another slave in the same year was sentenced to two hundred and fifty lashes before being dragged around the town following a conviction for stealing.[70] Despite such appalling treatment, the picture that is generally painted of the conditions of slavery in Belize is a very favorable one. Before discussing these conditions, however, it is necessary to examine the extent to which the law extended certain rights to the slaves of Belize.

The commissioners' report is somewhat more informative on the subject of slaves' rights than it is on punishments given by the courts. On the important question of property, the examinees stated that by custom the slaves of Belize could possess property for their private use, and that in cases where property acquired by or bestowed upon a slave was withheld by the owner, the slaves could seek redress to recover such property, except in matters of debt. The problem for the slave in such cases, however, would be to find someone willing to take up their cases, for though slaves could not be sued, they were entitled to sue only through their owners.[71]

A similar problem existed in cases of injury to a slave, when an action of damages could be undertaken by an owner to compensate him for injury done to his slave, but if the owner himself caused such injury, the slave had recourse only to criminal action, which would depend upon the willingness of someone to take up his case.[72] In such cases, therefore, it is likely that the customs of the settlement would be more influential in determining the outcome than would the vaguely defined legal rights of the slaves.

The situation was similar with regard to the sale of slaves. Though it was stated to be "the custom of the country" to sell slaves in families, there was "no law in existence to prevent the sale of slaves individually."[73] Consequently, if a slave should be separated from his or her immediate family through sale, the slave could have no legal recourse to prevent the separation.

With regard to the controversial question of the competence of slaves as witnesses and the admissibility of the evidence of slaves in the courts, it was stated that while their testimony could be received in cases directed against "persons of their own class," they were "not considered competent witnesses against white persons."[74] Such a disqualification would make it still more difficult, if not impossible, for slaves to achieve redress against their masters in cases of injury or the withholding of their property.

In summary, it may be said that though the slaves' possession of certain limited rights and their relatively high rates of manumission tend to substantiate the masters' claim of humanitarian and benevolent treatment, the slaves legally remained the property of their masters, and most limitations upon the masters' treatment of the slaves were customary rather than legal in nature. Consequently, the slaves were afforded little in the way of rights or protection by the law and remained, in their experience of actual conditions as in the definition of their status, entirely dependent upon their masters. Nor must it be forgotten that in the peculiar situation of the Bay settlement, the Crown's representative had very limited and ill-defined authority, while the masters, with their control of the Public Meeting and the magistracy, possessed great power in determining and executing the laws and customs of the settlement with regard to their slaves.

The masters' power over the slaves was not absolute, however. Though masters attempted to treat slaves as mere property, as objects, slaves possessed an immense latent power of which masters were frequently made aware. In various ways, the slaves resisted the institution within which their lives were organized, and through this resistance, they became the subjects of their own history.

5
The Slaves as Objects and as Subjects

THE CONDITIONS AND TREATMENT OF SLAVES

Shortly after the "apprenticeship" system ended in 1838, it was claimed that "for a great length of time slavery has existed in Honduras only in name; the very remembrance of it seems now certainly forgotten."[1] Later in the nineteenth century, the view that slavery in Belize had existed in name only and that slaves were well treated there was repeated: "Instead of the degraded bondage and grinding toil which was the lot of slaves on plantations, the logwood and mahogany-cutter was a slave only in name."[2] Recently, a historian has stated more guardedly that "it seems likely that slavery in British Honduras was, as has always been claimed, much less oppressive then elsewhere."[3] However, while the preceding account of the organization of slavery in a woodcutting establishment indicates conditions different from those prevalent on plantations elsewhere in the Caribbean, the evidence of the historical records, which heretofore has been barely examined, severely qualifies the masters' often repeated claims of benevolence and humanitarianism in the treatment of their slaves. Great difficulties lie in the evaluation of these records, of course, since they are mostly written by, or are in sympathy with, the masters themselves, who were concerned, particularly during the period of abolitionist agitation, with presenting their own behavior and the conditions of their slaves in the best possible light.

Henderson, whose account is such a rich source of material on the settlement in the early nineteenth century, claimed that "in no part of the world, where slavery prevails, can the condition of beings so circumstanced be found of milder or more indulgent form. The labour they undergo bears no proportion to that which they sustain throughout the islands: nor is it more to be compared with what they experience in the States of America."[4] Henderson estimated the cost of providing each slave with food, clothing, and other items, to be about £36 Jamaica currency, or over £25 sterling, per year. His itemization of these expenses is worth full quotation:

The Slaves as Objects and as Subjects 69

	£	s	d
Of Irish salt pork, to each negro, 5 lb per week, which on an average of price, may be estimated for 365 days at	8	10	0
Of flour, always the finest, 1 lb per day each, estimated at	10	0	0
Of rum, supposing a gill to be allowed to each slave per day, during the days that that work is carrying on, which may be numbered at 260: the spirits at 10s per gallon	4	1	3
Of sugar, 12 lb allowed, at each, to each, at 1s 3d per lb	0	15	0
Of clothing: two suits of fatigue, or working clothes, usually of osnaburgs, at about 1s 18d per yard to each, and making	1	3	4
One pair of coarse shoes ditto ditto	0	13	4
Miscellaneous: tobacco and pipes to each negro	1	10	0
Medical attendance, or medicine, per contract, to each	0	13	4
Saturday's labour, invariably the privilege of the slave, and which is generally engaged by his owner: established rates 3s 4d per day	8	13	4
Jamaica currency	35	19	7

In a note, Henderson pointed out that the considerable compensation paid for labor on Saturday, "though it be paid at the nominal rate of 3s 4d per day, seldom actually amounts to any thing like so much; it being in most instances accounted for in slops, trinkets, or liquors, of the most inferior kind; and which no doubt are given out in this way at a profit of more than 200 per cent. besides, the principal number of the persons engaged in the cutting of mahogany being also in trade, of course the above is provided for in the way of business."[5]

While Henderson's account of the expenses incurred in maintaining slaves indicates an unusual generosity on the part of the masters, his note concerning compensation for Saturday work shows that the masters were eager to find ways to reduce the cost of customary allowances. The account appears to be a statement of the "ideal" provisions made for slaves, and it is doubtful that such an ideal was often attained. In periods of economic hardship due to war or depression in trade, the masters would certainly require their slaves to tighten their belts, and even in peaceful and prosperous times there would be many ways by which the cost of maintaining slaves could be lowered, and the material conditions of slaves worsened. It is important, again, to emphasize that the masters who were engaged in the timber business were also the controllers of almost all the trade, wholesale and retail, in the settlement; they therefore had many opportunities to provide inferior provisions or, as Henderson indicates, to cheat by compensating for Saturday work in kind instead of in cash.

Nevertheless, the comments on provisions for the slaves are unanimous in stressing their adequacy, especially when compared with those made available for slaves elsewhere. In 1803, it was asserted that "there is not any part of the World where Negroes are better fed,"[6] and a few years later, at about the time of Henderson's visit, a similar account of slave provisions and conditions was given.

> The Slaves belonging to the Settlement are better treated than in the Colonies. . . . on arriving from Jamaica, the robust & healthy appearance of the Slaves is most striking—they are well fed by their Owners, generally receiving seven Pounds of Beef, & six pounds of Flour per Week, or in lieu of Flour fifty Plantains; two Gills of Rum per day, & if working in the Water, or rain, it is generally increased to three Gills per day, others give six pounds of Pork & six Quarts of Flour; if they are worked on Saturdays by their Masters, they are paid for it, that day being considered their own; Sunday is invariably at their disposal, & at Christmas they all have ten days, or a fortnight's holyday—Drivers are not known to any Gang; punishments are extremely rare.[7]

In 1816, Superintendent Arthur praised the generosity of the masters toward their slaves, a view he was shortly to modify considerably.

> All the Slaves are most abundantly fed by their Proprietors on the best Salted Provisions—Pork generally, at the rate of five pounds per week to each man, with Yams, Plantains, Rice, Flour, Salt, & Tobacco.
>
> Every Slave has a Moschetto Pavilion, Blanket, and Sheet found him—also, two suits of Osnaburgh annually. The Men and Lads work on account of their Owners five days in the week—for the Saturday's labour, they are entitled by usage, which has become a Law, to half a Dollar, and the Sunday is entirely their own.
>
> The Women are only employed in domestic purposes, and, if they have young Children, no work whatever is required from them by their Masters—in fact, my Lord, altho' I came to the West Indies three years ago a perfect "Wilberforce" as to Slavery, I must now confess, that I have in no part of the World seen the labouring class of People possessing anything like the comforts, and advantages of the Slave Population of Honduras.[8]

A few years later, when investigating the causes of a slave revolt up the Belize River, Arthur stated that the slaves "had been treated with very unnecessary harshness by their Owner, and had certainly good grounds for complaint."[9] In the same year, 1820, Arthur made "some observations upon the extreme inhumanity of many of the lower class of Settlers residing in the Town of Belize towards their Slaves," and drew attention to "the increasing severity and cruelty which is now practised with impunity"[10] because the offenders could not be punished under the current legal system. Having ascertained that "in many cases, the Slaves were severely oppressed," Arthur proclaimed the consolidated slave law of Jamaica to be in force in Belize. "Encouraged by the Proclamation . . . the numbers [of slaves] who came forward in a few days filled me with no less astonishment, than the fraud and injustice which had so long been secretly practised towards them."[11] By this time the settlers must have viewed Arthur as a "perfect 'Wilberforce' " and were doubtless relieved when his successor promptly asserted that "when compared with the Slaves in Jamaica, the Honduras Negro population may boast of great comparative comfort and good treatment from their Owners . . . the allowances to the Negroes and their Clothing are what very few, except the great proprietors could shew in Jamaica."[12]

Arthur's later account of the conditions and treatment of slaves in Belize is almost unique. Even the Reverend John Armstrong, who supported Arthur's appeal for legal protection of the slaves against ill-treatment, stated that the slaves were generally well-treated and adequately fed and clothed.[13] The general view of the conditions of slavery was contrary to Arthur's, though even Superintendent Codd's quite idyllic picture of slave life in 1823 included the fact that thirty-nine slaves had rejected the conditions he described and had fled the settlement in the ten weeks prior to his writing:

> Here the Negro is well fed, well clothed, and every comfort suiting his station is liberally provided for him; here he is at all times admitted into a participation of his industry; here are no Drivers with whips to urge him to his duty; nor regular systems of punishment, Here are no Workhouses; and I really believe in no part of the world where Slavery exists can the government of them be in a more indulgent form!! and the expense attending each Negro annually is beyond what I have ever known before; The best Irish Mess Pork, and good flour, are weekly delivered to him, and if not flour, Plantains which they in general prefer they have the unlimited use of; the Plantain yielding here in abundance, these with the addition of rum, tobacco, pipes, a knife, powder and shot and a short sword, here called a Mascheat, constitutes all their wants; he literally works only five days for his Master, he is allowed to saw boards, build Canoes, and flat bottomed boats, called here Pitpans, raise stock, and cultivate the soil to any extent for his own immediate profit, indeed his industry is always encouraged by the Owner, who purchases a large portion of the produce of his labour and its quite common for Slaves here, to lay by hundreds of pounds, with which they purchase themselves, or obtain a friend with that money to purchase their wives or children.[14]

Few travelers ever visited Belize, and of those few who did, one may safely assume that they would stay in the town, relying upon the reports of the richer settlers with whom they stayed and not visiting the remote lumber camps. An example is Captain McLean, who, arriving from Jamaica, "found abundance and cheerfulness domineering on every hand . . . every thing bespoke a state of comfort tranquillity and ease."[15] These highly favorable accounts of slave conditions and treatment in Belize, written by slave owners or their associates in a climate affected by the debate over reform and abolition, are clearly ideological in nature. Though the unanimity of their accounts with regard to the material provisions allotted to the slaves is impressive and certainly indicates that the ideal was an adequate allowance of food and clothing by the standards of the time, their accounts of slave treatment are somewhat more contradictory.

Moreover, it cannot be assumed that if the supply of provisions was adequate, slavery was therefore "much less oppressive then elsewhere," or that it "existed in name only." Such simple conclusions ignore the most important aspect of all, namely the slaves' own perception of their situation—the meaning that they attached to their status and treatment. The slaves, being human, were not objects or animals, but were men and women who engaged actively in relationships with their masters and with one another. A further evaluation of slavery in Belize, therefore, requires an examination of the actions of the slaves themselves. Such an examination may find that the slaves did experience a "degraded bondage" that was oppressive to them, that they did not share their masters' view of their situation, and that, consequently, they were inclined to react against an assigned status that, to them, was more than being "a slave only in name."

SOCIAL RELATIONS BETWEEN MASTERS AND SLAVES

Early in the nineteenth century, claims were made regarding "the good treatment, the extraordinary good Provision, & the attachment the Slaves shew to their Owners."[16] The assertion of good treatment was thereby extended to an assertion of good relations between masters and slaves. In 1809, it was stated that "the Slaves in this Settlement are much attached to it" and had "affection for their Owners."[17] Later in the nineteenth century, it was asserted that the relationship of slaves to their masters was one of "invariable fidelity,"[18] a view that was echoed by a more recent colonial apologist who wrote of the "humanity" and "egalitarianism" of the masters, and of an "attitude of mutual esteem, loyalty, and even affection."[19] The early assertion of "the devotion and zeal of the Negroes in the Defence of their Masters' lives and properties"[20] during the Spanish attack on St. George's Cay in 1798 was repeated in the twentieth century by a celebration of the same battle, called "Shoulder to Shoulder,"[21] which emphasized the supposed unity of interest between masters and slaves in Belize. Even a contemporary political scientist has accepted this evaluation, stating that there existed a "traditional good comradeship. . . . between the logwood cutters and their slaves."[22]

The claims that the slaves gave their masters "invariable fidelity," "affection," and "devotion," and that the relations between masters and slaves were characterized by "mutual esteem" and "good comradeship," are based upon an unquestioning acceptance of the ideological statements of the masters. An examination of the actions of the slaves themselves, including such desperate and drastic actions as suicide, murder of the masters, desertion, and revolt, demonstrates that the slaves did not share their masters' view of their situation or their social relationships. Suicide and abortion were known in Belize, and cases of the destruction of masters' property and even the taking of the masters' lives are quite frequently recorded. The most important evidence from the historical rec-

The Slaves as Objects and as Subjects 73

ords concerning the slaves' reactions to their situation, however, lies in the four slave revolts and the countless and continual desertions of slaves from the settlement.

One of the earliest references to slaves in the Bay settlement, dating from 1745, appealed for military assistance in the face of Spanish threats and exhibited a concern about the loyalty of the slaves, who then outnumbered the whites:

> We the Inhabitants of this Place shou'd be Assisted, and being now driven to the Highest distress that can be and reduced to a small quantity of People, not exceeding above Fifty white Men, and about a hundred and twenty Negroes, which Number of the latter we cannot tell how many may prove true in the time of Engagement... we are obliged to Fortifie our selves on shore with our slaves to hold our Liberties.[23]

The white settlers were always a tiny minority of the Bay settlement who, while depending upon "our slaves to hold our Liberties," were constantly haunted by the specter of slave revolts.

The lack of any permanent police in the settlement meant that despite Burnaby's Code, there was little "law and order" in Belize; the settlers had no power, apart from that provided by an occasional warship from Jamaica, to suppress disorder. During the economic crisis of the 1760s and 1770s, when the logwood trade was severely depressed but had not yet been replaced by mahogany, the settlement was said to be "in a State of the utmost disorder and Confusion."[24] During this period, the settlers had little ability to control their slaves, who, undoubtedly forced to bear a good deal of the hardship engendered by the economic crisis, rebelled at least three times between 1765 and 1773. The situation is described, and the settlers' fears intimated, in a letter of 1765:

> If His Majesty would be graciously pleased to appoint us some form of Government... some power to punish evil doers amongst ourselves, for as to the Spaniards they seem at present very quiet, and (excepting the circumstance of granting an asylum to our runaway Negroes) not bad neighbours. The want of power we lately very severely experienced in a very dangerous case viz the Negroes belonging to one Mr. Thomas Cooke late of Jamaica, rebelled, killed their Master and a Carpenter robbed the house of every thing that was valuable, and fled to the woods; a few days after they murdered three Men in a small Schooner of mine, that went into the New River to load Logwood, and the poor people unhappily falling into the hands of those inhuman wretches fell a sacrifice, and they sunk the vessell; For want of power to compel people to take arms against them we have not been able to raise a party, and they still continue in Rebellion and have entirely stopped the communication of the New River, altho there are not above ten or twelve men able to carry arms amongst them all, and if they do not destroy one another by their own Cabals (as we have some hopes they will do, two or three being killed by the others) we do not know when it will end.
>
> Many People tired of living in a state of anarchy are withdrawing their Negroes and effects, so that it appears as if this settlement would dwindle away.[25]

The absence of any government or police power, combined with the vastness of the territory, the remoteness of the timber camps, and the limited communications, made the white settlers very insecure and vulnerable to slave revolts. Even such small-scale revolts as those that occurred in 1765 and 1768 were sufficient to expose the helplessness of the disorganized settlers and to threaten the very existence of the settlement.

> Matters are come to this miserable pass, that [by 8 March 1768] Twenty three British Negroes, Armed, had gone off from the New River to the Spaniards, and many more were expected to follow them; so that Business of every kind was at a dead Stand, All his Majestys Subjects there being reduced to the last necessity, of protecting their Houses from being plundered, and themselves from being slain . . . being thus unprotected in their property & unredressed for the Injuries and Losses they have suffered, some of the Baymen have already quitted the Country, more of them are preparing to follow.[26]

As the economic problems reached crisis proportions in the early 1770s, social relationships in the settlement reached a critical climax. The settlers were petitioning the Governor of Jamaica in 1771, complaining of their indebtedness to the merchants of England.[27] As the indebted settlers struggled to survive the economic crisis, they must have had difficulty securing provisions at the same time that they were trying to increase the amount of logwood exported in order to compensate for its falling value. The brunt of these problems would have befallen the slaves of the settlement, then numbering over two thousand, who must have faced a combination of decreasing provisions and increasing work. The outcome of this situation was the biggest slave revolt of all which broke out in 1773; it lasted about five months and was suppressed only with the help of a naval force from Jamaica.

The uprising began in May 1773 on the Belize River. On 23 May a Captain Davey arrived at St. George's Cay and sent an officer and some sailors to quell the revolt. The following is from his report to Admiral Rodney on 21 June:

> The Negroes before our People came up with them had taken five settlements and murthered six White Men and were join'd by several others the whole about fifty armed with sixteen Musquets Cutlasses, etc. Our People attacked them on the 7th inst. but the Rebels after discharging their Pieces retired into the Woods and it being late in the afternoon we could not pursue them.[28]

Shortly afterward, fourteen slaves surrendered, but Davey was encountering difficulty in taking the rest. He organized a militia, in three parties of forty men each, "to endeavour to surround and destroy them, which if they do not effect they must give up the Trade, as they will be continually exposed to their incursions and there will be an Asylum for all the Negroes who choose to run away from their masters." Davey reported that apart from two settlements, trade in the Bay area was at a standstill, and settlers on the other rivers were apprehensive, particularly as he had been ordered to leave for Jamaica by 10 July. His report continued:

> The Inhabitants are in a very bad situation: they have neither Arms nor Ammunition and those that are here are obliged to keep Guard for fear of the Negroes on the Kay, and what is much worse their fears will not make them unite and there is not the least subordination—they are continually quarrelling and fighting.

The revolt continued, and on 8 August Admiral Rodney, commander of the British West Indian fleet, instructed Captain W. Judd, commander of H.M.S. *Garland,* to proceed directly to the Bay. His instructions included mention of three fugitive slaves who had killed someone called McDougal on the Rio Hondo, an incident that appears distinct from, but may have been connected to, the Belize River revolt. In October a committee of Baymen informed Rodney that nineteen of the surviving rebels were trying to reach the Spaniards in the north and that Judd had sent fifteen marines to cut them off. Eleven of the rebels were reported having reached the Spanish post on the Rio Hondo, however, and the Commandant of Bacalar refused to give them up, a position that the Baymen were concerned would "encourage other negroes to follow them." These rebel slaves had traversed probably a hundred miles of bush in the five months since the insurrection began. It was not until November that Judd arrived in Jamaica with the news that the revolt was over.

Though there were no reported revolts for several decades after the resettlement of the Bay area in 1784, the settlers were continually apprehensive about the possibility of such revolts developing. In 1800, for example, citizens at a Public Meeting discussed their "apprehension of internal convulsion and the horrors of St. Domingo."[29] Despite their continual assurances concerning the supposed loyalty and devotion of their slaves following the Spanish attack on St. George's Cay in 1798, the settlers clearly did not see themselves as exempt from the threat of slave revolt that, especially after the successful revolt in Saint Domingue, haunted all the slave owners of the Caribbean. In 1791, the settlement was said to be "panic struck" when a French ship carrying over two hundred of the Saint Domingue revolutionaries arrived. It was decided that "they should not be permitted to land so infectious a cargo."[30] In 1807, it was reported that "a French Black man" named Louis Sovereign, "who was for some time confined in Goal here, and not long since transported from hence, as a suspicious character... the said black man committed no crime here, but was sent from the settlement, merely on account of his being originally from St. Domingo."[31] Two years later, concern was expressed in connection with "the evil disposition of the Non Commissioned Officers belonging to the 5th West India Regiment, among whom are several who commanded Companies of black Troops in St. Domingo." It was feared that the "intimacy" between these soldiers and the slaves would be dangerous and that "there is great reason to apprehend that this Regiment will not easily be removed from Honduras without the assistance of

White Troops."[32] Clearly the masters did not perceive their slaves to be immune from influence and feared the "infectious" example of Saint Domingue.

In 1817, "the exposed and unprotected state of the settlers, surrounded by vast hordes of Indians who are all in the constant habit of breaking in upon their works" was thought to place the British settlers "entirely at the mercy of the Slave Population."[33] The Magistrates expressed their apprehension that the slaves would join the Maya, who for the previous thirty years had been attacking the timber camps in the interior, and that together they would destroy the settlement. They begged Bathurst to consider "the local situation of this Settlement, vulnerable and exposed as it is on every side, to the Incursions of the wild Indians, with which it is surrounded. A very small Gang of desperate runaway Slaves, who would join and lead these Indians, must instantly overpower us, and the destruction of every British Subject would be inevitable."[34]

Though there is no evidence that the Maya and the slaves ever undertook joint action, the slaves were once more demonstrating their rebelliousness at the time of the Maya attacks. In 1819, Superintendent Arthur reported that "the uneasy state of the Slaves during the last Xmas caused much alarm, and obliged me to take unusual measures of precaution at that time, and since then, to send Troops into the interior to dislodge some parties of these misguided men, who have collected on the Banks of the Rio Nuevo."[35] The following year another insurrection occurred, this time on the Belize and Sibun rivers. Arthur reported that the "Principal Wood-Cutters" were "earnestly praying for immediate protection" because "a considerable number of Slaves had formed themselves into a Body in the River Belize, and being well armed, and having already committed various depredations the most serious consequences were to be apprehended."[36] Arthur immediately declared martial law to be in force and sent parties of troops up the Belize and Sibun rivers. His own inquiries led to the discovery that "the Negroes who had first deserted and had excited others to join them, had been treated with very unnecessary harshness by their Owner, and had certainly good grounds for complaint."[37] The revolt having begun on about 24 April, Arthur issued a proclamation on 3 May, offering rewards for the apprehension of two black slaves, Will and Sharper, who were "reported to be the Captains and Leaders of these Rebels," but offering "a Free Pardon, to any of the other Runaways, who will at this time voluntarily come in and deliver themselves."[38] Arthur offered the reward as well as the pardon to runaways who would bring with them either of their leaders. Whether this attempt to divide the rebels succeeded or not is unknown, but by 22 May Arthur had issued a proclamation ending martial law, as "there no longer exists any Combination amongst the Slaves in the River Sibun."[39] The last slave revolt in Belize was over.

Apart from these revolts, the other major evidence of slave discontent is the continual complaints from the settlers that the neighboring Spaniards gave asylum to runaway slaves. These complaints are a continual refrain in the records from the eighteenth century right up to 1838. The Spaniards were certainly not being altruistic in promising freedom to runaway slaves; they adopted this policy with the intention of undermining the settlement by enticing away its essential labor force. The fact remains, however, that large numbers of slaves in the Bay area preferred the hope of freedom among the Spaniards to the certainty of enslavement under the Baymen.

The organization of timber extraction left small groups of slaves, much less supervised than were slaves in plantations, scattered in remote parts of the sparsely populated country. This form of organization and pattern of settlement, coupled with the expertise possessed by many slaves with respect to traversing the bush, provided many opportunities and facilities for their escape, especially when encouraged by the Spaniards' promise of asylum. In the words of Superintendent Hunter, in 1790:

> Slaves, in this Settlement, being so by choice only; for the Vicinage of the Spanish Out Posts and the encouragement held out to seek freedom, by embracing the Roman Catholic Religion, afford them temptations to elope from their Owners. Many of the Settlers of this Country have been entirely ruined by these circumstances, and all experience frequent and heavy losses.[40]

The Africans were, of course, slaves by compulsion rather than "by choice," but that so many slaves chose to seek freedom is further testimony to the fact that they were dissatisfied with their situation in the Bay settlement and that the relations between slaves and masters were not as harmonious as the latter generally professed them to be.

In the eighteenth century, most of the slaves who escaped went north to cross the Rio Hondo into Yucatán. This was partly because the south and west of the area that is now Belize were unsettled and unexplored, but it was also because the Spaniards had outposts just across the Rio Hondo, and the Commandant at Bacalar offered freedom and protection to the runaways. Some of the slaves who rebelled and escaped to Yucatán later helped the Spaniards in attacks against the British settlers. For example, when St. George's Cay was taken in 1779, it was observed that among the Spaniards "there were several negroes in arms, who had formerly run away from the inhabitants of the Bay; particularly a negroe man named Dover, formerly the property of Mr. John Tucker, who had, a few days before the Spaniards landed, killed a white man, Lawrence Rawson, in the New River."[41]

Just a few years before the battle of St. George's Cay in 1798, at which the slaves of the Bay were said to have demonstrated their "devotion" to their masters, there were many complaints from these masters that their slaves were deserting them.

> There is one circumstance which ... serves to discourage our Industry & even threaten the total ruin of the Trade of this Settlement, & that is the Desertion of our Negroes to the Spaniards which increases daily & that of late to such an alarming degree, that no one Man however well disposed he may consider his Negroes, can think his property safe for a single Night. It is but a Week ago since a whole Gang

> about Twelve in number... Deserted in a Body to the Spaniards, got safe in to the Look out & were as usual joyfully received, this last Desertion has caused a general dread & apprehension amongst the Inhabitants of this Settlement, who perceive nothing less than the total ruin of their Property, should a speedy Stop not be put to a practice so disgraceful to Society & so repugnant to Justice.[42]

It would appear that the slaves had different ideas concerning "Society" and "Justice," because they continued to flee the oppression they experienced in the settlement. In 1793, only a year after the above complaint was written, another appeared:

> That your Memorialists have very recently experienced an additional loss by having 24 of their Negroes revolted who have been enticed by the Spaniards (under a pretence of granting their Freedom) to Bacalar....
>
> That unless some means is speedily devised to render their conditions more safe, and to prevent the Desertion of the Negroes in future the Settlement at Honduras must be inevitably ruin'd.[43]

Fifteen slaves who escaped from "their master, Mr. Paslo, an Englishman, because of ill-treatment and starvation," reached the Spaniards north of the Hondo in 1813.[44] The same Thomas Paslow was one of the Baymen whose slaves were supposed to have fought by his side with "devotion and zeal" fifteen years earlier at the battle of St. George's Cay.

When the settlement expanded to the west and south early in the nineteenth century, the slaves went still farther, through the bush into the Petén, or by boat down the coast to Omoa and Truxillo. Shortly after the neighboring Spanish territories became independent in 1821, they abolished slavery, and the complaints that slaves were escaping to these republics increased. In 1823, for example, it was stated that in a little over two months thirty-nine slaves had absconded and fled to Petén, which "is believed to be well known to many of the Negroes, it has also been long known that Negroes who have absconded some years ago during the War are residing there."[45] A complaint from Superintendent Codd to the Petén authorities drew the response that there was "a Town of black People" which was joined by those who "emigrated from your Establishment" and who "already enjoy the privileges of Citizens."[46] In 1825 the settlers were becoming desperate, "having just learnt that 19 Slaves have left their employments up the River Belize in a body, and taken the road to the Town of Peten at the head of the River, and 13 to Omoa... instant ruin stares us in the face."[47]

Superintendent Codd's report in 1825, expressing fear of widespread desertion and revolt, is desperate in tone:

> From the Negroes own conduct, and declarations, my information is to the effect, that throughout the several works, the Negroes in their conversations among themselves make no secret of their thoughts on desertion; they speek freely, and it has been discussed whether it is not folly to desert to the Spaniards; as, when most of the *Whites* are scattered over the Country and where their avocations demanded their

The Slaves as Objects and as Subjects 79

presence, they could be destroyed, without them the Negroes leaving their families, or suffering any privation; for what resistance could the whites make when so situated. That those who have deserted frequently make secret visits to the Settlements on the River, from Peten, where they communicate with the Negroes there, and often rob. . . . and that the total number of deserters as near as can be ascertained with those already mentioned is about one hundred and twenty. . . . that in event of any sudden rising of the Slaves or attempt by the Runaways to come down upon us, secretly, instigated by the Spaniards; how far the Black portion of the Militia and also the Soldiers of the 2 West India Regt. might be affected by it . . . it is against the views of the Slaves we have now to guard, There is almost a total absence of all respect from the Slave to their Masters, a carelessness in their duty; and in the language often used by them, equality, is the burden of their conversation.

Our Militia composed almost wholly of Black Pensioners, have ever shewn great repugnance to interfere between Master and Slave in the apprehension of deserters, from the connexion of most of them with the female part; by whom many of them have families and become allied to the Males. That the Soldiers of the detachment of the 2 W I Regt. from their long residence here are many of them in a similar situation. . . . it is to be doubted how far they might be inclined to act with effect.[48]

Eighty years previously, the settlers, anxious about the loyalty of their slaves in the face of threatened Spanish invasion, had requested military assistance. In 1825 Superintendent Codd, dropping all pretense of good relations between masters and slaves and stating that the slaves even showed a lack of respect for their masters, expressed anxiety about the loyalty of the black soldiers and militia in the event of a slave revolt. Concerned that the black troops, many of whom had been "recruited" in Africa, might exhibit solidarity with the black slaves, whose talk was of freedom and "equality," Codd requested "that a white Regt. may be stationed here."[49] It was felt in 1825, as in 1809, that only white troops could be relied upon to defend the white settlers from their slaves.

Though the anticipated slave revolt did not materialize, the extensive desertions continued. George Hyde, a wealthy free colored man, reported the desertion of ten of his slaves in a six week period across the Rio Hondo into Mexico.[50] The settlers' London agent petitioned that "the defection of the Slaves continues to go on to a most alarming extent . . . as Christmas is a period at which the Negroes assemble at Belize from the distant works, the Magistrates tremble at the dismal apprehension of the Slaves clandestinely resolving on a simultaneous desertion of the Settlement."[51] Though no such simultaneous desertion took place, the whole situation of the settlement was becoming untenable: the slave trade had been abolished for two decades, and the slaves were unable or unwilling to reproduce themselves, so the continual emigration of slaves to the neighboring republics was reducing the settlement's labor force. James Stephen of the Colonial Office commented in 1830 that "Honduras is now in the center of Countries which have declared Slavery illegal, and if we persist in maintaining it we must look for a rapid depopulation of the Settlement by the Slaves passing the

Border line, and returning no more."[52] The 1826 census, the first enumeration made after the republics had abolished slavery, listed 215 of the total 2,410 slaves as "runaways," other censuses indicating that the slave population was reduced by about one half between 1823 and 1835.[53]

The abolition of slavery and the establishment of the "apprenticeship" system in 1834 did not give the slaves freedom and barely changed their status. Many of the "apprentices," who could earn wages in occupations of their choice only after giving about forty hours of unpaid labor per week to their masters, were dissatisfied with their situation. Superintendent Cockburn reported on the problems he foresaw in the "apprenticeship" period less than two weeks after its establishment:

> The period which has elapsed since the 1st of August has been unattended here by any actual disturbance, tho certainly much dissatisfaction has been evinced on the part of the manumitted Slaves. They do not, nor can they be easily made to understand the obligations attached to their freedom. Their idea is that the King has made them free & therefore that the making them work for Six Years longer without pay is an act of injustice. I have seen a great number of them & endeavoured to explain to their comprehension the real state of the case. They do not dissent from what is told them—& they so far seem to comprehend it, that altho several had avowed a disinclination to return to their work yet none have persevered in a refusal to do so. It is however quite evident that the Six Years apprenticeship has counter-balanced in their estimation all the ulterior advantages held out to them by the Bill. They look to the present only & therefore finding that they are not "to all intents & purposes set free & discharged from all manner of Slavery at once" They neither feel benefitted or gratified at what has been done for them. . . . I cannot but feel some apprehension that rather than meet the Six Years apprenticeship they will avail themselves of the facility which attends their quitting the Settlement & proceeding to the neighbouring Republics.[54]

The "apprenticed labourers" obviously had a very clear comprehension of "the real state of the case," namely, that though they were no longer called slaves they were to continue working for their masters without pay. It is not surprising that, dissatisfied with this "manner of Slavery," some of the "apprentices" sought real freedom by escaping to the Petén and Omoa.[55] In one case, eleven men who had escaped to live in the adjoining Central American provinces for many years prior to 1834 had returned to Belize on hearing of the so-called abolition of slavery. They returned "under the impression of being unconditionally free," but "finding their hopes disappointed by the Apprenticeship System they shortly after the first of August absconded and have ever since been absent."[56]

The historical records show that the slaves took group and individual action to reject their situations. Whether these actions took the form of revolt against or withdrawal from their enslavement, it is clear that—in contradiction to the ideological claims of the masters, which have been repeated in historical accounts of the settlement—the slaves were dissatisfied with their situation, their status, and their relations with the masters. Above all, in their periodic revolts and continual escapes, the slaves demonstrated their hatred of slavery, and by their actions, they frequently threatened the very existence of the settlement.

The geographical conditions in the Bay of Honduras certainly favored the slaves, should they have chosen to engage in protracted guerrilla warfare to destroy the whites or to establish independent communities on the fringes of the settlement area. Like the "Bush Negroes" of French Guiana and Surinam, the Maroons of Jamaica, and the escaped slaves of Palmares in Brazil, some runaways did establish independent communities in the Belize area early in the nineteenth century. In 1816, reference was made to such a community "near Sheboon River, very difficult to discover, and guarded by poisonous Stakes."[57] The following year, Superintendent Arthur reported that "a considerable body of runaway Slaves are formed in the interior,"[58] and, in 1820, he referred to "two Slave Towns, which it appears have been long formed in the Blue Mountains to the Northward of Sibun."[59] Apart from the settlements of escaped slaves in the neighboring countries, such as San Benito in the Petén, there were Maroon communities in the Belize area, particularly near the Sibun River, a tributary of which is still called Runaway Creek.

While these independent communities of escaped slaves were sometimes in communication with those who remained enslaved and, as they had done in 1820, provided a refuge for rebellious slaves on the run, they were never the bases for any organized, systematic, or protracted guerrilla action against white domination. Revolt was not such a pressing response to slavery in Belize, when freedom could be obtained by slipping away into the bush of the interior or over the borders of the settlement. Though the white settlers deplored the continual desertion of their slaves, the facility with which the slaves could withdraw may well have functioned as a safety valve (from the viewpoint of the masters) in letting out the most rebelliously inclined of the slaves and so reducing the likelihood of insurrections. Indeed, the revolt of 1768 can perhaps be more accurately described as an armed escape from the settlement, and even the 1773 revolt ended with the survivors forcing their way across the Rio Hondo.

Given the favorable geographical conditions and the great numerical superiority of the slaves, the fact that they never actually took over the settlement can best be explained not by a supposed devotion to their masters but by the availability of freedom beyond the bounds of British jurisdiction. Another factor that would have reduced the likelihood of successful revolt is that the productive enterprises in which the slaves were involved were small scale, the slaves working in small groups that were isolated from one another. Such a pattern of settlement, encouraging solidarity within each small group but inhibiting communication between groups, would favor small-scale revolts and escapes but would hinder the organization and coordination of a large scale insurrection like those that occurred in the plantations elsewhere in the Caribbean. The 1773 revolt, the largest and most prolonged in the settlement's history, appears to have spread like a forest fire, starting in one camp and moving on to others, killing the whites and gathering recruits as it moved.

Still another factor that detracted from the organization of a massive slave revolt was the very limited identification the slaves had with the Belize area as a possible permanent home. Africans who had been transported from their own land to the West Indies (where some would have stayed for a while before being resold in a Jamaican market), taken to the Mosquito Shore or the Bay settlement, and then continually shifted from camp to camp, could not be expected to have developed any commitment to the area. The limited time that most slaves had spent in the Bay, and the migratory nature of their work, must have inhibited any identification with the area. Had such identification been present, it might have induced the slaves to take over the settlement. The slaves, however, were concerned not with taking over a territory but with avoiding slavery, and where the latter could be more easily accomplished by withdrawal than by confrontation, slave revolts were less likely to occur.

Toward the end of the eighteenth century, a militia was organized in the settlement, and regular troops of the West India regiments were generally stationed at Belize. The presence of such military force (which had been directly experienced by some of the slaves, most of whom were from the Mosquito Shore where a major revolt had been crushed by force in 1780[60]) may have inhibited revolt, though the escapes continued on a large scale. Moreover, the savagery with which rebellious slaves were tortured and killed, "by burning, gibbeting & other methods of torture,"[61] may have functioned, as it was intended, as a deterrent to further revolt.

If the recorded actions of the slaves demonstrate that relations between them and their masters were not as harmonious as the latter claimed, what more can be said about the relations of masters and slaves? The accounts that emphasize the good treatment and conditions of slaves in Belize in comparison with their treatment in other slave societies, such as Jamaica, may be correct as far as they go. It certainly appears that life for the timber-cutting slave was less regimented, better provided for, and subject to less arbitrary and cruel punishment than was life for a slave on a sugar plantation. On the other hand, the work and experience of a slave in Belize was far from easy: the labor was arduous and frequently dangerous, the camps were isolated and destructive to family life, and the physical conditions of camp life were extraordinarily rough and uncomfortable. Moreover, the domestic slaves in Belize, primarily women, were often subject to ill-treatment and, occasionally, the most appalling tortures. The case of the sadistic Michael Carty has already been mentioned, but the records show that a number of cases of cruelty inflicted upon slave women were at the hands of the free colored concubines of the white settlers. Some of these women may have been prompted by jealousy when they felt they might be replaced in the favor of the master by a young slave girl; on other occasions, these free colored mistresses, feeling insecure in their status, may have treated the domestic slaves harshly in order to emphasize their social distance from them.

One such case of a cruel free colored mistress, Duncannette Campbell, occurred in 1820 when she was tried "for punishing her Slave named Kitty in an illegal, cruel, and severe manner, by chaining her and repeatedly whipping her for a considerable time in the said chains in the loft of her house."[62] A physician who examined the slave

> observed the scores of several wounds, which appeared to have been recently inflicted with a whip or cowskin; they were chiefly upon the shoulders, but there were also a considerable number on the left arm, the neck, and face; those on the face had produced considerable swelling and other symptoms of inflammation; one of the stripes had divided the ala of the left ear; another had wounded the left eye-ball; both eyes were much swelled and inflamed, and her whole countenance was so much disfigured that it was some time before I could recognize her.[63]

Despite this evidence of cruelty, the only question for the jury to decide was whether the legal thirty-nine lashes had been exceeded. Within five minutes they had acquitted the prisoner.

Armstrong summarized the situation when he stated in 1824: "It has been admitted that the condition of slaves in Honduras is comparatively comfortable; but there are instances, many instances, of horrible barbarity practised there."[64] Apart from such instances of brutality,[65] it would appear that the settlers of Belize, in general, treated their slaves with greater consideration for their physical welfare than did their planter counterparts in the Caribbean. Since the slaves had virtually no legal protection, and were thus subject to the whims and customs of their masters, it remains to be explained why these masters, who seemed at times to be as capable of cruelty as any others, were generally more restrained in their treatment of their slaves.

First, the settlers of Belize, who had no legal title to land, had most of their capital invested in their slaves: "The chief property of the settlers of Honduras... must be supposed to consist in slaves."[66] The slaves, being largely imported through the Jamaican slave markets, were expensive, and so, too, was their upkeep, since it was based largely on imported provisions. It was stated early in the nineteenth century that the value of a recently imported African was between £120 and £160 Jamaican currency, but a "seasoned" slave was worth £200 to £300.[67] With the difficulty and expense of obtaining new slaves, especially after the abolition of the slave trade, the settlers had a financial interest in taking care of their slaves. In addition, of course, the very nature of the arduous work and rough conditions experienced by the slaves in the timber camps meant that only strong and healthy slaves could be of any value to the settlers.

The fact that most of the Baymen seem to have considered the settlement their home may also have had some effect upon their attitude to their slaves. In the Caribbean many of the planters were men intent on making a quick fortune in sugar by the gross exploitation, and consequent exhaustion, of both land and labor. Many planters stayed on their estates only long enough to be able to employ a managing attorney, whereupon they would return to England to live in luxury as absentee landlords. Lacking contact with their slaves, they generally lacked any concern for their welfare either. The Bay settlers, on the other hand, had little contact with Britain and saw their future as dependent upon the upkeep of their property in the settlement.

A major factor that would inhibit the masters from treating their slaves poorly lay in the often demonstrated facility with which discontented slaves could escape. This point was clearly recognized by the settlers, who stated, in their attack upon Superintendent Arthur: "We hold our Slaves here merely from the affection they bear their Owners, and that, if they were not governed with mildness, kindness, and liberality, from the encouragement held out by the Spaniards to desert, and the facility with which they could do so, together with the improbability of their ever being again recovered, the country would be in a moment deserted, and the Settlers ruined."[68] In 1825, George Hyde, a leading free colored merchant and slave owner, stated that, "As for punishments or ill-usage, you are aware (if ever so deserved) we dare not inflict it, so easy is their retreat to the Spaniards."[69] Of course, the fact that hundreds of slaves did escape shows that they did not bear the affection for their owners that their owners claimed, but the ease of escape must have been a deterrent to ill-treatment.

Finally, the situation of the timber camps, in which one or two white men lived in remote isolation with between ten and fifty slaves, all of whom possessed machetes, axes, and sometimes muskets used for hunting, must have made the masters more cautious about rousing the slaves' anger. The fact that slaves were armed was the object of frequent comment. In 1788, for example, it was stated that "it has always been a Custom with us to allow our Negroes Firearms,"[70] and twenty years later it was noted that "the whole of the slaves of Honduras are permitted to use arms, and possibly a more expert body of marksmen could no where be found."[71] Superintendent Arthur, soon after his arrival in 1814, reported with amazement how some slaves, "leaving their Works in the interior of the Country came down in a Body to the Town of Belize to dictate who should be their Masters. . . . the several Thousand Slaves in this Settlement . . . by some unfortunate mismanagement, have been allowed to be provided with Arms, and therefore it requires additional attention to keep them quiet and peaceable, and certainly to give them no just grounds for discontent."[72] The slaves, who were armed and who knew the territory better than their masters, possessed something of the means that command a modicum of respect.

If the masters generally treated their slaves somewhat better than did the West Indian planters, they did so not from any spirit of egalitarianism or good comradeship, but for economic reasons or through their fear of the destruction of the settlement by insurrections or mass desertions. The slaves had frequently demonstrated their ability to act against their masters by revolt and escape, and the masters were continually haunted by the threat of "mass combinations" or "simultaneous desertions." Though the conditions of slavery in the Bay area differed somewhat from those on the Caribbean plantations, the slaves in the Bay, like other slaves, rejected and rebelled against their situation, some of them struggling for a freedom which they may never have experienced but for which they were willing to risk all.

6
The Laborers, Free and Enslaved, in the Early Nineteenth Century

THE FREEDMEN DURING SLAVERY

Following the resettlement of the Bay in 1784, the free colored and black groups rapidly increased. Already outnumbering the white settlers in 1790, by 1816 they were a quarter of the population, and in 1832 they outnumbered the slaves. The earliest estimates did not distinguish between the free colored and the free blacks, but the censuses that began in 1816 did make that distinction and showed that while the free blacks increased more rapidly than the free colored, they remained less numerous.

From table 6.1 it can be seen that the free colored and black population increased from 371 in 1790 to 1,788 in 1832 and that, as a percentage of the population, this group increased from 14 to 48 percent in that period. The 1835 census showed a dramatic reduction in their numbers (to 1,137), but since the population as a whole decreased, the free colored and blacks were about 44 percent of the total population.

Two features that differ notably between the slave and freedmen populations in this period are the sex ratio and the proportion of children to adults. While slave men always greatly outnumbered slave women, the reverse was generally the case among the free colored and black population. With the exception of 1806, the women were more numerous than the men, particularly among the free colored, where the ratio was about three women to two men in the 1830s. Also noteworthy is the relatively large number of children among the freedmen, which increased from 119 in 1790 to 804 in 1832; the number of slave children only increased from 418 to 453 in the same period. While slave women almost always outnumbered slave children, the reverse was the case among the freedmen, particularly the free colored.

It must be emphasized that the statistics on the freedmen need to be treated with extreme caution, as there is reason to believe that many of these individuals were not enumerated. In the late eighteenth century, it was stated that some "free

TABLE 6.1 Free Colored and Black Population of the Bay Settlement, 1790–1835

Date	Colored and Black			Total	Percentage of total population
	Men	Women	Children		
1790	120	132	119	371	14
1803	180	275	320	775	20
1806	238	207	332	777	22

	Colored					Black						
	M	W	C	Total	%	M	W	C	Total	%		
1816	157	171	234	562	15	128	158	85	371	10	933	25
1823	192	243	374	809	20	217	222	174	613	15	1,422	35
1826	190	260	398	848	20	193	262	220	675	16	1,523	36
1829	192	247	454	893	23	202	258	238	698	18	1,591	41
1832	190	295	484	969	26	240	259	320	819	22	1,788	48
1835	119	200	351	670	26	123	152	192	467	18	1,137	44

SOURCE: 1790, "General Return of the Inhabitants in the Bay of Honduras . . .," 22 Oct. 1790, CO, 123/9; 1803, "A Short Sketch of the present situation of the Settlement of Honduras . . . ," from Supt. Thomas Barrow, 31 March 1803, CO 123/15; 1806, Br. Gen. H. T. Montresor to Gov. Sir Eyre Coote, 22 Oct. 1806, CO 123/17; 1816, 1823, 1826, 1829, 1832, and 1835, Censuses of the Population, GRB.

Negroes, many of whom have no place of fixed Residence,"[1] had not been enumerated, and the 1823 census noted that "there are many free persons who have not returned themselves, or their Families, particularly the free Black Men."[2] The 1826 census, recognizing the difficulty of enumerating many of the "Free Black Settlers," stated that in addition to the returns given, there were 102 white, 189 colored, and 743 black men in the militia, but if they were added to the others "some might be twice returned."[3] There is reason to believe that many people, particularly among the free blacks, were not enumerated in these early censuses, but it is unfortunately impossible to suggest more accurate figures.

What were the origins of the freedman population in the Bay settlement? Where did they come from and why did they increase so rapidly? Most of the 371 freedmen who were first enumerated in 1790 must have come from the Mosquito Shore in the evacuation of 1787. A report on the evacuees from the Mosquito Shore stated that 537 of them were "White and Free,"[4] and since less than half that number were listed as white residents in 1790, most of them can be safely assumed to have been free people of color.

One important factor leading to the increase in the freedmen was the high incidence of manumission. Manumissions had been granted in the Bay settlement for almost as long as slavery had existed there; there are records of manumissions in 1737, 1772, 1788, and 1792,[5] but no statistics are available on manumissions until the nineteenth century. According to the censuses of 1816 and 1820, 178 slaves were manumitted between 1807 and 1816 and another 50 between 1817 and 1820.[6] Another report gave even higher figures: 201 manumissions between 1808 and 1816, and 62 between 1817 and 1820.[7] In the 1820s the rate of manumission increased, 141 slaves being manumitted between 1821 and 1825,[8] and 169 between 1826 and 1830.[9] These figures suggest that about six hundred slaves were manumitted in the settlement between the abolition of the slave trade in 1807 and the abolition of slavery in 1834. In comparison with other slave societies in the Caribbean, it is astonishing that about one-fifth of the slaves of Belize were manumitted in that quarter-century.

Of the 573 slaves who were manumitted between 1808 and 1830, about 57 percent were female (see table 6.2). Statistics from the late 1820s show that adult males were less likely to be manumitted than either adult females or children, despite the fact that they constituted the majority of the slaves. Between 1826 and 1830, less than one-quarter of the slaves manumitted were adult males, forty-one adult males, sixty-eight adult females, and sixty children being manumitted in those five years.[10] Two factors were probably influential in affecting this dispro-

TABLE 6.2 Manumissions in the Bay Settlement, by Sex, 1808–30

Date	Male	Female	Total
1808	4	6	10
1809	17	6	23
1810	22	24	46
1811	13	15	28
1812	20	6	26
1813	4	2	6
1814	12	14	26
1815	9	6	15
1816	9	12	21
1817	1	14	15
1818	1	5	6
1819	9	18	27
1820	7	7	14
1821	21	26	47
1822	15	24	39
1823	9	15	24
1824	10	8	18
1825	4	9	13
1826	20	27	47
1827	16	26	42
1828	8	26	34
1829	16	12	28
1830	2	16	18
Total	249	324	573

SOURCES: Returns of Manumissions by George Westby, 15 Dec. 1823, CO 123/34, and 31 Dec. 1825, CO 123/37; Supt. Cockburn to Lord Goderich, 25 April 1831, CO 123/42.

portion among the slaves who were manumitted. First, the adult male slaves, provided they were healthy and fit, were generally the most valuable to the slave owners, who would be reluctant to free them for fear of losing their labor. Second, adult white males outnumbered adult white females by at least two to one, so many of them took slave women as their concubines, subsequently freeing them and their offspring. For example, in 1792, one Johann Jacob Slusher, a blacksmith, manumitted four of his children, "mullatoes born of a Negro woman named Venus my property," and also Venus herself and her black daughter Luisa.[11] The high incidence of manumission and the greater likelihood that women and children would be manumitted helps to explain the rapid increase in, and the greater proportions of, women and children, especially free colored children, in the freedman population.

Another source of freedmen in the settlement was disbanded soldiers from the West Indian regiments. In June 1817, Superintendent Arthur informed the Magistrates that "His Majesty's Government have been pleased to determine on disbanding the 5th West India Regiment, and to provide for five hundred of the Men by removing them to this Settlement where they are to receive Grants of Land proportioned to their means of cultivation, or to engage themselves in the service of Wood-Cutters, or other Inhabitants as they themselves prefer."[12] By November 1817, some of the disbanded soldiers had arrived, and Arthur reported that "in the Distribution of the Disbanded Soldiers of the 5th West India Regiment the continuity of the situation decided me in giving grants of Land to a large proportion of them up the River Sibun, and in Manatee Lagoon."[13] A report dated February 1818, of "men discharged from the 2nd West India Regiment and the late 5th West India Regiment at present Settled in Honduras" stated that there was then a total of 412 men, 59 women, and 39 children in the settlement, and a further 144 men, 22 women, and 15 children arrived the following October.[14] This immigration of almost 700 people is not entirely shown in the increase (of about 500) in the freedman population between the censuses of 1816 and 1823. This fact was noted in the latter census and also in the census of 1826, which stated that "from the great number of Military Pensioners (disbanded Troops) and others Free Black Settlers who never could be depended upon for giving in Returns of themselves and Families it was found to be a work of almost impossibility to make a true and perfect Census."[15]

The ambiguous social position of the free people of color at the end of the eighteenth century, as described in chapter 3, was maintained in the nineteenth century. While a few of them became quite wealthy, they were legally discriminated against for the first three decades of the nineteenth century, during which time, though free, they occupied a position in the social structure that was distinctly inferior to that of the dominant white settlers. Despite the restrictions under which they suffered, Superintendent Arthur was astonished by what he perceived as the prominence of the "People of Colour" in the settlement's affairs when he arrived in 1814. He considered "the safety of the Settlement" to be "very considerably endangered," a fact that he attributed, first, to "an increase of Wealth and Prosperity [which] have been found to bring with them an increase of Independence," and, second, to "the decrease of the most respectable part of the Community, and the uncommon increase of People of Colour." He considered it "an unfortunate innovation [that] certain People of Colour who possessed considerable property" had been admitted to the Public Meetings, and deplored the fact that "an attempt has been made . . . with success once or twice, to introduce the Free Blacks and Charaibs. . . . At a Public Meeting convened during the last month above 30 of these Blacks and Charaibs were brought into the Meeting." He therefore recommended that the Public Meetings should consist "entirely of White Inhabitants British Born Subjects, possessing a clear and visible Property of Two hundred Pounds Jamaica Currency," and advocated that the influence of the free colored and blacks be diminished by denying them any "further Voice in Publick Measures."[16] Arthur followed this letter with another, stating that "the Population of the People of Colour has so much increased as to bear far too great a disproportion to the White Inhabitants."[17]

Though Arthur's views on the free people of color, like his views on the conditions of the slaves, were to change a great deal, and though the imperial government never acted on his advice concerning qualifications for membership in the Public Meeting, the freedmen of Belize were among the last in the British West Indies to achieve equal civil rights with the white settlers. In fact, as the proportion of the freedmen in the population increased during the first three decades of the nineteenth century, so did the restrictions on their activities. While wealthy colored men had held commissions in the militia during the struggle with Spain in the late eighteenth century, they could no longer do so in the nineteenth century. Permitted to possess mahogany or logwood works if the Magistrates unanimously consented to "naturalize" them in the eighteenth century, a law passed in 1805 excluded "free persons of colour" from locating a logwood works unless also possessing "four able negro men slaves." Such economic restrictions would force the freedmen into subsistence farming or fishing, or, as was certainly the intention of the regulations, into wage labor dependent chiefly upon white employers. In 1808 the Public Meeting was open to the free colored, but property and residence qualifications for colored men were at least twice those of white residents,[18] and they could not become Magistrates or even jurors. Despite these restrictions, Superintendent Arthur still advocated in 1815 that their privileges "should be curtailed rather than extended,"[19] on the grounds of "security."

The reaction of these free colored to their inferior social position and the discriminatory legislation was to petition the British government for fuller rights and privileges, generally emphasizing their loyalty, "respectable character," and "irreproachable conduct," and frequently stressing their "whiteness," both physical and cultural. A fine example of such a petition is that sent by William Usher to the king in 1815:

> That your Memorialist being a descendant of those Race of Indians who inhabit the Mosquito Shore, but in the sixth generation removed from said Indians to White....
>
> Your Memorialist was born upon the Mosquito Shore whose father was an Englishman, a native of London, he was sent to England at a very early age to the care and protection of his family, where your Memorialist was educated and brought up, and his birth was not only a secret to his relations and friends, but was unknown to himself, until he arrived in Honduras at which time, Your Memorialist was made acquainted with a situation in life he was to fill, which, however respectable might be his circumstances, connexions and character would for ever deprive him of those dearest privileges of an Englishman.... Your Memorialist having resided in Honduras fourteen Years during which time he has ever continued to conduct himself with that probity and honor which should and ought to be the first duty of a Subject, thereby rendering his conduct irreproachable, and obtaining the character of an honest man and good Citizen. From those mortifying and disgraceful distinctions, Your Memorialist is for ever deprived of the right of filling the office of Magistrate, of sitting as a Juror, or of holding any other public employment, not being considered White, although no visible distinction can be observed.[20]

Superintendent Arthur, commenting on this petition, stated that Usher's character was "unblemished," though "his remove from the Mosquito Indians is not quite so remote as he states."[21] Bathurst's reply simply suggested that the relevant laws and restrictions of Jamaica should be applied to "the Coloured Population of Honduras,"[22] but nothing appears to have resulted from his suggestion.

After living five years in the settlement, Arthur's opinion of the black and colored population had so changed that he reported: "The better description of people of Colour in the Colony, are infinitely superior to the lower class of white Inhabitants, who, for the most part, (there being so very few respectable Settlers) constitute the Jurors, and are altogether unworthy of such an Office."[23] By 1820, his concern had become one of trying to ensure protection and justice for the freedmen as well as the slaves:

> The great difficulty of forming a Jury in so small a Community of White Inhabitants ... I certainly consider that as the White Population bears no proportion whatever to the People of Colour, who can neither sit as Magistrates or Jurors, it is to them, an act of substantial Justice that as respectable a Bench as possible should be constituted, and it is moreover a protection which Humanity would willingly extend to the poor Slave Population, whose complaints have recently been the subject of my peculiar consideration.[24]

By the time of his departure, in 1822, Arthur's opinions had moved a full circle, from a perception of the free colored and blacks as a disruptive force to the view that they constituted "the main strength of the Colony," opposed by the "immoral habits and dangerous principles" of the whites:

> The People of Colour, as well as the Free Black Population in the Colony, although exceedingly indolent from causes which might both be explained and

remedied, I must ever represent as, orderly, tractable and well-disposed, indeed, nothing but their excessive submission can account for their having patiently endured the unjust Legislative and Judicial Authority by which they have been so long controled:—in this Class the main strength of the Colony consists, and they have certainly, my Lord, a proven Claim upon His Majesty's Government to be protected and relieved from the unjust, partial and over-reaching conduct of the generality of the White Population.[25]

Arthur's opinions may have changed, but the inferior social position of the free colored and blacks in the 1820s did not. Throughout the West Indies, the free colored were petitioning the British government for more rights and privileges, and Stephen Lushington advocated their cause in Parliament. The free colored population of Belize was no exception, and one of its most influential members, George Hyde, the son of a leading white settler who had been a judge of the Supreme Court and the Public Treasurer, sent a petition in 1827. Hyde emphasized that he was freeborn, was brought up and educated in England, and had become a successful merchant, but that "though his exertions might acquire him wealth, he must still remain in a condition of comparative degradation, on the sole ground of his Mother being a woman of colour, he is excluded from sitting as a Juror, serving as a Magistrate, from holding a Commission in the Militia, or from filling any Public Office of Trust, or Honor." He therefore enquired "by what power, or authority he and his other freeborn brethren of the mix'd race were deprived of any portion of the rights, and privileges, enjoyed by other of His Majestys Subjects."[26] Though Hyde emphasized his own personal qualities of birth and upbringing, and appeared to restrict his petition to the "freeborn brethren of the mix'd race," he was in fact interested in furthering the civil rights of all the free colored. Visiting London in 1827, he pressed his case in a series of interviews, letters, and petitions.[27] Dissatisfied with Bathurst's reply to his appeals, Hyde had his petition included in those that Lushington presented to Parliament on 12 June 1827. The case was subsequently made by Lushington that the current membership of the legislature, with qualifications at £250 for whites and £500 for colored, consisted of twenty-eight whites and twelve colored, despite the fact that "nearly two thirds of the whole property at Honduras in Land slaves & personalty belongs to the free coloured class exclusive of the free blacks."[28] He went on to give the opinion that

> it can never be supposed that the coloured class, who preponderate both in numbers and wealth would adopt any measures injurious to the interests of the Settlement, if all these restrictions were removed; & how the wealthy individuals of this class must feel, when they see their own clerks holding commissions in the militia, while they themselves are compelled to serve as serjeants & privates I need not attempt to prove. The same feeling of course arises both as to the Magistracy and Juries.[29]

Lushington then recommended that the Superintendent be directed to suggest to the legislative body that disabilities should be removed from the free colored and that "some person of colour" should be nominated to the criminal court.

The following year, Superintendent Codd reported on the deliberations of the legislative body. Prefacing his report with the comment that "the People of Colour of this Colony labour under less disabilities and indeed enjoy greater privileges than I believe any other," he went on to describe how the Public Meeting, far from lifting restrictions on the free colored as a class, which was the intention of Hyde and Lushington, merely granted them the right to petition as individuals:

> A Law was passed . . . declaratory that the Privileges and Immunities enjoyed by His Majesty's White Subjects should be Granted to persons of Color by going through the forms of Petition and Certificate of Character Honor and Probaty, that Education Long Residence and possession of Interest in the Country are the grounds on which they will obtain it.[30]

Since this was, in future, to be the only way in which free colored men could become members of the Public Meeting, it was in some ways a retrograde measure, contrary to the intentions of the Colonial Office. The part of the law that concerned qualifications for membership of the Public Meeting was repealed the following year, when it was decided in a Public Meeting that new members of that assembly were required to be elected by not less than twenty-five votes from the existing members, the qualifications for electing members being the same as when voting for Magistrates.[31] Such a measure would have ensured the self-perpetuation of the oligarchical Public Meeting, as was its intention.

The tardiness and indecision of the Public Meeting in Belize, which may well have been a deliberate attempt by the minority of white property owners to delay the imminent rise of the free colored in political affairs, was overtaken by events elsewhere in the British West Indies. While the Public Meeting continued to make free-colored participation in public affairs dependent upon decisions made by the white property owners on individual cases, the colored in the Crown Colonies of Trinidad and St. Lucia were relieved of all their civil disabilities. The Colonial Office having thus demonstrated its intentions, those colonies with their own legislatures, seeing the writing on the wall, reluctantly followed suit. The Jamaican Assembly passed an act granting civil rights to the free colored in 1830, and the legislature in Belize, itself under threat of dissolution,[32] passed a similar "Act to entitle all His Majesty's Coloured Subjects of Free Condition in this Settlement and their issue to the same Rights and Privileges with British Subjects born of White Parents" on 5 July 1831.[33]

The debate concerning this act is instructive. The act stated that the free colored "shall be entitled to have hold and enjoy all Rights, Privileges, Immunities and advantages whatsoever as if they were Born and descended of White Ancestors," thereby encouraging the idea, promoted for years by the free colored petitioners, that they could be considered "as good as white." The chairman of the Meeting, William Gentle, in proposing that the bill be adopted, praised the tractability and submissiveness of the free colored by saying that "this deserving Class of His Majesty's Subjects had long been debarred from various privileges and immunities which they had born with a degree of patient submission that reflected infinite credit.'' When an amendment was proposed that "Black Persons of Free Condition in this Settlement should also enjoy the like privileges as White Persons. . . . a considerable discussion here arose." The outcome of the discussion was the decision that because the bill referred to "persons of Color only," the amendment was really a new bill and it could not therefore be legally entertained. It was consequently withdrawn, and the attempt to extend the same civil rights to the free blacks was defeated.

It was noted in chapter 3 that the free colored, occupying an ambiguous position in the social structure, were ambivalent in their social identity. When they were enabled to hold commissions in the militia, to own slaves, and to participate in the settlement's political economy, they did so without hesitation, seeking thereby to join the white elite. But the white elite, though frequently related to the free colored, denied this sought-after identity. As the numbers of free colored rapidly increased, the white elite excluded them from participation in public appointments and from holding commissions in the militia, and discriminated against them in the area of economic opportunity. The free colored, faced with this situation, continued to deny their affinity to the slaves—and even to the free blacks. As in the confrontation of August 1787, the free colored chose not to involve the slaves but to seek redress for their grievances from the Crown's representative and the British government. In their petitions the free colored emphasized their loyalty, their "good character," their wealth, and their education. Above all, perhaps, they stressed their white ancestry, their racial proximity to the whites and distance from the slaves, in order to claim the same privileges as "His Majesty's White Subjects."

In summary, the free colored accepted the basic social distinctions of the society and exploited the white bias, both physical and cultural, which had been directed against them, in order to differentiate themselves from the blacks. It is therefore far from surprising that in 1831 the free colored were granted equal civil rights "as if they were Born and descended of White Ancestors" after being praised for the "patient submission" with which they had borne years of discrimination. Nor is it surprising that when the attempt to extend the same rights to free blacks failed, the free colored raised no objection. The racist ideology of the whites had so permeated the free colored sense of identity that the free colored were glad to have finally achieved social differentiation from the blacks. *The Honduras Almanack* for 1830, in describing what it called the "classes of society," distinguished between the free blacks and the free colored. While the colored were said to "partake more or less of the qualities of black and white, directly as their distance from either,"[34] of the free blacks it was said that "few of them are to be found entirely exempt from those low propensities which are exhibited in a state of barbarism."[35] Having accepted the whites' criteria of "barbarism," the free colored sought, and in 1831 achieved to some extent, to dissociate themselves from the "low propensities" of the blacks.

THE CULTURE OF THE SLAVES AND FREEDMEN

To what extent did the African cultural heritage, or to be more precise, the variety of African cultures, survive among the slaves and freedmen of African origin in the Bay settlement? The answer to this intriguing question must necessarily remain sketchy and incomplete. On the one hand, the blacks who were the practitioners of these cultures were mostly illiterate and left no record of their own. On the other hand, the white and free colored people, whether visitors, colonial administrators, or local settlers, showed little interest in understanding the strange African cultures that were, to them, evidence of the barbarism of their social inferiors. The few records that do exist referring to African customs and life are therefore biased by the racialist viewpoint of the writers, who were generally concerned with their "civilizing mission"—that is, with eliminating rather than understanding the culture of the blacks. Although the record, and hence the answer to the question, remains incomplete, there are nevertheless some interesting indications of the survival of certain aspects of African culture.

Although, as stated in chapter 4, there is no indication from the eighteenth-century records of the proportion of the imported slaves who were of African birth, there were certainly many African-born slaves, and several signs suggest that they were preponderantly from the Niger and Cross deltas in the Bight of Benin, or from farther south in the areas of the Congo or Angola. The only discovered estimate of the proportion of slaves who were of African and West Indian birth dates from 1823, when it was estimated that there were "near 1500 Africans" in a slave population of about 2,500, "the remainder being Creoles and Descendants of Indians."[36] The distinction made between these two groups in this case was in connection with the fact that "the African Negroes were all in commotion" over rumors of freedom, and it was asserted that "the ferment the envy and desire of liberty . . . could not be allayed or effaced in the Africans."[37] It was to be expected that one of the differences between those born free and those born in captivity would be a different understanding of the meaning of slavery.

It has been argued that there is a great emphasis on religion in African culture,[38] and that survivals of African customs could therefore be expected within this "culture focus." One problem that arises in connection with this conception, however, is that the boundaries between religion, magic, music, and dance were never distinct in Africa; music and dance were frequently an intrinsic part of religious ritual and magical practices. The records of the Bay settlement provide evidence of the survival of African music and dance, though it is far from clear to what extent these activities were religious in nature and to what extent they were secular entertainments.

One African survival that bridged the areas of religion and magic was the practice of obeah. Obeah was considered a means for manipulating or controlling the world, both natural and supernatural, and it could be associated with either good or bad intent. The whites were anxious to suppress the practice of obeah, which they believed, sometimes correctly, to be associated with revolt. The practitioners of obeah, which was generally an individual, as opposed to a group or cult, phenomenon, were Africans who claimed exceptional knowledge of charms and fetishes used for a number of purposes, including medicine. Not surprisingly, the obeah-men acquired a reputation for involvement in revolts, as they were frequently leaders within the slave community. "In the plotting of these rebellions," one writer has observed, "the obeah-man was essential in administering oaths of secrecy, and, in cases, distributing fetishes which were supposed to immunize the insurgents from the arms of the whites."[39]

In Belize a regulation regarding obeah was passed in 1791, at the time of the Saint Domingue revolt, which clearly indicated the white settlers' fear of the influence of obeah-men upon their slaves:

> In order to prevent the many mischiefs that may hereafter arise from the wicked art of Negroes going under the appellation of Obeah Men and Women, pretending to have communication with the Devil and other evil Spirits, whereby the weak and superstitious are deluded into a Belief of their having full power to exempt them whilst under their protection from any Evils that might otherwise happen; It is hereby Resolved that any free person of Colour or Slave, who shall hereafter pretend to any supernatural Power in order to affect the Health or Lives of others, or extorting Money or Effects under false pretences, or any way compassing the Life of any person by such means, or otherwise advising aiding or abeting any Slave or Slaves to depart their Masters Service, or shall harbour any runaway Slaves, or promote the purposes of Rebellion, shall upon conviction thereof, suffer Death or such other punishment as the Magistrates and Jury shall think proper to direct.[40]

The practice of obeah continued, however, as there is a report from 1816 of a Private Andrew Fife, who had deserted from the Seventh West India Regiment, practicing obeah in the settlement. "So great [was] his influence over the poor Slaves by virtue of his Obeah performances," noted Superintendent Arthur, "that the Country offered a public reward for his apprehension." His immediate execution was demanded as "the only means by which his pernicious principles can be eradicated from amongst the poor Slaves."[41]

To many Africans, death and burial constituted the most important phase of the human life cycle and were consequently accompanied by significant ceremonies. It is therefore not surprising that the funeral rites, or wakes, of the slaves were important occasions, marked by feasting, as described in 1830: "Wakes . . . are recreations of vivacity amongst the people . . . [and] present a tolerable resemblance of the Irish Wakes, where the house of mourning and the house of feasting are identified as one and the same."[42] Given the common African belief that at death one's spirit rejoined one's ancestors, it is understandable that death, as a release from slavery and a return to Africa, should be celebrated with feasting. An account written in 1850 is worth quoting at length, as it illustrates both the integration of feasting, music, and other recreation with religious ritual and the synthesis of European and African cultural elements in the wake and burial ceremonies:

If a slave-owner died, all his dependents and friends came together to be feasted; and the wife or mistress and her children prepared the house and provided provisions and plenty of ardent spirits. The corpse, dressed in its best clothes, was laid upon a bed and *waked* during the whole night. Cards, dice, back-gammon, with strong drink and spiced wine, helped to beguile its watches, during which the loud laugh and the profane oath were unrestrained. In the negro yard below, "the sheck'ka" and the drum "proclaimed the sport, the song, the dance, and various dreem"... [by] the different African nations and creoles, each in parties... Sometimes a tent was erected, where rum, coffee, and gingertea were dispensed to all who chose to come and make free. After a night thus spent, the corpse was carried in the morning to the churchyard, the coffin being borne by labourers, who in their progress used to run up and down the streets and lanes with their burden, knocking at some door or doors, perhaps visiting some of the friends of the deceased, professing to be impelled by him, or to be contending with the spirit who opposed the interment of the body. At length some well known friend came forward, speaking soothingly to the dead, and calling him Brother, urged him to go home, and promised him rest and blessing. They then moved all together towards the grave, and the sheck'ka's jingle, the voice of song, and latterly, the funeral service of the Established Church were mingled together in the closing scene.[43]

One final example of the survival of African religious influence in the settlement is especially interesting. Referring to the free blacks, the *Honduras Almanack* reported: "It is not rare to meet with black persons who possess an utter aversion to spirituous liquors, and can by no means be prevailed upon to taste a beverage in which they know anything of the sort to be a component part.... [they] in rejecting it, act not so much from a correct principle as from national usage, or original intercourse with Mahometan connexions."[44] Since between about 1770 and 1790 the majority of British slaves were exported from the Niger delta area, and many had been brought down river from the interior, it is quite possible that the Islamic influence remarked upon derived from the northern region of what is now Nigeria.

Concerning music and dance, there are a number of brief records. In 1790, "a favourite custom among the Slaves to amuse themselves, by dancing about in the streets"[45] was remarked upon, and at about the same time, "negroes diverting themselves playing the gombay" were reported.[46] The use of gombay or goombay drums was essential in African music and dance, but because their use disturbed the white settlers, they were frequently suppressed. In 1807, for example, Superintendent Hamilton complained about the slaves being accustomed "to beat Gumbays or other Instruments sounding like Drums, and to be strolling about the Streets at all hours of the Night."[47] A petition had previously been sent to him complaining of

> a very large assemblage of Negroes either free or Slaves... who have resorted to certain appointed Huts situated in different parts of the Swamps on the South side of this Town, whose apparent motive for which is Dancing. Whatever may be their real motive for such Meetings, certain it is these Nightly revels are productive of much

noise and occasion much disturbance in the Neighbourhood, as to deprive the Inhabitants therein from enjoying their natural rest.[48]

They therefore requested the Superintendent to instruct the military to break up these nocturnal meetings and to lodge the participants in the public jail. By 1809, the slaves, who had engaged in "their Country Plays on musical Instruments until 12 o Clock... were in the first instance limitted to 9 every night... to which restriction they punctually submitted, tho' not without murmuring."[49] The slaves protested because what was being suppressed was clearly one of their major modes of recreation, involving important elements of their African culture.

A description of the "gumby" in 1830 shows that these nocturnal meetings survived repression. They were recognized as

> being importations from the coast of Africa; large parties meet at night, at some appointed negro yard, where they commence dancing to the beat of the drum, and the music of their own voices... there can be nothing more calculated to impress a stranger with surprise, than the different formations of their drums and the variety of their dances.[50]

Since the timber camps were so isolated, and much of the trucking of logs was done at night, the slaves must have had few opportunities for such communal recreation during most of the year. There is reference to a slave owner who inspired "the Negroes when at work to make him the burden of their songs,"[51] quite probably satirical in nature, but generally the slaves would have waited for their return to the town before engaging in community festivities.

The greatest opportunity for communal recreation occurred at Christmas, between the long seasons of intense and arduous labor in isolated camps in the bush. The occasion was one that seemed to bring together all the blacks in a street festival of music, songs, and dances. A description of the event is provided in an early nineteenth century account:

> The morning of Christmas-day is invariably ushered in by the discharging of small-arms in every direction, every thing now from established custom being free and unrestrained; and the master's house (where the festivity commences) and whatever it contains is now open to all. The members of the several African tribes, again met together after a long separation, now form themselves into different groups, and nothing can more forcibly denote their respective casts of national character than their music, songs, and dances. The convulsed rapid movements of some, appear inconceivably ludicrous; whilst the occasional bursts of loud chorus, with which all are animated, contribute greatly to heighten the singularity of the entertainment.
>
> The endurance of the negroes during the period of their holidays, which usually last a week, is incredible. Few of them are known to take any portion of rest for the whole time; and for the same space they seldom know an interval of sobriety. It is the single season of relaxation granted to their condition; and that it should be partaken of immoderately may therefore appear not altogether so extraordinary.
>
> At this season water-sports are also common, and Dory-racing affords a very general amusement; and on these occasions large sums are freely betted both by

owners and slaves. This species of diversion has no small share of utility attached to it, as it contributes to render the latter highly expert in a kind of exercise that is inseparably connected with the labour in which they are principally engaged.[52]

Another description, more than twenty years later, demonstrates the continuity of the event:

> At Christmas, the slaves enjoy a saturnalia which continues without interruption for the space of a fortnight. During this time there is an entire relaxation from all toils; negroes of all conditions join in sets, and perambulate the streets from morn till night, with colours flying and music playing, to which they keep time in graceful movements, waving their flags and umbrellas to the measured beats of their drum. Each slave has an unlimited increase of allowance during this joyous period. The Christmas gambols, however, are not carried on with the same vivacity as heretofore. The practice is evidently on the decline.[53]

The suggestion that the Christmas festival was declining in 1830 is contradicted somewhat by an account written half a century after the abolition of slavery:

> At Christmas, when the season's work of cutting, hauling, manufacturing and bringing out was over, the slaves were allowed from three weeks' to a month's license to enjoy the pleasures of town in Belize, according to the respective ideas of what was enjoyment peculiar to the several tribes. These congregated in separate bodies, and followed the African rites they had brought with them, but all displaying the same wonderful endurance in undergoing the fatigues of dissipation that they undoubtedly did in sustaining those of toil—"keeping it up" day and night. Amongst other questionable results deducible from slavery-times, this of keeping festivity going all night as well as all day, clings to the celebration of the Christmas holiday still. Music and dancing and the extravagant consumption of gunpowder by discharging it from their shot-guns, were common to all the tribes. Pitpan-races on the river formed a much more interesting and agreeable feature of the carnival, and a prettier aquatic sight cannot be witnessed in any quarter of the globe.... On race-days the largest pitpans are manned by crews of from twenty to forty paddlers, appropriately dressed and representing rival mahogany firms.[54]

A number of aspects of these descriptions are worth emphasizing. First, the obvious relaxation of discipline and the license for slave behavior otherwise forbidden is apparent from the very opening of the Christmas Day festivities when guns were fired in the streets. Secondly, the dory or pitpan races on the river appear to have been an item strongly encouraged by the masters; this was a competitive event between rival groups of slaves that was valuable to the masters because it developed required skills and a feeling of teamwork and solidarity among the slaves of a gang. Thirdly, the "convulsed rapid movements" of the slaves' dances seemed "ludicrous" to the European observer because they were characteristic of African dancing, as were the use of the drums and the "bursts of loud chorus." The use of flag-men in the street dancing, who keep time to "the measured beats of their drum," is reminiscent of the flag-men of Trinidad's carnivals. Last, but by no means least, is the reference to the blacks, free and enslaved, joining in "sets," which was itself a common feature of slave street festivals from Jamaica to Brazil, and which generally involved a degree of rivalry in costumes and dancing between the groups. In Belize there seems no doubt that these sets were organized on a tribal basis, the Africans regrouping on this annual occasion according to their "respective casts of national character" and each set emphasizing its particular music, songs, dances, and whatever other "African rites they had brought with them." This phenomenon also appeared in Jamaica; a nineteenth-century observer noted that, during the Christmas festivities, the slaves of various tribal origins "formed into exclusive groups competing against each other in performing their national music."[55]

The Christmas event, then, was an occasion of great importance to the Africans because it enabled them to reunite after long periods of separation and isolation, and, in an atmosphere of relaxation and license, to recreate aspects of their original cultures in an extended street festival. According to the descriptions, Christianity itself had no part in this festival, which was a public display of energy and endurance, an outburst of long-suppressed creativity.

Sometimes the excitement and drunkenness would lead the slaves to direct some antagonism toward their masters, but the masters were aware that this great reunion could easily become an occasion for concerted desertion or revolt, and the militia were always kept in readiness. Sometimes, also, the rivalry between the "sets" would lead to squabbles: "It was found necessary to institute a guard to control the slaves during the annual Christmas holidays, the different African tribes, no doubt, occasionally indulging in faction-fights."[56]

The extent to which these "different African tribes" persisted in the settlement was closely related to the persistence of elements of African culture; indeed, the persistence of such differentiation was itself a phenomenon of survival. It was mentioned in chapter 4 that many of the names of slaves recorded in the 1790 census indicated African birth and identified slaves with particular areas, sometimes with specific tribes. This kind of identification endured and extended to the free blacks, who were reinforced in 1817 and 1818 by discharged members of the West India regiments, many of whom had been "recruited" in West Africa. The Eboes, or Ibos, of Nigeria seem to have been particularly distinctive, possibly because they were present in relatively large numbers. In 1826, for example, one John Charles, "an African free Negro of the Eboe Country"[57] was mentioned, and the free Eboes even had a section of the town of Belize named after them. It has been recorded that, in 1819, "Eboe Town, a section of the town of Belize reserved for that African tribe, was destroyed by fire,"[58] but a map of Belize in the 1829 *Honduras Almanack* still identified an area west of Saint John's Church as "Eboe Town."[59] A description of Belize in 1850 also mentioned a section called "Eboe Town, consisting of numerous yards, flanked with long rows of what are called negro houses, being simply separate rooms under one long roof, which used to be appropriated to slaves, and now accommodate the poorer labourers."[60]

An account of the free blacks in 1830, though characterized by the racial prejudice of the author, indicates clearly the extent to which these people attempted to maintain their tribal identity and customs, and even to recreate some political organization, in the repressive context of the Bay settlement:

> The Blacks . . . present almost as many varieties as there are countries whence they come; and seem to uphold their original systems, prejudices, superstitions, and amusements, to as great a degree, as they can be allowed consistently with the regulations of civilized society. . . .
> As they have come to this and other neighbouring regions from various places, so they maintain, as far as in them lies, the customs of the countries whence they came; and hence their habits in a great measure continue. In order to preserve themselves distinct and to uphold their customs, each nation selects one from their body to whom they give the title of king. This is observed by almost every tribe or nation; consequently we have a variety of sable monarchs, who exercise a certain species of lordship over their respective subjects, and receive, in return, the most marked attention and respect. Their affection for their countrymen is very conspicuous; a black man will share his last plantain with another native of his own land, and seldom distinguishes or addresses him by any other appellation than countryman.[61]

In 1850, it was stated that there were in Belize "Congoes, Nangoes, Mongolas, Ashantees, Eboes, and other African tribes,"[62] indicating that tribal identification persisted well after emancipation.

While differences were certainly recognized between African slaves according to their tribal origins, differences were also recognized between the African-born as a whole and the West Indian born, or "Creoles." If, as has been suggested, the African-born slaves constituted about three-fifths of all the slaves in 1823, then it can be assumed that the Creoles were always in the minority. If the Creoles had been a majority they might have formed a more substantial Creole slave society into which the newly arrived Africans would have been socialized. Though a good deal of socialization, known as "seasoning," certainly took place, during which the Africans were taught to adjust to their slave status, the fact that the African-born were always a majority would make it easier for them to support and maintain some of their customs and beliefs. The Creole slaves may have learned from their masters to devalue the African cultural heritage, but there is no evidence from Belize that they viewed the African-born with the degree of contempt that was a characteristic of their fellows in some of the plantation societies. Indeed, it has even been suggested that free colored women sometimes married Africans who had been discharged from the West India Regiments:

> No Antipathy however exists on the part of the Creole Women to the Native African Men every thing depending upon the degree of Civilization at which the Africans shall arrive, and his competency to support the Woman in Comfort. It is no uncommon occurrence for the free Creole of Color to marry the African Soldier of the West India Regiment.[63]

In addition to the maintenance of some tribal solidarity, one of the ways aspects of African culture could be sustained in Belize was through the existence of stable families, sometimes including several generations. It was mentioned in the section on slavery and the law that though no relevant law existed, it was considered contrary to custom to sell slaves in such a way that families would be broken up. Since the slave proprietors in the settlement had a greater degree of interest in their slaves than did the sugar planters, and since the expense of importing and maintaining slaves in the Bay settlement was greater, some of the masters may even have encouraged the development of stable families. Not only would familial stability have encouraged the slave women to have, and care for, children, but it would also be a way of tying the men to the town of Belize and discouraging them from escaping into the interior. Whatever may have been the motives of the masters, there is no question that some of the slaves experienced a fairly stable family life.

The 1834 slave register lists slaves, by name, belonging to each owner, and states the relationship of such slaves to one another where such a relationship was known to exist. Though the register rarely includes deceased members of the family, members of the family who belonged to another master, or members who had escaped, there are many instances of families who may have had the opportunity of living together, sometimes through several generations. For example, one slave woman, Mary France, a fifty-eight-year-old black "plantation keeper," was owned by Alexander France, as were six of her children and seven of her elder daughter's children (Appendix B). In another case, Quashie Cunningham, a sixty-seven-year-old laborer, was owned by Sarah Keefe, along with seven of his children, ranging in age from thirty-seven to twenty-three years, and nine grandchildren, aged between eleven and three years (Appendix C).

Some of the slaves also lived in stable conjugal relationships, as can be seen from the records on the family of Jane and Sam Burn, belonging to William D. Burn. Jane was recorded as the wife of Sam, and they were listed with five of their children and one grandchild. Jane also had an older daughter by a previous relationship. That daughter, Betsy, was described as a mulatto, as were her three children, while Jane and Sam and their offspring were all black (Appendix D). In another case, Ann Smith was the owner of a forty-year-old washerwoman, Nancy Gambqunil, described as "lately married to a Pensioner, Jean Gambqunil," Nancy's nine children, her sister Eve and Eve's son, and a nephew, Robert (Appendix E). In one case there were two generations of apparently stable conjugal relationships between slaves belonging to the same owner: Hannah, one of the two children of Murphy and Mary Anne Black, was living with and had two children by a man called Glasgow (Appendix F).

The largest family reported by the 1834 slave register consisted of the twenty-eight slaves of the estate of Sarah Goff, all of whom were related. The eldest was a thirty-seven-year-old mahogany cutter, Sammy Goff, who had eleven cousins and sixteen second cousins (Appendix G). This appears to be a long-established family; it dates back to the eighteenth century when a slave woman had a large number of children, who, in turn, produced Sammy Goff and his cousins. The existence of large families who maintained contact for several generations provided the opportunity for the transmission of African cultural traditions down through the century of the settlement's existence prior to the abolition of slavery.

Since the slaves of the Caribbean, unlike their masters, could not communicate with their homelands, their only continued contact with Africa was through new arrivals. While it is possible that many of the slaves imported to the settlement in the first years of the nineteenth century were born in Africa, and could therefore reinforce African cultural traditions, the flow of slaves into the settlement was reduced to a trickle after the abolition of the slave trade in 1807, and not all of those few who were brought would have been African-born. Thus, between 1816 and 1825 only forty slaves were imported, mostly from Jamaica.[64] With such small reinforcements, the maintenance of African cultural traditions depended heavily upon the persistence of tribal solidarity among the free blacks and at the communal Christmas festivals, and upon socialization in the slave families. (A major reinforcement arrived just prior to emancipation, however; 459 Africans, "liberated" from Spanish and Portuguese slave ships, landed in Belize in 1836.)[65] At the same time that these factors tended to maintain certain aspects of African culture, other factors were operating to repress and eliminate them.

In addition to the specific acts of repression directed against aspects of African religion, music, and dance, which were mentioned previously, the whole structure of slavery must be seen as one which militated against the survival of African culture. The economic and political organization of the settlement, created by the masters, was imposed upon the African slaves. Though some of the free blacks appear to have attempted to recreate some tribal political organization, they nevertheless had to operate within the limits imposed by the British administration—or, in the words of the 1830 *Almanack,* as far "as they can be allowed consistently with the regulations of civilized society." Even in that aspect of life which was so important to the Africans, and which was quite insignificant with regard to the maintenance of the settlement's political economy—namely, religion—the whites were active in attempting to divest the Africans of their traditions and to convert them to Christianity.

The white settlers seem to have paid little attention to religious affairs, either their own or their slaves', during the eighteenth century, and it was not until the early nineteenth century that an Anglican chaplain was appointed to the settlement. Though the chaplain busied himself baptizing hundreds of people, the Anglicans were not very concerned with encouraging religion or spreading it among the slaves. The first Baptist missionary arrived in 1822, followed three years later by the first Wesleyan. Both came before the Anglican church, Saint John's, was consecrated, the settlement having been incorporated into the Jamaican diocese in 1824.

In 1822, when handing the superintendency to Major General Pye, Arthur, a religious man who had attempted to promote religion and education in the settlement, complained that "the Religious Instruction of the Slaves as well as of adults of the lower class, generally has been almost systematically opposed."[66] Nevertheless, in the preceding decade the chaplain had succeeded in baptizing 1,478 people, of whom 709 were slaves. In the years 1812 to 1829, about three thousand persons were baptized by the Anglicans, and about half of them were slaves. As can be seen in table 6.3, the rate of baptism was generally not above one hundred a year for the first few years of the chaplaincy's existence, but in 1819, 1820, and 1821 a special effort seems to have been made to baptize the slaves. Once again, from 1825 to 1827, over a hundred slaves were baptized each year by the Anglicans, who were then competing with the Baptist and Wesleyan missionaries. The burials of slaves were less likely to be seen to by the Anglicans, however, as only about three hundred of the approximately two thousand burials solemnized by the chaplains between 1812 and 1829 were of slaves.[67] As far as marriages were concerned, these were extremely rare between slaves, only three taking place between 1812 and 1823, compared to twenty-one among the free blacks and fifteen among the free colored.[68] Three marriages recorded were of slave men to free women.[69] A major inhibition to the solemnization of marriage by the Anglican chaplain lay in his fee of thirteen shillings and four pence for performing the ceremony. In 1828, in the face of "the great and general desire of the Inhabitants to promote Christianity," the chaplain agreed to perform

TABLE 6.3 Baptisms of Whites, Free Colored, Free Blacks, and Slaves by the Anglican Chaplain in Belize, 1812–29

Date	White	Free Colored	Free Black	Slave	Total
1812	2	13	5	13	33
1813	5	32	13	49	99
1814	3	31	25	54	113
1815	5	28	30	28	91
1816	9	37	5	23	74
1817	4	38	17	77	136
1818	7	35	30	55	127
1819	6	70	61	100	237
1820	10	73	76	177	336
1821	9	49	41	133	232
1822	6	39	36	92	173
1823	14	43	34	53	144
1824	....	....	...	....	....
1825	7	52	34	112	205
1826	4	62	70	114	250
1827	10	50	95	152	307
1828	10	50	39	79	178
1829 (to 19 Oct.)	10	40	20	74	144

SOURCES: 1812–23, "Return of Baptisms..." by Rev. John Armstrong, 16 Dec. 1823, CO 123/34; 1825–29, "Return from the Church Register..." by Rev. Mathew Newport, 19 Oct. 1829, AB, R.2.

such services for slaves gratuitously.[70] Under pressure from the Colonial Office, the Public Meeting finally passed a law abolishing all fees for the marriage or baptism of slaves in 1829.

The Baptist and Wesleyan missionaries, like the Anglicans, centered their congregations in the town of Belize, though the latter had been instructed to take the gospel to the slaves in the mahogany camps. These missionaries, unlike their counterparts in places like Barbados and Jamaica, did not experience hostility or persecution to any extent. While missionaries in the islands were blamed for creating unrest among the slaves in the 1820s, such charges were unknown in Belize, where the missionaries were generally permitted to preach without hindrance. The missionaries were active in the area of education, the Methodists particularly so among the Caribs in Stann Creek; the only activity denied them was that of conducting marriage ceremonies, Anglican marriages alone being considered legal in the settlement.

The effect of this missionary activity upon the population of African origin is hard to evaluate. The number of baptisms among the free colored, free blacks, and slaves is impressive, but many of these baptisms may have been simply nominal and may not reflect any real involvement with the church or with Christianity. On the other hand, many of those who remained unbaptized may have been influenced considerably by Christian beliefs and practices. There does not seem to have been any equivalent of the Jamaican "native churches" in Belize, though doubtless some degree of reinterpretation and synthesis of African and European religious elements occurred in the settlement. Though the influence of the established church and the dissenters seems to have been less potent in Belize than elsewhere, it was certainly the intent of the clergymen to suppress and eliminate African beliefs and practices and to replace them with Christianity. Over many years their intention was largely realized.

It has been said that the Jamaican slave at the time of emancipation had "a way of life, with a system of education, social ties, habits, and modes of thought, but these had all been developed out of an African heritage in a way that fitted him to be a slave in a European-dominated society."[71] Much the same can be said of the slave, or the free black, in the settlement at Belize. Though elements of African culture survived the "middle passage" from Africa to the New World, were maintained or recreated in Belize, and there helped preserve some sense of identity and solidarity among people of African origin, these elements survived in a hostile context. The structure of the society itself militated against the persistence of African forms of social organization, whether economic, political, or familial, and the dominant Europeans continually repressed African cultural traditions.

7
Apprenticeship and Emancipation

THE LABORERS DURING THE APPRENTICESHIP PERIOD

The Abolition Act, passed in June 1833, contained two important elements that were calculated to appease the proprietors of slaves. One element was the provision introducing the system called "apprenticeship," under which all registered slaves over the age of six years were to become "apprenticed laborers" who would be compelled to work without pay for the same masters as they had prior to abolition. (Full freedom was to be received by non-field workers in 1838 and by field workers in 1840, but the apprenticeship system was abolished entirely in 1838.) The other element concerned compensation; the act empowered the treasury to raise twenty million pounds to be paid to the slave owners as compensation for their loss of property. There can be no question that these elements of the Abolition Act were intended, generous and sympathetic as they were to the slave owners, to produce a minimum of social change and to ensure the continued dependency of the freedmen, as a labor force, upon the master class. In order to evaluate to what extent the intentions of the act were fulfilled in Belize, it is necessary to examine a number of factors, including the extent to which alternatives to wage labor were available to the freedmen. But first, let us look at the nature of the slave population at the time of emancipation.

One consequence of the provisos referred to above was the requirement that slaves be registered, both in order that they could become "apprenticed laborers" and in order to calculate the compensation due to the slave owners. Accordingly, notices were issued "to all Owners of Slaves to be prepared to submit to the Auxilliary Commissioners Returns shewing the name, Sex, Colour, Age, employment and Country of their Slaves."[1] With the exception of the last item mentioned, the slave register of Belize, begun 8 May and ended 1 September 1834, contains a wealth of information on the age, sex, color, and occupations of the slaves of Belize, and also provides valuable data on the familial relations of the slaves and of the distribution of slave ownership. Just two thousand slaves were registered in 1834 (more than were enumerated in the 1832 census) and it can be assumed, given the vested interest of the slave owners in registering their slaves, that it was a virtually complete registration. Consequently, it is possible to create a demographic profile of the slave population as it existed immediately prior to emancipation.

According to the slave register, the slave population was predominantly black, 91.3 percent of the slaves being listed under that category. Of the remainder, 4.9 percent were described as "sambo," 2.1 percent as "mulatto," 1.4 percent as "coloured" or "brown," three people as "quadroon," and one as "mustee." While some of these terms had a specific meaning in the Jamaican context,[2] one cannot be certain that they had the same meaning in Belize, or even that they were used with consistency.

An analysis of the slave population by age (see table 7.1) shows that over half the slaves were under the age of thirty. However, there were almost as many slaves in their forties (18.8 percent) as there were slave children under the age of ten (19.0 percent). This can be explained by the fact that many of the slaves who were forty years of age or more in 1834 had been brought into the settlement in their youth, prior to the abolition of the slave trade in 1807. This fact is also reflected in the sex ratio shown in table 7.1; at age forty years or more, men outnumbered women by ten to three, but under the age of forty they outnumbered women by only seven to six. During the years when slaves could still be imported emphasis was placed upon importing young men who could be mahogany cutters, the result in 1834 being that about half of the entire slave population consisted of men aged thirty-five years or more.

Table 7.2, showing the occupations of the slaves, demonstrates the preponderance of one kind of work for the men and another kind of work for the

TABLE 7.1 Slave Population of Belize, by Age and Sex, 1834

Age in years	Male	Female	Total	Percentage
70 and above	18	6	24	1.3
65–69	13	3	16	0.8
60–64	43	9	52	2.7
55–59	62	15	77	4.0
50–54	93	24	117	6.1
45–49	134	40	174	9.1
40–44	133	53	186	9.7
35–39	82	47	129	6.7
30–34	75	51	126	6.6
25–29	78	77	155	8.1
20–24	109	95	204	10.7
15–19	82	67	149	7.8
10–14	76	64	140	7.3
5–9	86	77	163	8.5
0–4	104	97	201	10.5
Total	1,188	725	1,913	99.9

SOURCE: Slave Register, 1834, AB.

TABLE 7.2 Occupations of the Slave Population of Belize, by Age and Sex, 1834

Occupations	Male, Age in Years								Female, Age in Years								Total
	0–9	10–19	20–29	30–39	40–49	50–59	60+	Total	0–9	10–19	20–29	30–39	40–49	50–59	60+	Total	
Woodcutter	1	88	158	144	244	121	39	795	…	…	…	…	…	…	…	…	795
Waiting boy or girl	56	42	2	…	…	…	…	100	40	14	1	…	…	…	…	55	155
Laborer	…	2	4	2	9	13	8	38	…	…	…	…	…	…	…	…	38
Carpenter or carpenter's boy	…	5	12	5	5	2	1	30	…	…	…	…	…	…	…	…	30
Plantation man or woman	1	2	…	…	4	11	19	37	…	…	3	2	1	1	4	11	48
Sailor or boatman	…	3	3	3	…	3	1	13	…	…	…	…	…	…	…	…	13
Cattleman	…	3	3	1	1	1	1	10	…	…	…	…	…	…	…	…	10
Footman	5	3	1	…	…	…	…	9	…	…	…	…	…	…	…	…	9
Washerwoman	…	…	…	…	…	…	…	…	…	9	52	37	47	14	1	161	161
Housemaid, servant, or domestic	…	2	…	…	…	2	…	4	6	48	47	10	6	4	4	125	129
Chambermaid	…	…	…	…	…	…	…	…	2	30	12	1	…	…	…	45	45
Cook	…	…	…	…	…	…	…	…	…	4	34	38	28	9	4	117	117
Seamstress	…	…	…	…	…	…	…	…	10	17	18	6	2	…	…	53	53
Drudge	…	…	…	…	…	…	…	…	…	2	3	3	8	9	5	30	30
Other	…	2	4	2	3	1	2	14	2	…	2	1	1	3	…	9	23
No occupation	140	1	…	…	…	…	3	144	122	1	…	…	…	…	…	123	267
Total	203	153	187	157	266	154	74	1,194	182	125	172	98	93	40	18	729	1,923

SOURCE: Slave Register, 1834, AB.

women. The sexual division of labor is strongly marked, only young children, and to a lesser extent, older men and women, sharing similar employment: the children waited table and the older people worked as plantation laborers employed in cultivating provisions. Among the men the dominant employment was woodcutting, chiefly in the extraction of mahogany, which accounted for over 80 percent of all the males aged ten years or more and over 87 percent of all the men in the most physically mature age range of twenty to fifty-nine years. Even some of the other occupations for men, such as carpenter and cattleman, were part of, or closely associated with, the business of mahogany extraction. Eight men were stated to be the managers or captains of woodcutting gangs, seven of these being fifty years old or more. The only other male occupations represented were laborer (38), sailor or boatman (13), footman and other domestic (13), blacksmith or blacksmiths' boy (5), drayman (2), penkeeper (2), cooper (1), bankkeeper (1), stove boy (1), and butcher (1). The slave women, with the exception of 11 plantation women, were employed in domestic work, primarily as housemaids, chambermaids, or domestic servants (170), washerwomen (161), cooks (117), seamstresses (53), or drudges (30). There were also 5 nurses, 3 bakers, and 1 vendor among the women.

One feature of the employment patterns of slaves, revealed in table 7.2, is the transition from one occupation to another undertaken by the slaves as they grew older. As has already been remarked upon, the young boys and girls first worked in the domestic realm where, waiting on the master's table, they would be taught to be subservient in their relations with the master. The majority of the boys would then become "attached to the Mahogany Works" as assistants, a few of them becoming assistants to blacksmiths or carpenters. The physically mature men, as has been noted, were almost all engaged in woodcutting, but as they became older or infirm they would be more likely to be shifted to agricultural or some other, less arduous labor. Among the female slaves the transition was from one kind of domestic work to another: from waiting girl to housemaid, chambermaid, or seamstress, and then, as the girls attained their twenties, to the more skilled or heavy work of cook, washerwoman, or drudge.

The patterns of employment experienced by the slaves, men and women, were fixed and must have appeared as a binding and unalterable necessity. Alternatives, particularly for the women, were few, though some of the men could hope to become captains of gangs or huntsmen in mahogany extraction, or to acquire a skilled trade. For most of the slaves, however, their only experience, and hence their apparent prospects, remained woodcutting for the men and domestic work for the women. The same was true for most of the freedmen, both before and after abolition. In 1833, it was pointed out that "the Free Labourer and Slave work together, but tho' with the Gangs for months together, it would be impossible to discover the one from the other unless they were separately pointed out."[3] The free laborers worked with the slaves in the mahogany gangs because there were few alternative means of livelihood, and the masters hired free laborers because their diminishing number of slaves could not provide as much labor as was required. In 1836, it was stated that between twelve and fifteen hundred "foreigners and free Labourers are hired annually for the Mahogany Works, and they are by no means sufficient to answer the demand. . . . the importation of Africans would in a high degree be conducive to the Interests of the Settlement. The demand for labourers has been for many years encreasing."[4] The same report stated that Caribs were also employed in mahogany cutting. If the figure of free laborers employed on the mahogany works is accurate, then they outnumbered the slaves in the 1830s by almost two to one. Since the censuses of the early 1830s enumerated only about three or four hundred adult male freedmen, colored and black, it can be assumed that many of these, with Caribs and "foreigners" in addition, constituted the free laborers in the mahogany works.

A description of the conditions of labor, both slave and free, in the mahogany camps in 1833 was included in a memorial from the slave proprietors to the Superintendent, the memorialists arguing that the generosity with which they had treated their laborers should be repaid with generosity in the allocation of compensation money. They emphasized the common conditions and treatment of slaves and free laborers, and indicated that few of the free blacks—that is, those who had experienced mahogany cutting as slaves—could be induced to continue such work; hence the necessity of relying upon foreign labor.

> The Slaves of this Settlement receive by custom the benefit of one sixth part of their labour or one day in the week, for this they are paid by their Master whether sick or well, every six months, without any deduction at the rate of ¾ per day or £8.13.4 per annum. They receive stipulated quantities of clothing yearly.
>
> The Slave and the Free Labourer whether in the mahogany works or at Belize are provided with an *equal* weekly allowance. . . .
>
> The use of the cart whip as a stimulus to labour, if ever in use has entirely ceased, the present generation know nothing of its existence as the best proof of this the hired free labourer voluntarily submits to and is under the same management as the Slave.
>
> During nine months of the year labour is performed by task work both by the free labourer and the Slave and this is generally finished in five and seldom exceeded 6 hours, the remaining part of the day is spent as the Slave thinks fit . . . there are no gangs at present employed in cutting mahogany exclusively composed of Slaves, half of each gang being free labourers . . . the freeman and slave labour together side by side, are subject to the same restraint and management in every respect, eat, drink, and sleep together. . . .
>
> It is however necessary to remark that the free labourers alluded to, are for the most part foreigners, few of the native free Blacks possessing sufficient industry to induce them to engage as labourers in the cutting of Mahogany.[5]

In 1836, one of the cutters reported to the settlement's secretary that his mahogany gangs were composed of Free and liberated or apprenticed Africans and free and Creole Blacks and of the coloured inhabitants of the Settlement, all of whom are, necessarily, worked, in united masses, without any distinction whatever being known betwixt the freemen and those, hitherto, denominated Slaves and now apprenticed labourers. . . . in a great number of instances, Gangs are headed and immediately directed by Africans or immediate descendants of such under whom the free blacks and Creoles work with cheerfulness.[6]

While the final assertion of the "cheerfulness" with which all went about their work must be treated sceptically, it does appear that few distinctions were made between the laborers on grounds of color, place of birth, or legal status. In other words, laborers were treated alike whether they were free or not, and it is therefore not surprising to find that the free laborers reacted in much the same way to the situation as did the slaves.

One of the problems faced by the employers was what would today be called absenteeism, but which was then termed "desertion," and the offender was called a runaway, whether he was a slave or a free laborer. The minutes of a Public Meeting in 1833 report the masters' concern about "runaway Caribs and other deserters from their employers," and the Meeting resolved to appoint a constable in Stann Creek "for the apprehension and bringing to Belize of all such Caribs and deserters."[7] It is clear, then, that even before emancipation, the masters were well acquainted with some of the problems of hiring wage labor, and the free laborers were equally aware of some of the problems of being employed as mahogany cutters.

The minimal development of educational opportunities in the settlement was one of the reasons for the absence of alternatives to employment in mahogany cutting for the freedmen. The wealthier settlers had sometimes sent their children to be educated in England, and they showed little interest in developing institutions of formal education in the settlement. A free school was started early in the nineteenth century and was encouraged by Superintendent Arthur. A Public Meeting in 1819 voted that £300 in Jamaica currency should be given annually from the public funds "in Aid of the Free Schools of this Settlement," and a further sum of £700 in Jamaica currency was allocated for the construction of a new schoolhouse.[8] The purpose of the school was less that of developing practical skills than of instilling what were considered appropriate values, attitudes, and behavior patterns, and education consequently consisted largely of religious instruction. As Superintendent Cockburn put it in 1833, he wished "to encourage an increasing system of morality amongst the Inhabitants,"[9] by inducing higher attendance in church and school. He and his wife took a personal interest in obtaining "a numerous and constant assemblage of White, coloured, & Black at the Public Schools. . . . The number of Boys daily receiving instruction varies from 90 to 120."[10] Cockburn added that children were "enticed from our Schools" by the "Dissenting Ministers," and it appears that the missionaries, both Baptist and Wesleyan, were active in promoting education.

By 1835, the Wesleyan missionary, Thomas Jefferies, reported the existence of two schools: a day school in Stann Creek Town attended by about seventy children, "but of late it has been much Neglected for want of Teachers,"[11] and a Sunday school in Belize Town. At the same time the Baptist missionary, Henderson, reported the existence of three Sunday schools and the recent establishment of two day schools, the combined attendance of which was "upwards of one hundred children." Henderson, too, stated that there was "a deficiency in the number of School Teachers," and that the school buildings were "inadequate."[12] The Anglican chaplain, meanwhile, reported that the number of children registered at the Free School was 218, and he also expressed the need for more teachers and supplies. The stress on religious instruction is evident in the fact that he asked for four teachers to "give instruction in chanting & lead the children in psalmody," and his request for supplies consisted of bibles and prayer books.[13] In the following year, attendance at the Free School was stated to consist of only eighty-five boys.[14]

The religious emphasis in the curriculum and the control of education by religious authorities have been constant features of education in the country to the present day; the goal of Belizean education has not been to promote either critical intellects or practical skills but to instill an awareness of the correct modes of conduct and the sense of duty deemed appropriate in obedient colonized peoples. In 1835 Lord Glenelg pointed out to Cockburn "the important interest which the Proprietors of Land in Honduras have in the religious Instruction of the Labouring Population, and the diffusion among them of those principles which afford the best Security for good order, and the right discharge of every social duty."[15]

In 1836, the Public Meeting, feeling the need for some educational facilities for the apprentices who were shortly to become free citizens, voted that £100 should be placed at the disposal of the Superintendent and chaplain "for the purpose of procuring Teachers, Books etc. for a School to be opened for any Apprenticed labourer, desirous of attending the same, either by day or in the evening, for the purpose of receiving moral and religious Instruction."[16] Education was therefore not intended, nor did it provide, a means of independent advancement among the freedmen. The entire system of apprenticeship had actually been designed as a means of securing the labor force for a further period of years, during which time the apprentices, in the words of Superintendent Cockburn, would be "made to understand the obligations attached to their freedom."[17] The "moral and religious Instruction" was simply perceived as a necessary element in this training for citizenship.

The settlers' response to the news that their slaves would soon be freed was to voice concern that they be adequately compensated for the loss of their property and to point out that any attempt to regulate the hours worked by the apprentices would be detrimental to the enterprise of mahogany cutting.[18] Further, they expressed anxiety about the appointment of Special Magistrates, whose duty it would be to enforce the scheme of apprenticeship and to settle disputes arising between masters and apprentices. The settlers anticipated "serious obstacles" in the way of the Special Magistrates carrying out their duties, and they advocated that complaints and disputes could be settled, as before, in the "Courts of Judicature established in the Settlement."[19] Superintendent Cockburn, however, realizing that such an arrangement would simply enable the masters themselves to rule over cases between them and their apprentices, felt that the appointment of Special Magistrates was an essential prerequisite to the success of the apprenticeship system. He wrote:

> I should by no means feel warranted in recommending that the faults & omissions of apprenticed Labourers or the complaints made by them against their Owners, should continue to be heard & decided upon by Courts unavoidably composed, as the Courts here must be, of Persons who for so many years have been Slave Owners themselves.[20]

Nevertheless, since the arrival of the Special Magistrates was delayed, Cockburn appointed two of the chief settlers and Magistrates, William Maskall and William Coffin, to act in their place.[21] That appointment was never sanctioned by the Colonial Office, which sent out a Lieutenant Grigg; he died only a few months after his arrival in Belize in April 1835. A second man, William Gow, was sent out to replace someone called Williamson in the Southern District. Meanwhile, one L. M. McLenan was acting as Special Magistrate in the Northern District. Given the confusion in their appointments, and the lack of information on the men themselves, it is virtually impossible to assess either their personal caliber or the work they undertook. Despite the series of monthly reports they produced, many of them almost duplicates, it is hard to evaluate to what extent they were acting independently, were prepared to defend the apprentices, or were subservient to the masters.

The general tenor of the Special Magistrates' reports was that "a good feeling generally prevails between apprentices and their employers" and that the apprentices "perform their work in general with great willingness."[22] As a later report noted, "The relative position of Master and Servant being now well understood by all parties, my attention is drawn but to few complaints, and those chiefly of a trifling nature principally amongst the females in the Town a few of whom form the chief delinquents."[23] It seems that the women were more often punished than the men, generally for disobedience, absenteeism, or other minor offenses. Typical is a monthly report that stated: "There have been six convictions, of which number, five have been females. . . . The offences were generally absence from work."[24] Returns of punishments inflicted on apprentices by the Special Magistrates between September and December 1835 showed that among 1,677 apprentices, a total of 25 were punished, 15 of whom were women. The kinds of punishment included thirty stripes with a whip, one month's hard labor, and two week's solitary confinement on bread and water.[25] Since the Superintendent had stressed that the Magistrates were to be primarily concerned with controlling the slaves, with preventing "idleness, profligacy and insubordination,"[26] rather than with protecting them, it is not surprising that most of the complaints they dealt with were from the masters, and most of the punishments they inflicted were on the apprentices. However, it is remarkable that there is no record of a complaint registered against the masters. Since it is unlikely that the apprentices considered their masters' behavior entirely beyond reproach, it is probable that they perceived the Special Magistrates as a disciplinary instrument of the masters (the first two Magistrates were local slave proprietors) to whom it would be pointless to address complaints. The contemptuous attitude of the Magistrates toward such a possible course of action may be inferred from the comment of one of them, in connection with complaints made by some "liberated Africans," that the complaints seemed "to arise principally from mistaken notions of their duty."[27]

In 1833, the slave owners had expressed concern about the limitation of hours to be worked by the apprentices, maintaining that the peculiar nature of the business of mahogany extraction required a more flexible system. For example, the business of trucking the huge trunks was generally carried out at night, by the light of torches, in order to avoid the period of greatest heat for this particularly arduous labor. The Order-in-Council had instructed that the apprentices could only be required to work forty-five hours per week, but this was disregarded in the settlement, where "the hours of labour are from six in the morning until six in the evening with interval of two hours,"[28] making a total of fifty hours in the week. Despite the fact that this disregarded the terms of the Abolition Act, and the abuse was even extended to the town and domestic workers, the slave owners' offense had no effect upon the compensation awards.

Slaves had always been valued highly in the Bay settlement. In 1809, a "seasoned" male slave was worth between £200 and £300,[29] and some of the slaves who purchased their own freedom paid £200 or more; one paid as much as £450 in 1829.[30] While the average price for a slave in the 1820s was about £120, individual prices ranged from 10s. for an old man to £610 for "Blacksmith Joe," clearly a skilled worker. An estate of thirty-one slaves, four of whom were described as "very old," realized £9,710 in 1820, an average of over £300 per slave.[31] When the value of slaves in the settlement was assessed in 1835, it was estimated to be £230,840, and the portion of the twenty million pounds of compensation money that was set aside for the proprietors in Belize was £10-1,958.19.7 ½.[32] The rate of compensation per slave in Belize, £53.6.9 ½, was higher than the rate for any British colony. In Jamaica the compensation per slave was £19.5.4 ¾, and in Barbados it was £20.13.8 ¼. The only comparable compensation rates were in Trinidad and British Guiana, where they were £50.1.1 ¼ and £51.17.1 ½, respectively.[33]

Although they had been promised their full freedom in the near future, many of the apprentices could not wait. By saving the wages they had earned in overtime, or selling the various articles they had manufactured in their spare hours, many apprentices accumulated enough money to purchase their freedom, a fact that the Special Magistrates continually remarked upon. Thus, in 1836 it was reported that there seemed to be a "very general desire among the apprentices to purchase their discharge,"[34] and, in the following year, a Magistrate commented that "the desire to purchase their Discharge still prevails, indeed is evidently increasing."[35] Though anxious to obtain liberty, the apprentices had severely limited opportunities to achieve an independent means of livelihood, with the result that most of them continued to work for their former masters. "The men generally take to their former employment of mahogany cutting.... The females many of them become sempstresses, bakers, or hire themselves as domestic servants."[36] Less than a year before the general liberation of the apprentices, a Special Magistrate reported:

> The desire to purchase their Discharge continues very general—in this District five have been released from servitude since my last Report.
> Those who have obtained their Discharge for the most part betake themselves to their old employments either in the service of their former employers or those from whom they can obtain the most advantageous terms.[37]

Only six months prior to the termination of the apprenticeship system, Special Magistrate McLenan reported that "during the last month Eleven Apprentices have received their Discharges—the desire to purchase which seems to increase as the eventful 1st of August approaches."[38] Evidently, the slaves, as Eric Williams has expressed it, "were not prepared to wait for freedom to come to them as a dispensation from above."[39]

With the approach of the termination of the apprenticeship period (on 1 August 1838), a number of preparations were undertaken to ensure a smooth transition, particularly in the legal regulation of the relations of masters and servants. An early attempt to regulate the practices of hiring laborers having been "negatived by a large Majority,"[40] a committee was established, on the Superintendent's recommendation, to consider proposals for "regulating the relative duties of Master and Servant."[41] In response to a dispatch from the Colonial Office, the clerk of the courts reported to the Superintendent and clearly expressed the nature of the problem, particularly emphasizing the absence of adequate legal protection for the laborers:

> The employment of Household and all other servants, whether Journeymen or otherwise, within the Town of Belize, is regulated upon much the same principle as in England. The great bulk of the Lower Classes, however, and almost all the Charibs and Spaniards who resort to the Settlement, are employed in the Mahogany Works in the Interior, and with them it is the practice to enter into Contract by which they hire themselves generally for six or twelve months. This is usually done at the commencement or middle of the year, when the servant goes before a Magistrate, & volunteers a Contract for his services.
> It is in the enforcement of these Contracts, however, that the great evil lies. There is no law on the subject further than what custom has sanctioned. That custom

has been, that where the Servant has failed in his Contract, the Master has had the power to bring him up at once on Warrant, and have him summarily punished by Imprisonment and public Whipping. If however the breach of Contract lay with the Master,—If for example, the Master was deficient in the payments he had contracted to make to his servant, the Servant could only sue the Master as in the matter of a common debt.

To send the Servant into Court for the recovery of his wages amounts to an absolute denial of justice to him. People in his condition are not supposed to possess the means of their remaining for months at Belize to prosecute their suits for those very earnings which would enable them to reside there for a little. They only add to their embarrassment by being debarred from leaving the Town and entering into another contract.[42]

A Public Meeting proposed a law to settle disputes between masters and servants in March 1838, but the Superintendent found it "in a shape which I could not approve, for it was stripped of its most valuable provision . . . for the recovery of Servants Wages and petty debts."[43]

In response to a demand from the Colonial Office that the apprenticeship period be ended before its legal termination in 1840, Superintendent Macdonald met with the "Proprietors of Praedial Apprentices" on 30 June 1838 and requested their approval of "the complete, unrestricted and immediate emancipation of the Apprenticed Labourers from involuntary Servitude."[44] Their approval having been secured, Macdonald next addressed a Public Meeting on 9 July 1838 and informed the members of the strength of opinion in Britain, and of the decisions made in Jamaica, Barbados, Antigua, and other colonies, to end apprenticeship on 1 August. He eloquently called on the members "to imitate these examples, and prevent Honduras from possessing the dishonourable distinction of being almost the only place where a number of our fellow creatures were unjustly kept without the pale of the common brotherhood of humanity."[45] The settlers having promptly concurred, regulations for resolving disputes over wages and other contractual matters between masters and servants were hurriedly agreed upon. Not only could the employer take his employee to court for "absenting himself from his duty, or for unruly and disobedient conduct," but the employee could take his employer to court, before three Magistrates empowered to fine him, for "unlawfully withholding any wages due to such complainant." It was further stipulated "that every servant or labourer shall be henceforth hired in writing," and the contract was to be registered at the clerk of court's office, "in order to remedy the great evil and inconvenience which has of late arisen to masters or employers by reason of labourers engaging themselves to several individuals at or nearly the same time to work for and during the same periods, and receiving considerable advances from each person on account of their wages." The Meeting also agreed "that all Sunday markets in this Settlement be from henceforth totally abolished."[46]

Though the forthcoming termination of apprenticeship on 1 August was

Apprenticeship and Emancipation 117

viewed with some trepidation by the settlers, the event actually passed without disturbance, as Superintendent Macdonald's account makes clear:

> As immense assemblage of apprentices, of all classifications, having met, by agreement, at the court-house, proceeded to church, when the bells commenced ringing, with a variety of banners appropriate to the occasion, and attended by a band of music. After having heard the service, and a most suitable discourse, which they listened to with a serious and respectful deportment, they marched into the green fronting my house, where one of their number addressed me, thanking me, in the name of his assembled brethren and sisters, for what the Queen had done for them, and making every profession of loyalty and good conduct for the time to come. After I had informed them that they were now so far free agents, and exhorted them to demean themselves with propriety, they departed, and spent, by the kindness of their recent owners, the remaining part of the day in festivity and mirth. . . . the emancipated persons were all industriously pursuing their usual avocations on the morning of the 2d, no complaint, of any kind whatever, having been as yet preferred against one of them, clearly proving the change is a good one.[47]

In assessing the nature of the apprenticeship period in Belize, one encounters the same problem that existed before 1834, namely, that the welfare of the laborers depended primarily on the custom of their masters rather than on the law. The Trinidad Order (an Order-in-Council which was intended to implement the Abolition Act throughout the colonies and which was to have been followed in Belize with certain specified modifications), was in many respects completely ignored. The Special Magistrates, for example, certainly visited the mahogany works only occasionally, if they did so at all, and not with the regularity required by the order. The Anti-Slavery Society criticized and condemned the "mutilated" Trinidad Order, as it was applied in Belize, and concluded by saying, "If, under such a system, the Negroes enjoy a comfortable servitude it certainly can be attributed to no legislative precaution on their behalf but will be owing probably to the neighbourhood of the Republics whose proximity produces at least one salutary influence in their favour."[48] The fact that so many of the apprentices either took advantage of the proximity of the republics, or took the trouble and expense of purchasing their freedom, shows that they found their so-called apprenticeship to be far from a "comfortable servitude."

Moreover, although the Superintendent had expressed the expectation that all would be well following emancipation, labor problems continued in the settlement. Though a general amnesty had released all prisoners from jail on 1 August, the jail was full again a few months later, with 103 prisoners. The most common offense was riotous behavior and drunkenness (36 prisoners), but 9 prisoners were listed as "runaways" and 24 were guilty of insolence, disobedience, or breaking an agreement. A typical example of the severity of sentencing in such cases is that of Pedro Chabia, found guilty of "breach of contract," and sentenced on 5 February 1839 to "six months' imprisonment with hard labor on the Public Works."[49] It is clear that the struggle between former masters and slaves was continuing, although in new forms.

INHIBITIONS ON THE DEVELOPMENT OF A PEASANTRY AFTER EMANCIPATION

Emancipation was a watershed in Belize, as in the rest of the West Indies, not because it changed the basic class-color differentiations of the society, which it did not do, but because it changed the forms in which the struggle between exploiter and exploited was expressed. Most of the freedmen of Belize continued to work in the mahogany camps, where their struggle to influence wages and conditions was opposed by the employers' power over rents and the prices of necessary subsistence articles. Above all, the employers' power lay in their ability to withhold land from the freedmen, thereby depriving them of the possibility of becoming independent subsistence farmers.

Some of the freedmen had produced provisions while they were slaves. Slaves who were allowed to cultivate, and sometimes to market, food crops were engaged in peasant-like production and marketing—but they were still slaves. This situation, in which the masters reduced their costs of production by having the slaves provide for themselves, gave rise to what has been termed a "proto-peasantry."[50] After emancipation, in many parts of the Caribbean, such proto-peasants rejected their former masters whenever conditions permitted and became a real or "reconstituted" peasantry. The alternative was to be forced into a wage-earning, proletarian position, still dependent upon the masters. Whether the slaves became peasants or proletarians depended upon a variety of factors, including the availability of land.

In a territory like Belize, with such a low population density (about four thousand people in almost nine thousand square miles), it would appear that a probable alternative means of livelihood to the continuation of labor in the timber forests would be the pursuit of agriculture. Even during slavery the people of African origin had shown their interest in making plantation grounds for growing subsistence crops, despite the existence of many obstacles. With emancipation in 1838, all the freedmen required in order to be able to escape the need to cut mahogany—that is, for freedom to become a reality rather than merely a change in legal status—was land.

Most of the land between the Hondo and Sibun rivers had been claimed by the white settlers during the eighteenth century and was therefore beyond the reach of the freedmen. But in 1817, as a result of a proclamation by Superintendent Arthur,[51] all unclaimed lands were vested in the Crown. Although many grants of Crown land were made before 1838, there were still vast tracts of land belonging to the Crown within the settlement, which then extended from the Rio Hondo to the Sarstoon River. There was a real possibility, therefore, of an independent peasantry arising, based upon the lands belonging to the Crown.

Hitherto many Crown grants had been made, and they had all been gratuitous. If similar grants had been made to the new freedmen, many of them would undoubtedly have chosen to cultivate provision grounds rather than continue to perform the arduous tasks of woodcutting, which they must have resented for its associations with slavery.

Such prospects were soon severely inhibited, however. Six weeks after emancipation, Lord Glenelg, Secretary of State for the Colonies, issued a circular relating to the new laws that must be passed, which were "calculated to meet the new exigencies of Society" consequent on the termination of the apprenticeship system. One of the laws referred to was "the Law for preventing the unauthorized occupation of Land," and an Order-in-Council on the subject was promised.[52] On 12 November 1838 another circular was despatched from the Colonial Office, this time "directing that grants of land are only to be made on payment of £1 per acre."[53] Thus, at the very time that the newly freed men became eligible for grants of Crown land, such grants were declared to be no longer gratuitous.

Superintendent Macdonald was not in agreement with the imposition of a price of £1 an acre on Crown land. Having earlier received permission to grant lands south of the River Sibun, he had a much larger area of land to dispose of than his predecessors, and he had in fact issued many grants, some for quite large areas of land, in the southern parts of the settlement. These had all been issued gratuitously, and he was disturbed by the instruction to sell at £1 an acre. In 1839, Macdonald urged the Secretary of State to allow him to continue "to act with regard to the disposal of land as my predecessors and myself have hitherto done"[54]—that is, to make large grants of land in the hope that they would be developed into plantations. He argued that "by making free grants of land encouragement has been given to those disposed to cultivate the soil," and pointed out that, with the depletion of mahogany resources, "the permanent welfare of this place must mainly depend upon the rearing of colonial produce." He claimed, without substantiation, that free grants of land had encouraged the movement of capital and labor toward agriculture.

Macdonald's emphasis on capital and labor, and the hopes he voiced for the extensive cultivation of such plantation crops as cotton, show that he was concerned with developing the large-scale cultivation of export crops as a substitute for the export of mahogany, the supplies of which he felt were rapidly diminishing. He clearly did not have in mind the possibility of the freedmen developing into an independent peasantry. However, the Secretary of State's reply indicates that the instruction to sell Crown land at £1 an acre *did* have the freedmen in mind, and that it was intended to inhibit them from developing an independent means of livelihood by preventing them from acquiring land:

> The argument which you have urged against the sale, in preference to the gratuitous donation of Lands in Honduras, is, in substance, that the demand of a price for Land would discourage or prevent the extension of the cultivation of it.

> This opinion is however opposed to the universal experience which has been obtained in every other part of the Colonial Possessions of the Crown in which the same question has arisen. The effect of alienating the waste lands of the Crown by a mere gift of them has always been in fact the same. It has tended to create indolent habits, *to discourage labour for wages,* and to leave large tracts of Territory in a wild & unimproved state.[55]

Macdonald's attempt to continue the free granting of Crown land was firmly rejected. The result of Colonial Office policy was that no Crown land was sold in the period up to 1855,[56] and by 1869 the total amount sold was said to be "utterly insignificant."[57]

Though the slaves had become legally free in 1838 and possessed in theory the freedom to choose whether to continue working for their former masters in the forests or to seek alternative employment, in reality their inability to acquire land, among other factors, ensured their continued thralldom to the mahogany lords. Nor was this situation a matter of chance. It was a calculated policy, since the Colonial Office felt that ownership of land would "discourage labour for wages"; and in Belize, as in the West Indian colonies, it was thought imperative that the freedmen continue to labor in the same sectors and for the same master class as they had during slavery. And yet, despite the attempts of the planters to retain the freedmen as laborers, a large peasantry developed in many West Indian territories, notably Jamaica, Trinidad, and British Guiana. That such a development failed to occur in Belize may be shown to be the result of a number of factors, including the imposition of a price on Crown land.

In the years after emancipation, the economic situation of sugar cultivation and that of mahogany extraction were markedly different. As sugar cultivation became less profitable, particularly after the Sugar Duties Act of 1846, by which the preferential duties for sugar from British colonies were to be gradually withdrawn, the sugar planters of the West Indies tried to reduce their costs by increasing productivity through reorganization and new techniques. In the depressed state of the market many planters sold their estates, and among those who continued operations, many were willing to release some of their land and their laborers. The mahogany cutters of Belize, however, experienced a boom in the late 1830s and 1840s, as a result of the demand in Europe for mahogany for building railway coaches. Exports rose from 7.7 million feet in 1827 to 8.5 million feet in 1837 and to a peak of 13.7 million feet in 1846[58]—almost doubling in twenty years. Moreover, the mahogany cutters were unable to reorganize their enterprises or to introduce new techniques to make their laborers more productive; in fact, the methods of felling and trucking mahogany trees hardly changed until mechanization was introduced in the twentieth century.

As long as there was a boom in the mahogany trade, and as long as the extraction of the giant trees depended upon human labor, augmented by oxen, the mahogany houses were not only determined to retain every laborer they had previously possessed but were also anxious to acquire more laborers, either neighboring Caribs or "Spaniards," or immigrants.

In 1834 a Public Meeting decided to apply for 1,800 Africans captured from slaving ships, and a petition by the "most influential & respectable Inhabitants" was sent to the Secretary of State in 1835, asking for 825 "of the captured Africans condemned by the British and other Commissioners at the Havanah, being sent to this Settlement." It was suggested that they should be "apprenticed" for a period of eight to sixteen years, "or at the option of the Employer," and noted that their labor was "required in the Cutting of Mahogany."[59] In August 1836, Major Anderson, the acting Superintendent, reported the arrival of 256 "liberated" Africans from Havana,[60] and in December 203 Africans, destined for Cuba on a Portuguese slaver, were landed. Of the latter it was said, "The greater part of the Males finding Countrymen amongst the Soldiers of the 2nd W.I. Regt. quartered here became desirous of enlisting in that corps," and forty-five men were so enlisted, the remainder being "portioned out amongst the Inhabitants."[61]

The intention behind encouraging the immigration of more Africans, whose status was to be virtually that of slaves, was not only to increase the supply of labor but also to make the apprentices more tractable after emancipation. This intention is made explicit in a report from a Special Magistrate to the Superintendent in 1838:

> I entertain confident hopes, that after the whole of the female apprentices have obtained their complete emancipation, they will return with greater willingness, to their former employments, and become a more useful body than they have hitherto been. The introduction of the successive Cargoes of Africans which have arrived in the Settlement, will tend to depreciate the services of the Apprentices after August next, and will render it the more necessary for the latter to conduct themselves with increased activity and attention, to enable them to obtain employment.[62]

Nevertheless, these "liberated" Africans could not have satisfied the mahogany cutters' demand for labor. Shortly after their arrival many died of cholera, five were drowned, and two committed suicide, leaving only 357 alive on 31 December 1837, and only 229 of those were male.[63] When the settlers objected to their recent acquisitions being emancipated at the same time as the other apprentices, orders were sent from London to the Havana Mixed Commission that no more Africans should be sent to Belize. This attempt to augment the labor force during the 1830s seems to have been a very limited success, and it certainly did not fulfill the early hopes of the settlers.

The labor force at the time of emancipation was not only small, but it may also have been actually diminishing. The number of adult male slaves in the settlement declined from 1,645 in 1816 to 686 in 1835, according to the censuses, and the 1839 census enumerated only nine hundred men, of whom the healthy laborers could not have numbered much more than eight hundred. With labor becoming such a scarce "commodity," and with the mahogany trade booming, the mahogany houses were anxious to secure every able-bodied laborer they could, both from within and without the settlement.

Granted that the wealthy mahogany cutters were strongly motivated to keep the labor force tied to their enterprises after emancipation, it remains to be seen how they succeeded in doing so. After all, many of the planters in Trinidad, Jamaica, and British Guiana attempted to keep their ex-slaves on the sugar plantations, but with less success. In Trinidad and British Guiana there was such a massive withdrawal of plantation labor, the freedmen preferring to cultivate idle Crown land for their own benefit, that the planters resorted to the equally massive importation of indentured East Indian laborers. In Jamaica, too, where planters had failed to control the freedmen with a system of rents for the huts and grounds that the slaves had formerly occupied without charges, there was an exodus of plantation labor. It has been argued that this led to the development of "two different Jamaicas—the planters' Jamaica of the coastal plains and inland valleys, and the settlers' Jamaica of the mountain freeholds. The two were separated by culture and racial caste."[64] It has been said of the West Indian freedmen generally that, "where there was opportunity of a living off the estates, they departed in large numbers. Where they had little option, they continued as hired labourers for the planters."[65]

The wealthy cutters of Belize reduced the options of their ex-slaves with a system of labor laws and practices designed to keep the laborers under very firm control. At the heart of this system of control was the practice of paying wages in "advances." The hiring period for mahogany work was generally the Christmas holidays, when both employers and laborers congregated in the town of Belize. The advance system was ostensibly intended to permit the laborer to purchase his supplies prior to going to the forests for the season, but the employers knew that the advances they gave were rarely used for this purpose. Instead, the money was spent in "keeping Christmas" in the festive fashion traditional in the settlement, with the result that the laborers would have to purchase their supplies on credit and at exorbitant prices from the employers' stores in the forests, a practice known as the "truck system." The effect of the combination of the "advance" and "truck" systems was to bind the laborer to his employer by keeping him in debt. Often, the balance of the wages a worker received in the forest was insufficient to meet his expenses, he ended the season in debt to his employer, and he therefore had to work off his debt to the employer in the following season.

These practices, which originated in relation to the free laborers prior to emancipation, were certainly an effective mechanism of control even before they became incorporated into the laws of the settlement in 1846 (and were subsequently amended in 1852).[66] The laws imposed a penalty of imprisonment with hard labor for three months on a "servant" failing to fulfill a contract after receiving advances, and among other repressive measures, it allowed the employer, or his agent, to apprehend a laborer without warrant and remove him forcibly to his designated place of work.[67]

This system of debt servitude could be enforced within the settlement because the population was so small. It would have been very difficult for an indebted laborer to remain undetected in Belize, and his position would have been aggravated by the undeveloped internal market situation. A laborer in Jamaica who wanted to avoid an employer could move to another parish in the island and could exchange his produce at any one of a number of markets, while his Belizean counterpart was restricted to the town of Belize if he wanted to sell his produce. The undeveloped market situation in the settlement inhibited the creation of a peasantry more directly. The Public Meeting that agreed to emancipate the apprentices on 1 August 1838 also abolished all Sunday markets, thereby destroying the marketing institution generally preferred by the small cultivator for the sale of his products.

The great reliance upon imported food that characterized the period of slavery has remained a feature of Belize, much to the advantage of the commercial sector. While some slaves and free blacks had always cultivated foodstuffs and had managed to sell some of their produce, the small population of the settlement and the dominating influence of the merchants had restricted the development of an internal market. Many of the biggest mahogany cutters, like Marshall Bennett, were also large-scale merchants; and there was an affinity of interests between the timber and commercial sectors, which were not as differentiated as the planters and merchants of, say, Jamaica. The merchants of Belize certainly benefited from the cutters' advance system, and they were opposed to the development of locally produced foods or of a self-sufficient peasantry.

The underdevelopment of the internal marketing system, combined with the unavailability of accessible land, meant that few of the freedmen, even if they avoided debt servitude, could have depended on small farming as a practical means of livelihood. This is in great contrast with Jamaica, for example, where the development of an internal marketing system during the period of slavery had provided an incentive for the freedmen to buy plots from abandoned or ruined sugar estates and to make a living by small farming. Between 1840 and 1845, the number of people in Jamaica owning freehold plots of less than nine acres increased from 883 to 20,724.[68] In Berbice, British Guiana, of the fifteen thousand landless slaves who were emancipated in 1838, almost five thousand had bought and were cultivating a total of seven thousand acres of land within four years.[69]

It has been stated that "land prices throughout the British Caribbean ranged from about £4 to £10 per acre, depending on the territory and the quality of the land. These prices were not beyond the pockets of those who had saved during slavery and who had been working for good hourly wages during the apprenticeship period."[70] In the different circumstances obtaining in Belize, however, the £1 per acre demanded for Crown land, in remote, wild, and unexplored parts of the country and a long way from the only market in Belize Town, was not an attractive or practical proposition for the freedmen. When private land did change hands, it was sold by the smaller settlers to the bigger; the latter, wanting to keep their laborers, were unwilling to sell to the freedmen. As a consequence, the freedmen, denied access to private land and offered only the virtually useless Crown lands, remained landless and thus wholly dependent upon the merchant-cutter elite.

While many of the other British West Indian territories developed an independent peasantry after emancipation, therefore, no comparable development occurred in Belize, despite the apparently attractive ratio of population to land area. The freedmen of Belize had always shown that they were interested in cultivating the soil, like their counterparts elsewhere in the West Indies, but because of their small numbers, the undeveloped state of the internal market, and the monopoly of land ownership by those who required their labor, the means of an independent existence were scarcely available to them. Although these factors were instrumental in inhibiting the growth of an independent peasantry, few observers then or since have acknowledged their importance, and many have attempted to explain the lack of development of a peasantry by suggesting that the laborers had an "invincible distaste" for agriculture and an "inherent preference" for mahogany cutting.[71] The fact is that the majority of the freedmen, like the slaves, were coerced to work in the mahogany gangs. When slavery was abolished, new methods were developed to maintain the submission of the labor force to the masters; primary among these methods was the combination of the "advance" and "truck" systems, which trapped the freedmen in a form of debt servitude while the monopoly of land ownership denied them access to the means of an independent existence.

The considerable redistribution of land that followed emancipation in Jamaica and elsewhere did not occur in Belize, and the growth and diversification of agricultural production that could have been expected had a peasantry developed did not materialize. Superintendent Fancourt reported in 1847:

> Of Agriculture in British Honduras little that is satisfactory can be said. ... the cultivation of the soil has been almost entirely neglected, a few of the labouring classes alone having their small plantations in which they raise plantains, yams & Indian corn, the first two in quantity barely sufficient for their own maintenance, the last mentioned in still smaller proportions.[72]

The fact that the freedmen were given little option to leave the timber works meant that the settlement remained dependent upon imported food. In summary, the situation after emancipation remained very much to the advantage of the wealthy mahogany cutters and merchants, both of whom benefited from the existence of a landless proletariat controlled by the advance system, and both of whom were opposed to the development of an independent and self-sufficient peasantry.

8
Post-Emancipation Society—1

THE RETURN OF THE MAYA TO WESTERN BELIZE

In chapter 2 an account was given of the Maya resistance to British incursions in the late eighteenth and early nineteenth centuries, and of their retreat into the forests of the interior in the 1820s and 1830s. Little was heard of the Maya by the British settlers in those two decades. Beginning in 1847 this situation changed dramatically, however, and in the 1850s and 1860s the Maya were a significant force with which the colonial administration had to contend.

The resurgence of the Maya of Yucatán that began in 1847 was paralleled by a revival of anti-colonial activity among the Maya of the upper Belize River valley. A newspaper report of 12 June 1847 stated that while Bacalar was threatened in the north,

> on several occasions recently we have heard of depredations being committed on the property of the Mahogany Cutters in the Belize River, and in one or two instances attacks on individuals, by what are called the "wild Indians" ... some two or three weeks since, a party of them attacked and plundered several of the storehouses of the gangs employed on the Eastern and Western Branches, and fears are entertained that unless some effectual means are at once resorted to, this system of pillage will be continued.[1]

It is uncertain whether Maya activity in and inhabitation of this area had been continuous since the early nineteenth century or whether the Maya moved in and out of the area, sometimes retiring from the intruding mahogany cutters and at other times retaliating against their camps. But from the middle of the nineteenth century on, the Maya greatly increased their activity and settlement in the north and west of Belize.

A raid on a mahogany camp on the Rio Bravo was reported later in 1847,[2] and in March 1848 some "Indians ... armed with bows and arrows" attacked Hill Bank on New River Lagoon.[3] These raids probably originated across the Rio Hondo in the north and not in the Belize River valley. The events taking place in Yucatán were to influence profoundly the pattern of Maya settlement and the nature of Maya relations with the British in the west and north of Belize. The interaction between the Maya and the British, and between the various groups of Maya themselves, was complicated and frequently changing.

The Santa Cruz Maya, who were engaged in the prolonged war with the Spanish-Mexicans known as the *Guerra de las Castas*,[4] made a few raids across the Rio Hondo into the northern districts of Belize but never attempted to lay claim to any of the territory. The Santa Cruz generally preferred to maintain good relations with the British as they needed the supply of arms and ammunition that came to them from the merchants of Belize. The British colonial officials were frequently willing to turn a blind eye to this munitions trade, despite complaints from the Mexican government, as long as the Santa Cruz were the de facto rulers of the territory just north of the settlement's border. The British were very apprehensive of the dangers of alienating their powerful neighbors, who had forcefully demonstrated their dislike of *los blancos* in Yucatán. Throughout the *Guerra de las Castas,* therefore, the British and the Santa Cruz, with brief exceptions, perceived a mutual interest in keeping the Rio Hondo a peaceful channel of communication. Not so the Mexicans, however, who wished to cut off the military supplies of their enemies, the Santa Cruz Maya.

In 1853, apparently on the intervention of Superintendent Wodehouse, who had succeeded Fancourt in a mediating role between the Santa Cruz and the Mexicans, a contingent of Maya to the south and west of Santa Cruz submitted to the Mexican authorities. These Maya, known as *los pacíficos del sur,* consisted of various groups, including the Ixcanha, the Lochha, and the Chichanha, who formed and re-formed in a series of alliances, splits, and realliances between the two centers of power, the Mexicans of Campeche and the Maya of Santa Cruz. At one time, Pablo Encalada, the leader of the Lochha, claimed control over all *los pacíficos,* with the support of the Mexicans but basing his authority on the "votes of the Indians in the different villages."[5] One group of Maya, the Chichanha, located close to the northwest border of Belize, proved particularly independent of any such alliances, however.

Chichanha was a Maya settlement with a long history. In 1695, the Maya of Chichanha were discovered plotting to massacre the Spaniards who resided in their town. The leader was executed in the town plaza and many of the Maya scattered into the surrounding jungle.[6] Said to have been reestablished in 1733, it was first referred to in the British records as "a considerable Town named Chechenha" in 1826.[7] The Maya of Chichanha had been among the first to sign a treaty of peace in 1851, but peace with the Mexican authorities meant war with the Santa Cruz. José Maria Barrera, founder of the cult of the speaking cross, marched on Chichanha with about five hundred men, burned the village, and captured the headman, Angelino Itzá.[8] By signing the treaty, the Chichanha Maya had gained no protection from remote Campeche or Merida, but had brought the wrath of the Santa Cruz upon themselves. Under the treaty of 1853 *los pacíficos del sur* were to fight against the Santa Cruz, Maya against Maya;

the Chichanha agreed to furnish four hundred men for the Mexican cause. In particular, the Mexicans wanted the Chichanha to halt the trade in war materials between Belize and Santa Cruz.

The Chichanha Maya, led by Luciano Zuc, raided the mahogany works of Young Toledo & Company at Blue Creek in September 1856. They demanded rent for cutting on Mexican territory and ransom for the prisoners they had taken.[9] This action, which was repeated in May of the following year, appears to have been motivated not so much by Mexican interests as by a desire for gain on the part of the Chichanha themselves. But in 1857, the Santa Cruz again attacked the Chichanha, and the village disintegrated.

A division took place among the survivors of Chichanha, some of them, under Zuc, moving toward the border of Belize and settling at Icaiché, a village in an inaccessible swampy region; others, "nearly one half... of the whole force, accompanied by women & children, under the guidance of Asunsion Ek" marched southward and settled "in the territory of Guatemala and of British Honduras."[10] These latter Chichanha Maya appear to have been motivated by a desire for peace, retiring from the struggles of Yucatán and settling in an area probably thinly populated by other Maya.

On 15 May 1857 Superintendent Seymour reported:

> On a visit which I recently made to the Northern & Western frontiers of this settlement I fell in with some Indian residents of British Honduras, who communicated to me the intelligence that several bodies of Indians of another tribe; the Chichenhas,—numbering in the aggregate... 8000 individuals, forsaking the neighbouring province of Yucatan have immigrated to our side of the Hondo where they are employed in burning & otherwise destroying bush & mahogany trees with a view to the cultivation of the soil, contemplating permanent occupation.[11]

Seymour himself stated an unwillingness "to make myself responsible for the accuracy of the numbers reported," and eight thousand is certainly an overestimate. At the time of Seymour's report these Maya were settling near "the remoter mahogany works" from New River Lagoon west to Booth's River and over the boundary in the Petén. Seymour made a point of insisting that the immigrants "must not be allowed to destroy the trees which alone give value to the land on which they are squatted,"[12] since the exploitation of the timber resources of Belize was the sole raison d'être of the British settlement's existence at that time. Seymour wanted to "persuade them to accept work & wages in the interior,"[13] believing that by incorporating them into the labor force, "much ultimate benefit to the settlement"[14] might ensue.

In the following years, Ek's Chichanha Maya drifted farther south toward the Belize River, away from Zuc, who seemed anxious to reestablish his authority over them. In 1862, a commissioner sent by Seymour found them in the Yalbac Hills just north of the Belize River in the Western District.[15] Their main village was San Pedro, lying less than ten miles northwest of Young Girl and inhabited by about three hundred and fifty people. Their villages extended northward to include San José, Chunbalché, and Naranjal, and Ek's authority extended west, beyond Chorro and San Domingo, to villages within the Petén. The population of ten of the villages was estimated by the commissioner to amount to over nine hundred persons.

Though the area into which Ek's Maya migrated may have been already populated, Eric Thompson is misleading, and possibly incorrect, in saying that "Indians . . . inhabiting villages such as Yalbac were probably the descendants of the Maya of Tipu culture."[16] Yalbac was not a Maya village, as Thompson implies, but a mahogany camp on Labouring Creek. Moreover, Thompson makes no distinction between the Maya who may have already inhabited the area (though not necessarily uninterruptedly since the Tipu period) and those who migrated with Ek from north of the Rio Hondo and who may have borne no relation whatever to the Tipu Maya. That Ek may have settled in an area that was already inhabited by Maya is indicated by a reference to the village of "San Pedro on the River Belize," shown in a Guatemalan map of 1832[17] to be in the vicinity of Ek's village. So, while it cannot be denied that there *may* have been some continuity between the Tipu and nineteenth-century settlements, first, there is no evidence to support such a claim, and second, we do know that a considerable number of the Maya in that area had migrated from the north.

Ek's group had moved into the last area of western Belize that had not been penetrated by the woodcutters—the Yalbac Hills. British settlers, whose sole goal was the extraction of timber, had always restricted themselves to camps on the rivers and creeks, down which they could float the huge mahogany logs to the coast. The frontier of their exploitation, for it was hardly a settlement in any permanent sense, had moved west from New River Lagoon and Roaring Creek since the early nineteenth century. By the middle of the century, the mahogany cutters had penetrated the northwest up the Rio Bravo and Booth's River, and west along Labouring Creek to Yalbac and up the Belize River as far as Duck Run, near present-day San Ignacio el Cayo. The Maya settled just beyond this frontier, in the Yalbac Hills, but they were close enough to the mahogany camps to make the mahogany cutters and the colonial administrators apprehensive about them. Superintendent Seymour attempted to control these new immigrants, and to bring them under the authority of the colonial administration, by appointing Ek as their *commandante* and appointing other individuals in the various villages as *alcaldes,* giving them all symbols of their offices.[18] Though, in fact, this amounted merely to a recognition of Ek's own previously established authority among the Maya, Seymour attempted to make them dependent upon British protection. The Superintendent's intention was only fulfilled with difficulty, however, after a period of struggle and armed conflict.

The Icaiché Maya had been led, since the death of Zuc in 1864, by Marcos Canul, a man who showed little respect for British authority and did not recognize British territorial claims in the northwest of the colony. Canul's raid on a mahogany camp at Qualm Hill on the Rio Bravo in April 1866 was considered very serious by the timber companies and the colonial administration. Two men had lost their lives, rent was demanded for the use of land considered to be British territory, and a considerable ransom was demanded for the prisoners taken in the raid.[19] Six months later the administration was afraid that the Icaiché Maya were about to join those in the Yalbac Hills, thereby threatening the Belize River camps. It appears that Canul was under some pressure from both the Santa Cruz and the Lochha Maya in the north,[20] while Ek expressed apprehension at the approach of the Icaiché,[21] probably fearing that he would be displaced if the two groups of the Chichanha Maya became reunited. In any case, a hasty march on San Pedro by one Captain Delamere actually precipitated the very realliance it had been intended to prevent. The San Pedro Maya, feeling they had somehow earned the disapproval of the British, could only turn to Canul for support. Canul and his troops arrived in San Pedro early in December, promptly demanded rent from a mahogany camp,[22] and protested to Lieutenant Governor Austin that "English troops had been scouring the country... with a view of molesting the Indians."[23] A detachment of British troops was sent up the Belize River under the command of Major McKay, but on the morning of 21 December, they were routed on their way to San Pedro by the combined Maya forces led by Canul's second-in-command, Rafael Chan.[24] The British casualties were five dead and sixteen wounded, and the civil commissioner, Mr. Edward Rhys, was abandoned in the precipitate retreat and never heard from again. Though the situation appeared serious to the British at the time, and caused considerable panic throughout the colony,[25] the repercussions were in fact to prove far more serious for the Maya of the Yalbac Hills.

After troop reinforcements arrived in Belize early in 1867, a field force of over three hundred soldiers, complete with incendiary rockets, was organized and led by Lieutenant Colonel Harley. Entering San Pedro without opposition on 9 February, they burned the village to the ground. San Pedro had been a village "of some 50 houses most of them well built and substantial, beside larger buildings, which were of a solid construction, such as the Fiesta House, Chapel, etc.—but nothing of San Pedro now remains except the Chapel, its population... was not less than between 3, and 400 people."[26] Harley went on to destroy the "rich and ample provision grounds of San Pedro covering a large extensive plain, about 3 or 4 miles from the Town... as also their corn houses."[27] The British troops also destroyed the Maya villages of Santa Teresa, San José, Naranjal, Cerro, Santa Cruz, and Chunbalché, burning the adjacent corn and provision grounds and the granaries in order to drive the Maya out of the district.[28] The Maya appear to have fled, and the area remained sparsely occupied for a while, but soon they drifted back, rebuilding and reoccupying some of their old villages.

Canul kept up his struggle against the British during the next five years. In April 1870 Canul and his men marched into Corozal and occupied the town, and on 31 August 1872, leading about one hundred and fifty men, Canul attacked the barracks at Orange Walk (New River). After several hours of fighting, the Icaiché were unable to dislodge the garrison, so they retired. Canul, who had been fatally wounded, was carried over the Hondo, where he died on 1 September 1872.[29] That was the last serious attack on the colony, and more peaceable, but still uneasy, relations continued between the Icaiché Maya and the British throughout the 1870s.

The Maya who had migrated to the Yalbac Hills in the mid-nineteenth century were a splinter from one of the several groups of the Maya of Yucatán who had been divided against each other during the *Guerra de las Castas*. But this group, the San Pedro Maya under Ek, had avoided one area of conflict only to be drawn into another. Escaping the conflict between the Spanish-Mexicans and the Santa Cruz Maya, which had developed into a fraternal struggle between groups of Maya, Ek and his followers were unable to remain neutral in the conflict between the British and the Icaiché Maya, despite the fact that they had settled in a remote region. The realliance between the San Pedro Maya and the Icaiché Maya was a temporary affair, at first precipitated but later destroyed by British military action. When the San Pedro Maya were joined by the Icaiché they were able to win the battle of San Pedro in 1866, but they were to lose the subsequent war. Driven out of the Yalbac Hills area in 1867, these Maya, upon their return, were dominated by the British colonialists, while the Icaiché Maya were beaten back across the northern border during the following five years.

The zeal with which the British crushed the San Pedro Maya in 1867 is in part explained by their desire to revenge the rout of the previous year, but it was also caused by their desire to secure the outlying areas of the colony for the settlement of potential immigrant Confederate refugees from the American Civil War.[30] Most of the immigrants who came stayed only a few years in the south of the colony, but the policy of attracting white settlers remained. This policy was influenced by a desire to develop agriculture in the Western District and the upper Belize River valley, but it was also intended to increase the proportion of whites in the population, which, by the second half of the nineteenth century, had fallen to about 1½ percent. The Maya, who were trying to develop the interior of Belize for their own agricultural purposes, were thus the victims of a racialist scheme of colonization. In the colonial scheme, the Maya were seen not as the agricultural pioneers that in fact they were but merely as a nuisance to the mahogany business and as a potential source of labor for white-owned plantations.

In 1857, Superintendent Seymour had worried about the Maya destroying the mahogany trees, "which alone give value to the land," and sought to make them into wage laborers. At that time "British Honduras" was still not officially a colony, there was little interest in agricultural development, and even the registration of land titles had not been instituted. Within the next decade, however, all this was to change, and the place of the Maya within the colonial structure had to be more defined and systematized. Even before the declaration of colonial status, an act was passed in Belize "to provide for the more speedy Administration of Justice in the rural districts of British Honduras,"[31] giving a legal basis to the position of *alcalde,* which had been adopted from the Spanish colonial system. When the appointment of *alcaldes* was approved by the Secretary of State in 1864, and their monthly salary fixed at $5.00, the administrative system for controlling the Maya was established.

In 1867, Lieutenant Governor Austin issued the following regulation: "No Indian will be at liberty to reside upon or occupy, or cultivate any land without previous payment or engagement to pay rent whether to the Crown or the owner of the land."[32] The following year, in his lengthy "Report on the Land Question," Lieutenant Governor Longden discussed what could be done with the Maya villages that had been reestablished in the western district:

> Several of these villages are situate upon lands claimed either by the British Honduras Company or Messrs. Young Toledo and Company, but whenever they are situate on Crown Lands I think the villages and a sufficient surrounding space should be reserved *in the hands of the Crown* for the use of the Indians,—no marketable titles being issued to them to enable them to dispose of such lands.[33]

Thus it was made clear that whereas the largest landowners of the country, who only a few years before had obtained firm titles to their vast lands, were not to be disturbed, the Maya should not be allowed to own land but were to be confined to the reservations created by the Crown Lands Ordinance in 1872.

The settlement of the Maya in the west of Belize in the latter part of the nineteenth century took place within the discriminatory restrictions of the colonial framework. With a decline in the timber trade, the formalization of the colonial status of the territory, and the growth of agricultural interests, the land itself was seen for the first time by the colonizers as being intrinsically valuable, and the interior was seen as a potential site of agricultural exploitation. The Maya, who had first been driven back and kept away from the valuable mahogany trees, were then perceived as potential agricultural wage laborers to be exploited by immigrant white capitalists. In the colonial scheme of things, therefore, the Maya had to be denied the right to own land in order to deprive them of their independent means of livelihood and make them dependent upon the prospective employers. A late-nineteenth-century account of the Maya described them as subsistence farmers but stressed their potentiality as plantation laborers:

> The Indians... are baptized, but mix up idolatrous rites and superstitious beliefs with the Christian creed and ceremonies.... They live industriously and inoffensively in villages scattered over the district, cultivating their patches of maize and pulse, their pigs and poultry.... The indigenous Indian... might be made available to some extent could he be induced to quit his scattered village-homes, and this is perhaps the cheapest labour to be procured.[34]

Spanish contact with the Maya of Belize in the sixteenth and seventeenth centuries was significant but sporadic because the Spanish never settled in the area. For the first century after the arrival of the British there was little or no contact between the two peoples, but there followed a century of skirmishing and warfare at the end of which the British established their dominance over the Maya. By the time "British Honduras" was declared a Crown Colony, the Maya had been incorporated into the colonial social structure as a dispossessed and dominated group.

CARIBS AND CREOLES

Just as the Maya were incorporated into the colonial social structure in the 1860s as a dominated and dispossessed group, so too were the Caribs, as the colonial administration extended its jurisdiction into the southern parts of the settlement. The Caribs, or "Black Caribs," of Belize are of predominantly African racial origin, descendents of Africans who escaped from slavery in the Windward Islands and mixed with the Carib Indians of St. Vincent, from whence five thousand of them were transported by the British in 1797 to the island of Ruatan, off the coast of Honduras.[35] Some of them later moved onto coastal areas of Honduras, and by 1802 there were about one hundred and fifty Carib settlers in the Stann Creek area.[36] The British settlers had some years previously gone as far south as Deep River, which is about twice the distance from the Belize River mouth to Stann Creek, so that the Caribs soon found themselves being affected by the jurisdiction of the Magistrates. The Caribs were principally engaged in fishing and the cultivation of ground foods, and it is possible that they took some of their produce up to Belize town to market. Certainly they were visiting the town by 1811, as a Magistrates' meeting in that year directed that all Caribs arriving at the fort (in Belize town) must get a permit or ticket from the Superintendent or quit the settlement within forty-eight hours.[37]

In 1835, when there were about five hundred Caribs in the sourthern part of the settlement, they were said to be "carrying on a constant traffic by sea with Belize, in plaintains, maize, poultry, etc. The men in great part hire themselves by the year to Mahogany cutters."[38] In the following year it was observed that "most of them speak English, and from them the Mahogany Cutters derive their best labourers,"[39] though a few years before, a Public Meeting had referred to the problem of "runaway Caribs" and resolved to appoint a constable in Stann Creek for their apprehension.[40] In 1841 "Stand Creek" was described as a "flourishing village... which now probably contains one half of the entire tribe" of Caribs. "This village is now their largest settlement, and is rapidly increasing, both from natural causes and immigration."[41] There were said to be a thousand Caribs, three hundred of whom were employed as woodcutters and seventy as fishermen, chiefly catching the hawksbill turtle. At about the same time, the American traveler Stephens described the Carib town of Punta Corda, which

> consisted of about five hundred inhabitants. . . . Besides cotton and rice, the cahoon, banana, coconut, pineapple, orange, lemon, and plantain, with many other fruits

which we do not know even by name, were growing with such luxuriance that at first their very fragrance was oppressive.[42]

Although, in the 1830s, the Caribs were being employed as mahogany cutters and were being converted by the Wesleyan missionary, Thomas Jefferies, they were still largely independent, self-sufficient, and unincorporated into the colonial social structure. With the southward expansion of the settlement, and the growing demand for labor caused by emancipation and the growth of interest in commercial agriculture, the semi-autonomy of the Caribs was overcome, and they were rapidly integrated into the society as yet another repressed and disenfranchised group.

For about fifty years the Caribs had occupied lands in the south for the cultivation of subsistence crops, but when the Laws in Force Act of 1855 provided unequivocal official recognition of the validity of location titles, the Caribs' provision grounds were not included. The Laws in Force Act gave retroactive legitimacy to the ownership of land that had been occupied by the settlers, or had been simply appropriated by them under the old location laws, before 1817. It was further enacted that any person who had been in quiet and undisturbed possession of a location since 1 January 1840, "shall have good right to such possession as against any grantee or other person whomsoever."[43] The Bill received the royal assent and was proclaimed on 8 March 1856, the British government thereby confirming the titles to land held under the old location laws. This act fulfilled its purpose of giving proper freehold titles to the old settlers, but it was never applied to people like the Caribs, despite the fact that many of them had occupied their land without challenge since before 1817 and certainly since 1840.

Shortly after the Laws in Force Act had recognized the validity of the old settlers' occupation of land and had given them freehold titles, the decision was taken to deny the Caribs any title to their lands. In 1857, J. H. Faber, the Crown surveyor, issued the following notice in the Carib town of Stann Creek:

> Leases for the town lots in Standing Creek and plantation ground on the neighbouring Crown lands will be issued at the Colonial Secretary's Office in Belize.
>
> The leases will be for the term of seven fourteen or twenty one years at the annual rate of one dollar.
>
> It is not compulsory for the present inhabitants of Standing Creek to take out a lease—but in the event of their leaving this place without having obtained one, they will forfeit their right to the houses or other buildings they may have erected, and the constable has received instructions to take possession of said buildings and keep them at the disposal of the Crown.[44]

In a letter to the Superintendent explaining his reasons for issuing the notice, Faber argued that "it is generally known that the Caribs are of a very erratic and nomadic disposition & for the slightest reason they will immediately emigrate to another part of the coast & there form the nucleus of another settlement," and that his intention was "to give .... to each householder such document as will ensure him a peaceable enjoyment of his house and plantation on our territory, and that for the small stipend of one dollar paid yearly." He expressed the hope "that we will by this measure attract near Belize a valuable body of labourers," and concluded that "several Caribs in Standing Creek have already applied for their papers (as they call the lease) which proves that my object has been rightly understood."[45]

The Caribs, of course, felt obliged to apply for the leases through fear of losing their houses and plantations unless they complied with the notice. If the intention was really to give "each householder such document as will ensure him a peaceable enjoyment of his house and plantation," an enjoyment that had been disturbed only by the interference of the colonial officials, then the appropriate document would have been a Crown grant giving freehold title to land long occupied, and not an annual lease the cost of which would in a few years exceed the value of the land. But Faber expressed his real motive, which was to convert the Caribs from a largely self-sufficient peasantry into a labor supply for the mahogany gangs. Later the Caribs were also in demand to work on the developing sugar estates in the south of the colony. Accordingly, the Caribs had to be deprived of their independence and curbed in their "erratic and nomadic disposition" in order to make of them a more disciplined and tractable labor force. Made annual tenants on Crown land in 1857, they were later, along with the Maya, deprived of the opportunity of holding lands by freehold title when reserves were established by the Crown Lands Ordinance of 1872. Since the Caribs had occupied lands in the south before 1857 without molestation from the colonial authorities, the notice of 1857 and the subsequent establishment of reserves must be regarded as a move to dispossess the Caribs from their lands.

By the late 1850s the number of Caribs in the settlement had increased considerably. A rough census indicated that there were eleven hundred Caribs in Stann Creek town and four hundred more in Punta Gorda. A number of villages, such as Sibun Creek, Seven Hills, Lower Stann Creek, and Jonathan Point, were said to have between one hundred and one hundred and fifty Caribs each. In all, there were said to be about twenty-two hundred Caribs in the settlement, or about one-tenth of the whole population.[46]

The population of African origin, apart from the Maroon communities, some disbanded soldiers, and a few freedmen, had never possessed land. The chief occupation of this group was still mahogany extraction, and as this occupation was seasonal and involved shifting camps, most of the members of mahogany gangs had their permanent homes in the town of Belize. Especially after the depression in the mahogany trade in the late 1840s and 1850s, there was an increasing tendency for these people, who became known as the "Creoles," to reside and work in the town of Belize, performing various urban occupations. By 1881 Belize town contained 5,767 people, or about 21 percent of the colony's population, and these were predominantly Creoles.[47]

There were nevertheless some people of African origin who engaged in subsistence farming and in production for the internal market. Their small farms were principally in the Belize District or along the rivers or the coast, from whence the peasants could transport their produce to the market in the capital by dugouts or dories. Daniel Morris, curator of the Jamaica Botanical Gardens, who visited Belize in 1882, described the produce of such small farms: "The settlements along the coast, inhabited by Creoles, Caribs, or Spaniards, are generally surrounded by patches of bananas, plaintains and coconuts; with cassava, sugarcane, sweet potato, rice and wanglo, to supply their daily wants."[48] When their daily wants could not be satisfied directly by their produce, or by the sale of their produce in the market, these people would sell their labor power as more or less temporary farm or forest workers. Only a few of them owned any land; most were squatters with no title and very precarious possession. Lieutenant Governor Longden stated in 1868 that such small plantations, though occupied for over fifty years by the disbanded soldiers, could, where there was no title, be "sold ... over the heads of the present occupiers to large proprietors."[49] The small cultivators were thus susceptible to dispossession, and despite their sometimes lengthy occupation and utilization of the land, they were perceived by the colonial administrators and the "large proprietors" as "unauthorized occupants," squatters, and trespassers.

The insecurity of tenure experienced by these peasants, coupled with limitations of their technology (the chief tools at their disposal were machetes, axes, and fire) and the habit established during slavery of shifting from camp to camp, encouraged the adoption of swidden agriculture and the reliance upon quickly maturing rather than permanent crops. These conditions, along with the undeveloped marketing and transportation systems and an extraordinary monopolization of land resources, have militated against the development of sedentary peasant farming in Belize. One effect of this has been the continued reliance of the population on expensive imported foodstuffs, which has been much to the advantage of the commerical sector. Another effect, particularly among people of African origin, is that farming activity has come to be devalued and is perceived, at best, as a part-time venture and a stand-by if employment opportunities become scarce—a situation which has benefited the employer class.

For a variety of reasons, therefore, the majority of the non-white colonized, whether Maya, Carib, or African, was dependent upon finding employment as wage laborers, a situation resulting both from the actions of the employers and a deliberate colonial policy.

9
Post-Emancipation Society—2

AGRICULTURE

From the start of British occupation, the extraction of timber, first logwood and then mahogany, had been the chief economic raison d'être of the emerging colony. Though some of the slaves and freedmen, the Caribs, and the Maya had engaged in cultivation, chiefly for subsistence purposes, the settlement's elite had shown little interest in the development of agriculture. This was due in part to the prohibition of the cultivation of commercial crops in the treaties with Spain, and the occasional requests made to the British government for permission to cultivate such crops for export were denied. But, given the shortage of labor and the abundant supplies of mahogany, there was also little incentive in the first decades of the nineteenth century for the elite to become involved in plantation agriculture in Belize. Following emancipation and the rapid depletion of mahogany reserves due to the increased demand for the timber in the 1830s, however, some individuals began to consider agriculture as an alternative economic base for the settlement.

An "agricultural company" was formed in 1839 to encourage and promote agricultural activity,[1] but nothing came of that effort. In the same year, some of the settlers had petitioned the Secretary of State, requesting that the produce of the settlement be admitted into English ports at the same rates of duty as that of other dependencies. The reply was discouraging, though a very guarded permission to grant lands for cultivation was given.[2] This did not satisfy the settlers, however, and at a Public Meeting in 1841 they decided to forward a petition to the House of Commons. The petition stated that previous memorials had been sent in 1833, 1835, and 1839, and noted that:

> The Cutting of [mahogany and logwood] having become a precarious Employment, your Petitioners are desirous of acquiring the unquestionable right of cultivating this extensive soil, with a bona fide Title of Propriety [sic] in the Arable Lands thereof; and with unrestricted permission to export such cultivated products from this and to have them Imported into the United Kingdom, at the same rate of Duties as from the British West India Islands.[3]

No reply to this petition has been found.

In 1847 the Superintendent had to report that "of Agriculture in British Honduras little that is satisfactory can be said."[4] He went on to say that although "two or three individuals have recently applied themselves to the manufacture of rum," sugar was still "almost exclusively derived from the Town of Bacalar in Yucatan." He concluded that "the existing body of Merchants & Mahogany Cutters" would probably never invest capital in the cultivation of the soil, despite the fact that "sugar cane grows luxuriantly." The prospects for agricultural development were thus very dim in 1847. The population was small, the freedmen were confined to forestry work by their inability to obtain land, there was no export market and the internal market was undeveloped, and the major merchants and mahogany cutters had little interest in investing in agriculture.

However, when the Maya of Yucatán rose in revolt against the white settlers of Spanish origin in 1847, a series of events was set in motion that was to have major consequences for the economy and social structure of Belize. As a result of the chaos and bloodshed of the *Guerra de las Castas,* during which the population of Yucatán was almost halved,[5] thousands of Maya and *mestizos* fled into Belize. Many of these refugees returned to Yucatán, but a large number remained and settled—some, as has been described, in the west, but most in the north. An official report of 1856, which estimated a total permanent population of about twenty thousand, stated that over one-quarter of the people were in the Northern District,[6] most of whom would have been Yucatecan refugees. That report indicated that there were an estimated seven thousand people living permanently in the town of Belize, four thousand people in the Southern District, three thousand in the Western District, and fifty-five hundred in the Northern District. In 1857, it was noted that the town of Corozal, "now in the sixth year of its existence already possesses 4500 inhabitants,"[7] and that the population of the Northern District, excluding Indians, was between ten and twelve thousand. "Tickets of residence" were issued at Corozal to two thousand adult male immigrants in 1857; it was estimated that they were only one-quarter of the refugees.[8]

In 1858, a census taken by the Fathers of the Society of Jesus "of such towns villages & mahogany works as are partially or entirely inhabited by Roman Catholics"[9] showed the enormous growth of villages in the Northern District, populated by Yucatecan refugees. Corozal contained forty-five hundred people "Yucatecos principally but some Indians & Creoles." San Estevan, populated by thirteen hundred "Yucatecos," was the next largest town in the north and, larger even than Stann Creek with eleven hundred Caribs, was the third largest town in the country. A number of villages, such as San Pedro, Sarteneja, Punta Consejo, Lowrys Bight, Orange Walk, San Antonio, and Corosal Chico, each contained two hundred or more persons, mostly from Yucatán. In the first of the regular modern censuses, taken in 1861, the total population was said to be 25,635, and the 1871 census recorded 24,710 persons in the country,[10] a high proportion of them having come from Yucatán.

The Maya and *mestizo* refugees who came to Belize in the decade or so after 1848 had for the most part been small-scale cultivators in Yucatán. The value of their continuing agricultural activity was recognized as early as 1852 by the Superintendent:

> They have already commenced the cultivation of Sugar, Corn, Tobacco, and other articles for which there must always be great demand in this market; and looking to the almost entire absence of agricultural undertakings in the other Districts, as well as to the general scarcity of labour which exists here, it cannot be disputed that the retention of these settlers, and their general absorption into the permanent population of our territory, is a matter of great importance to this community.[11]

Four years later, in 1856, Superintendent Stevenson, in his speech to the Assembly, urged support of the Northern District, "the first ... in which there has been any attempt at establishing villages, peopled by small and independent cultivators."[12] He spoke of them growing "considerable quantities" of rice, corn, and vegetables, and by 1857 the Yucatecan refugees were already supplying enough sugar for the local market and for export.

A report of 1859 distinguished between the Maya and the *mestizo* refugees in terms of their characteristic economic activities. The Maya were said to be either employed in mahogany gangs or engaged on their own account in logwood cutting, "which has passed principally into their hands," and in *milpa* farming and pig raising. The *mestizos,* on the other hand, were described as those who, "with a sprinkling of Indians, are our sugar growers."[13]

While these immigrants from Yucatán had been able to cultivate land to produce foodstuffs for subsistence and sale, and even for export, the African freedmen, still dominated by the landowning companies, remained almost entirely dependent upon wage labor in the mahogany works. The freedmen had been prevented from obtaining land in the decade after emancipation as part of a conscious policy designed to maintain a sufficient labor supply for the mahogany business, so they also found it impossible to rent land from the big landowners. Yet some of these same landowners tolerated, and even encouraged, the settlement of Maya and *mestizo* refugees in the north by renting them lands. Why were the Yucatecans allowed to develop as a peasantry, and why were they not, like the ex-slaves, promptly forced into wage labor?

The answers seem to lie in a number of related factors, chief among which was the labor supply situation as seen by the landowning elite. In the first place, the refugees were a new element in the settlement's population. The landowners did not view them with that same sense of ownership with which they still saw their former slaves, and did not feel as if they were losing labor if the immigrants were allowed to cultivate the soil. No doubt there was also a degree of racial stereotyping involved in this perception, as is evident in the Superintendent's comment in 1859 that the Maya, "more robust than the Spaniard, less addicted to pleasure than the negro ... are admirably adapted to the monotonous drudgery of logwood cutting."[14] The employers probably considered the Yucatecans inherently unsuited to such heavy work as mahogany cutting, just as they considered the Africans particularly suited to it.[15]

Secondly, the landowners do not appear to have needed the labor of the Yucatecans in the circumstances of the mid-nineteenth century. The immigrants came at a time when the mahogany trade was declining, and the labor supply was probably then reasonably adequate in relation to the current demand. The Northern District, into which the majority of them came, was considered to be virtually denuded of mahogany, so, though some of the Maya worked on mahogany gangs, the immigrants were not perceived as a whole as potential laborers in such gangs.

Thirdly, some of the landowners in the Northern District, who had not developed any real interest in plantation agriculture (because of the undefined and insecure status of the settlement and the absence of colonial duty privileges in the metropolitan markets) and who therefore had no need for plantation laborers, were in possession of large idle estates. The Yucatecans were anxious to work on the land, and these landowners were prepared to rent their land to them; it was a simple and effective way of exploiting this new population. Little information has been found to date to describe with precision the tenurial relations between the landowners and the immigrants, the distribution of tenancies, or the land tenure systems preferred or adhered to by the Maya and *mestizos*. However, it is clear that most of the land cultivated by the immigrants in the north was rented from the big landowners.[16]

The landowners were no doubt encouraged to accommodate the refugees by the Superintendents, who had an interest in establishing an agricultural base in the settlement. Belize had for long been dependent on imported foodstuffs, partly from Bacalar and other neighboring areas. The sentiment expressed by Superintendent Macdonald in 1839 that "from the exhaustion of Mahogany the hitherto staple commodity, the permanent welfare of this place must mainly depend upon the rearing of colonial produce,"[17] was repeated in the following two decades by succeeding Superintendents, who were eager to encourage agriculture both for export and for internal consumption. As late as 1856, Superintendent Stevenson, in his speech to the Assembly, remarked that "we are at present wholly dependent on neighbouring countries" for rice, corn, and other foodstuffs, and since any break in the fragile friendly relations with those areas would create problems of supply, "it requires but little foresight to encourage Agricultural Industry, wherever it can be profitably pursued."[18]

The *Guerra de las Castas* introduced uncertainties into this supply situation, and since the Yucatecan refugees no doubt included some of the very people who had been engaged in such trade with Belize, the Superintendents perceived it to be in the interests of the settlement to allow and encourage them to continue to supply the market from within the settlement itself. Moreover, when the Yucatecans began to produce sugar, as well as vegetables and other subsistence crops, the Superintendent was plainly overjoyed at the development, for sugar was a tropical export crop *par excellence*. In the same speech to the Assembly, in 1856, Stevenson referred to the "small and independent cultivators" of the Northern District, who were making it "an improving Agricultural country."[19] Later that year, he reported that apart from subsistence plots, agriculture had never been successfully pursued, and continued:

> But within the last few years—the cultivation of the cane has been attempted by the recent Spanish and Indian Settlers in the Northern District, who, by their own rough means have succeeded very fairly in establishing small but rather profitable plantations near Corosal on the margins of the principal Rivers in that district,—and, although in no one place is there a large field of cultivation or anything like scientific agriculture or Manufacture, yet the result has shown . . . a pressure on the Revenue on "Spirits" and "Sugar." The aggregate amount produced and sent in small quantities from time to time to Belize being very considerable.[20]

The following year, Stevenson reported that eight hundred acres were under cane cultivation in the north, and that "the wants of the Settlement, in the two articles of Sugar and Rum, will soon be more than fully supplied by the Northern District alone."[21] In fact, performance was such that later in 1857, the new Superintendent, Seymour, was able to report:

> The first shipment to Europe of sugar the produce of Honduras was made, to the extent of a hundred barrels, about a fortnight ago, in the ship "Byzantium" for Liverpool. It is but very recently that our planters were able to satisfy the demands of our own market.[22]

The Yucatecan refugees, with their little *ranchos* on rented lands, had shown that sugar could be successfully cultivated and exported, and before long the big landowners followed in the footsteps of these small farmers and took over the business. This development was foreseen by the settlement's treasurer, who predicted in 1860 that agricultural enterprises "will soon be valued by Capitalists, now that the capabilities of the Soil have been practically tested by small Planters."[23] Thus the big landowners became agricultural entrepreneurs, forcing some of their tenants into wage labor and quickly dominating sugar exports.

Table 9.1 shows that sugar exports from Belize more than quadrupled in the

TABLE 9.1 Exports of Sugar from Belize, in Pounds, 1862–68

Year	Pounds
1862	397,176
1863	451,966
1864	694,231
1865	478,865
1866	1,336,496
1867	1,218,560
1868	1,706,880

SOURCE: Longden to Grant, 19 June 1868; Longden to Grant, 17 May 1869, AB, R.98.

seven years from 1862 to 1868. Lieutenant Governor Longden stated that in 1867, three thousand acres of land were under cane, 868 tons of sugar were produced, 544 tons of which were exported, and 53,914 gallons of rum were produced, 4,800 of which were exported.[24] In 1868, 1,033 tons of sugar were produced, of which 762 tons were exported.[25] In the report on 1868, it was stated that "there are Ten Estates, devoted to the cultivation of Sugar, on which steam machinery has been erected ... the present acreage is only a small part of that which it is intended to cultivate." These ten estates with steam machinery had an estimated total of 1,683 acres in cane, of which 1,176 acres were in the north and 507 in the south. By far the biggest sugar producer was the British Honduras Company, whose four estates, at Santa Cruz, Trial Farm, Tower Hill, and Indian Church, had an estimated 746 acres in cane. The report added:

> Besides these ten large Estates there are 32 small Estates or Milpas cultivated partly in Sugar and partly in Indian corn by the Spaniards who immigrated into the Northern District from Yucatan. On these "Milpas" as they are called the extent of land in cane varies from 5 acres to 110 acres. In the whole of the Milpas together there are 1,015 acres of cane land giving an average of nearly 32 acres to each Milpa.

There can be no question that within a decade of the first export of sugar from Belize by the *mestizo rancheros,* the production and export of sugar had become dominated by the five companies that had steam machinery on their extensive estates.

The system of production on the *ranchos* was quite different from that on the plantations. Whereas the former utilized the traditional swidden techniques of cultivation associated with the Maya *milpa,* animal power and simple processing equipment, the plantations used a short-term fallow system, steam power, and more sophisticated machinery. Both plantation owners and *rancheros* cultivated sugar cane and subsistence crops, such as corn and vegetables, though one may expect that the shift in emphasis from subsistence to cash crops was associated with an increase in the size of the production unit; only a little space of the smallest *milpas* was devoted to cash crops, and the largest plantations were primarily involved in the production of sugar.

The growing dominance of the plantations over the *ranchos* and *milpas* caused changes in the cultural ecology as well as in the social structure of the district. Many of the traditional Maya crafts, for example, were neglected as the Maya became increasingly dependent upon goods bought from the company store. Many of the Maya and *mestizos* became a rural proletariat dependent entirely upon the wages, in cash and food, provided for plantation work. Others, however, became a part-proletariat and part-peasantry, their low cash wages being underwritten by their continued subsistence agriculture on rented land. As long as the population remained small and the expansion of sugar production did not strain land resources, this arrangement suited the employers, who could thereby simultaneously reduce the wages and collect rents. The maintenance of this form of land use and land tenure enabled the Maya to develop into small-scale cash crop producers when the plantations declined and also established a precedent for the coexistence of peasant-*milpa* and industrial-estate types of agriculture when the plantations were reintroduced in the twentieth century.[26]

IMMIGRATION

One of the chief reasons for the belatedness of agricultural development in Belize was the small population and, from the viewpoint of the big landowners and mahogany cutters, the scarcity of labor. In 1835, Thomas Miller, the keeper of the records, wrote a lengthy memorandum "relating to the labour which might be made available for the proposed cultivation of the soil in Honduras."[27] Miller emphasized that, "if it were intended to encourage a rapid and extensive scheme of Agriculture in Honduras . . . it would be necessary to provide labour on a great scale." He suggested that the neighboring territories could furnish a supply of labor, from Yucatán, the Petén, Charibs from Truxillo, and West Indians after the termination of apprenticeship. In addition, Miller suggested the authorization of transport for "about 1500 negroes who are yearly condemned by the Mixed Commission" at Havana, and the encouragement, through "the granting or sale of lands on favourable conditions, and a reasonable protecting duty on the produce which might be raised on them," of emigration from England. Above all, however, Miller advocated that "an extensive supply of labour might be supplied from the British Possessions in India." The principal crops that Miller had in mind for the proposed agricultural development were sea-island cotton and indigo, but nothing developed from his proposals. With the development of sugar plantations twenty-five years later, however, the idea of large-scale immigration was once more important.

The need for a supply of labor was foreseen by the big landowners as soon as they began cultivating sugar cane. The bigger estates put many of the *mestizo rancheros* in the north out of business and reduced them to a rural proletariat, along with the Maya. Given the seasonal nature of the demand for labor and the absence of pressure upon land resources, many of the Maya and *mestizos* who constituted most of the laborers for the big estates continued to cultivate their *milpas* on small rented plots, their subsistence agriculture underwriting the plantation agriculture by maintaining the required labor force through the long "dead" season. Such an arrangement was to the advantage of the landowners, of course, as it helped secure a cheap labor force, whose wages were being subsidized by *milpa* production, and, through the systems of tenancy and debt peonage, made the tenant-laborers more dependent and tractable. Nevertheless, very little of the land held by the large landowners was planted with cane, and this was partly because of the shortage of labor. The landowners, led by the British Honduras Company, attempted to acquire an adequate supply of labor by immigration. On 7 February 1860 the Assembly passed a bill to encourage immigration from China, but the British government disallowed it, not favoring emigration "to a Settlement exposed to so much risk of disturbance as British Honduras."[28] After the territory was declared a colony in 1862, however, assent was given to an act "designed to facilitate the immgration into the Colony of free negroes from the United States."[29]

In 1863, John Hodge, a major stockholder and manager of the British Honduras Company, went to London and Washington to arrange for the immigration of black Americans who had been emancipated that year. Hodge brought four commissioners from the United States to examine the lands and circumstances in the colony and to report to the authorities in Washington. The official American agent in Belize, Dr. Charles Leas, did not favor the immigration proposals, however; he later stated that it was fortunate the American freedmen had not been sent to Belize "to be subjected to a species of slavery and demoralization far worse than ever existed in our country."[30] As a result, the U.S. government turned down the proposals.

Attempts were then made, with rather more success, to import Chinese laborers. In 1865, 474 Chinese immigrants arrived from Amoy and were put to work on the sugar estates, chiefly those of the British Honduras Company.[31] By 1868 "only 211 were left," over a hundred having died and about a hundred more having fled to the Santa Cruz Maya due to bad food, overwork, and cruel treatment by the manager of the British Honduras Company's estates on the New River.[32] The number of Chinese immigrants continued to decline in the following years. In 1869, Lieutenant Governor Longden mentioned "the small remnant of the Chinese immigrants still working on the larger estates, about 193 in number,"[33] and in the 1871 census only 133 persons were listed as having been born in China.[34]

A number of laborers were brought from the West Indian islands: for example, a good many came from Barbados in 1865.[35] In 1871, 905 people were listed in the census as having been born in the West Indies, though many of these may have been brought to Belize much earlier. Aware of the example set by Trinidad and Guyana, the big landowners also attempted to obtain laborers of Indian origin, but their efforts did not succeed until after 1871. In 1868, further legislation was passed to encourage the immigration of agricultural and other laborers into British Honduras. Commenting on this act, Longden reported that:

> By this act any person may import into this colony labourers from any place whatsoever... [and] shall receive from the Immigration Funds a bounty of one third of the passage money of such labourers, not exceeding, however, in any case £5 for a man or woman, or £3–6–8 for each child....
>
> If a few hundred negroes accustomed to the actual cultivation of the sugar-cane, can be brought from America or from any of our own colonies, where there is an excess in the supply of labour over the demand, I have reason to believe that sure and rapid progress would be made in agriculture. There appears to be no lack of capital

here . . . but the great want of all the landowners is a supply of labourers accustomed to the cultivation of the sugar cane.[36]

Since the export of timber was still more valuable than that of sugar, the big landowners kept the laborers of African origin at work in the forests and employed Maya and *mestizo* laborers on the northern sugar estates, and Caribs in the south. In 1869, Longden stated:

> In the Northern District the number of the population which appears to be increasing both from natural causes and by the influx of Indians from Yucatan, will perhaps be found able to furnish a sufficient number of labourers capable of being trained into efficiency. In the Southern district the planters must either import their labour or employ the native Charibs.[37]

The efforts at encouraging immigration having met with little success, Longden concluded in 1869 that "the principal difficulty in the way of an extended growth of Sugar on a large scale will probably be found to consist in the want of steady intelligent and reliable labour."[38]

The immigration plans of the 1860s were chiefly designed to bring nonwhite workers into the colony as agricultural laborers, but the colonial administrators also wanted to attract white immigrants who would become independent cultivators and establish estates. A clearly racialist double standard was operative: whites, even whites without capital, were perceived as independent and development-oriented, while all nonwhites were viewed simply as backward and dependent, suitable only to be organized as laborers by the whites.

Major efforts were made to attract Confederate planters from the southern United States, Lieutenant Governor Austin in particular being strongly committed to this policy. He is reported to have told the U.S. consular agent that the only hope for the future of the colony was southern immigration, and that if enough Confederates came to the colony, Great Britain would grant it independence.[39] Though the official price for Crown land remained five dollars an acre, Austin's enthusiasm for encouraging the immigration of white southerners led him to attempt to sell 500,000 acres of Crown land at Icacos for twenty cents an acre. It is clear from Austin's letter to the Colonial Office in 1867 regarding the Icacos grant that he was seeking not white persons with capital but "impoverished" whites:

> . . . the imperative necessity of making some provision for the immigrants who may soon be expected in very large numbers has compelled me to assume an individual responsibility and to act in a manner which in my opinion is only justly liberal towards those who are too much impoverished to be able to give much save in those physical services which will change this Colony from an unknown wilderness into a garden teeming with all the wealth & beauties of the tropics.[40]

The nonwhite population—Maya, Caribs, and Africans—who had pioneered agriculture in the colony and had changed areas like the Yalbac Hills from an "unknown wilderness" to an area of extensive cultivation, were either denied titles to land altogether or had to pay twenty-five times as much for Crown land as the white immigrants.

As well as virtually giving away Crown land to the Confederate refugees, Austin went out of his way to urge "the great landed proprietors of the Colony" to dispose of their lands to these "Anglo Saxon" immigrants. In 1867, he reported:

> At last... the great house of Young Toledo & Co. has been driven as well by the force of public opinion as by a proper appreciation of their own interests to alter their line of conduct, and... they are now offering 100 acres of land gratuitously to every male adult from the Southern States of America or of Anglo Saxon Origin who will settle on those lands on the Western Frontier which we are now heard of for the first time as being of unexampled richness and beauty.
>
> I need hardly point out... that if carried out to any extent such plans of immigration should not only benefit the Colony but be a great relief to the Imperial Government in the way of defence.[41]

In the colonialists' racialist scheme of things, only white settlers, whether humble homesteaders or big planters, were perceived as a source of agricultural development or as reliable in relation to defense. In the 1860s the western frontier was being secured, and the interior was perceived as suitable for colonization, but the interior, which had been agriculturally developed by the Maya, was to be settled by people "of Anglo Saxon Origin," while the Maya pioneers, like the Caribs and people of African origin, were to be dominated and dispossessed. The whole nonwhite population of the colony, and also nonwhite immigrants, were perceived only as potential wage laborers, to be organized and exploited by the whites, in relation to whom they would remain in a condition of perpetual dependency.

Many Confederate refugees came to the colony in the period from 1864 to 1870, but most of them went on to Guatemala or Honduras, or returned to the United States. Apparently the major reason for the refusal of these immigrants to remain in the colony was the high price of land. At first the price was maintained at five dollars (£1) per acre for both Crown and private lands, but in 1867 some of the landowners changed their policy and offered to sell land cheaply to the southerners. As already mentioned, Lieutenant Governor Austin was selling huge tracts in the south for a nominal sum, and the official price of Crown land was halved. Immigration of southerners was said to average fifty persons per month for the years 1867 to 1869, but by June 1869 the U.S. agent reported that the immigration had ceased, and that more were returning to the United States than were arriving.[42] In the end, very few of the southern immigrants remained in Belize. Some of those that remained (such as the group that formed the "Toledo Settlement" in the south[43]) acquired quite large areas of land and started agricultural estates, but in the long run their impact on agricultural development was minimal.

In summary, it may be said that there were two radically different and even contradictory conceptions of agriculture in Belize. The colonial elite, which had for so long been committed exclusively to the business of timber extraction, turned only belatedly to the possibilities of agriculture. When the colonial administrators and big landowners did concern themselves with agriculture, they considered only the large-scale production of tropical crops for export, and such a conception required large supplies of dependent agricultural wage laborers. Hence, schemes for the colonization of the interior, for the development of agriculture, and for mass immigration were simultaneously conceived in the 1860s. But in the meantime large numbers of Maya had reoccupied the western interior, where they developed extensive subsistence agriculture, and in the north the Maya and *mestizo* refugees of the *Guerra de las Castas* were producing corn, vegetables, and sugar cane as the tenants of the big landowners. The colonial schemes of the 1860s were developed at the expense of these small farmers and peasants, who, while independent, were perceived as a threat, but, reduced to dependency, could become wage laborers to be exploited on the plantations. In fact, though the conflict was resolved in favor of the white colonizers, their schemes for extensive immigration and agricultural development did not flourish. The population increase that occurred in the 1850s was not the result of immigration policies, and the immigration acts of the 1860s had little effect. As for agriculture, the pioneering aspirations and efforts of the Maya, Carib, and African peoples went unrecognized and unrewarded, while the efforts at plantation agriculture, though temporarily successful, soon faltered and declined, leaving the colony dependent once again on its timber resources.

LABOR CONDITIONS IN THE COLONY

Despite the decline in the mahogany trade that had taken place since the middle of the nineteenth century, the export of mahogany remained the primary economic base of the colony and the chief sector of employment. It is therefore worth quoting the lengthy and colorful account by Gibbs of the process of mahogany extraction, an account which shows that the technique and experience of forest work had changed little in over a century:

> A form of contract between the parties, called a hiring-sheet, is signed before the police-magistrate, according to the ordinance made and provided, and the labourer is bound until next Christmas—longer, of course, or shorter, if he chooses—to his employer. The gangs for mahogany works are generally from twenty-five to fifty strong, with one or more captains, carpenters, foremen, bookkeepers, and, over several works, a manager. The labourers are allowed to take their families with them, and seldom see town again until the season's toil is accomplished. Pork, flour, groceries, clothing for the hands, tools, and reserves necessary, are forwarded up to the banks by pitpans from Belize, and before the dry weather has fairly set in, work begins. . . .

The situation of the bank or work, the headquarters of the gang, depends on the operations of an individual called the "hunter," but it must necessarily be on an eligible site on the river. About the month of August, the huntsman or treefinder starts, machete in hand, to cut his way through the thick bush to some rising eminence, and, climbing the highest tree he can find, examines the surrounding forest. As at this season of the year, the leaves of the mahogany are of reddish-yellow tint, they are easily distinguishable by the hunter when making his survey. He is, where the lands he is working are not very clearly defined as to proprietory limits, compelled to proceed craftily, so as not to be over-reached, especially in placing his marks for recognition, by a rival. The trees are not found in clumps, but singly, sufficiently adjacent, however, to circumscribe the area of operations about to be undertaken.

The bank on the river being conveniently arranged to his discoveries, a main truck-path is opened up in their direction, with branch paths diverging right and left to the trees selected for felling that season. In determining this part of the year's plans, great judgement is required to avoid cutting paths to trees that will not pay for the time and labour necessary to clear a passage to them.

At the bank are the store-houses, bush dwellings, cattle-sheds, and "bar-quadier." The hands spend most of their time away in the bush, only meeting at the banks at certain intervals.

The truck-paths having been properly prepared and levelled—work generally given out in tasks of about 100 yards per man per day to clear—the hands are away in the bush, felling. The axe is applied to the trunk about twelve feet from its base, the axe-men standing on a platform skillfully constructed, and attached to the tree. At the moment of falling, a firm nerve and quick eye is required to avoid accidents, which do sometimes occur. The tree felled, the branches are lopped, and they with the trunk reduced from their rounded to a four-sided form. But there they lie, huge cumbersome timber-giants, and the river, eight or ten miles off, on whose bosom they are to float, sometimes with a sluggish current, anon at a speed of ten miles an hour.

There are two, or properly speaking, three, modes of hauling the precious logs from the depths of their native forests, and of course it depends entirely on the nature of the country and the distance from navigable waters, which mode has to be adopted. Rolling is the original process, long followed with pecuniary success, before cattle-trucks and truck-paths were found necessary. Sliding on skis is practised where the lie of the country, the ground declining gradually to the bank, will admit the logs being hauled over skids, and it is adopted in bringing out the wood from the branch paths into the main truck-path. Trucking is, of course, where the logs are hoisted on to suitably-constructed vehicles, which run on broad wooden truck-wheels, the hindmost higher than the foremost pair. The three modes of carrying away the logs are frequently combined, a season's cuttings being got out partly by trucking, partly by rolling and sliding. To a gang of forty hands there will be a complement of six trucks, with a team of seven or eight pairs of oxen, and two drivers to each truck. The mahogany logs are elevated on the trucks by inclined platforms, the logs having been sawn into sizes to equalize the loads for the yokes of oxen. Twelve men are told off, in trucking, to load, and sixteen to cut food for the teams and to perform miscellaneous duties on the works.

> Night is the time selected for trucking out, and the scene is an animated and characteristic one.
>
> Upon the heavy background of the dense, tropical foliage, the torches carried by the workmen make a flickering clear-obscure, by whose light their dusky forms, naked to the waist, are made phantasmagorically visible, moving round the huge, inert mass of timber as it lies on what may readily be mistaken for a gigantic catafalque, while the patient oxen wait for the crack of the driver's whip, and the shouts of the gang break the deathlike stillness of the surrounding forest. The signal given, the whole rude cavalcade starts off at a rapid pace, with wild whoopings, crackings, and shouts, for the river's bank.
>
> The logs once arrived at the bank, they are roughly squared on the river "barquadier," "manufactured," the hands call it; but this work is frequently postponed until the timber arrives at the river-mouths, where are more extensive and convenient "barquadiers," especially when advantage has to be taken of sudden high flood....
>
> On the Old River, the logs are floated down independently until they reach the point called the Boom, twenty-three miles up-river from Belize, where they are collected, formed according to marks into small rafts as wanted for shipment, and thence floated to Belize, to be towed alongside the vessels. Previously to being shipped, the "butts" and "fans" are sawn off, the wood further (sometimes entirely) prepared for shipment, bad wood picked out, and the good measured by sworn measurers.[44]

Apart from the migratory gangs, chiefly composed of Creoles whose permanent residence was in the town of Belize, the population of the Northern District consisted largely of recent immigrants from Yucatán, and in the Southern District the majority of the people were Caribs. To what extent did the laboring people of Belize, of different racial and ethnic origin, and living in different districts, experience different living and working conditions? An evaluation of this intriguing problem is made possible by a group of reports made by the District Magistrates in 1870 on the general conditions and treatment of laborers in their districts.

According to the official census of 1861, the number of people living in the Northern District (13,547) was over half the total population of the settlement (25,635).[45] Lieutenant Governor Austin reported in 1864 that there were 2,883 people on the Rio Hondo and 10,664 on the New River, and "of these 3933 are pure Indians, 1129 Spanish and 6737 Mixed, and consequently with exception of the wood cutting gangs which are migratory, & consist to a great extent of Creoles, there is but little labour available in the rivers, save for the Yucatecan & Indian villages scattered here and there on the banks."[46] At a time when sugar estates were expanding in the north, the question of a labor supply was of great concern. Austin commented that both "Medical & Magisterial supervision in the New River... are even now lamentably deficient" and he expressed his desire "of placing the rights of employers & employed generally on a more satisfactory basis. I had several opportunities of observing how at such a distance masters could be successfully defied by their people, & how in many ways the labourer was completely at the mercy of his employer."[47] It is apparent from the report of Edwin Adolphus, the Magistrate at Corozal, on the treatment of the Indian laborers five years later, that "Magisterial supervision" meant enforcing the rights of employers, not of the employed. *All* of the 286 cases decided by him under the colony's labor laws in 1869 consisted of discipline imposed upon the employees: 245 were punished for "absenting themselves from work without leave," 30 for "insolence and disobedience," 6 for "assaults on masters and book-keepers," and 5 for "entering into second contracts before the expiry of the period of former ones."[48]

Though the Magistrate clearly functioned in his legal capacity as an instrument of discipline for the employers against the employed, his report on labor conditions is not uncritical of the behavior of the employers, and particularly of the advance and truck systems whose use had been extended from the mahogany cutters to the Maya and *mestizo* agricultural laborers. Adolphus stated that the *mozos,* or "Indian labourers," were "without exception, always in debt to their Employers," and he described the causes and effects of their indebtedness:

> During the annual fair, held in Corozal at Christmas, when much carousing takes place, the greater part of the mozos squander their money advances for the following year: the advances in goods are usually supplied after Christmas on their proceeding to work.
>
> The system of advances to which they have become so accustomed, and without which the Indians cannot be got to hire, is the main drawback to their regular attendance to work; for, knowing at the commencement of their engagements that they already are in debt, the chief incentive to labour is thereby removed. The Employer, though able of course to cause the idle to be arrested and punished by the Magistrate, is frequently deterred from so doing by reason of the great probability that, on liberation from gaol, the recently punished Indians will take the earliest opportunity of crossing the border into Yucatan, but a few miles distant, where the Indian Commandants gladly receive them.... There are at present scores of runaway mozos living on the opposite bank of the Rio Hondo, who are largely indebted to their former masters, some of whom have actually been ruined by this practice. Another reason that they are so seldom imprisoned for misconduct, as compared with the black laborers, is that they are paid by the task and not by the month as are the latter....
>
> The Spanish system of hiring, or as I may truly call it semi-slavery, was originally brought to this Colony by the Yucatecans when they took refuge here, some twenty years back, after having been driven out of Bacalar by the Indians. It is still practised to a great extent. The Indian laborers, all being overwhelmed with debt, become regarded, in course of time, as a portion of the value of the various ranchos or Estates on which they live and work, and actually themselves imagine, in many instances, that they have no right to leave the same unless they satisfy their Master's heavy claims against them, which belief is naturally of course much fostered by the employers, as it is their principal security for the payment of the servants' debts ... but if the mozo fails to obtain, within a limited period, a new

master, who will pay the debt for him, he unhesitatingly returns to the old service under the impression that there, and no where else, is he obliged to work.... it is always clearly understood between the Indian and the Ranchero, when the latter pays the debt of the former, that before he can leave his new Master's service he must repay either in cash or by labour the heavy money advance made ... a complaint by an Indian against his master is a matter of very rare occurrence indeed.[49]

The debt peonage created by the advance system, combined with rents for annual tenancies in a context of land monopolization and a truck system in which the workers receive "the greater portion of their wages in goods," did amount to semi-slavery. But Adolphus was wrong in placing the responsibility for the introduction of this system upon the Yucatecan refugees. Though a similar system had been practised in Yucatán, it had existed in the settlement long before the immigration of the Yucatecans. The combination of the advance and truck systems had been utilized by employers to control the Creole laborers in mahogany gangs even before, but particularly after, emancipation in 1838. In fact, Adolphus stated that "the Creoles and Caribs receive about the same advances as the Indians, from three to four months—half goods, half cash," but that their contracts were attested before a Magistrate. When breaking a contract, they were likely to be brought to the summary court, charged with "non-performance of tasks, disobedience, absenting themselves from their work, sick and idle time etc." The Creoles and Caribs were actually more likely to be punished for such infractions than were the Indians because escape was more difficult for them. Thus we see that the relative ease of escape, the deterrent that had to some extent mitigated the masters' harsh treatment of slaves, also influenced the behavior of the employers of the *mozos* in the 1860s.

The living conditions of Maya and Creole laborers were said to be similar: "Their houses, or rather hovels, are... entirely devoid of any the slightest appearance of comfort." Adolphus stated that the Creoles and Caribs received more substantial rations than the *mozos*—"four pounds of salt pork or fish and fifty plaintains per week"—but that they also received "nominally much larger tasks than the Indians." According to Adolphus, "the Indian labourers... are much sought after," and he gave four reasons: first, "cheapness"—their rations consisted of only twelve quarts of corn per week; second, they were considered to be "tractable and obedient... more easily managed than the Creoles and Caribs"; third, "they finish their work in a better style than the other laborers, although they perform less"; fourth, "they will work at night willingly where but seldom the blacks can be got to do so. In fact they will attend for weeks together, during the night, at the mill without murmuring."

The problem facing the employers was the organization of a plantation labor force among people whose work experience had been either slave labor in the mahogany forests or primitive subsistence cultivation. While the laborers could be made thoroughly dependent upon their employers through the imposition of rents and the use of the advance and truck systems to induce indebtedness, such dependency did not ensure their regular attendance or disciplined behavior at work. The employers seem to have preferred the *mozos* for plantation labor because they perceived them as more amenable to discipline, though less susceptible to punishment, than the blacks.

Adolphus described how the Creoles, receiving their advances in Belize town, "fritter away every fraction on their mistresses" and arrived at their place of work broke and requesting further advances. The employers generally refused to make further advances, so "at the very commencement of their contract a spirit of disaffection and disinclination to work" was engendered and the employers resorted to the Magistrate "to enforce the fulfilment of the contracts." The employers, judging that the blacks would quit at the end of their contract whether they remained in debt or not, did not extend advances exceeding the value of their labor, with the result that the blacks were generally free from debt at the termination of their contracts. "The black labourers... knowing full well that, at the expiry of their contracts, they cannot be detained, cause, but too frequently, considerable trouble by impertinence and disobedience," while the *mozos*, encouraged to believe that they had "to continue working in the respective estates until the debts they have contracted are liquidated," were more easily intimidated and disciplined. However, it was thought that there was a limit on the punishment it was profitable to apply to the Maya, because a runaway *mozo* was of no value to a plantation.

The Magistrate at Orange Walk on New River, Downer, wrote a similar report of labor conditions in 1869. He emphasized, however, that the Maya's "love of independence" and "reluctance to enter into written contracts of service" made them "not so easily imposed upon, as some persons are inclined to think.... Those that seek employment, or are prevailed upon to undertake it, are perhaps barely equal, numerically, to those that remain at home."[50] Downer also described wages, indebtedness, and the functioning of the truck system:

> The average rate of wages paid to Indian laborers varies with the nature of the work they are required to perform. For cutting logwood, which is their principal occupation, they are paid at the rate of three dollars per ton with rations, or four dollars, they feeding themselves. The mule drivers, or those employed in bringing out the logwood, are paid at the rate of ten dollars per month with rations. For ordinary labor, such as working on the ranchos etc. they are paid according to the work done... average at the rate of from $7 to $8 per month, and rations....
>
> There is... a considerable percentage charged upon goods supplied to a laborer.... the Indian laborer is scarcely ever out of debt... even where an estate laborer signs for all cash, he generally places himself in the same position as one who hires "half and half," by taking from the Estate's store such goods as he stands in need of.[51]

The wages were not only low, they were also frequently paid partly in rations, or "half and half," a practice that was obviously to the advantage of the employer. But even when the laborer was paid entirely in cash, the charges for goods at the estate's store would be excessive, thereby benefiting the employer and leading inevitably to the indebtedness and further dependency of the employees.

The Magistrate of the Southern District, referring to the truck system, stated that it was the same in the south as throughout the colony, "and has the same baneful effect here, as elsewhere."[52] The custom of providing a portion of the wages in goods was being discontinued on the two principal sugar estates (Regalia and Seven Hills, belonging to Young Toledo & Co.), the men being said to be "more satisfied to take Six dollars per month in cash, than eight dollars half in goods and half in cash." The account of the wages paid to laborers on the Regalia estate shows a large differential according to skill and also according to race, the Chinese being the most poorly paid workers. Out of a total of 187 employees, 148 were Creoles and Caribs, 32 "Spaniards," and 7 Chinese. Seventy-nine of the Creoles and Caribs received from six to seven dollars in cash per month, and sixty-one of them received from seven to eight dollars per month, half in cash and half in goods. Ten of the Spaniards received six dollars in cash per month, and twenty of them received from seven to eight dollars, "half and half." Of the seven Chinese workers, six received only four dollars in cash per month, the other getting seven dollars in "half and half." There were four "Captains," three of them Creole and one Spanish, who received between ten and twenty dollars in cash per month, and four Creole carpenters who received from thirty to forty dollars in cash per month. The most highly paid employee was a Creole carpenter who received fifty-five dollars in cash per month, or about fourteen times as much as the Chinese laborers. Laborers on the Seven Hills estate, consisting of 124 Creoles and Spaniards and 52 Chinese, were said to be "paid in the same proportion as those on Regalia Estate."[53]

The Police Magistrate in Belize, who was responsible for overseeing many of the labor contracts of mahogany workers, stressed in his report the impact of a recent decline in the mahogany trade. A decline in the demand for mahogany produced a decline in the demand for labor, leading in turn to increased unemployment, a reduction of wages and labor migration:

> The number of labourers always fluctuated more or less. In 1865 & 66 for instance, 1633 hands were employed . . . but 1868–69 2273 were hired, at reduced rates, of which no less than 685 received small advances in Cash; and in 1869–70 only 1169 have hired at somewhat lower wages, and with the same number of Cash advances; showing thereby the gradual decline of the Truck system, and the extent to which the fall in mahogany has affected the Labor market; and although a great number has left for the projected Railway at Puerto Caballo, in Spanish Honduras, the local Employers have obtained the full complement of the limited hands they required for the few remaining works in active operation.
>
> The disbanding of the 4th West India Regiment which threw about 90 extra hands into the labor market, and the abandonment of the mahogany works occurred almost simultaneously, about the middle of last year, and the rate of wages as well as of advances at once fell to a minimum, and would have continued so were it not for

the hands required for the Railway. The higher wages (all above $12) are given to Captains of Gangs, Tradesmen, and Mechanics.[54]

The gradual decline of the truck system resulted from the employers' perception that it was no longer required in a depressed market in which the supply of labor had become more than sufficient for their needs. When labor was scarce, the truck system was an intrinsic and vital part of the system of labor control instituted by the employer class, but, with a changed market, the employers themselves began to question the utility of a system that no longer functioned in their interests. The Police Magistrate in Belize described this situation in which the smaller mahogany cutters were getting squeezed out by their merchant suppliers, the latter being careful to protect themselves from a fall in the value of mahogany:

> A Merchant who has no land, agrees to disburse a mahogany Cutter who possesses land but no means, on condition of receiving in Belize all the wood cut at a certain fixed price. The mahogany Cutter hires his men, and the merchant advances them 3 to 4 months wages, half in cash and half in goods, at enhanced prices, and when he comes to settle he discounts 5 p cent on the goods in favor of the mahogany Cutter, and charges him 10 p cent Commission on the whole business. But those Houses who have mahogany works of their own (principally the British Honduras Company and Messrs. Young Toledo & Co. who possess between them, almost ⅔ of the Colony) dealt more liberally with their laborers with respect to the advances in Goods; and sometimes disbursed parties on more moderate terms, and gave permission to others, who had no lands, to cut in their Forests at the rate of 5$ for every tree felled.
> Since the abandonment however of the mahogany works the Truck System has been in some measure given up.... Employers are anxious to do away with the system altogether, and have made comparatively trifling advances this year, and appear to think that the Custom is so engrafted in the Labor system that nothing but Legislative enactment will effectually eradicate it.[55]

Needless to say, the changes in the market brought no benefits to the laboring class. In fact, the declining demand for labor meant that many more were unemployed, some had to seek work abroad, and those who were able to secure work in the colony were exploited as badly, if not worse, than before. In 1868 fifty-five employers hired 2,273 laborers in Belize town (70 percent of whom were paid in goods and cash, the remainder in cash only) and in 1869 twenty-two employers hired 1,169 laborers (56 percent of whom were paid in goods and cash). While the median cash wage in 1868 was eight dollars per month, it had fallen in the following year to six dollars, and the mean cash wage fell from nine dollars to seven dollars and fifty cents.[56]

Under the labor laws of the colony, the Magistrates could deal severely with laborers who broke their contracts or were disobedient. One man convicted of disobeying his overseer was sentenced to fourteen days of hard labor, and another, convicted of refusing to work and attempting to strike his employer, was fined one month's wages (eight dollars) and costs (two dollars). A laborer who hired himself to another employer before the expiration of his first contract was sentenced to two months of hard labor in Belize jail.[57] In 1868 and 1869, 146 cases were brought by the masters against servants at the police court in Belize. Only one of these cases was dismissed; a common punishment among the others was three months' imprisonment with hard labor. In the same period ten cases were brought by servants against masters, only one of these resulting in punishment, namely a two dollar fine.[58] The severity of the sentences and the lack of cases involving complaints by laborers against their employers show that the labor laws and the Magistrates who enforced them were operating to the distinct advantage of the employers and were chiefly a means of disciplining and controlling the labor force.

The high incidence of absenteeism, "neglect of work," and disobedience shown in the Magistrates' records is a demonstration of persistent dissatisfaction and discontent among the laborers and of continuing labor problems for the employers. Sometimes the discontent was expressed in the form of group action; strikes, though illegal, were utilized by the workers at critical moments of the production process in the attempt to improve their situation. An interesting example of this type of action is recorded in a case tried on 16 November 1869 by Magistrate Hamilton. One Lucas Howel and thirty others were tried for having left work "without leave or lawful excuse":

> The defendants were put by the Manager of Regalia Estate to cut canes by day work, which they did not like, wishing to work by task, but which the Manager would not consent to, as they hurried through their work and did not cut the canes properly. The defendants then left off working at 10 o'c in the morning and came down to Allpines to ask me to compel the Manager to give them task work.... I think their principal reason for striking was to try and frighten the Manager into what they wanted. This happened during crop and the Mill had to be stopped for the day. They were by my advice arrested and tried and I ordered each of them to pay their employers the sum of $2.50 and the costs of $1.50 which they consented to do, and the Manager agreed to stop it out of their wages.[59]

A number of voices were periodically raised against the advance and truck systems. Magistrate Adolphus gave his opinion that "until the present most pernicious truck system is abolished by legislative enactment, there will not, nor can not, be strict justice done between the master and servant."[60] A dozen years later Gibbs, in a lengthy description of the colony's employment practices, also called it "a most pernicious system":

> The first principle in this system ... is the advance of three or more month's wages at the time of hiring. The labourer engages himself some time during the Christmas holidays for the ensuing year at say nine dollars per month. But he has just entered upon, or is in the height of, his few weeks' annual festivity, and he and the woman he lives with, and the children, if any, require money "to keep Christmas."

He applies for, and is granted four months' advance of wages; probably taking three to begin with, and spending it out, returning for another month's advance. But by his agreement he is bound to take half of his wages in goods from his employer, who keeps in his store a stock of such goods as his hands require, and of a certainly inferior quality. First of all there is an undue advantage on the employer's side ... the evil of his purchasing in the dearest market, instead of being allowed to take his money where he likes, is the lesser one only; the greater is that he receives these goods and the cash in the middle of a saturnalia of dissipation, and the consequences are the hard cash disappears like butter before the sun, finding its way into the tills of the rumsellers. The goods are next sold at one half what he is charged for them; that money, or the greater part of it also disappears, and another advance follows. The labourer has therefore to start his year's engagement three, four, or even five months in debt. On the works the same rule of half goods half cash is pursued, but he sees no more cash although he gets goods. The bookkeeper of the gang keeps his account, debiting so much for every day he is absent from work, even for sickness, and exacting fines rigorously, the contract being in every way a tight one for the labourer. It is hardly necessary to add that when his season's work is over he finds himself in debt when he comes down to Belize for his Christmas spree. At no time is he capable of understanding his accounts clearly, and the time chosen for settling his year's accounts is when he is enjoying a continuous carousel ... the system is a most pernicious one in every way.[61]

Even though colonial administrators and colonial apologists like Adolphus and Gibbs could agree on condemning the perniciousness of the advance and truck systems, it was unreasonable to expect them to be abolished by legislative enactment. The Legislative Assembly and, after 1871, the Legislative Council were dominated by the great landowners and employers in whose interest it was to maintain a hiring and remuneration system that was "in every way a tight one for the labourer."

Fifty years after emancipation, the colony's handbook was humanely but vainly critical of the predominant employment practices:

It is well known that a system has prevailed in the colony unchecked ... of labourers being kept in debt by their employers for the purpose of securing a continuance of their labour, as such labourers consider themselves bound to serve until such debt is extinguished. Advantage has been taken ... to keep them in debt by either supplying them with goods or drink for the purpose, and they thus become virtually enslaved for life.[62]

Though the institution of slavery had been declared abolished half a century previously, the laborers of Belize, whether Maya, Carib, or Creole, plantation or forest workers, were far from being emancipated. The so-called free laborer, like the slave, remained "completely at the mercy of his employer."

10
The Political Economy: The Dominance of the Settlers, 1765-1830

THE PROBLEM OF THE COLONIAL SETTLERS

The history of Belize is a classic tale of colonial dependency and exploitation. The demands of the metropolitan market created the raison d'être for colonial occupation and settlement, and the changing needs of the market crucially affected the system of land tenure, the pattern of land use, and the structure of land distribution.[1] The developing colonial economy required a large and dependent labor force, resulting in massive immigration and dispossession, coupled with a variety of coercive measures to control the laborers. One way of ensuring the continued dependence of the laborers upon their employers was through the monopolization of land ownership, a feature of the Belizean political economy that, leading to the underutilization of both land and labor, perpetuated the dependence of the entire economy upon the metropole. The demands of metropolitan capitalism have thus created and perpetuated the dependent satellite economy of Belize: the development of the former is structurally linked with the underdevelopment of the latter.

The political economy of a colonial society is not an autonomous reality, therefore, but an intrinsic part of the whole metropolis/satellite system. The history of a colonial society can be adequately understood only within the relevant systemic whole of the greater capitalist system of which it is a part. But it must not be assumed that the metropolis/satellite system is reflected in a dichotomous social structure consisting simply of the imperialists and the colonized. Such a simplistic conception not only fails to appreciate important distinctions within the social structure of the metropolis, but it is also a deficient conception of the social structure of the colonized society. Such "traditional schemas," according to Arghiri Emmanuel, are characterized by "their failure to recognize a third factor that intervenes between imperialist capitalism and the peoples of the exploited countries, i.e., the colonialists themselves."[2] The colonialists themselves, in other words, constitute a social formation capable of acting as an independent factor in the imperialist process. Settler communities, in particular, distinguished from the colonized peoples by economic, political, cultural, and racial qualities, and often highly cohesive internally, are capable of undertaking significant societal action.

The colonial settlers clearly exist in an antagonistic relationship with the colonized peoples—their entire raison d'être consists of the exploitation of such peoples—but Emmanuel has stressed that "the most difficult struggles of the imperialist countries since the 18th century had not been with the natives in their colonies but with their own settlers."[3] The problem that requires further illumination is: What are the circumstances under which, and what is the extent to which, the settler communities come into conflict with the metropolitan interests?

In analyzing the reasons for the decolonization of Africa since the Second World War, Emmanuel has argued that "the *extraordinary haste* with which independence was granted in many cases, particularly in the Congo . . . can only be explained by a positive motive, i.e., the home countries' need at a certain moment *to steal a march on their own settlers who were threatening nearly everywhere to secede and form White States.*"[4] While this generalization may be valid in several instances, there are other examples of recent decolonization in which it appears inappropriate, particularly in those cases where *the struggle between the colonial settlers and their home countries was fought, and lost by the settlers, in the nineteenth century*. It can be demonstrated that Belize is such a case.

THE SETTLER OLIGARCHY

While the number of settlers in Belize remained small, and profits from the logwood trade remained lucrative, the settlers made little attempt to formalize their customs or to regulate their occupation and disposal of land. With the drastic decline in the profitability of logwood in the 1760s, however, competition between the settlers increased, some of them, in the process, becoming indebted to London merchants and to the wealthier cutters and traders of the Bay. The 1763 treaty having given the British the right to extract logwood from the Bay of Honduras, the British government took a tentative step toward controlling the situation by having Admiral Burnaby codify the settlers' customs and establish a rudimentary civil government with an official blessing. At the same time, in 1765, the settlers passed resolutions defining their method of making a logwood location, and they assumed the authority to allocate lands to themselves. Though the treaty's assertion of Spanish sovereignty precluded the establishment of an unequivocal system of freehold tenure, the settlers being granted merely usufructory rights to the logwood trees in the settlement, the logwood works allocated by their regulations soon came to be treated as freehold property. They were sold, devised, and dealt with in all respects as such from at least 1765 on.[5]

However, just at the time that the settlers were given the right to cut logwood and had devised an appropriate system of land distribution, overproduction for a limited market produced such a drastic fall in prices that the market price did not cover the expenses incurred in sending logwood to Europe.[6] By 1765, however, mahogany accounted for about a quarter of the total value of exports, and by the 1770s it was by far the more important export. Though mahogany remained the chief export of Belize for almost two hundred years, the demand for it, and consequently its price, fluctuated enormously on the English market, with the result that the economy of Belize was chronically unstable. As Gibbs expressed it in the late nineteenth century, "an admiralty board could send the market up at once by advertising for tenders: a change in the taste for furniture to maple or black walnut, would send it down for years."[7]

At the beginning of the nineteenth century the mahogany exported from Belize amounted to about three and one-half million feet annually, but in 1819 over six million feet were exported. That peak was followed by a slight decline over the next six years, but 1826 and 1827 were boom years, almost seven million feet of mahogany being exported in the latter year. That peak, in turn, was followed by a more serious decline, "in consequence of overtrading and a glut in the home market,"[8] which did not begin to reverse itself until about 1834. The second major export, logwood, though reaching a peak of over four thousand tons exported annually in 1824 and 1825, averaged only 2,650 tons per annum between 1819 and 1830, and never regained the importance it had held in the mid-eighteenth century (see table 10.1).

The shift from the preeminence of logwood to the preeminence of mahogany in the settlement's economy encouraged the tendency for control of the economy to concentrate in the hands of a few settlers, because the extraction of mahogany was a much larger-scale operation, requiring more land, labor and capital, than that of logwood. In 1787 just twelve of the old Baymen claimed possession of four-fifths of all the land between the Rio Hondo and the Sibun River,[9] or about two thousand square miles. They were able to claim all this land, despite the regulations specifying the size of mahogany works and limiting possession to no more than two in any one river,[10] because these regulations "were not complied with strictly; but were constantly evaded by means of fictitious, and collusive copartnerships, between the Masters or owners of Slaves, and their kind Servants."[11] By using such evasions, and by discriminating against the poor whites and free colored and blacks, most of whom were evacuees from the Mosquito Shore, a handful of old settlers were able to monopolize land ownership in the settlement before the end of the eighteenth century.

Superintendent Despard, having attempted to execute Lord Sydney's instructions that the Mosquito Shore evacuees were to be "accommodated with lands ... in preference to all persons whatever,"[12] came into conflict with these old settlers who successfully defied the authority of the Crown's representative,

TABLE 10.1 Exports of Mahogany and Logwood from Belize, 1798–1830

Date	Mahogany in 1,000 Superficial Feet	Logwood in Tons
1798	1,347	1,114
1799	3,355	2,712
1800	3,102	1,612
1801	3,061	1,216
1802	4,646	1,348
1803	4,582	1,544
1804	....	....
1805	2,434	1,268
1806–18	....	....
1819	6,142	2,112
1820	5,692	1,895
1821	4,234	1,830
1822	....	....
1823	4,250	3,562
1824	5,574	4,391
1825	5,083	4,166
1826	6,386	2,602
1827	6,905	1,853
1828	5,462	1,278
1829	4,631	1,767
1830	4,557	2,696

SOURCES: 1798–1802, "A Short Sketch of the present situation of the Settlement of Honduras..." by Supt. Barrow, 31 March 1803, CO 123/15; 1805, Br. Gen. Montresor to Gov. Coote, 22 Oct. 1806, CO 123/17; 1803, 1819–21, 1823–30, Quarterly Returns of Exports from Belize, in CO 123/15, 123/16, 123/28–31, 123/34–42.

particularly on the crucial question of the authority to allocate lands. Given official permission to extract mahogany by the Convention of London in 1786, the Baymen felt their monopoly threatened by the arrival of the first appointed Superintendent and the relatively large number of evacuees. After the resolutions regarding mahogany works were passed in 1787, Despard commented on the concentrated possession of land by a few settlers, noting "the partiality of this law to rich people," and pointing out that "there being in the River Wallix [Belize] not above sixty miles of Mahogany ground in length, which according to this rule would be entirely occupied by a very few of the old Settlers."[13] Despard explained how the old settlers managed to control the land between the Belize and Sibun rivers, which had just been allocated under the 1786 Convention:

> Until the late Convention, the cutting Mahogany was always held even by the Old Baymen to be contraband, and, therefore, they cut it where ever they could find it; and they now claim all the wood which they can find in or near the Places which they formerly held in this illegal manner.... Messrs. Hoare, O'Brien, McAuley, Bartlett, Potts, Meighan, Armstrong, Davis, Tucker and Sullivan and Garbutt... alone possess at least nine parts in Twelve of the present augmented District.[14]

In 1791, after he had been recalled from the settlement, Despard wrote that "the district both old and new was so taken up by the Old Settlers, that not one of the

Mosquito Shore or other new Settlers have to this day been able to get a Mahogany work of any value, without purchasing it from some old Bayman."[15] The few wealthy old settlers were thus able to negate Sydney's instructions to Despard, defy the authority of the Crown's representative, and continue to allocate land to themselves.

When Superintendent Arthur arrived in 1814, he discovered a situation in which the monopoly of land ownership existed as part of a monopoly of power in the political economy of the settlement. The chief settlers, through their Public Meetings and magistracy, had succeeded in defying the authority of Superintendents since 1787, when they had asserted their power to dispose of the land against the clear instructions of Lord Sydney. A handful of the settlers had used this authority to secure for themselves almost all of the available land, and this in turn increased their power vis-à-vis the Superintendent and the other inhabitants of the settlement. To resolve the conflict over the location of executive authority in favor of the colonial administration, it was first necessary to break the monopoly of the few wealthy settlers over the land.

By 1814 the problem of the authority to allocate land was more urgent than ever, since the de facto limits of the settlement by then extended much farther to the south than the boundaries permitted by the Convention of 1786. Except for the town of Belize and St. George's Cay, none of the lands in the settlement were yet recognized or treated as Crown lands because of the reservation of Spanish sovereignty in the treaties. If the settlers were to maintain their power to dispose of the land, the entire enlarged settlement would soon be claimed by the same small group of wealthy cutters. By 1816, Arthur had come to the conclusion that drastic action was necessary and suggested to Earl Bathurst that the Crown be made the only authority competent to dispose of land in the settlement. Arthur explained that there was

> ... a monopoly on the part of the monied cutters, to the almost entire exclusion of the poorer class of His Majesty's subjects.... an adventurer explores the interior, discovers a Batch of Wood, fells a Tree, which is considered sufficient to give a Title to the Lot, or Work ... which he afterwards disposes of as his property to some more wealthy Cutter, and this possession is acquired without any communication whatever being made to the King's Superintendent, regardless of the district being within or without the British Limits.[16]

Apart from his concern at the monopolization of land in the settlement, his goal being to "prevent any undue advantage being taken by the opulent over the poorer Class of Settlers,"[17] Arthur doubtless felt that in Belize, though it was not yet officially recognized as a colony, the Crown, not the settlers themselves, should have the authority to dispose of the land. He therefore advocated that "the Cutters should be called upon to register in the Superintendent's Office, all their Works in the Country—their Titles to such Works, and whether they have been confirmed to them as Grants from the Crown; and that, in future, no occupancy shall be esteemed valid, without a Grant from His Majesty through His Representative in this Settlement."[18]

The Dominance of the Settlers, 1765-1830   161

Bathurst approved of Arthur's suggestion and authorized him not to permit "any occupation of Land at Honduras without the Sanction of the Superintendent being previously and formally obtained under his written authority specifying the extent and situation of the Land to be occupied."[19] Bathurst's instruction effectively countermanded the authority assumed by the Public Meeting on 24 July 1787, when it was declared "that the inhabitants of this country are adequate to the division of the lands, works, or other emoluments and privileges, granted to them by the definitive treaty or convention,"[20] and made the Crown, through the Superintendent, the sole authority to dispose of lands. Arthur accordingly issued a proclamation on 18 October 1817 forbidding any future appropriation of land by location and requiring all settlers to state under what title the lands they claimed were held.[21]

The immediate effect of Arthur's proclamation was to designate all unclaimed land as Crown land, the authority to dispose of which lay exclusively with the Superintendent as the Crown's representative, and to require registration of existing claims within six months, stating under what title they were held, on penalty of their invalidation. Arthur perceived his proclamation as only the initial stage of a struggle to break the monopoly of the monied cutters—thus attempting what Despard had signally failed to achieve thirty years before. But Arthur was aware of the inadequate definition of the Superintendent's powers and prudently avoided any major confrontation with the settlers by confining his proclamation to future acquisitions of land. However, by demanding the registration of claims and a statement concerning under what title the works were held, Arthur sought to expose the basis of these titles and to obtain the information required to present a case for expropriation to London.

The registration of claims was to take place before 10 March 1818, and on 9 March 1818 Arthur appointed a commission "to examine into the several Claims of Lands, Works and Lots in the British Settlement of Honduras."[22] In providing the commission's terms of reference, Arthur referred to the proclamation's requirement that claims on land be registered, and continued: "And Whereas, in obedience thereto Returns have been made to the Secretary's Office, purporting to be the claims of Individuals to Such Property; and . . . it is expedient that the validity of such claims should be ascertained before any Title can be given on the part of the Crown. . . ."[23] Arthur thus revealed his intention of examining the claims put forward before deciding whether or not to issue Crown grants in support of such claims. In other words, all the claims were regarded as in jeopardy, and if some of them were later to be admitted, it would be the subsequent issuance of a Crown grant, and not the old location laws, that would give the claimant a proper and secure title. Arthur was therefore seeking to make the exclusive authority of the Superintendent regarding the allocation of land retroactive, by denying the authority of the Public Meeting and denying the monopolistic claims of the settlers, and then to expropriate the land and reallocate it by making Crown grants.

The commissioners' report being completed by July 1820, Arthur sent it to

London with a covering letter interpreting the results and supporting his case for imposing the Crown's authority on all the lands in the settlement. Referring to Despard's attempt to follow Sydney's instructions in settling the Mosquito Shore evacuees, Arthur commented:

> The Resolutions by which they professed to be governed (which the Old Settlers for their further advantage soon found it convenient to break through in several important points) were of course framed so as to confirm the usurpation of the Old Settlers to the great injury of the Inhabitants from the Mosquito Shore and almost to the total exclusion of all other His Majesty's Subjects.[24]

Referring to the 1787 resolution that "no person shall possess more than two Mahogany Works in any River,"[25] Arthur observed:

> ... the covetousness of the Old Settlers soon led them to break through it, for so soon as they had located one Work, and thereby obtained what they chose to consider freehold possession, they moved to another, so that by Location, or Purchase, or Bequest, or Partnership, or under some cloak or other there are Cutters who hold, at least, eight or ten Works, and, as the front line of a Work is no less than three miles, each must comprehend a very large tract of Country. ... such has been the rapacity of the Old Settlers, that, by the claims now before me, it does not appear there remains any unclaimed ground on which Mahogany is to be found.[26]

Arthur's argument was based upon the fact that the "covetousness" and "rapacity" of the settlers had led them, first, to usurp the authority to dispose of land and, second, to violate their own regulations in order to monopolize land ownership. Consequently, though the Superintendent had been invested in 1817 with the authority to dispose of land within the treaty limits, no lands of value remained unclaimed within that area, and the Superintendent was thus unable to grant land to those who required it. (For example, when the disbanded soldiers from the second and fifth West India Regiments arrived in 1817 and 1818, Arthur located them around Manatee Lagoon, south of the Sibun River and outside the treaty limits, without giving them formal grants of land. Consequently, the descendants of these old soldiers still suffered from insecurity of tenure fifty years later when Lieutenant Governor Longden suggested that he should be authorized to give them gratuitous Crown grants of the plots of land in their possession.)[27]

Arthur's sweeping recommendations were intended to abolish the old settlers' monopoly and give substance to the Superintendent's authority to allocate land:

> ... no Cutter shall possess more than two Works at one time ... and he should hold those under a Grant from the Crown, only so long as he Chooses to fell Wood thereon. ... no Lands or Works whatever shall be considered Freehold Property, unless specially granted as such by His Majesty's Representative, in His Majesty's Name. ... This, whilst it would place Cutters in the full temporary possession of such Lands as they require for cutting Mahogany and Logwood, so long as it is in

The Dominance of the Settlers, 1765-1830

> their interest to hold them for that purpose, would also admit the Inhabitants and Settlers in general to enjoy, as Freehold Property, such land as they may require either for their Dwellings, or, for the purpose of cultivation.[28]

Had Arthur's recommendations been effected, a more equitable distribution of land, based upon the capacity for its utilization, might have resulted—but this did not occur. When Arthur was preparing to leave the settlement in 1822, he reported that he had not issued any grants because the British government had not reached a decision on the commissioners' report,[29] and in 1831 Superintendent Cockburn requested in vain that Arthur's recommendations be implemented. Cockburn recommended to the Secretary of State for the Colonies that

> ... no further delay should take place in a matter of such consequence and that your Lordship should direct that all Persons holding Mahogany or Logwood Works, Plantations or Town Lots should be called upon to send in returns of the same to the Superintendents Office with a view to giving regular Grants to those whose claims are valid.[30]

Cockburn's call for action, like Arthur's, went unanswered, and it was not until the 1850s that a regular system of land tenure was instituted in the settlement. The Laws in Force Act of 1855[31] provided retroactive legitimacy to ownership of land that had been appropriated prior to 1817, under the old location laws, thereby confirming the monopolistic distribution of land established during the preceding century.

Although Arthur failed in his attempt to destroy the monopoly of land ownership and to secure the invalidation of titles based on location, he did succeed in asserting the Crown's sole authority in respect to all future dispositions of unclaimed land. After his proclamation in 1817, therefore, no new locations were deemed to give valid titles to land. This fact is of great significance with respect to all the land south of the Sibun River and outside the treaty limits. Although some settlements had been made as far south as the Moho River by 1817, very little land south of the Sibun had been given over to locations, so most of this area was saved by Arthur from the "rapacity" and "covetousness" of the "monied cutters."[32]

A major reason for the indecision of the British government regarding Arthur's recommendations was its continuing reluctance to assert British sovereignty over the territory. The eighteenth-century treaties were very emphatic in reserving the sovereignty over the land to Spain, and while the settlers dealt with the land as though it were their freehold property, it was difficult for the British government to ignore a fundamental aspect of the treaties to which it was a signatory. Although the British government exercised a large degree of de facto sovereignty, particularly after 1796, it continued to vacillate until the 1840s, sometimes insisting on the fact of Spanish sovereignty while at other times taking actions which in effect asserted British sovereignty. (For example, Superintendents, responsible to the Governor of Jamaica, were regularly appointed after

1796; troops were stationed and fortifications built in Belize; and as early as 1809, land grants were made for town lots.)[33] The anomalous constitutional position of the settlement, which inhibited the British government from asserting its sovereignty and from defining and insisting on the authority of its representative, enabled the settlers to persist in their monopolistic control of the land.

Through their monopolization of the settlement's primary natural resource, a handful of settlers were able to dominate the economy. In fact, the same settlers who owned most of the land also owned most of the people, there being a great concentration of slave ownership. In 1790, twenty estates possessed between them over a thousand slaves, or about half of all the slaves in the settlement, while over one-fifth of the free heads of families possessed no slaves at all.[34] The 1816 census showed that a mere eleven free heads of families owned 1,013 slaves, while 108 owned 185 slaves and 125 owned none.[35] In other words, at the two extremes of the structure of slave ownership, 3 percent of the free heads of families owned 37 percent of the slaves, while 62 percent of the free heads of families owned less than 7 percent of the slaves.

The 1820 "Census of the Slave Population" recorded that 211 owners possessed 2,563 slaves, an average of 12 slaves each. The five biggest owners, however (Marshall Bennett, James and George Hyde, Grace Tucker Anderson, Thomas Paslow, and Potts and Farrell) possessed 669 slaves, or over one-quarter of the total, while 31 percent of the owners possessed a mere 4 percent of the slaves.[36] The biggest slave owner in the early nineteenth century was Marshall Bennett, who owned only 22 slaves in 1790 but had 211 slaves in 1816, 250 in 1820, 247 in 1823, 271 in 1826, 266 in 1829, and 253 in 1832; his proportion of the total slave population increased from 1 to 14 percent. The 1835 census showed an even greater inequality than that of 1816, 3 percent of the free heads of families owning 40 percent of the so-called apprenticed laborers and 81 percent of the free heads of families owning a mere 7 percent of the apprenticed laborers.[37]

The great concentration of ownership of both land and slaves in the hands of a few settlers encouraged the domination of the settlement's political economy by a tiny minority. An illustration of this phenomenon can be seen in the case of Marshall Bennett, who, in addition to being the biggest slave proprietor, acted as one of the Magistrates for twenty-two of the thirty years between 1798 and 1828,[38] and was the senior judge of the Supreme Court. He was a colonel of the militia, was the president of Arthur's commission on land, was frequently the chairman of the Public Meeting, and was one of the chief mahogany cutters and merchants of Belize. (Involved in a dubious company called the Eastern Coast of Central America Commercial and Agricultural Company, to which the Guatemalan government attempted to grant 14 million acres of Vera Paz and all the land between the Sibun and Sarstoon rivers in 1834, Bennett retired to Guatemala, where he was the most important British merchant, with interests in mining, manufacturing and shipping throughout Central America, where he lived until his death in 1839.)[39] Also important were the Hydes, James and his "colored" son, George. The 1790 census named James Hyde as a co-owner, with three others, of 82 slaves, and in 1816 he was named as the sole owner of 120 slaves. Subsequent censuses named James and George Hyde as the owners of a hundred slaves or more, making them among the largest proprietors of slaves in the settlement. In 1806 James Hyde was one of the Magistrates[40]; in 1814 his name appeared on several mahogany works on various rivers in Du Vernay's map of the settlement[41]; in 1818 he was one of the commissioners appointed by Arthur to report on land tenure; and he was later a Supreme Court judge. In 1830 he was the settlement's treasurer,[42] and in 1832 he was appointed the settlement's agent in the United Kingdom at an annual salary of £300.[43] Meanwhile, George Hyde, educated in England, well propertied in both land and slaves, and a successful merchant, was busily petitioning in London in 1827 for an extension of civil rights to his fellow "freeborn brethren of the mix'd race."[44] In 1830, Superintendent Cockburn wrote that George Hyde was "a Person of colour, but a more loyal, zealous or intelligent Inhabitant, the Settlement does not possess," and characterized him as one of "the Persons whose advice & assistance I should consider myself as likely to be most benefited by."[45] But in this same letter Cockburn stated:

> ... for some years past, the prosperity of this Settlement has been retarded by the influence of some five or Six Individuals who have monopolized the management of offices & held in subjection the rest of the Inhabitants.[46]

The monopoly in the management of the settlement's affairs about which Cockburn complained was the same phenomenon to which Despard had drawn attention almost half a century before, namely, the concentration of political and economic power in the hands of "a very arbitrary aristocracy."[47] This aristocracy kept the rest of the population in subjection by using its political power to enforce and maintain its economic monopoly. The Magistrates and their close associates not only owned most of the land and much of the population of the settlement, but were also "almost our sole importers, exporters, and retailers, too; and they had the equity to import, just what served themselves"; their "private purposes" involved "keeping the people poor and totally dependent upon them."[48] Some of the victims of the Magistrates' legislation complained that "these Laws or regulations seem also (to us) to be partial and in favour of one sett of people, and palpably calculated to enslave another,"[49] while Despard pointed out that many of the Mosquito Shore evacuees were "entirely excluded from any means of gaining a Subsistence, unless they will become the Servants of these Legislators, which really seems to be the principle intention of this partial rule."[50]

Through their total control of the settlement's political economy, therefore, the oligarchy of wealthy settlers controlled not only the slaves they owned but also the majority of the free population, white, colored, and black, by forcing them into a dependent situation. The wealthy settlers legislated against land acquisition by other free people in order to deny them an independent means of livelihood, thereby forcing them into some employment. The oligarchy monopolized landownership not in order to utilize all the land (which, despite their possession of hundreds of slaves, they could not do) but in order to deny its use to others.

Though the chief source of the wealth of the settler elite lay in the export of timber, their commercial activities, both within the settlement and with neighboring territories, were also important. Despard had mentioned their control of the import, export, and retail trades in 1788, and though the population of the settlement remained small, their monopoly of the internal market must have enabled them to engage in lucrative profiteering. Of developing importance, however, was the trade carried on between Britain and Central America via Belize.[51] While the neighboring territories were dominated by Spain, much of this trade was illegal, but during the 1820s the trade greatly increased, Belize becoming in the process something of an entrepôt.

Table 10.2 shows that the value of exports from the United Kingdom to Belize increased from about thirty thousand pounds in 1806 to almost eight hundred thousand pounds in 1829, much of this being reexported from Belize to Central America. Commission houses were established in Belize in 1824, and in 1825 the first British consul was appointed in Guatemala. An attempt was made to negotiate a commercial treaty between Britain and the Central American Republic in 1826, but this attempt, and a later effort in 1830, failed to bring official approval to the burgeoning and lucrative contraband trade. During the 1820s four-fifths of Central American trade went through Belize, the value of exports through Belize to Central America and certain Mexican ports being estimated at nearly £260,000 annually in the years 1825 to 1828.[52] Central America imported chiefly manufactured goods, such as cotton textiles, dry goods, and hardware, while the merchants in Belize bought and exported indigo and cochineal (used for dyeing in the booming English cotton industry) and other natural products such as sarsaparilla and tortoise shell.

Although some of the old settlers, like Marshall Bennett, were able to exploit these expanding trade opportunities, most of the merchants of Belize

TABLE 10.2 Value of Exports from the United Kingdom to Belize, 1806, 1823, 1829

Date	British Manufactures and Produce (in pounds sterling)	Foreign and Colonial Merchandise (in pounds sterling)	Total
1806	27,010	2,723	29,733
1823	342,940	14,893	357,833
1829	753,710	38,568	792,278

SOURCE: Memorial from London Merchants to Lord Goderich, 20 Sept. 1832, CO 123/43.

The Dominance of the Settlers, 1765-1830   167

lacked the contacts and credit, and probably the skills and initiative as well, to survive in this entrepôt business. The Commission houses were established by British commercial companies specifically to trade with Central America and hence were in competition with the settler-merchants of Belize. During the 1820s, therefore, the expanding trade between Britain and Central America, while providing some opportunities for the established settler-merchant oligarchy of Belize, also introduced a direct conflict between these settlers and metropolitan commerical companies.

Until about 1830, the leading settlers controlled not only the land, labor, and commerce of the settlement, but also the instruments of its government and the agencies of its administration. In the late eighteenth and early nineteenth centuries the Superintendents were placed in a weak and anomalous position when opposed by a united and determined merchant/mahogany-cutter settler elite. As late as 1838, James Stephen stated: "The Crown is represented by a Superintendent who is not much more than a Looker-on, and who supplies the want of authority by dexterity and address in acquiring and using influence over the general meeting and the Magistracy."[53] It is true that the authority of the Superintendent was never clearly defined by the British government, but it is inadequate merely to say that "the basic weakness of his position was implicit in the lack of authority delegated to him,"[54] implying that a clearer delegation of authority would have resolved the problem. Because Britain had agreed not to create any formal government in the Bay settlement and, through the first decades of the nineteenth century, was unwilling to assert its sovereignty over Belize, the commission issued to the Superintendent was always phrased in very general terms, providing him with no specific rights, powers, or privileges. But this ambiguity in the location of executive authority only became a *problem* when the Crown's representative was challenged by the settlers.

The first Superintendent, Despard, had, after all, been given specific authority to dispose of land to the new settlers—but the old settlers successfully challenged and annulled that authority. The instructions given to succeeding Superintendents appear to have been oriented less toward avoiding misunderstanding with the Spaniards than toward avoiding confrontation with the settlers. For example, in 1810 Lord Liverpool instructed Colonel Smyth, on his appointment as Superintendent, that "His Majesty's Subjects shall be left in the full enjoyment of their ancient Customs in the convening of public Meetings, the election of Magistrates and other Public Offices; and in the raising and application of the Money required for the public Service."[55] Since just two years earlier the sum voted annually by the Public Meeting for the Superintendent had been withheld from Superintendent Hamilton because of his unpopularity with the settlers, the settlers' control over finances—a control authorized by the British government—gave them control over the Superintendent. As late as 1829, Superintendent Codd, in response to an instruction from the Secretary of State that he should pay himself an annual salary of £1,000, complained that as all expenditure of the settlement's funds remained in the hands of the Magistrates, he could not actually pay himself a salary at all.[56]

The problem was not so much that the British government had delegated insufficient authority to the Superintendent, but rather that it had recognized the authority assumed by the settlers. Only gradually, and largely as a result of the action of particular Superintendents, did successive holders of the position acquire more power—power that, just as gradually, came to be accepted and supported by the Colonial Office. Superintendent Arthur, for example, made use of proclamations on important issues[57] such as the treatment of slaves, the illegal enslavement of Indians, and the allocation of lands, and though his instructions did not specify the use of such an instrument, succeeding Superintendents periodically issued proclamations as a means of exercising an assumed legislative authority. In this way, the authority of the Superintendent was expanded, but at the expense of, and only after conflict with, the settlers.

One of the most frequent loci of disputes concerned the Superintendents' use of their military authority. Until 1851, the Superintendents were all military men seconded from their regiments, usually for two or three years, to supervise the settlement. In part these disputes arose because of the attitude taken by men of military training toward the administration of the settlement (Superintendent Hamilton, for example, stated in 1807 "I consider this completely to be a Garrison Town"[58]), but the problem was also caused by the ambiguous constitutional status of the settlement. It was not clear whether or not the courts of the settlement were actually legally established tribunals, such as those of the West Indian colonies, and there was consequently much dispute as to whether military offenders could be tried in civilian courts[59] or civilians tried by court martial.[60] In 1812 the law officers of the Crown advised Lord Liverpool, in response to a query concerning the competence of the settlement's courts, that "we cannot trace the authority of the Magistrates at Honduras, or the Laws by which their decisions are governed, to any legal origin, and therefore we do not conceive that such decisions can be legally enforced."[61] In other words, the strict view being expressed was that the courts could be established only through the authority of the British Parliament and Crown, not simply by the mutual consent of the settlers. The settlers' judicial system, nevertheless, continued to exist and function.

In the matter of the judicial system, as in that of land tenure, the period during which Superintendent Arthur and Earl Bathurst were in office saw some important changes. In 1815, Bathurst directed that while the ancient customs of the settlement were to continue to be enforced, the powers of the civil courts were to be restricted. Criminals could be punished only by fines, imprisonment, or transportation, and the civil authorities were to have no jurisdiction over military and naval personnel in civil or criminal cases.[62] While Bathurst's directions certainly clarified the limits of civil jurisdiction, they did not specify the proper procedure to be undertaken in cases of murder and other crimes subject to

The Dominance of the Settlers, 1765-1830   169

the death penalty. Consequently, when, in 1817, it became known that a slave had "during the late Xmas made an attempt upon the life of one of the oldest Magistrates in the Country," Arthur reported to Bathurst: "It is not probable that the inability of the Bench to proceed against offences of so serious a nature can be kept long a secret from the lower orders of this extensive community, and the consequences are certainly to be dreaded when the Slave Population are apprized of it. . . . Crimes of this nature, which have been so frequent of late, will accumulate upon us very fast."[63] The following year the Public Meeting drew attention in a petition to the fact that "there is no Authority by which the hand of the Assassin can be legally stayed,"[64] and Arthur supported their petition. The outcome was the passing, in June 1819, of the "Act for the Punishment of Certain Offences in the Bay of Honduras" and the establishment of a Supreme Court in Belize the following year.

The establishment of the Supreme Court in 1820 was an act of great significance not only for the judicial system but also in the broader political-administrative structure. The court, consisting of four or more persons issued with a Royal Commission, was limited in its jurisdiction to the consideration of murder, manslaughter, rape, robbery, and burglary, and therefore filled most of the gaps (except the offense of attempted murder) existing in the prior judicial system. The act was more important, however, in that it constituted legislation in the British Parliament of formal government institutions in Belize without either prior consultation with or subsequent complaint from Spain. It thus amounted to an effective and unchallenged assertion of British sovereignty over the territory of Belize—*before* Central America achieved its independence from Spain.

Of even greater importance to our current concern with the political-economic structure of the settlement, however, is the fact that this court was the only legally established tribunal in the settlement (and, until 1862, it remained so). Despite this fact, the Colonial Office permitted the continued existence of the other civil courts, thereby implicitly authorizing the persistence of the settlers' own judicial system alongside that established by the British government. These other courts, the Grand Court, the Summary Court, and the Slave Court, were described by the Commission of Legal Enquiry as administering English law with a few adaptations made to suit local conditions.[65] The generally approving tone of the commissioners' report, and the absence of any action by the British government following the report's reception in 1829, meant that the judicial system established by agreement between the more wealthy and powerful settlers was left undisturbed.

Within the settlers' judicial system, the elected Magistrates played a central and crucial role, but they were also important in an executive capacity, and it was chiefly in the latter role that they clashed with the settlement's Superintendents. The Magistrates corresponded with the London agent and with merchants and financiers in London who were concerned with the settlement. These contacts in the metropolis were frequently used as a lobby to pressure and petition the

Secretary of State in accordance with their interests. Until 1830 the power of the Magistrates was almost unlimited. They were responsible for initiating legislation in the Public Meeting and for allocating the money voted from public funds by the Meeting. Some appointments of public officials, such as the clerk of the market and the high constable (and, in 1806, even the Public Treasurer) were made by the Magistrates until Superintendent Arthur succeeded in getting an unequivocal instruction from Bathurst "in no case to recognize or admit any person in any public capacity whose actual nomination or appointment shall not have originated with yourself."[66] This was only a very limited assertion of the power of the Crown's representative, however, as long as the Magistrates themselves, with their crucial control over legislation and expenditure, remained elected officials.

The custom of the election of Magistrates clearly existed prior to 1765, when Burnaby's Code gave it some, albeit vague, official approval. Between 1791 and 1796 the government of the settlement was by Magistrates, and a Superintendent was only reintroduced in the war emergency of 1796 when Earl Balcarres appointed Major Barrow. In 1800 the Public Meeting decided that there should be seven elected Magistrates and that, while no one could be forced to act as Magistrate for two successive years, the refusal to accept election for one year, or reelection after an interval of a year would result in a fine of £100.[67] In 1809 the Public Meeting made the qualifications for election to the Magistracy more stringent: in future, Magistrates were to be British-born white male residents possessed of at least £500 in visible property.[68] Though these restrictions defined the office as an exclusive and elitist institution, they do not appear to have improved the quality of the occupants. Only five years later, Superintendent Arthur wrote:

> The most illiterate Men of the worst Characters are placed on the Bench, and such Men ... are but ill-qualified for the Duties they have to perform. Their decisions are consequently most gross, and they of course fall into the most abject Contempt; their Authority is ridiculed, and even the semblance of a Court of Justice is with difficulty supported. ... one of these Magistrates ... has been iniquitously employed in carrying on the Slave Trade to a considerable extent, in defiance of the Laws of the Settlement, of an Act of Parliament, and in direct contempt of my orders. ... I cannot shut my Eyes to the self-interest and ignorance that influence their decisions.[69]

In 1819 Arthur wrote to a friend, "you can form no idea of the depravity of some of the Inhabitants who are raised to the Magistrates Seat."[70]

The fact that Magistrates were unpaid does not seem to have attracted public-spirited men to the office. On the contrary, settlers seem generally to have been willing to undertake the considerable volume of work entailed by the role because of the opportunities it offered to discover their own rewards, as well as to use their position to influence the Superintendents and the British government in line with their interests as merchants and mahogany exporters. In 1793 a court gave "Letters of Administration upon the Estate and Effects of William

Penn. . . . deceased'' to Marshall Bennett (then the foreman of the jury), ''on Condition that he account with the Magistrates . . . and pay over to them whatever balance may appear to be in his hands from time to time and he to be allowed the usual Commissions as an Administrator.'' The next day Bennett was ''granted according to the customs of Honduras'' the letters of administration on the estate and effects of another deceased settler.[71] As an example of the maladministration of the Court of Ordinary, Arthur noted that the property of deceased persons ''continued in the hands of the Magistrates'' and their friends as administrators or coadjustors, despite the existence of worthy claimants.[72] The office of Magistrate, then, provided a source of greater wealth for those already wealthy enough to qualify for the position, thereby encouraging the concentration of the settlement's wealth. Similarly, the institution of the magistracy, combining as it did executive and judicial powers and limiting access to these powers to a handful of rich white settlers, maintained the concentration of power in the hands of the settler oligarchy.

The claim that the ''democratic practice'' of electing the Magistrates ''stopped the Bench from becoming an irremovable oligarchy,''[73] appears unsupportable in the face of the extraordinarily restrictive qualifications and the narrowness of the franchise. Irrespective of the ''most abject Contempt'' that might be directed at the Magistrates, very few people were qualified to replace them, and few people were able to express effectively their desire for a change in the bench. It was recounted in chapter 3 how, in 1790, four Magistrates were defeated when the electorate was temporarily increased from forty to two hundred and fifty, the subsequent reaction of the ''arbitrary aristocracy'' being an appeal for the restriction of ''democratic practice.'' Once elected, of course, these wealthy settlers could utilize the power concentrated in their position to help ensure, through such positive and negative sanctions as patronage and victimization, their own perpetuation in office.

The power of the Magistrates to summon the Public Meeting was yet another source of friction between them and successive Superintendents. When Sir Richard Bassett challenged this power, the Magistrates asserted that ''the right of calling the Public Meeting has always been inherent in the Magistrates.''[74] Once again it was Superintendent Arthur who attempted to resolve this problem, by agreeing on the formality that he should be informed when the Public Meeting was assembled and that, in practice, this should take place on the Monday following the closure of the Supreme Court. This compromise was no real solution, however, and the question of the responsibility for summoning the legislative assembly was not really resolved until the constitutional changes of 1854.

The Public Meeting itself, developing out of an informal gathering of leading inhabitants in the eighteenth century, took on some of the characteristics of a legislative assembly. As it became a more formal institution early in the nineteenth century, the qualifications for membership were more precisely specified. In 1808 membership in the Public Meeting (and hence the electorate for the bench of Magistrates) was limited to male British subjects who, if white, had to prove one year's residence and own £100 in visible property; if colored, a candidate had to prove five years' residence and possession of £200 in visible property.[75] These highly restrictive qualifications, like the even narrower qualifications for becoming a Magistrate, were intended to keep legislative powers in the hands of the privileged elite, but they did not ensure the existence of a "respectable" legislative body. The fact that, once qualified, a man became a member of the Public Meeting for life meant that he did not lose his place even if he went bankrupt or was convicted of criminal behavior. Consequently, the Superintendents, without exception, criticized the social composition of the Public Meeting, which included disreputable and criminal elements. Superintendent Arthur reported that the "disgraceful exhibition" of the courts was "harmony itself in comparison with the proceedings of the Publick Meetings."[76]

Under pressure to reform itself, the Public Meeting became more restrictive, rather than less, in its qualifications for membership. In 1820 it decided to limit membership to white British males with one year's residence and property valued at £500, and colored men born in the settlement and possessing £1,000 in property.[77] The membership of the Public Meeting was thereby restricted to a tiny elite, said to consist of twenty-eight whites and twelve colored in 1827,[78] and attendance at the Meetings does not seem to have risen above fifty men before 1830: in 1823 there were reported to be twenty-nine persons present, in 1829 there were forty present, and in 1830 there were forty-seven and forty-six present.[79] In other words, only about 1½ percent of the adult population was enfranchised in the 1820s. The chief power of this minority lay in its control of legislation and of public finance. At the same time, the members of the Public Meeting constituted the electorate who selected the magistracy, and the Magistrates had the power to introduce legislation and allocate government expenditure. Any attempts made by a Superintendent, "who is not much more than a Looker-on," to encroach upon the power of the oligarchy were resented and vigorously resisted.

Superintendent Arthur, who succeeded in asserting the Crown's authority regarding dispositions of unclaimed land, introducing the proclamation as a legislative instrument, acquiring the authority to appoint public officials, and establishing the Supreme Court through legislation in the British Parliament, did more than any other Superintendent prior to 1830 to infringe upon the powers of the settler oligarchy. In general, however, these powers remained essentially intact and unchallenged, and following Arthur's departure in 1822, the settlers were in almost complete control of the settlement for the rest of the decade. Major General Edward Codd, who was Superintendent from 1823 to 1829, lost control of public affairs and his own mental faculties. On assuming the office of Superintendent in 1830, Lieutenant Colonel Francis Cockburn reported:

> For some years past the prosperity of this Settlement has been retarded, by the influence of some five or Six Individuals, who have monopolized the management

of offices & held in subjection the rest of the Inhabitants—Nothing but imbecelity of mind with which it seems pretty certain Maj. Gen. Codd was for many months afflicted could have admitted for so long a time of such a state of things.[80]

In a critical and vigorous manner, Superintendent Cockburn was to supervise a period of significant change in the political-administrative structure of the settlement.

During the 1820s, particularly after Arthur's departure, the settler oligarchy must have felt very secure in its control of the settlement. The Spanish threat, turned back at St. George's Cay in 1798, had not been renewed in the nineteenth century; the Maya, after a series of struggles, had retreated into the interior after 1817; and the slaves, apart from one easily quelled revolt in 1820, had been quieter than in the previous century. The eight years during which Arthur was Superintendent (the longest tenure of any Superintendent) brought some challenges, but the settler oligarchy survived virtually unscathed, with its monopoly over land and its control over government expenditure and legislation and over the judiciary essentially unimpaired. The 1820s, with the booms in logwood and mahogany exports and the expanding trade with Central America, were mostly years of economic prosperity for those settlers who were already wealthy and powerful enough to take advantage of the expanding opportunities. Though the movements for the extension of civil rights to the free colored and for the abolition of slavery were gaining momentum in the metropolis, the more frightening specter of slave revolt, which had haunted the settlers at the turn of the century, had become less pervasive as the number of slaves diminished. In fact, there appeared to be little on the settlers' horizon to challenge their vision of their continuing and unimpeded dominance of the settlement. But within four decades the settler oligarchy would itself be dispossessed, both of its political privileges and its economic dominance.

11

The Political Economy: The Decline of the Settlers, 1830-1871

THE DEPENDENT ECONOMY

The depression in the mahogany trade that followed the boom of 1826/27 lasted until about 1834. In 1830 Superintendent Cockburn reported that there was "a large supply of mahogany the product of this Settlement now on hand in England which in consequence of the Market being overstocked & the high Duty, cannot be sold at a remunerating price."[1] According to a nineteenth-century account:

> In 1830–31 the export of mahogany fell two and a half millions of feet, having retrograded since 1826–27, in consequence of overtrading and a glut in the home market. It began to increase again to three, four, five, six millions of feet each successive year, until 1837, when it reached eight and a half millions. This 1837 was a particularly prosperous year. Other articles increased also in the amount exported....[2]

According to the quarterly returns of exports from Belize, about 5 million feet of mahogany were exported in 1832 and 4½ million feet in 1833,[3] whereupon the trade increased to about 8½ million feet in 1837. In the 1840s the exports of mahogany continued to increase, to almost 10 million feet in 1845 and a peak of 13,719,075 feet in 1846,[4] in response to the railway boom in which mahogany was used for building carriages.

The great boom in the export of mahogany from 1835 to 1847 produced its own depression. Over-exportation had meant the cutting of young trees and the exhaustion of all easily accessible trees, with a consequent serious depletion of the settlement's timber resources. The result, as the cutters moved farther and farther into the interior in search of mahogany, was a rise in the cost of production, which, combined with a fall in prices,[5] led to a decline in profitability. Gibbs provided this analysis:

> It was about ... 1850, that permanent depression of the mahogany trade may be said to have begun. Prices not only fell, but, as the larger trees became more difficult to

find in situations near the creeks and rivers handy to the port of embarkation, the expense of bringing out the wood after it was felled and squared was much increased.[6]

The persistence of the chronic depression in the mahogany trade, however, may be accounted for chiefly by a fall in demand, an important factor in which was the substitution of iron for wood in the construction of ships. Table 11.1 shows that, from the peak of almost 14 million feet in 1846, exports declined to about 5½ million feet in 1859. Following a brief recovery from 1860 to 1862, exports declined still further, to about 4 million feet in 1867. Though this sudden decrease was attributed to "the incursions of the Indians, which cause the withdrawal of the mahogany gangs from the infested District,"[7] exports continued to decline to about 3 million feet in 1868. In 1870 only 2¾ million feet of mahogany were exported from Belize, the lowest recorded annual figure since the beginning of the century.[8]

Meanwhile, the export of logwood, while fluctuating greatly from a low of fifteen hundred tons in 1859 to a high of fifteen thousand tons in 1864, took up some of the slack in timber exports. Thus, in 1868, the value of the logwood exported was almost the same as that of mahogany, Longden's comment being that "the decline in the export of mahogany is in value more than balanced by the additional export of Logwood."[9] However, Longden's statement, which did not

TABLE 11.1 Exports of Mahogany and Logwood from Belize, 1832–68

Date	Mahogany in 1,000 Superficial Feet	Logwood in Tons
1832	5,015	2,359
1833	4,565	1,776
1834–36	....	....
1837	8,500	....
1838–44	....	....
1845	9,320	....
1846	13,719	4,314
1847–56	....	....
1857	7,267	6,681
1858	6,275	5,034
1859	5,436	1,502
1860	8,090	6,845
1861	8,657	7,000
1862	8,885	7,802
1863	6,196	8,471
1864	7,135	15,238
1865	5,240	7,352
1866	5,167	8,036
1867	4,156	4,528
1868	3,007	9,271

SOURCES: 1832–33, Quarterly Returns of Exports from Belize, CO 123/43–45; 1837, 1845–46 (mahogany), Archibald Robertson Gibbs, *British Honduras* ... (London, 1883), pp. 93, 102; 1846 (logwood), Narda Dobson, *A History of Belize* (London, 1973), p. 129; 1857–67, Lt. Gov. Longden to Gov. Grant, 19 June 1868, AB, R.98; 1868, Longden to Grant, 17 May 1869, AB, R.98.

take account of the decline in the price of both logwood and mahogany, obscured the fact that the value of both products had declined drastically. In 1866, 5,167,167 feet of mahogany, valued at 4½d. per foot, was worth £96,884, and 8,036 tons of logwood at £5.2.8 per ton was worth £41,252. Two years later, 3,006,619 feet of mahogany, valued at 2¼d. per foot, was worth only £28,187, and the logwood exported, though increased in quantity to 9,271 tons, had declined in value, at £3 per ton, to £27,813. The combined value of these export products, therefore, had dropped from about £140,000 in 1866 to a mere £56,000 in 1868. While the export of sugar had increased substantially (762 tons were exported in 1868), the contribution it made to the total value of exports in 1868, as can be seen from table 11.2, was minor. Despite the precipitous decline in the value of mahogany and logwood, these two woods, accounting for 82 percent of the total value of the colony's exports in 1868, still dominated the economy.

The fluctuations in the demand for mahogany and logwood in the European market, and the subsequent fluctuations in the profitability of the trade for the cutters of Belize, had a pervasive effect upon the social life of the colony as well as its economic life:

> When London and Liverpool prices current showed an advance in the rates for logwood and mahogany, there were cheerful, smiling faces in the countinghouses, and bustle and activity around the wharves of Belize—when prices fell there was dullness everywhere; lounging woodcutters on the bridge or around the grog-shops, instead of being away in the woods, axe in hand; clerks eating up their salaries, and principals looking glum.[10]

Meanwhile, the transit trade with Central America was also declining. The fact that the Central American Republic was for so many years the location of civil strife and unstable governments had encouraged many of the British merchants to establish themselves in Belize. These branch and commission houses were in competition with those of the older settlers who had engaged in the contraband trade for so long. In 1830 Superintendent Cockburn wrote, "In the Town of Belize there are already several British Merchants who import annually a large supply of Goods for Guatemala, and there is a constant trade established on that account between this Port & Omoa Truxillo etc."[11] But with the collapse

TABLE 11.2   Value of the Produce of Belize Exported in 1868

Product	Value (in pounds sterling)
Mahogany	28,187
Logwood	27,812
Sugar	9,908
Rum and molasses	550
Cedar and fustic	1,149
Cocoa nuts	735
Turtle	53
Total	68,394

SOURCE: Lt. Gov. Longden to Gov. Grant, 17 May 1869, AB, R.98.

The Decline of the Settlers, 1830–1871

of the federal government in 1839 and the rise of Rafael Carrera, the master *caudillo* of Guatemala, in the 1840s, the greater political stability encouraged British merchants to settle in Guatemala City and to establish direct connections with London, thus threatening the entire commercial status of Belize as an entrepôt port. The opening of the Panama railway in 1855, changing the routes of Central American trade and developing commercial centers on the Pacific coast, was another serious blow to Belize, whose once-favored trading position was rapidly being bypassed.

For a long time one of the problems of the growing British trade with Central America had been the absence of a return cargo. The merchants of Belize had imported agricultural merchandise, such as foodstuffs and the cattle needed for hauling logs, from Honduras and Guatemala, and as long as the demand for mahogany and logwood lasted in Europe, the ships' cargos of British manufactured goods could be replaced with timber. But with the establishment of direct connections between Britain and Guatemala, the disruption of trade with Yucatán following the *Guerra de las Castas,* and the depression in the mahogany trade, both imports and exports suffered a decline in the 1850s and 1860s (see table 11.3).

The "permanent depression" that developed in Belize in the 1850s affected all sectors of the economy because the economy was dominated by the merchant/mahogany companies. A decline in the mahogany trade, and in trade in general, affected these companies adversely; some reacted by closing altogether and others reacted by employing fewer laborers at lower wages. The consequent unemployment and poverty meant less retail trade, so the small shopkeepers, suffering a reduced turnover, would cut back on their largely imported stock. This cycle of depression was described by the Public Treasurer in 1860:

> The commencement of the year 1859 was remarkable for the uneasiness and apprehension which pervaded the whole community, and originated in the recent

TABLE 11.3 Value of Imports and Exports from Belize, 1857–70

Year	Imports (in dollars)	Exports (in dollars)
1857	1,343,450	2,201,360
1858	1,039,540	1,901,360
1859	876,465	1,440,805
1860	1,004,345	1,579,595
1861–62	....	....
1863	1,328,755	1,953,215
1864	....	....
1865	1,053,375	1,615,845
1866	....	....
1867	952,475	931,345
1868	....	....
1869	755,945	875,165
1870	921,685	859,885

SOURCE: Lindsay W. Bristowe and Philip B. Wright, *The Handbook of British Honduras for 1890–91* (London, 1890), p. 175.

failures of two extensive Houses engaged in the Mahogany Trade. The calamitous consequences of these commercial disasters were widely diffused, and injuriously afflicted every branch of our local industry....

... the Mahogany Trade has been entirely engrossed by four or five influential Firms, who employ large numbers of Foremen, Laborers, and Mechanics in their different Works.... the retail Stores have always mainly depended for their annual profits upon the sums disbursed by the Gangs, when they return to Belize in the month of December, for the purpose of entering into fresh Contracts for the ensuing Season....

The natural result followed the reverses.... The operations of the embarrassed Houses were restricted. The Labor Market became crowded with Persons seeking employment, and the price of Labor fell—It is true that the few who could command Capital were enabled to hire their Workmen at a remunerative rate—but, as the usual amount of money was not in circulation, the Shopkeepers suffered in proportion, and failed to realize their customary emoluments.

Another Interest was also languishing and depressed—Those Merchants, who imported with a view to principally disposing of their Goods to Purchasers from the contiguous States of Central America, had found that modern facilities of communication with Europe had gradually induced many Foreigners to resort directly to the home manufacturers for their supplies, instead of dealing as heretofore with their Correspondents in Belize—and thus, simultaneously, all Classes looked forward with a gloomy foreboding, and distrust of the future.[12]

The remainder of this chapter seeks to indicate and evaluate the extent to which the economic depression affected "all Classes" in Belize by examining the ways it reflected changes occurring in the distribution and structure of power within the metropolis/satellite colonial system.

CHANGES IN THE POLITICAL-ADMINISTRATIVE APPARATUS

In the late 1820s the Public Meeting, as chapter 6 demonstrated, was struggling to maintain its exclusivity against the demands for political privileges made by members of the free colored group. In 1828 the Public Meeting declared that "the Privileges and Immunities enjoyed by His Majesty's White Subjects should be Granted to persons of Color by going through the forms of Petition and Certificate of Character Honor and Probaty,"[13] and the following year it was decided that new members of the Meeting were required to be elected by not less than twenty-five votes (i.e., a majority) from the existing members.[14] This was clearly an attempt by the white settler oligarchy to delay the rise of the free colored in political affairs and to perpetuate the exclusive nature of the legislative body.

Within a year of his appointment, Superintendent Cockburn launched a major attack upon the Public Meeting. He began his offensive not, however, on the grounds that the meeting was an undemocratic oligarchy, but on the grounds that it included "too many classes." Cockburn, like some of the "Wealthier &

more respectable Inhabitants," was concerned with the threat of a "democratization" of political affairs. His suggested solution, however, was not to perpetuate the privileges of the settler oligarchy by increasing the restrictiveness of the qualifications for membership of the Public Meeting, but to abolish the Meeting altogether, replacing it with a Legislative Council headed by the Superintendent. In this connection he also criticized the control exercised by the Magistrates over the public funds:

> I beg leave to urge on your consideration the pressing necessity of at once doing away with the Body entitling itself the Legislative Meeting of Belize. The number of Persons now composing this Assemblage is about Seventy with every prospect of a continued and most inconvenient increase. The description of its Members includes but too many classes and ... those who have the least at stake in the interest and advancement of the Settlement are the most talkative and troublesome.... They seemed immediately to consider themselves invested with a degree of first rate consequence & authority.... The Wealthier & more respectable Inhabitants are however I am happy to say, still ready and anxious to meet the views and wishes of Government.... The Members of [the Meeting] assemble three times a year, as it is termed, according to Law, and as they meet without the interference of the Superintendent, so they in like manner close their proceedings previous to the account of them being even submitted for approval.... until reference can be made to the Imperial Parliament, an Order in Council or an Authority from the Secretary of State should be sent out doing away with the present Legislative Meeting & in lieu thereof placing all the financial and other arrangements of the Settlement under the direction & control of the Superintendent and a Council of Government.... until some final arrangement with respect to the internal Government of this Settlement is determined on, the Magistrates might be considered ex officio as the Council of Government.
>
> There is one other point ... requiring some alteration, & that is the power which the Magistrates are invested with, or rather which the Legislative Meeting assumes the power of investing them with, of disposing of the Public Funds without any control on the part of the Superintendent, all accounts of every description are submitted to the Magistrates for their decision, and an Order on the Public Treasurer signed by any three of them is considered valid.[15]

Three months later Cockburn repeated his criticism of the Public Meeting in the following terms:

> The more I see of it, the more I am warranted in assuring you that unless it is put a stop to, the Public business of the Place cannot be carried on. At every Meeting fresh Members are admitted, and the number thus increasing without any limitation leads to such absurd discussions and opinions as exceed belief. If the Meeting cannot be done away with altogether, I would recommend that ... it should only be assembled and dismissed by His Majesty's Superintendent as occasion might require and that the Members should take their qualification Oath once in every year if called on so to do—there are now many Members of the Meeting who tho' qualified when admitted are known at this time not to be worth one farthing in the World ... it would be much better if the operation of it were put a stop to altogether.[16]

Cockburn was advocating the abolition, or at least the drastic reform, of the Public Meeting on the grounds that there could be "no representation without taxation," and because the membership was increasing to include some poorer settlers. In fact, the records of the Meetings at that time show there was no increase in the number of members and that at no time did "the Assemblage" consist of more than fifty persons. At the Meetings on 1 March and 5 July 1830 (prior to Cockburn's claim that the group consisted of about seventy persons) there were forty-seven and forty-six members present, respectively, and at the Meetings of 3 November and 4 November 1830 (immediately preceding Cockburn's second letter, in which he claimed that the membership was increasing) the attendance was forty-two and thirty-four, respectively.[17] The following year, at the Meeting of 4 July 1831, when the crucial bill "relative to the Privileges of People of Colour of Free Condition" was debated, forty-four members were present, only thirty-six of whom returned to vote on the bill the next day.[18]

Cockburn's concern was not so much with this imaginary breadth of franchise as it was with imposing his own authority as Superintendent over the settlers. In so doing, he was actually following instructions given to him by the Colonial Office in 1829. The Colonial Office, while still wary of initiating a major constitutional reform that would violate the terms of the treaties with Spain, was clearly concerned about the power exercised by the settlers and the lack of authority of its own representative. Cockburn was therefore told that while he should exercise great tact in controlling the subjects of discussion, "it seems indispensable that the power of initiating all Laws, which are to be debated and enacted at Meetings should be vested in H. M.'s Superintendent."[19] He was also instructed that in future all laws passed by the Public Meeting were to be sent to the Colonial Office and were not to be considered in effect unless and until they were approved and sanctioned by His Majesty's government. It is by no means certain, however, whether this imperial control over the settlers' legislature was ever exercised.

In 1831 the Public Meeting, under pressure from the Colonial Office, accorded the "Coloured Subjects of Free Condition... the same Rights and Privileges with British Subjects born of White Parents," but an attempt to extend the same civil rights to the free blacks was defeated,[20] and the social composition of the Meeting does not appear to have changed significantly. Superintendent Cockburn continued to attack the Public Meeting in 1832, again complaining about its supposed lack of exclusivity:

> The unlimited number to which it may extend is also highly objectionable, for the only requisites on becoming a Candidate are, that the signature of Twenty five of the old Members shall be given in favour of the Person proposed, & then on his taking the Oath before alluded to at the next assemblage of the Meeting he is considered as duly elected—so that if any election really takes place it is merely that of the Members electing one another—The present number of Members amounts to

about Sixty or about 1 for every 100 including the Slave Population or One for every Fifty of the Free population even including the Blacks who are not allowed to vote for the return of Magistrates.—Were this Meeting restricted in its numbers—were the Oaths acted up to & the Members returned by a Majority of Votes in the same way the Magistrates are now elected—it would indeed be a benefit to the whole Settlement.[21]

Both the Superintendent and the white settler elite felt threatened in the early 1830s by the increasing and increasingly influential free colored and black people. The "civil rights" campaign of the free colored and the movement toward abolition constituted a democratic threat to the settlers' status quo. The response of the settlers and the Superintendent to the threat of democratization was different, however: the settlers attempted to maintain their privileges by building the barriers around their oligarchy still higher, while the Superintendent advocated the abolition, or at least the restriction, of the power of the settlers' institutions with a consequent increase in the powers of the Colonial Office and its representative.

As far as the Public Meeting was concerned, this three-way struggle reached a stalemate. The Public Meetings persisted without being democratized but also without securing official recognition and legal sanction from Britain. In 1832 Lord Goderich, the Colonial Secretary, wrote: "If His Majesty's Government are disposed to acquiesce in the system which has hitherto prevailed, that acquiescence must not be construed into approbation of it; still less into an acknowledgement that it rests upon any legal basis."[22] Almost a decade later it was even suggested that the unsettled constitutional problems were advantageous because the "Public Meeting does not feel itself strong and can at any time be told that it has no legitimate existence."[23] So long as the settlers would concede the major changes introduced through the Crown's representative—changes like the abolition of slavery—the Colonial Office preferred to ignore the constitutional and diplomatic problems surrounding the institutions of government in the settlement.

In 1832, with the abolition of slavery approaching, and the consequent necessity of appointing suitable Special Magistrates, it became essential to resolve the problem of the responsibility for the appointment of public officials. Lord Goderich informed Superintendent Cockburn "that the King would no longer recognize in the Settlers of Honduras the claim to appoint the subordinate Officers of Justice by election of the Inhabitants."[24] Cockburn, interpreting this dispatch in accord with his own predilections, promptly issued a proclamation stating that the election of Magistrates was henceforth abolished and that they would in future be appointed by the Superintendent. Cockburn reported:

> The appointment of Magistrates having so long depended on a popular election, I felt it possible that some ill-feeling or some partial opposition might have arisen against the alteration which was about to take place, but such was not the case.[25]

The bench of 1833 was thus appointed by the Superintendent without apparent complaint or protest by the settler oligarchy at this major curtailment of their customary rights. Goderich's reply to Cockburn, however, made it clear that while the right to appoint public officials should clearly not reside with the settlers, neither should it rest in the hands of the Superintendent. Goderich argued that public appointments were to be made, possibly based on nomination by a Superintendent, by Her Majesty's government in England. Bathurst's instructions to Arthur in 1819, "in no case... recognize or admit any person in any public capacity whose actual nomination or appointment shall not have originated with yourself,"[26] were not to be interpreted as vesting all power of appointment with the Superintendent. Goderich emphasized that the object of the instructions had been "an exclusion as against the Settlers not as against the Crown."[27] In practice, it appears that subsequent appointments were generally made by the Governor of Jamaica giving approval to the Superintendent's nominations, with occasional officials, such as qualified legal specialists, being appointed directly from England.

Despite Goderich's qualification, the "exclusion as against the Settlers" amounted to a considerable encroachment upon the customary power of the settlers by the Superintendent. The decline of the magistracy, key-stone of the settler oligarchy's political-administrative institutions, meant the decline of the authority of the settler oligarchy itself, and may be dated from the first appointment of Magistrates in the settlement in 1832. Caught at a time when its membership was weakened by economic depression and threatened by an extension of democratic practices, the settler oligarchy was dealt a blow in the central institution of its political power. Through the 1830s and 1840s the settlers continued to struggle to maintain political supremacy in the settlement, but, undermined by developing economic forces, they were ultimately to lose the struggle. Henceforward, the authority of the Crown's representative increased as that of the magistracy and Public Meeting decreased, while economic control shifted decisively from the settler colonialists toward the metropolis.

THE CONSOLIDATION OF METROPOLITAN OWNERSHIP

During the second quarter of the nineteenth century a change occurred in the form and organization of land ownership in Belize. The big landowners were originally settlers or settler families and partnerships, and they constituted a settler elite who were referred to as the "Principal Inhabitants" or "the monied cutters." This elite generally had connections with, and was sometimes indebted to, London merchants, but they maintained sole ownership of their extensive lands in Belize. The new development involved the direct participation of the London merchants in land ownership in the settlement through partnerships with the old settlers. It is inaccurate to speak of "the monied cutters" as a settler elite after this change took place, because these cutters had been incorporated into firms with a pronounced absentee or metropolitan element.

The Decline of the Settlers, 1830-1871

The outstanding example of this new kind of company was James Hyde & Company, a partnership between the local landowning Hyde family and a London merchant, John Hodge, who, in acknowledging his appointment as agent for the settlement in 1848, stated that his interests in Belize had existed "for more than twenty years."[28] The earliest date that can be placed on the existence of this firm is 1846, for a letter written in 1860 mentions that in 1846 "Messrs. James Hyde, John Hodge, and James Bartlett Hyde (who then traded together in Honduras under the Firm name of James Hyde & Co.) purchased from a William Alexandre France a mahogany and logwood work situate on the New River."[29] Such a partnership, with access to more capital than a settler would have on his own, was able to increase the quantity of land it possessed by purchase. Particularly after the depression in the mahogany trade in the 1850s, many of the old settlers, like France, were unable to meet their debts to London merchants and were forced to sell their lands. Those settlers who had such merchants as their partners, however, were able to survive and sometimes to become more powerful by engrossing the property of the indebted settlers. Several large landowning firms of this type were recorded in the land titles registry in the 1860s, chiefly partnerships between local settlers and metropolitan merchants, such as Young Toledo & Company, Carmichael Vidal & Company, and Sheldon Byass & Company.

With the increase in market demand in the mid-1820s and particularly in the 1840s, production and trade expanded considerably. The demand for mahogany by the rail companies led to the expansion of mahogany cutting operations up to, and frequently across, the boundaries of the settlement in the north, west, and south, and also to a ruthless exploitation of young and even immature trees. The direct involvement of a more pronounced absentee element in this expansive market encouraged a get-rich-quick mentality that fostered a drastic exploitation of the forest resources. With a complete absence of planning or any attempt at reforestation, the expansion of production in the 1840s drove the woodcutters into less accessible areas and severely depleted forest reserves. As long as the market was strong and the price high, this unsystematic exploitation was profitable, but when demand and prices fell, the rising production costs made many of the mahogany cutting enterprises unprofitable. In addition, many of these mahogany houses were involved in the import-export trade with Central America and Mexico, a trade that, for the reasons previously stated, declined rapidly in the 1850s. Deteriorating economic conditions in the 1850s resulted in a number of financial failures and bankruptcies. The failure of some of the mahogany cutters meant that their assets, chiefly land, were put up for auction, mortgaged, or taken over by creditors. The trend, described by the Public Treasurer in 1860 when he said that "the Mahogany Trade has been entirely engrossed by four or five influential firms,"[30] was clearly one of increasing consolidation and the intensification of metropolitan ownership.

A similar pattern was in evidence in the sugar islands of the Caribbean, where there was "an ever-growing toll of failed estates and planters selling out to any available buyer."[31] The same combination of circumstances—foreign competition, overproduction for a declining market, price declines, exhaustion of resources, and increasing production costs—resulted in the same pattern of failures, mortgages, bankruptcies, and credit foreclosures. The consequence was a centralization of capital, a consolidation of the production enterprises into fewer and larger units. Through both concentration (the accumulation and expansion of the amount of capital) and centralization (the change in the distribution of capital by the merger of existing sources of capital), firms like James Hyde & Company, constituting a partnership between landowning settler and metropolitan merchant elements, became dominant in the settlement's economy.

The trend toward the consolidation of capital and the intensification of metropolitan ownership took place at a time when the organization of capitalism was changing in the metropolis itself. The old mercantilist notions of trade, which protected colonial products in the metropolitan market, were being overthrown in the 1840s in favor of the economic principle of free trade. The abolition of the Corn Laws and the Sugar Duties Act of 1846 and the repeal of the Navigation Laws of 1848 were major victories of rising industrialism in Great Britain. The Joint Stock Companies Act, passed in 1856, marked the further development of the concentration of corporate capital within the prevailing economic philosophy of laissez faire. This act encouraged the growth of capital accumulation and the concentration of capital by allowing large numbers of people to invest with limited liability in joint stock companies. Within six years 2,479 companies registered in Britain under this act,[32] one of them being the British Honduras Company, Limited, registered as such in 1859.

With the decline of forestry and the growth of an agricultural interest in the 1850s, there was a renewed concern over the validity of titles to land. Titles to most of the privately owned lands had their roots in the old locations, dating back to 1817 and before, but the validity of titles by location had never been unequivocally accepted. In a petition of 1841 the settlers, having referred to a desire to cultivate cotton, rice, coffee and tobacco, complained that they were "debarred by the uncertain tenure of their lands, except for Mahogany and Logwood cutting."[33] Though the British government remained ambivalent in its assertion of sovereignty over the settlement in the 1840s, by the mid-1850s international considerations had altered sufficiently to remove Britain's restraint in openly asserting its sovereignty. In the course of the 1850s Britain signed a number of agreements with the United States (chiefly the Clayton-Bulwer Treaty of 1850) and other countries with the intent of regularizing its relations with the Central American republics. By 1854 Britain was confident enough to approve the settlement's first recognized constitution, providing an elected Legislative Assembly of eighteen members and clearly defining the Superintendent's authority.[34]

One of the first acts of the new Legislative Assembly, the Laws in Force Act of 1855, regularized the legal system generally, and two sections dealt specifically with the validity of land titles by location. The effect of sections two and three of the Laws in Force Act[35] was to provide retroactive legitimacy to ownership of land that had been appropriated by the location laws up to 1817. The Laws in Force Act, proclaimed on 8 March 1856, and two other acts (one, passed in 1857, concerned with the mode of conveyance of land, and the other, passed in 1858, called "the Act for Quieting Title,")[36] confirmed the titles to land held under the old location laws. While these acts were perhaps adequate to satisfy the settlers, who had intimate knowledge of the history of the lands they occupied as well as of the location laws, the acts were very vague and did not lend themselves to precise legal definition. The uncertainties of the application of the location laws remained even after the Laws in Force Act confirmed their validity, with the result that many titles remained open to question, thus giving rise to abundant litigation. Though this resolution of the problem may have been satisfactory to the old settlers, it could not be expected to have satisfied those abroad who were interested in investing in the land of the settlement. At this time a group of English capitalists were interested in such investment, but they were not prepared to risk their capital until titles to land could be acquired that were as safe and secure as those they were accustomed to hold in England. The result was that, beginning in 1858, the Honduras Land Titles Acts were passed, their object being "to render land marketable even where the title could not be conclusively established."[37]

An adviser to the Colonial Office, writing in 1858 on the Honduras Land Titles Act, referred to the Laws in Force Act and the conveyancing act, and noted:

> But before these Acts have had time to work their full effect circumstances have brought the uncertainty of the Honduras Titles into inconvenient prominence. An attempt has been made to form a Company for the purpose of bringing large tracts of the Colony [sic] into cultivation and the question has been immediately submitted to English Conveyancers, how that Company is to be secured in the possession of its lands. To solve this question and to enable the present proprietors to give secure Titles to the proposed purchasers, the present Act has been drafted in England and passed by the Legislature of Honduras.[38]

When the settlement's Attorney General wrote his report on the act he explained that the object of the act was "to give a perfect title to persons whose estates are registered, such a title that is, which parties would be disposed to accept who have been accustomed to invest their money on property only to which there is an absolute and indefeasible title." He was quite clear on the origin of the act: "This Bill was introduced . . . to forward the views of a proposed European Land Company, and framed . . . by one of the most eminent conveyancers in England."[39] Because of various objections made to it, the 1858 act did not receive the royal assent, but a register of land titles was nonetheless instituted in that year. The 1859 act did receive the royal assent,[40] but it was amended in 1861, and it was the 1861 act that became the final draft of the Honduras Land Titles Act.[41]

The "proposed European Land Company" to which Attorney General Ball had referred became the British Honduras Company in 1859 and the Belize Estate and Produce Company in 1875. From its inception until the present day this company has completely dominated the private ownership of land in Belize and has been the chief single force in the colony's political economy. The company, which had procured a famous English conveyancing lawyer to draft the most important law relating to land tenure in the settlement, and which immediately took advantage of the terms of the law, had its roots in one of the oldest of the settler families, that of James Hyde. Almost all the lands held by the British Honduras Company, as recorded in the land titles register,[42] were transferred to it by John Hodge and James Bartlett Hyde, and the early claims book dating from 1859 enters these same lands in the names of "John Hodge, of London, merchant, presently residing in Belize, on behalf of himself and James Bartlett Hyde, the surviving copartners of the late firm of James Hyde & Co., who lately carried on business in this Settlement as Merchants and Mahogany cutters."[43]

James Hyde & Company, one of the several firms that developed in Belize as partnerships between settler landowners and metropolitan merchants, was the only one of them to take advantage of the Joint Stock Companies Act. Registering as the British Honduras Company, Limited, in 1859, the company entered a new stage in its organizational development, distinguishing it from other settler-merchant partnerships such as Young Toledo & Company. All the other firms then extant have since disappeared, some of them collapsing in the 1860s, but the British Honduras Company survived and even expanded. Of particular interest is the contrasting case of Young Toledo & Company, a firm that had been in operation since at least 1839.[44] Identified by contemporary sources as one of the two great land monopolists in the 1860s and 1870s, Young Toledo & Company went into bankruptcy in 1880, and the British Honduras Company bought nine of its mahogany works the following year.[45]

The reorganization of James Hyde & Company as the British Honduras Company enabled it to accumulate more capital, and it is this feature that distinguishes it from the other large firms of the time. The availability of more capital provided the company with a distinct advantage in two important respects. First, it had a greater capacity for investment not only in mahogany extraction but also in agricultural production. Second, the company was able to hold its land idle, speculating on long-term gains, while other firms were forced to dispose of some of their land in order to obtain fluid capital. The British Honduras Company was therefore able to make adjustments enabling it to survive the extended depression in the mahogany trade, and it was also able to purchase yet more land from those firms, like Young Toledo & Company, that were forced by the depression into bankruptcy. One result of the continuing depression in the colony's economy, therefore, was the further concentration and centralization of capital in the hands of metropolitan companies.

The Decline of the Settlers, 1830–1871

The structure of land ownership, which had been highly concentrated since the late eighteenth century, became one of increasingly extreme monopolization in the nineteenth century. The primary source for the study of the structure of land distribution in the 1860s is the land titles register. The earlier claims book (1859–62) notes 191 claims on mahogany works, 158 of which were held by three firms: eighty works were claimed by Hodge & Hyde as the surviving copartners of James Hyde & Company, fifty-five by Young Toledo & Company, and twenty-three by the liquidators of Carmichael Vidal & Company. The names of the mahogany works claimed indicate that these firms had bought the works of many of the old settlers; for example, those claimed by Hodge & Hyde include the names Young, Gabourel, Hickey, Gentle, White, Swasey, and Craig.

The land titles register, the first entries in which date from 1863, shows an almost complete division of the colony's private land between the British Honduras Company and Young Toledo & Company, all the works of Carmichael Vidal & Company having been transferred to the latter in 1864. Since Hodge & Hyde had transferred all their registered works to the British Honduras Company by 1875, the latter had eighty-nine registered mahogany works in that year, compared to seventy-six for Young Toledo & Company. When the British Honduras Company became the Belize Estate and Produce Company, Limited, in 1875, it registered ninety works in its name, all of which had been transferred to it by the former. The 1888 handbook stated that the Belize Estate and Produce Company owned one million acres in the Northern District alone,[46] and with their lands in other areas, their holdings must have amounted to about half of all the privately owned land in the colony.[47]

The monopoly of land ownership in 1871 was thus very marked. The British Honduras Company owned well over one million acres, and Young Toledo & Company owned about one million acres. Sheldon Byass & Company owned four works, or about fifty thousand acres, and John Carmichael[48] owned about twenty-five thousand acres, including the town of Corozal. These, with a handful of others who each owned several thousand acres, together possessed almost all the land held as private property in the country. Above all, the British Honduras Company had consolidated its wealth and succeeded in becoming the most powerful organization in the country. Since its formation, this company has influenced the legislation and dominated the economy of Belize.

The powerful influence of the British Honduras Company upon legislation in Belize was apparent even in the course of the company's formation, when, as the "proposed European Land Company," it arranged for the enactment of the most important land law in the settlement's history, thereby providing the security of tenure demanded by the British investors. Other legislation enacted in the company's interest and at its instigation included the acts of 1862 and 1868, which encouraged the immigration of labor at the colony's expense, and the 1863 act, which allowed the duty-free importation of machinery to be used in agriculture and manufacturing. The company also exercised its power by opposing legislation, most notably in its effective resistance to the implementation of land taxes. It even went so far as to interfere in international affairs with regard to the boundaries of the colony and relations with Mexico.[49]

The concentration of about half of all the freehold land in that company's hands has meant that the pattern of land use and the direction of the colony's economy have been largely determined by the metropolitan owners of the British Honduras Company. Moreover, the consolidation of the metropolitan ownership of the colony's economy meant the almost complete elimination of the settler class as a major element within the colony's social structure. In 1845, before the great immigration of Yucatecan refugees, the 399 whites amounted to 4 percent of the total population of 9,809,[50] but by 1881 only 375 of the total population of 27,452, or a little over 1 percent, were white.[51] As 271 of those whites were males, it is apparent that very few white families were settled in Belize and that most of the whites were probably transient adult males. It was remarked upon that "white people but look upon it as a resting, not an abiding place, one from which they hope eventually to return enriched to their native soil."[52] At the same time that "British Honduras" became a colony, therefore, it ceased to be a place of settlement for whites.

THE CREATION OF A CROWN COLONY

At the same time that the white settlers of Belize were losing control of the settlement's economy to metropolitan companies, they were losing control of the political-administrative apparatus through increasing disenfranchisement. In the late 1820s the white settler oligarchy faced a serious political predicament. Threatened by the growing demands of the free colored group, the white oligarchy accepted a curtailment of its political privileges, reluctantly conceding greater authority to the Superintendent as the representative of the metropolitan government. Having lost control of the magistracy, which had been the keystone of the settlers' political-administrative system, the oligarchy was fighting a losing battle after 1832. The insistence of the metropolitan government that the abolition of slavery should be applied in Belize was an important assertion of British control over the territory and was thus contrary to the settlers' system as well as the Spanish claims. Moreover, the insistence of the Colonial Office on the use of Special Magistrates during the "apprenticeship" period in Belize, as in Britain's official colonies, was a further indication of increasing metropolitan control.

Throughout the 1830s and 1840s there appears to have been a mutual reluctance on the part of both Britain and Spain to reach any agreement over, or even to openly discuss, the question of sovereignty. Spain, having lost its Central American empire, was certainly no longer, if it ever had been, an effective power in the Belize area, and when Spain recognized Mexican independence in 1836, no mention was made of the British settlement. Britain, on the other hand, made no reference to its own settlement in 1849 when it recognized the independence of the Guatemalan republic. The settlers themselves had been agitating for a firm and unequivocal assertion of British sovereignty for some years, partly in order to obtain preferential tariff treatment, and there can be no doubt that the metropolitan partners of the developing companies in the settlement were concerned about the security of their investments, particularly in land.

In the late 1840s a number of broader international issues combined with the internal situation of the settlement to produce a resolution of the question of sovereignty. The United States, having expanded into the Southwest and seized over half of Mexico's territory, began looking for a site for a Central American canal to link its eastern and western seaboards. At the same time Britain, also concerned with questions of interoceanic transit, revived its interest in the area, including the Bay Islands and the Mosquito Shore. In the Clayton-Bulwer Treaty of 1850 these two powers agreed to promote the construction of a canal and, at the same time, to refrain from colonizing any part of Central America. The British government interpreted the latter as applying only to any future occupation, but the American government, particularly after 1853 when an aggressively expansionist administration emphasized the Monroe Doctrine, claimed that Britain was obliged to evacuate the area. Britain did yield on the Bay Islands and the Mosquito Shore but, in 1854, provided a formal constitution for its possession at Belize. The exigencies of international diplomacy coincided with the agitations of the Superintendent to produce these constitutional changes.

It had been stated of the Public Meeting in 1838 that "a Majority of the Members of the Meeting as now constituted, consists of coloured men," though membership was restricted to male British subjects who possessed visible property worth £400. The electorate was restricted to male British subjects who had been resident in the settlement for a year and who possessed property worth £100.[53] Throughout his eight year incumbency as Superintendent (1843–51), Colonel Fancourt, Cockburn's successor, had been very critical of the Public Meeting.[54] It appeared that any British-born resident with property worth £300 could inform a member of the Public Meeting that he wished to become a member. The provost marshall would then open a poll, and if, at the end of seven days, twenty-five registered voters had voted for him, the applicant was elected for life. If he suffered a loss of his property he would remain a member but would lose his voting rights. Fancourt reported that of the sixty-four members in 1848 only thirty-three were qualified to vote. He concluded that "the real governing body consists of 5 or 6 Mahogany Houses in Belize whose operations are almost entirely dependent on certain other Houses in London."[55] Thus the care with which the oligarchy had protected itself against the free colored, by instituting a restrictive and self-perpetuating membership, had resulted in the shift of the real locus of decision-making from the Public Meeting to the metropolis-dominated companies.

Another reason Fancourt pressed for a constitutional change was the massive increment in the settlement's population as a result of the immigration of refugees from the *Guerra de las Castas* after 1848. This sudden influx of Maya and *mestizo* refugees led to the prompt innovation of local government when a paid magistrate was appointed in the Northern District in 1849. The following year there were three magistrates in the Northern District, one in the Southern District, and one each in the Sibun and Belize river areas. In 1856 the payment of these district magistrates was regularized and the basis of the local administrative and judicial system legally established.

A combination of reasons, therefore, led in the early 1850s to the widespread desire for an unequivocal assertion of British sovereignty and an unambiguous constitution. Various proposals were circulated between Belize, Jamaica, and London until, by the end of 1853, an act "To amend the system of Government of British Honduras" received the royal assent.[56] The act stated:

> That the Legislative Assembly shall consist of twenty-one members, of whom eighteen shall be elected, and three appointed by the Superintendent.... That no person shall be capable of being elected a member of the Legislative Assembly, who shall not be of the full age of twenty-one years, and a natural born subject of the Queen, or naturalized by law, and who shall not be lawfully possessed, over and above any debts or incumbrances to which he may be liable, of real or personal property in British Honduras to the value of Four Hundred Pounds Sterling.[57]

The old Public Meeting, which had been in existence for about a century, was disbanded, and the new Legislative Assembly was introduced in 1854. The franchise was restricted to males with real property yielding an income of £7 per year or with a salary of £100 per year. The Assembly was to last for four years, though it could be prorogued or dissolved by the Superintendent at any time. The constitutional change clearly gave the Colonial Office, through the Superintendent, greater power in the settlement and correspondingly reduced still further the political influence of the settlers. Since the Superintendent could originate legislation, give or withhold consent to bills introduced by the Assembly, and even dissolve the Assembly at will, the legislature was little more than a talking body, a chamber of debate rather than decisions.

In the 1850s, therefore, "British Honduras had become a colony in all but name."[58] The remaining settlers, stricken by the severe and prolonged economic depression, petitioned through the Legislative Assembly for colonial status in 1861.[59] They felt that the unequivocal assertion of British sovereignty might, by removing doubt as to the territory's status, encourage development through the immigration of people and an influx of capital. It is quite probable that the favorable reaction of the Colonial Office to this petition was influenced by the wishes of the British Honduras Company, which, since its formation in 1859, had been concerned with the security of its extensive real estate. In 1862, some two centuries after the first British settlements were established near the Belize River, the British government declared "British Honduras" a colony and made its Superintendent into a Lieutenant Governor. Within nine years, however, a further constitutional development occurred: the Legislative Assembly abolished itself after a life of only seventeen years, and the British government established its total control over the colony.

The pattern of consolidation that had occurred throughout the West Indies, as it had in Belize, in the 1840s and 1850s, was the result of a common set of circumstances. Similarly, the pattern of constitutional changes that followed in the 1860s was the result of a shared, and interrelated, combination of factors. In the islands, the decline of the sugar trade, which preceded the abolition of slavery, had meant the decline and eventual demise of the planter class. Following emancipation in 1838 and the abolition of imperial tariff protection after 1846, the old social system of the sugar producing islands was disrupted. In places like Jamaica, the declining planter class attempted to maintain its social position through the maintenance of political power, but with a disintegrating economic basis, the planters abandoned their old representative institutions. In Jamaica it was the particular crisis of the Morant Bay rebellion in 1865 that caused the Legislative Assembly to abolish itself in favour of Crown Colony government.[60] In Belize the particular circumstances that precipitated the crisis were, of course, different, but a similar general combination of conditions was present.

In the late 1860s the expenses of administering the colony had increased, largely as a result of the costly military expeditions against the Maya, undertaken at a time when the economy was severely depressed. Consequently the public debt, being "chiefly for military expenditure,"[61] rose to about $150,000 by 1870. The great landowners, whose mahogany camps in the west and northwest had been attacked and were continually threatened by the Icaiché Maya under Marcos Canul, were at last moved by this state of affairs to allow the Legislative Assembly to impose a land tax in 1867. However, the tax was imposed for only two years, to meet the immediate emergency, and its terms were actually very favorable to the big landowners.[62] In the crisis of 1866–67 the great mahogany companies were willing to support a temporary measure for raising revenue by the taxation of land, but they had no intention of continuing to pay such a tax.

The Legislative Assembly, which controlled the colony's revenues and expenditure, was dominated by the great landowners and merchants. Though the landowners were themselves often also involved in commerce, some antagonism existed between them and the other merchants of the town of Belize: the former resisted the taxation of land and favored an increase on import duties, and the latter preferred the opposite. Moreover, the merchants of Belize town felt relatively secure from the Maya attacks and were therefore unwilling to contribute toward the military expenditure necessary to resist them. At the same time, the landowners were unwilling to bear the expense themselves and held the view that it was unjust to require them to pay taxes on lands that were given inadequate protection. These conflicting interests produced a stalemate in the Legislative Assembly, which failed to authorize the raising of sufficient revenue.

Unable to agree among themselves, but pressed by the necessity of raising additional revenue, the members of the Assembly attempted to convert British Honduras into a Crown Colony in 1869 so that the imperial government could bear more of the burden of defense. In 1870 the Assembly agreed to surrender its privilege of self-government in return for greater security against the persistent Maya threat, in much the same way as the Jamaican Assembly had abolished itself after the crisis of the Morant Bay rebellion in 1865. The Legislative Assembly having "committed political suicide,"[63] the new colonial constitution was inaugurated in April 1871. Under the new constitution, the colony was governed by the Governor-in-Council, the Council consisting of five official and four unofficial members, all nominated.[64]

The constitutional change of 1871 confirmed and completed a change that had been taking place during the preceding half century. The old settler oligarchy, which had confidently dominated the settlement at the beginning of the nineteenth century, was progressively undermined by a number of factors. The rising status of the free colored group and the emancipation of the slaves were major developments in the structure of social relations that threatened the social dominance of the white settlers. At the same time, the beleaguered white oligarchy was attacked by the Colonial Office, which succeeded in gaining control over much of the settlement's administrative apparatus, notably in the appointment of Magistrates in 1832. The struggle of the settlers to maintain their social and political supremacy was therefore two-sided. On the one hand, they opposed the rising democratic tide of the emancipated masses, and on the other, they sought to maintain their traditional executive authority against the Crown's representative.

The factor that was "ultimately decisive"[65] in bringing about the demise of the settler oligarchy was economic. The decline in the mahogany trade and the subsequent prolonged depression in the 1850s and 1860s not only removed the basis of the settlers' power but also virtually eliminated the settler group. The consolidation of economic enterprises in the middle of the nineteenth century was achieved by a reorganization of capital ownership, first in the form of partnerships between landowning settlers and metropolitan merchants, and eventually, in the dominance of the entire economy by one metropolitan company. This transfer of economic power from the settlers to the metropolis-based companies made the Legislative Assembly, the legatee of the old Public Meeting, little more than a debating society that carried out the wishes of the major economic interests. When, in the crisis of the late 1860s, induced by the combination of severe economic depression and the military threat from the Maya, the Assembly was unable to solve the colony's problems, it simply abolished itself and handed all formal political power to the Crown, thereby carrying out the recommendations made by Superintendent Cockburn three decades previously.

The de facto power of the metropolitan landowners in the colony was recognized when three of the four unofficial appointees to the new Council

The Decline of the Settlers, 1830–1871   193

represented the landed interests, while only one represented the commercial interests. (The effect was felt immediately, when the Legislative Council raised import duties from 4 to 10 percent.)[66] The metropolitan companies, particularly the British Honduras Company/Belize Estate and Produce Company, continued to have a dominant influence, either through nomination or through election on a narrow franchise, for most of the following century. The manager of the Belize Estate and Produce Company frequently sat on the Council, and it is fair to say that "relations between the company's representatives and the United Kingdom's representatives were always extremely close, and the B.E.C.'s influence on policy and administration can hardly be overestimated."[67] From the time when the "proposed European Land Company" succeeded in introducing the Honduras Land Titles Act, the British government and its representatives in the colony have frequently felt the pressure of the company's stockholders. After Marcos Canul's last raid in 1872, for example, the chairman of the British Honduras Company not only addressed a complaint to the Colonial Office but also lodged a formal complaint and demand for compensation with the Mexican government, though the British and Mexican governments had no diplomatic relations at the time. Since the investors were demanding the protection of their property, the company pressured the British government to respond and to provide effective protection.[68] The company's chairman stressed "the claims of our company and of the Colony of British Honduras, the interests of both being nearly identical."[69]

For over thirty years the declining settler oligarchy of Belize had struggled with a combination of social, political, and economic problems. Some time in the middle of the nineteenth century they lost that struggle and left the emerging colony firmly in the grasp of metropolitan control. With the demise of the settler class, the stage was set for the struggle between the colonized masses and the metropolitan forces. The establishment of crown colony government in 1871 confirmed and clarified, but did not create, the contradiction between these two great hostile camps.

12
Conclusions

All of the most significant socioeconomic factors of the Caribbean historical experience were present in Belize, though they existed in forms that sometimes differed from those found elsewhere in the region. Colonial domination was a relatively late development in Belize because of the inaccessibility of the territory and its physical and, initially, economic unattractiveness to Europeans. In addition, the competitiveness between Spain and Great Britain was not decisively resolved; Spain continued to assert its sovereignty but never settled Belize, while Britain developed its settlement without asserting sovereignty. Nevertheless, with the development of the logwood and mahogany trades, the subsequent dependence of the settlement upon the metropolis was unavoidable.

The entire raison d'être of the settlement depended upon the state of the European market for a particular tropical product, and fluctuations in the market had substantial effects upon the political economy and the social structure of the colonial satellite. The rise of the logwood trade early in the eighteenth century produced a demand for labor that was resolved by importing thousands of African slaves, thereby establishing the racial/ethnic composition of the early settlement. The crisis in the logwood trade in the 1760s and 1770s produced a crisis in social relations, culminating in the slave revolt of 1773, which threatened the very existence of the settlement. The rise of the mahogany trade saved the settlement but also transformed it, as the exigencies of mahogany extraction led to an even greater concentration of property, both land and slaves, and the development of a dominant white settler oligarchy. That this oligarchy remained dependent upon metropolitan markets, however, became apparent in the middle of the nineteenth century, when a depression in the mahogany trade led to a further consolidation of the settlement's economy and its domination by metropolitan companies.

The monopolization of land ownership, the tendency toward tropical monoculture, the dependence on metropolitan markets both for exports and imports, and a social structure polarized between a generally white minority and a black majority, are all typical features of a plantation economy. The colonial experience of Belize was characterized by the presence of all these features, even

Conclusions 195

though the economy was not based upon plantations in the strictest sense. The organization of the predominant production unit in Belize differed in many ways from, for example, the sugar plantations of the islands, and the experience of slaves and wage laborers in the mahogany gangs was in a number of ways quite markedly different from that of the slaves on sugar plantations. Nevertheless, the "macro-features" of the society have been similar to those of the Caribbean colonies that have been dominated by sugar plantations.

The demands of the metropolitan market create the plantation economy, an economy that depends upon the centralized control of the primary resources of land, labor, and capital. In a situation where labor is scarce and land is plentiful, the capitalists find difficulty in securing the labor they require for their enterprises. The initial solution was to import slaves by the thousands, but in Belize this did not solve the masters' "labor problem," because so many slaves escaped to the neighboring areas.

In the late eighteenth century the settler elite instituted a series of regulations by which they succeeded in allocating all the land to themselves in order to deny an independent means of livelihood to the many poor free evacuees from the Mosquito Shore who were perceived as potential laborers. Through their control of the political-administrative apparatus, the settler elite was able to monopolize the land even after emancipation and thus to prevent the ex-slaves from becoming an independent and self-sufficient peasantry. The ex-slaves in Belize, unable to acquire land and indebted to their masters by the advance and truck systems, continued to be tied to labor in the mahogany forests. The Caribs and the Maya, too, were denied freehold titles to land in order to make them available as a source of labor for the sugar plantations that were being developed in the third quarter of the nineteenth century.

During the formative century that preceded emancipation in Belize, the fundamental social distinction was between the free and the enslaved. This legal differentiation overlapped extensively with racial distinctions, with the result that the basic categories of white master and black slave affected the social status of those, like the poor whites or the free colored and blacks, whose social position was more ambiguous. Though it would seem that the majority of whites were neither rich nor powerful, to be white meant to identify and to be identified with the rich and powerful white elite. On the other hand, though not all blacks were slaves, to be black meant that one was undoubtedly associated with the status of slavery. Between the tiny elite and the masses of slaves were the free persons with limited civil rights, both colored and black, who were denied identity with the whites yet who themselves denied any affinity with the slaves.

The institution of slavery was revived by the colonizers of the New World as a way of dealing with the problem of a labor supply. Having captured and possessed the land, the colonial proprietors captured and possessed people to work it for them. But, though the origin of slavery may have been primarily economic in nature, the existence of the institution gave rise to persistent cultural traditions as well as patterns of social relationships. John Rex has argued that "the violence used by those who ran the slave trade is the most important underlying fact in the structure of race relations situations even when what we are studying is a society in which emancipation has long since been carried through."[1] There is no doubt that in Belize, as elsewhere in the New World, the persistent low status of blacks is in part a consequence of the fact that they were historically the victims of systematic degradation under slavery. This traditional assocation of blacks with slave status is compounded by a devaluation of the African cultural heritage accompanied by an elevation of European culture. More important than these cultural traditions, however, is the persistence of structural discrimination that has kept the black majority of the population poor and dependent even after legal emancipation.

Gordon Lewis has suggested that after emancipation in the West Indies, "the economic struggle between former master and slave continued but in new forms,"[2] and that emancipation simply "removed the gross features of the slave system without basically upsetting the underlying class-colour differentiations of the society."[3] These comments are equally applicable to Belize, where the masters, who needed all the laborers they could get during the mahogany boom of 1835–46, added the advance and truck systems to their monopolization of the land as the means of compelling the ex-slaves to continue to work in the mahogany forests. The result was the almost complete failure of an independent peasantry to develop, and it was not until the arrival of the Maya and *mestizo* immigrants from the north that any major agricultural developments occurred in Belize. Emancipation, though an important event, did not influence the development of the social structure of Belize in any essential manner. In 1838 the legal status of the slaves, who were then a minority of the population, was changed, but their conditions, their prospects, and their relations with the masters remained essentially the same, because they lacked the means to achieve a real emancipation.

In one sense, the abolition of slavery did eliminate a contradiction, however. "The essential and unanswerable problem," as Douglas Hall has put it, was "that although the slaves were accounted as capital equipment, they were people, and their masters were torn by conflict between these two views of their property."[4] After emancipation the masters were torn by no such contradiction, but were able, quite simply, to perceive all the laborers, present or potential, of whatever race or ethnicity, as inferior people. In fact, the white elite, who after the middle of the nineteenth century were not so much a settler class as the bureaucratic representatives of metropolitan organizations, held racial stereotypes of the various colonized peoples. An example of the unflattering distinctions made between the non-white segments of the colony's population is provided in a report from the Police Magistrate of Belize to the Lieutenant Governor in 1870:

Conclusions 197

> The Laborers consist of Creoles (natives of the place) and Caribs, natives of Jamaica, and Spaniards from the neighbouring Republics. In the Northern District the Laborers are principally aboriginal Indians. Of the whole the Indians are the most docile, passive, and abstemious. The Creoles and Caribs come next in degree of patient submission and endurance, but the latter are Clannish, cunning and dishonest. The Jamaicans hard working but insolent, insubordinate, and dissipated—The Spaniards bloodthirsty and revengeful.[5]

In a colonial society such as Belize the various racial/ethnic groups are to some extent occupationally specialized and geographically segregated, and though they participate in the same economy and are subject to the same polity, it is clear that they do not subscribe to a common culture, ideology, or value system. The factor that held such a variety of groups together was the monopoly of power held by the colonizers—in other words, the colonial society was bound together by the political and economic institutions of the dominant colonizing group. However, these institutions changed in accordance with changes in the nature of, and the relations between, the chief social formations that constitute the social structure of the colonial society.

The series of developments that took place in the 1850s were crucial for the future history of Belize. The massive influx of refugees from Yucatán doubled the population, established the basic racial/ethnic dichotomy of present-day Belize, and introduced agriculture into the economy. In that decade, also, the depression in the mahogany trade critically undermined the old settler elite, which, under political pressure from two directions, finally succumbed to the power of the metropolis. The result was a further consolidation of capital, a reorganization of the colonial political and economic institutions, and a restructuring of the distribution of power in Belize, away from the declining settler oligarchy and toward the bureaucracies and board rooms of the metropolis. One of the major social formations of Belize, the white settler class, was virtually eliminated, and henceforth the historic colonial confrontation was to develop between the forces of the metropolis and the colonized people. The establishment of crown colony rule in 1871, though providing a convenient point at which to limit this account, was not in itself decisive, for it merely confirmed a development that had been in process for decades and that has defined the basic problems of contemporary Belize.

Appendixes

APPENDIX A.
LAWS AND CUSTOMS RELATING TO SLAVERY

In the case of a black or coloured person, *bona fide* in possession of liberty, but unable to produce a document of his manumission, on the trial of a civil action instituted by him, if an objection to that effect were taken by the defendent, the *onus probandi,* the examinants declared, would lie with the party so objecting.

This is a proof of the liberality of the settlement in matters regarding liberty. . . .

Slaves are allowed to sue in the courts, through their owners, and are held exempt from being sued. They are also, by the custom of the country, allowed to possess property for their private use.

They may, through their owner, or any other person they choose to select, get redress for any such property taken or wrongfully withheld from them; and may, even against their owners, obtain redress in every case except in matters of debt.

In the event of personal injury done to a slave, an action of damages would, (the examinants said) lie to compensate the owner for such injury, and the offending party would likewise be amenable to criminal process.

Slaves are considered alike subjects to the payment of debts as other property.

All transfers of slaves are required to be in writing.

With regard to the sale of slaves, whether taken under execution or other judicial authority or sold by private contract, it appears to be the usual and very laudable custom (there being no express regulation on the subject) to sell them in families and not individually; the relationship, however, not being considered in this respect beyond the immediate issue, but no distinction is made with respect to the legitimacy or illegitimacy of such issue.

Appendix

Owners in this settlement conceive that they have the power of inflicting, at their discretion, corporal punishment upon their slaves to the extent of thirty-nine lashes; and also, for petty misdemeanors, to imprison them without a warrant from a magistrate, paying themselves the expenses of the slaves during such confinement....

Slaves are not considered competent witnesses against white persons, but their testimony is received in all the Courts of the settlement against their own class. They are sworn in the usual form....

Slave evidence must, the examinants concurred in stating, be received with caution from their low state of civilization; and they were disinclined to recommend any extension of the competency of this class of persons as witnesses.

In answer to our enquiry, whether the circumstance of the same offence being committed by a free person or a slave caused any difference to be made with respect to the punishment, the examinants said, "Free black persons and slaves are liable to the same punishment; the courts exercise discretion in this case, and generally give it in favour of the slave from the low state of his intellectual cultivation."

This seems a wise departure from the principle of the Roman law....

Slaves are not held personally responsible for criminal offenses committed by them by the order of their owners, except in cases of felony....

The examinants say, that an owner cannot be compelled to sell his slave on tender of a reasonable price for his freedom, but that they have never known the circumstance of a refusal in such case to sell.

In cases of manumission directed by will, such bequest of freedom, it is stated, is invariably made known to the slave. Indeed it is declared to be the general practice to read the wills at the funeral of the testators, and to record the same in the record office, where slaves are permitted to have ready access to them. The examinants are therefore of opinion, that it does not lie in the power of an heir or executor to defeat the benevolent intention of a testator in this respect. A slave, they also state, could in such case enforce his rights by writ of replevin; and on the issuing of such writ, although a bond is required in double the value of the slave, yet the Court invariably order the same to be executed on the security of the public chest; thus humanely facilitating the assertion to freedom.

There is no fine or tax here on the manumission of a slave; nor, on the gratuitous manumission of a slave by an owner, is the latter obliged to enter into any security to the settlement, to prevent its being burthened with the slave in the event of his subsequent incapacity, by sickness or otherwise, to support himself.

In the cases of clauses in deeds or wills granting manumissions, where the expression is obscure, such clauses are, it is said, invariably interpreted favourably to the slave.

Bequests in favour of freedom are considered as specific legacies.

No public notice is required of the intention to manumit.

The consent of the owner or his representative is held to be necessary before the marriage of a slave can be solemnized; but such consent, it would appear, is seldom refused. . . .

No commixture of the blood of whites with that of coloured persons, is considered here, as it is to a certain extent in Jamaica, to give a title to freedom.

Extracts from the report of the "Commissioners of Inquiry into the Administration of Criminal and Civil Justice . . . on the Settlement of Honduras," 24 February 1829, CO 318/77, pp. 9–11.

APPENDIX B.
FAMILY OF MARY FRANCE BELONGING TO ALEXANDER FRANCE, 1834

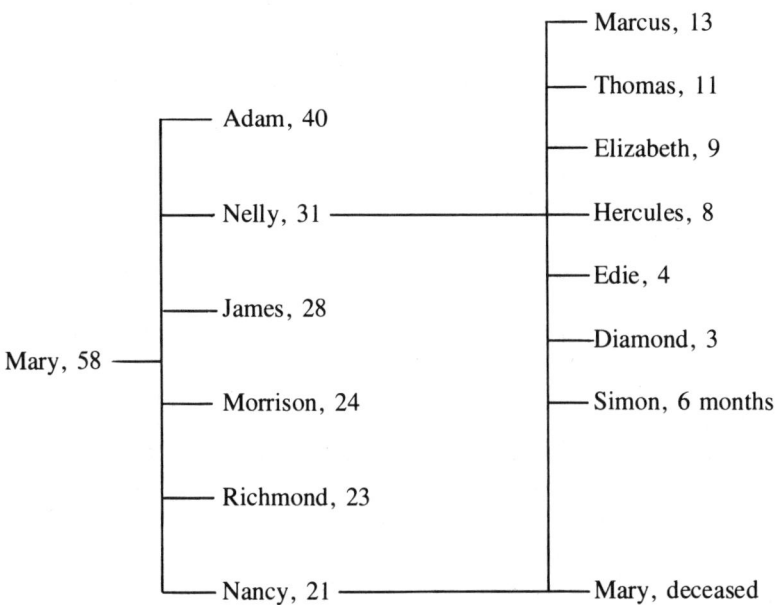

APPENDIX C.
FAMILY OF QUASHIE CUNNINGHAM BELONGING TO SARAH KEEFE, 1834

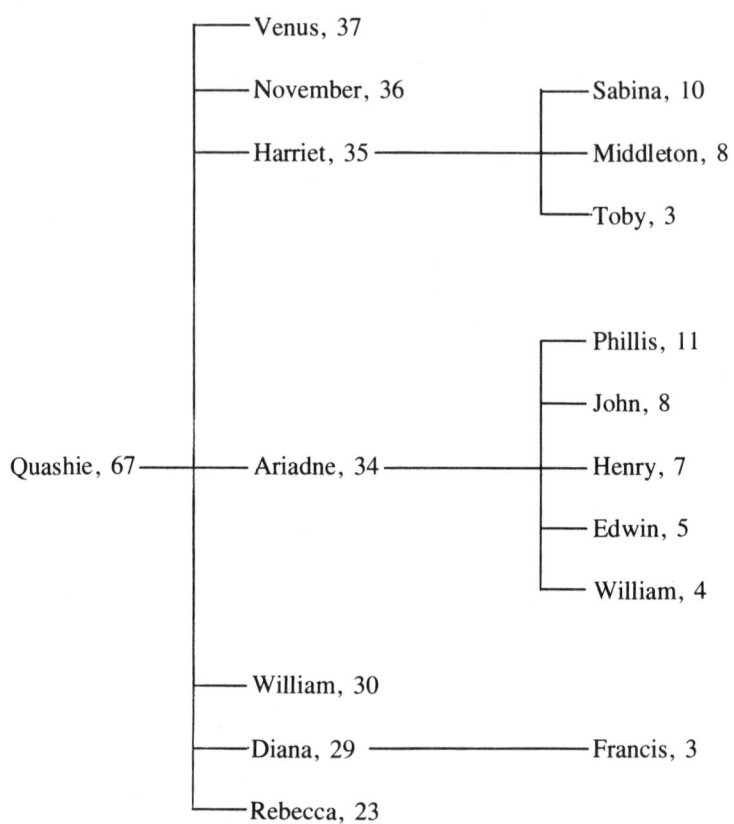

APPENDIX D.
FAMILY OF JANE AND SAM BURN BELONGING TO WILLIAM D. BURN, 1834

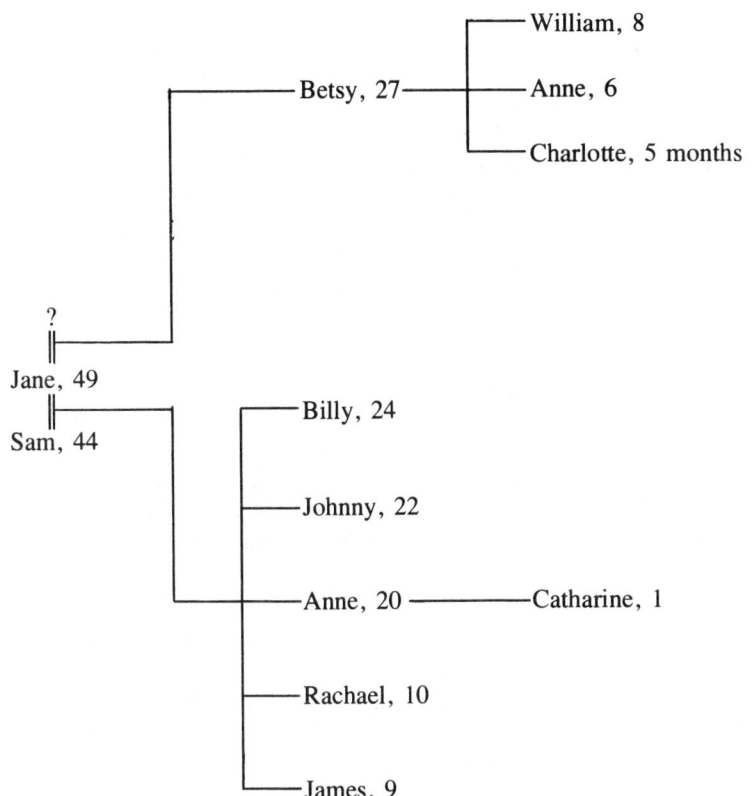

APPENDIX E.
FAMILY OF NANCY GAMBQUNIL BELONGING TO ANN SMITH, 1834

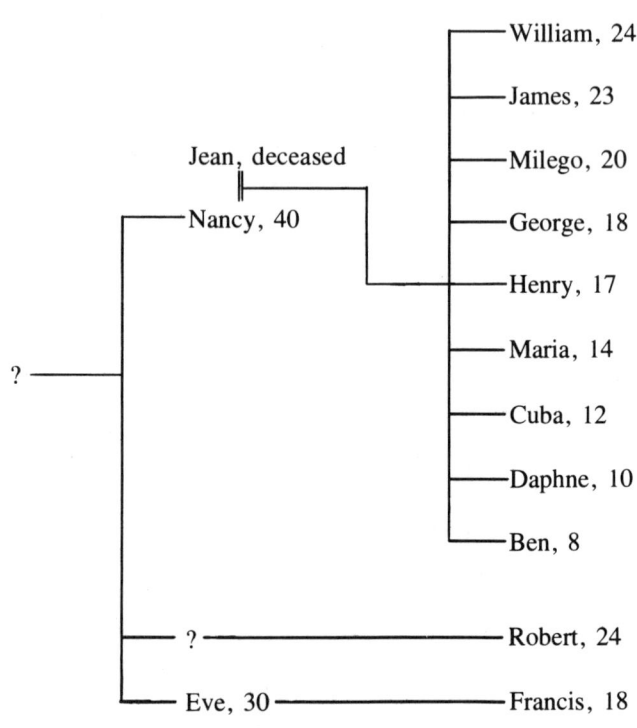

Appendix

APPENDIX F.
FAMILY OF MARY ANNE AND MURPHY ANDERSON BELONGING TO RICHARD JOHN AND ANNE ANDERSON, 1834

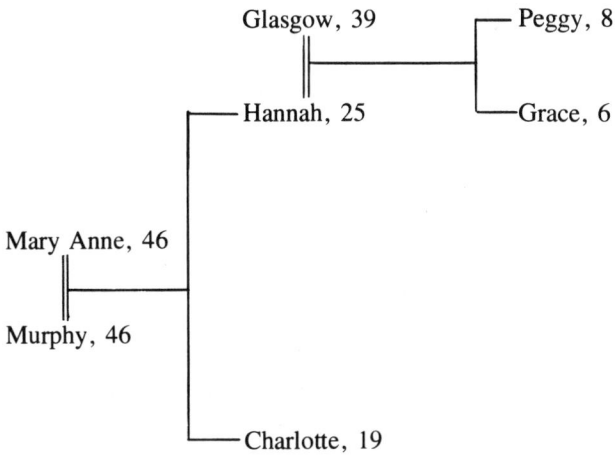

APPENDIX G.
FAMILY OF SAMMY GOFF BELONGING TO ESTATE OF SARAH GOFF (DECEASED), 1834

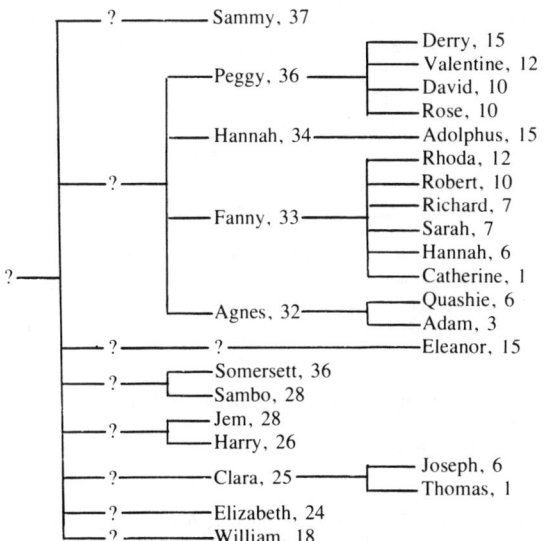

Notes

PREFACE

1. Sidney W. Mintz, Foreword to *Afro-American Anthropology: Contemporary Perspectives*, ed. Norman E. Whitten, Jr. and John F. Szwed (New York, 1970), p. 6.
2. See Sidney W. Mintz, "The Caribbean as a Socio-Cultural Area," *Journal of World History* 9, no. 4 (1966):912–37.
3. Stephen L. Caiger, *British Honduras, Past and Present* (London, 1951), and Algar Robert Gregg, *British Honduras* (London, 1968).
4. D. A. G. Waddell, *British Honduras: A Historical and Contemporary Survey* (London, 1961), and Narda Dobson, *A History of Belize* (London, 1973).
5. Wayne M. Clegern, *British Honduras: Colonial Dead End, 1859–1900* (Baton Rouge, 1967), and R. A. Humphreys, *The Diplomatic History of British Honduras, 1638–1901* (London, 1961).
6. N. S. Carey Jones, *The Pattern of a Dependent Economy: The National Income of British Honduras* (Cambridge, 1953); A. C. S. Wright et al., *Land in British Honduras: A Report of the British Honduras Land Use Survey Team* (London, 1959); Grant D. Jones, *The Politics of Agricultural Development in Northern British Honduras* (Winston-Salem, N.C., 1971); Norman Ashcraft, *Colonialism and Underdevelopment: Processes of Political Economic Change in British Honduras* (New York, 1973).

CHAPTER 1

1. Belizean Independence Secretariat, *Belize: New Nation in Central America* (Belize City, 1972), p. 3.
2. Sir John Alder Burdon, *Archives of British Honduras*, 3 vols, (London, 1935) 2:57, 60.
3. *Census of British Honduras, 9th April, 1946* (Belize, 1948), p. xxix.
4. *Census of British Honduras, 1960* (Kingston, n.d.) 2:65.
5. Statistics from the census reports and the registrar general's annual Blue Books.
6. Ibid.
7. Census of 1946, p. xxix.
8. Great Britain, Colonial Office, *Report of the British Guiana and British Honduras Settlement Commission, Cmd. 7533* (London, 1948), p. 223.
9. Provisional census figures for 1970.
10. Ibid.
11. Belizean Independence Secretariat, *Belize*, p. 37.
12. O. Nigel Bolland and Assad Shoman, *Land in Belize, 1765–1871: The Origins of Land Tenure, Use, and Distribution in a Dependent Economy* (Jamaica, 1975), p. 104.

13. Lindsay W. Bristowe and Philip B. Wright, *The Handbook of British Honduras for 1888–89* (London, 1888), p. 81.
14. Goverment of Belize, *Belize: New Nation in Central America* (Belmopan, 1976), p. 26.
15. Belizean Independence Secretariat, *Belize*, p. 39.
16. Ibid., p. 37.
17. Ibid., p. 37.
18. Ibid., p. 37.
19. Ibid., p. 35. By 1975 the balance of trade deficit was U.S. $28 million.
20. *Latin America and the Caribbean: A Handbook,* ed. Claudio Veliz (London, 1968), p. 173.
21. A. A. Hunter, *Rural Land Utilization Tax... A Beneficial Just and Equitable Piece of Legislation* (Belize, n.d.), p. 8.
22. Bolland and Shoman, *Land in Belize,* p. 114.
23. Ibid.
24. "The Definitive Treaty of Peace," 1763, CO 123/1.
25. Burdon, *Archives of British Honduras* 2:330.
26. Ibid., pp. 410–11.
27. Belizean Independence Secretariat, *Belize,* p. 19, shows a facsimile of the opening sections of the 1853 "Act to amend the system of Government of British Honduras."
28. *The Handbook of British Honduras,* ed. M. S. Metzgen and H. E. C. Cain (London, 1925), pp. 67–68.
29. "British Honduras Constitution (Amendment) Ordinance, 1932," Ordinance no. 17 of 1932.
30. "An Ordinance to provide for the Constitution and Legislative Council of the Colony," Ordinance no. 13 of 1935.
31. T. D. Vickers, *The Legislature of British Honduras* (Belize, 1953), p. 26.
32. For an account of the early years of the P.U.P., see Assad Shoman, "The Birth of the Nationalist Movement in Belize, 1950–1954," *Journal of Belizean Affairs,* no. 2 (1973), pp. 3–40.
33. "The British Honduras Constitution Ordinance, 1954," Ordinance no. 13 of 1954.
34. "The British Honduras Constitution (Amendment) Ordinance, 1960," Ordinance no. 12 of 1960.
35. See C. P. Cacho, "British Honduras: A Case of Deviation in Commonwealth Caribbean Decolonization," *New World Quarterly* 3, no. 3 (1967):33–44.
36. N. S. Carey Jones, *The Pattern of a Dependent Economy: The National Income of British Honduras* (Cambridge, 1953), p. 18.
37. Belizean Independence Secretariat, *Belize,* p. 59.

CHAPTER 2

1. Eric R. Wolf, *Sons of the Shaking Earth* (Chicago, 1959), pp. 67–68.
2. Gordon R. Willey et al., *Prehistoric Maya Settlements in the Belize River Valley,* Papers of the Peabody Museum of Archaeology and Ethnology no. 54 (Cambridge, Mass., 1965).
3. Ibid., p. 570.
4. Gordon R. Willey and Demitri B. Shimkin, "The Collapse of Classic Maya Civilization in the Southern Lowlands: A Symposium Summary Statement," *Southwestern Journal of Anthropology* 27, no. 1 (1971):12.
5. Ibid., p. 15.
6. J. Eric S. Thompson, "Sixteenth and Seventeenth Century Reports on the Chol Mayas," *American Anthropologist* 40, no. 4 (1938):603.
7. Ibid., p. 592.
8. Ibid., p. 593.
9. Doris Zemurray Stone, *Some Spanish Entradas 1524–1695,* Middle American Papers no. 4 (New Orleans, 1932), pp. 259–69.
10. J. Eric S. Thompson, *Maya History and Religion* (Norman, Okla., 1970), p. 59.
11. Robert S. Chamberlain, *The Conquest and Colonization of Yucatan 1517–1550* (Washington, D.C., 1948), pp. 120–24.
12. Sylvanus Griswold Morley, *The Inscriptions of Petén,* 5 vols. (Washington, D.C., 1937–

38), 1:27–33; William R. Bullard Jr., "Stratigraphic Excavations at San Estevan, Northern British Honduras," Art and Archaeology Occasional Papers no. 9, Royal Ontario Museum (Toronto, 1965), pp. 9–10; Thompson, *Maya History,* pp. 70–71.

13. Juan de Villagutierre Soto-Mayor, *Historia de la Conquista de la Provincia de el Itzá* (Madrid, 1701), quoted in Charles St. John Fancourt, *The History of Yucatán from Its Discovery to the Close of the Seventeenth Century* (London, 1854), p. 221.

14. Morley, *Inscriptions of Petén,* 1:49.

15. Ibid., 1:56.

16. Thompson, *Maya History,* p. 70.

17. Morley, *Inscriptions of Petén,* 1:70.

18. Woodrow Borah, "New Spain's Century of Depression," *Ibero-Americana,* no. 35 (1951), p. 3.

19. "An Account of the Spaniards landing at and taking of St. George's Key, by the subscriber, who was then on the place, and an Inhabitant," Edward Felix Hill, 1 Oct. 1779, CO 137/76.

20. Unsigned letter to Gov. Dalling, 3 Sept. 1779, CO 137/75.

21. See, for example, three maps: "The Bay of Honduras" by Thomas Jeffreys, 20 Feb. 1775, CO 123/14/1; "A Map of A Part of Yucatan or of that Part of the Eastern Shore within the Bay of Honduras Alloted to Great Britain for the Cutting of Logwood, in consequence of the Convention Signed with Spain on the 14th July 1786. By a Bay-Man," London, 1787; "A Sketch of the British Settlement of Honduras and course of the Southern Coast to the River Dulce" by H. C. Du Vernay, 9 March 1814, CO 123/23.

22. Thomas Graham, "Journal of my Visitation of Part of the District granted by His Catholic Majesty for the occupation of British settlers . . . ," 27 Oct. 1790, CO 123/9; "A Narrative of the Publick Transactions in the Bay of Honduras from 1784 to 1790," Edward Marcus Despard, 8 March 1791, CO 123/10.

23. Sir John Alder Burdon, *Archives of British Honduras,* 3 vols. (London, 1935), 2:58.

24. Ibid., 2:101.

25. Capt. G. Henderson, *An Account of the British Settlement at Honduras* . . . (London, 1809), pp. 18–19.

26. Minutes from the public record, 25 Feb. 1817, CO 123/26.

27. Supt. Arthur to Major Fraser, 12 June 1817; see also Magistrates of Honduras to Earl Bathurst, 26 Feb. 1817, and Arthur to Bathurst, 12 July 1817, CO 123/26.

28. Thompson, *Maya History,* p. 71.

29. See *The Defence of the Settlers of Honduras against the unjust and unfounded representations of Colonel George Arthur* . . . (Jamaica, 1824), pp. 45–46.

30. *The Honduras Almanack* (Belize, 1830), pp. 11–13.

31. David M. Pendergast, ed., *Palenque: The Walker-Caddy Expedition . . . 1839–40* (Norman, Okla., 1967), pp. 52, 159.

32. Burdon, *Archives of British Honduras* 1:4.

33. Stephen L. Caiger, *British Honduras, Past and Present* (London, 1951), pp. 126–27.

34. D. A. G. Waddell, *British Honduras: A Historical and Contemporary Survey* (London, 1961), p. 18.

CHAPTER 3

1. E. O. Winzerling, *The Beginning of British Honduras 1506–1765* (New York, 1946) pp. 33–44.

2. J. A. Calderon Quijano, *Belice 1663(?)–1821: Historia de los establecimientos britanicos del Rio Valis hasta la independencia de hispanoamerica* (Seville, 1944), pp. 34, 46–49.

3. See also G. W. Bridges, *The Annals of Jamaica,* 2 vols. (London, 1828), 2:134–37, and "A Map of A Part of Yucatan. . . . By a Bay-Man" (London, 1787), which names the "River Wallis or Balleze."

4. Alan K. Craig, "Logwood as a Factor in the Settlement of British Honduras," *Caribbean Studies* 9, no. 1 (1969):53–62.

5. Sir John Alder Burdon, *Archives of British Honduras,* 3 vols., (London, 1935), 1:50.

6. Ibid., 1:52.

7. CO 137/5.

8. Anonymous and undated paper, CO 137/48.
9. Board of Trade report to George I, 25 Sept. 1717, CO 123/3.
10. Letter from Robert Hodgson, 10 April 1751, CO 137/59.
11. "The Memorial of His Majestys Subjects driven from the Bay of Honduras in September 1779, on behalf of themselves and the Merchants formerly Trading to the Said Bay... ," Robert White to Thomas Townshend, 10 Feb. 1783, CO 123/2.
12. Gov. Knowles to Sir Thomas Robinson, 13 April 1755, CO 137/60.
13. "The Definitive Treaty of Peace," signed 10 Feb. 1763, CO 123/1.
14. Joseph Maud to Gov. Littelton, 7 Oct. 1765, CO 137/62.
15. White to Townshend, 10 Feb. 1783, CO 123/2.
16. Capt. Nathaniel Uring, *A History of the Voyages and Travels*... 2d ed. (London, 1727), pp. 354–58.
17. Archibald Robertson Gibbs, *British Honduras: An Historical and Descriptive Account of the Colony from Its Settlement, 1670* (London, 1883), pp. 124–25.
18. Minutes of the Public Meeting, 10 April 1765, CO 123/5; "Laws of Honduras 1806–1810," GRB.
19. Minutes of the Public Meeting, 6 May 1766, CO 123/5; "Laws of Honduras 1806–1810," GRB. By "parallel" the resolution actually means the opposite—"perpendicular"—as was made clear in the Minutes of a Public Meeting on 3 March 1812 referring to the "Ancient and established usage of the Settlement" in "establishing Division lines of Mahogany Works"; Meetings of Magistrates B, 1808–1815, GRB.
20. Unsigned letter to Gov. Dalling, 3 Sept. 1779, CO 137/75.
21. "An Account of the Spaniards landing at... St. George's Key... ," CO 137/76.
22. See White to Lord Shelburne, 2 July 1782, and White to Lord North, 8 April and 11 Dec. 1783, CO 123/2.
23. Bartlett to Dalling, undated, CO 137/76.
24. Article 3 of the Convention of London, 1786, from "A Map of A Part of Yucatan.... By a Bay-Man."
25. "Remarks upon the Situation Trade etc. etc of the District occupied by the British Subjects in the Bay of Honduras," ex-Supt. Barrow, 1 May 1809, CO 123/18.
26. Burdon, *Archives of British Honduras* 2:92.
27. Enclosed in Supt. Smyth to Earl Bathurst, 24 May 1814, CO 123/23; see also Burdon, *Archives of British Honduras* 2:167.
28. Supt. Codd to Horton, 8 July 1825, cited in R. A. Humphreys, *The Diplomatic History of British Honduras, 1638–1901* (London, 1961), p. 18.
29. White to Lord Sydney, 28 May 1787, CO 123/5 and CO 123/14.
30. Letter from Supt. Despard, 23 Feb. 1787, CO 123/5.
31. John Atkins, *A Voyage to Guinea, Brasil, and the West Indies*... (London, 1735), p. 227.
32. The Inhabitants of the Bay of Honduras to Major Caulfield, 8 June 1745, CO 137/48.
33. Unsigned letter to Dalling, 3 Sept. 1779, CO 137/75.
34. Sydney to Despard, 31 July 1786, CO 137/86; and 26 June 1787, enclosed in Supt. Arthur to Bathurst, 13 Sept. 1820, CO 123/29.
35. Letters from Despard, 23 Feb. and 31 Oct. 1787, CO 123/5 and CO 123/6.
36. Letter from Despard, 23 Feb. 1787, CO 123/5.
37. CO 123/5.
38. Despard to Sydney, 17 Aug. 1787, CO 123/5.
39. Despard to Sydney, 23 Feb. 1787, and Despard to Col. Grimarist, 14 Aug. 1787, CO 123/5.
40. Settlers to London merchants, 26 Aug. 1787, CO 123/5.
41. 27 Aug. 1787, CO 123/5. Emphasis in original.
42. Despard to Sydney, 17 Aug. 1787, CO 123/5.
43. Settlers to London merchants, 27 Aug. 1787, CO 123/5.
44. Ibid.
45. An account of 18 Aug. 1787 by Bartlet, Douglas, Pitts, and O'Brien, 12 March 1791, CO 123/13.
46. "A Narrative of the Publick Transactions in the Bay of Honduras from 1784 to 1790" by Despard, 8 March 1791, CO 123/10.
47. Settlers to London merchants, CO 123/5

48. Despard to Sydney, 24 Aug. 1787, CO 123/5.
49. Burdon, *Archives of British Honduras* 1:1.
50. 17 Dec. 1839, CO 123/55.
51. Burdon, *Archives of British Honduras* 1:104.
52. Lords of the Admiralty to Lord Hillsborough, 27 July and 23 Aug. 1768, CO 137/63; Admiral Parry to Sec. Stephens, 12 Dec. 1768, in Burdon, *Archives of British Honduras* 1:116.
53. Petition to Admiral Rodney, 12 Sept. 1771, CO 137/67.
54. Sydney to Despard, 6 Feb. 1788, CO 123/6.
55. Gordon K. Lewis, *The Growth of the Modern West Indies* (London, 1968), pp. 289–90.
56. N. S. Carey Jones, *The Pattern of a Dependent Economy: The National Income of British Honduras* (Cambridge, 1953), p. 136.
57. Burdon, *Archives of British Honduras* 1:31.
58. "Regulations framed by the Committee chosen by the British Inhabitants of the District," 10 June 1789, CO 123/12.
59. "Minutes of a meeting of the Magistrates," 23 April 1790, CO 123/12.
60. "A Narrative of the Publick Transactions . . . ," CO 123/10.
61. CO 123/9.
62. The account by Bartlet et al., CO 123/13.
63. James Bannantine, *Memoirs of Edward Marcus Despard* (London 1799), p. 29; letter from Despard, 26 Dec. 1800, CO 123/14; Sir Charles Oman, *The Unfortunate Colonel Despard and Other Studies* (London, 1922), pp. 1–21; E. P. Thompson, *The Making of the English Working Class* (New York, 1963), pp. 478–84; O. Nigel Bolland, "Despard's Conspiracy, 1802: The Social Composition, Organization, and Ideology of a 'Pre-Industrial' Secret Society" (in preparation).
64. D. A. G. Waddell, *British Honduras: A Historical and Contemporary Survey* (London, 1961), p. 12.
65. "A Narrative of the Publick Transactions . . . ," CO 123/10.
66. Despard to Sydney, 24 Aug. 1787, CO 123/5.
67. Memorial from White to Sydney, 21 Feb. 1788, CO 123/6.
68. Sydney to Despard, 6 Feb. 1788, CO 123/6.
69. Petition to William Pitt, 13 Aug. 1793, CO 137/92.
70. 18 May 1790, CO 123/9.
71. Burdon, *Archives of British Honduras* 1:184.
72. Supt. Hamilton to Gov. Coote, 26 Nov. 1807, CO 123/17.
73. Smyth to Lord Liverpool, 31 Aug. 1810, CO 123/19.
74. Arthur to Bathurst, 31 July 1819, CO 123/28.
75. Col. Lawrie to Evan Napean, 26 Jan. 1788, CO 123/6.
76. "Return of such of the Inhabitants from the Mosquito Shore as His Majesty's Superintendent has found it necessary to issue a further supply of provisions to," 24 Aug. and 20 Oct. 1787., CO 123/5.
77. Hodgson to Gov. Trelawny, 14 April 1771, CO 137/76.
78. CO 123/11.
79. CO 123/9.
80. Orlando Patterson, *The Sociology of Slavery* (London, 1967), p. 53; Edward Brathwaite, *The Development of Creole Society in Jamaica, 1770–1820* (London, 1971), p. 121.
81. Despard to Sydney, 17 Aug. 1787, CO 123/5.
82. Petition from the Bay settlers to Trelawny, 19 Feb. 1771, CO 137/76.
83. Letter from Despard, 11 Jan. 1788, CO 123/6.
84. Robert English, Samuel Harrison, and Abraham (or Absalom) Bull to Despard, 20 Aug. 1787, CO 123/5.
85. Despard to Sydney, 24 Aug. 1787, CO 123/5. Emphasis in original.
86. "A Narrative of the Publick Transactions . . . ," CO 123/10.
87. "Plan of Police . . ." proposed by Supt. Hunter, 18 May 1790, CO 123/9.

CHAPTER 4

1. H. H. Bancroft, *History of Central America,* 3 vols. (San Francisco, 1883–87): 2:626.
2. Archibald Robertson Gibbs, *British Honduras: An Historical and Descriptive Account of the Colony from Its Settlement, 1670* (London, 1883), p. 34.

3. The Inhabitants of the Bay of Honduras to Major Caulfield, 8 June 1745, CO 137/48.
4. Capt. G. Henderson, *An Account of the British Settlement at Honduras*... (London, 1809), p. 59.
5. *The Honduras Almanack* (Belize, 1830), p. 6.
6. "Memorial of the Magistrates & Principal Inhabitants settled at the Bay of Honduras" to Lord Hillsborough, 1769, CO 137/65.
7. "General Return of the Inhabitants...," 22 Oct. 1790, CO 123/9.
8. Orlando Patterson, *The Sociology of Slavery* (London, 1967), pp. 129–33.
9. Br. Gen. H. T. Montresor to Gov. Sir Eyre Coote, 22 Oct. 1806, CO 123/17.
10. Ibid.
11. G. W. Roberts, *The Population of Jamaica* (Cambridge, 1957), p. 225.
12. Henderson, *An Account of the British Settlement*..., p. 92.
13. Census, 1816; census of the slave population, 31 Dec. 1820, GRB.
14. Return of manumissions by George Westby, 31 Dec. 1825, CO 123/37; Supt. Cockburn to Lord Goderich, 25 April 1831, CO 123/42.
15. Henderson, *An Account of the British Settlement*..., p. 39.
16. Supt. Despard to Lord Sydney, 17 Aug. 1787, CO 123/5.
17. Henderson, *An Account of the British Settlement*, pp. 46–47, 50–51, 53–54, 74–75.
18. Montresor to Coote, 22 Oct. 1806, CO 123/17; see also Maj. Gen. Pye to Earl Bathurst, 26 July 1822, AB, R.2: "The Name of Driver is here unknown...."
19. Henderson, *An Account of the British Settlement*..., pp. 47–50.
20. "An Account of the Spaniards landing at... St. George's Key," Edward Felix Hill, 1 Oct. 1779, CO 137/76.
21. Henderson, *An Account of the British Settlement*..., p. 13.
22. Unsigned letter to Gov. Dalling, 3 Sept. 1779, CO 137/75.
23. George Dyer to Evan Napean, 18 Oct. 1787, CO 123/5.
24. Robert White to Napean, 18 Sept. 1788, CO 123/6.
25. Count de Floridablanca to Anthony Merry, 30 May 1789, CO 123/7.
26. Richard Hoare to White, 25 Aug. 1788, CO 123/7.
27. White to Duke of Leeds, 31 July 1789, CO 123/7.
28. Montresor to Coote, 22 Oct, 1806, CO 123/17.
29. Henderson, *An Account of the British Settlement*..., p. 42.
30. Magistrates meeting, 4 April 1803, MM A2, GRB.
31. Meeting, 26 June 1805, GRB; "Laws of Honduras 1806–1810," GRB.
32. Public Meeting, 29 Oct. 1805, MM B, GRB.
33. Meeting, 30 June 1810, MM B, GRB. Emphasis in original.
34. Public Meeting, 29 Oct. 1805, MM B, GRB.
35. "Remarks upon the Situation Trade etc...," by ex-Supt. Barrow, 1 May 1809, CO 123/18.
36. Gibbs, *British Honduras*, p. 175.
37. "The Laws Regulations and Customs of Honduras... as abstracted from the whole...," 18 March 1803, CO 123/15.
38. Patterson, *Sociology of Slavery*, p. 77.
39. Supt. Smyth to Bathurst, 12 Nov. 1813, CO 123/22.
40. Report of the "Commissioners of Inquiry into the Administration of Criminal and Civil Justice... on the Settlement of Honduras," p. 3, 24 Feb. 1829, CO 318/77.
41. *The Defence of the Settlers of Honduras*... (Jamaica, 1824), p. 67.
42. Robinson, Gifford, and Copley to Bathurst, 24 Aug. 1822, CO 123/32.
43. Bathurst to Arthur, 22 Sept. 1821, AB, R.3.
44. Report of the "Commissioners of Inquiry...," 24 Feb. 1829, CO 318/77.
45. Ibid., p. 1.
46. Ibid., p. 9.
47. Cockburn to Goderich, 25 April 1831, CO 123/42.
48. C. L. R. James, *The Black Jacobins* (1938; rpt. New York, 1963), p. 11.
49. Cockburn to Goderich, 25 April 1831, CO 123/42.
50. Report of the "Commissioners of Inquiry...," p. 93.
51. Ibid., p. 94.
52. Ibid., Appendix E, pp. 106–12.

53. Ibid., p. 109.
54. Ibid., p. 110. In another case, however, the Magistrates appeared to emphasize that the fact of freedom, no matter how long it had been established, did not constitute legal freedom. A slave named Patty Crawford who had escaped and lived in Omoa for forty-three years in freedom returned with her children to the settlement. The Magistrates decided that the children were free and that "Lawrence Crawford had no just claim on them," but by purchasing the woman's freedom the Magistrates inferred that her one-time owner continued to have a legal right to her (Cockburn to Goderich, 23 March 1833, CO 123/44).
55. Ibid., p. 94.
56. Ibid., p. 95.
57. Ibid., p. 95.
58. *Honduras Gazette,* 19 May 1827, quoted in Narda Dobson, *A History of Belize* (London, 1973), p. 155.
59. Dobson, *History of Belize,* p. 155.
60. Smyth to Bathurst, 12 Nov. 1813, CO 123/22.
61. "Proceedings of a General Militia Court Martial...," 4 Aug. 1813, CO 123/22.
62. Letter from Thomas Potts, 30 Aug. 1806, CO 123/17.
63. "A Narrative of the Publick Transactions in the Bay of Honduras from 1784 to 1790," Edward Despard, 8 March 1791, CO 123/10.
64. James Bartlet to Despard, enclosed in Despard to Napean, 21 Oct. 1787, CO 123/5.
65. Sir John Alder Burdon, *Archives of British Honduras* 3 vols, (London, 1935), 1:210.
66. John Armstrong, *A Candid Examination of the "Defence of the Settlers of Honduras"* ... (London, 1824), p. 59.
67. Arthur to Bathurst, 21 Oct. 1816, CO 123/25.
68. Ibid.; see also minutes of Magistrates' meeting, 29 Aug. 1816, CO 123/25.
69. Ibid.
70. Summary court records, 1817–21, GRB.
71. Report of the "Commissioners of Inquiry...," p. 93.
72. Ibid., p. 94.
73. Ibid.
74. Ibid.

CHAPTER 5

1. Supt. Macdonald to Lord Glenelg, 18 March 1839, CO 123/55.
2. Archibald Robertson Gibbs, *British Honduras: An Historical and Descriptive Account of the Colony from Its Settlement, 1670* (London, 1883), p. 37.
3. D. A. G. Waddell, *British Honduras: A Historical and Contemporary Survey* (London, 1961), p. 14.
4. Capt. G. Henderson, *An Account of the British Settlement at Honduras* ... (London, 1809), pp. 59–60.
5. Ibid., pp. 57–59.
6. "A Short Sketch of the present situation...," by Supt. Barrow, 31 March 1803, CO 123/15.
7. Br. Gen. Montresor to Gov. Coote, 22 Oct. 1806, CO 123/17.
8. Supt. Arthur to Lord Bathurst, 7 Nov. 1816, CO 123/25. It is rather surprising that this generous account of the slaves' good treatment was sent a little over two weeks after Arthur had sent his account (Arthur to Bathurst, 21 Oct. 1816, CO 123/25) of Carty's trial for grotesque cruelty to a young female slave.
9. Arthur to Bathurst, 16 May 1820, CO 123/29.
10. Arthur to Bathurst, 7 Oct. 1820, CO 123/29.
11. Arthur to Bathurst, 10 Jan. 1822, in *The Defence of the Settlers of Honduras*... (Jamaica, 1824), p. 68.
12. Letter from Act. Supt. Pye, 25 July 1822, CO 123/31.
13. John Armstrong, *A Candid Examination of "The Defense of the Settlers of Honduras"* ... (London, 1824).

14. Supt. Codd to Bathurst, 8 March 1823, CO 123/34.
15. Extract from the *Royal Jamaica Gazette,* 6 March 1824, CO 123/35. See, however, Armstrong's criticism that McLean never visited any of the camps but only "paid two or three short visits to the dwelling-houses, and dined with two or three of the richer inhabitants, without probably making a single enquiry of such few of the slaves as might be present in the town" (Armstrong, *A Candid Examination,* p. 62). Armstrong also pointed out that McLean, a slave proprietor in Jamaica, was requested by the chief proprietors of Belize to help them in their case against Arthur.
16. Montresor to Coote, 22 Oct. 1806, CO 123/17.
17. "Remarks upon the Situation Trade etc . . . ," ex-Supt. Barrow, 1 May 1809, CO 123/18.
18. Gibbs, *British Honduras,* p. 37.
19. Stephen L. Caiger, *British Honduras, Past and Present* (London, 1951), pp. 26, 125.
20. "An Account of the Descent of the Spaniards on the Settlement in the Year 1798," in *The Defence of the Settlers of Honduras . . . ,* p. 93.
21. Monrad Sigfrid Metzgen, ed., *Shoulder to Shoulder, or the Battle of St. George's Caye 1798* (Belize City, 1928). Metzgen's pamphlet, popularizing the view of the mutual interdependence of blacks and whites in Belizean history, appeared shortly after a visit by Marcus Garvey to encourage development of a branch of the Universal Negro Improvement Association in Belize.
22. Gordon K. Lewis, *The Growth of the Modern West Indies* (London, 1968), p. 292.
23. The Inhabitants of the Bay of Honduras to Major Caulfield, 8 June 1745, CO 137/48.
24. Petition from the principal subjects of the Bay of Honduras to Admiral Rodney, 12 Sept. 1771, CO 137/67.
25. Joseph Maud to Gov. Littelton, 7 Oct. 1765, CO 137/62.
26. "The Memorial of Allan Auld of London Merchant, & Trading to the Bay of Honduras" to Lord Hillsborough, July 1768, CO 137/63.
27. Petition from the Bay settlers to Gov. Trelawny, 19 Feb. 1771, CO 137/66.
28. The extracts from reports on the 1773 revolt are from Adm. 1/239 in Sir John Alder Burdon, *Archives of British Honduras,* 3 vols. (London, 1935), 1:121–24.
29. Burdon, *Archives of British Honduras* 1:282.
30. James Bartlet to Dyer, Allan & Co., 26 Nov. 1791, CO 123/13.
31. Supt. Hamilton to the Magistrates, 5 April 1807, CO 123/17.
32. Dyer to Edward Cooke, 29 May 1809, CO 123/18.
33. Minutes from the public record, 25 Feb. 1817, CO 123/26.
34. Magistrates to Bathurst, 26 Feb. 1817, CO 123/26.
35. Arthur to Bathurst, 1 April 1819, CO 123/28.
36. Arthur to Bathurst, 16 May 1820, CO 123/29.
37. Ibid.
38. Proclamation, 3 May 1820, CO 123/33.
39. Proclamation, 22 May 1820, CO 123/33.
40. "Plan of Police" proposed by Supt. Hunter, 18 May 1790, CO 123/9.
41. "An Account of the Spaniards landing at . . . St. George's Key . . . ," Edward Felix Hill, 1 Oct. 1779, CO 137/76.
42. Letter from Thomas Potts, 28 May 1792, CO 123/13.
43. "The Memorial of Benjamin Garnett and Charles Armstrong late of Honduras Bay" to Henry Dundas, 11 June 1793, CO 123/13.
44. Manuel Melendez to Manuel Artazo, 15 March 1813, in "An Inventory of the Manuscript Collections of the Middle American Research Institute" (New Orleans, 1939, mimeo.), pp. 120–21.
45. Codd to Bathurst, 8 March 1823, CO 123/34.
46. Leon Baldison to Codd, 15 Nov. 1823, CO 123/34.
47. Magistrates to Codd, 28 Jan. 1825, CO 123/36.
48. Codd to Bathurst, 18 Feb. 1825, CO 123/36. Emphasis in original.
49. Ibid.
50. George Hyde to Marshall Bennett, 12 Feb. 1826, CO 123/37; for country of origin, Hyde listed three as being from "Moco," two from "Mandingo," one from "Eabo," three from "Mungola," and one from "Dago."
51. Henry Cooke to Lord Dudley and Ward, 27 Aug. 1827, CO 123/38.
52. James Stephen to Horace Twiss, 13 Oct. 1830, CO 123/41.
53. Censuses of 1823, 1826, and 1835, GRB.

54. Supt. Cockburn to John Lefevre, 13 Aug. 1834, CO 123/45.
55. See, for example, Cockburn to Commandant of Petén, 6 Sept. 1834, and Macdonald to Commandant of Omoa, 28 Sept. 1837, AB, R.8.
56. L. M. McLenan to Macdonald, 1 Feb. 1838, CO 123/53.
57. Burdon, *Archives of British Honduras* 2:184.
58. Arthur to Major Fraser, 12 June 1817, CO 123/26.
59. Arthur to Bathurst, 16 May 1820, CO 123/29.
60. See affidavit of Joseph Everett, 3 June 1780; letter from Richard Hoare, 5 July 1780; Hoare to Gov. Dalling, 8 July 1780, CO 137/78.
61. "A Narrative of the Publick Transactions in the Bay of Honduras from 1784 to 1790," Edward Marcus Despard, 8 March 1791, CO 123/10.
62. Arthur to Bathurst, 7 Oct. 1820, CO 123/29.
63. Ibid.
64. Armstrong, *A Candid Examination*, p. 61.
65. See also the case against Miss Mary Ann Uter for having her slave, Phyllis, cruelly flogged with a tamarind whip, in Cockburn to Lord Stanley, 1 July 1833, CO 123/44.
66. Henderson *An Account of the British Settlement*, p. 59.
67. Ibid., p. 60.
68. *The Defense of the Settlers of Honduras* ... , p. 11.
69. Quoted in Frederick Crowe, *The Gospel in Central America* ... (London, 1850), p. 321.
70. Hoare to Robert White, 25 Aug. 1788, CO 123/7.
71. Henderson, *An Account of the British Settlement*, p. 73.
72. Arthur to Bathurst, 2 Dec. 1814, CO 123/23.

CHAPTER 6

1. "Precis of the former state of the Settlers on the Mosquito Shore, and of the recent Settlement in the Bay of Honduras," n.d., CO 123/14/1.
2. Census of 1823, GRB.
3. Census of 1826, GRB.
4. Col. Lawrie to Evan Napean, 26 Jan. 1788, CO 123/6.
5. Sir John Alder Burdon, *Archives of British Honduras* 3 vols., (London, 1935), 1:69, 118, 167, 197–99.
6. Censuses of 1816 and 1820, GRB.
7. Return of manumissions by George Westby, 15 Dec. 1823, CO 123/34.
8. Return of manumissions by Westby, 31 Dec. 1825, CO 123/37.
9. Supt. Cockburn to Lord Goderich, 25 April 1831, CO 123/42.
10. Ibid.
11. Burdon, *Archives of British Honduras* 1:197–99.
12. Supt. Arthur to Magistrates, 18 June 1817, CO 123/26.
13. Arthur to Lord Bathurst, 20 Nov. 1817, CO 123/26.
14. CO 123/27.
15. Census of 1826, GRB.
16. Arthur to Bathurst, 2 Dec. 1814, CO 123/23.
17. Arthur to Bathurst, 3 Dec. 1814, CO 123/23.
18. Qualifications for membership for whites were possession of £100 Jamaica currency and one year's residence. For colored men the qualifications were possession of £200 Jamaica currency and two year's residence; see memoranda of Arthur, 31 May 1823, CO 123/34. Another reference states that the colored had to show five years' residence; see minutes of Public Meeting, 20 Oct. 1808, in Burdon, *Archives of British Honduras* 2:123.
19. Arthur to Bathurst, 16 Feb. 1815, CO 123/24.
20. "The Memorial of William Usher one of His Majestys loyal Subjects settled in the Bay of Honduras ... ," 20 Jan. 1815, CO 123/24.
21. Arthur to Bathurst, 16 Feb. 1815, CO 123/24.
22. Bathurst to Arthur, 28 Nov. 1815, AB, R.1.
23. Arthur to Bathurst, 4 Nov. 1819, CO 123/28.

24. Arthur to Bathurst, 16 May 1820, CO 123/29.
25. Arthur to Bathurst, 5 March 1822, CO 123/31.
26. George Hyde to Bathurst, 3 Feb. 1827, CO 123/38.
27. Hyde to R. Wilmott Horton, June 1827; Hyde to Horton, 11 June 1827, CO 123/38.
28. Letter from Stephen Lushington, 28 Oct. 1827, CO 123/38.
29. Ibid.
30. Supt. Codd to R. Hay, 12 July 1828, CO 123/39.
31. Minutes of the Public Meeting, 6 July 1829, CO 123/40.
32. Cockburn to Horace Twiss, 9 Aug. 1830; Cockburn to Twiss, 8 Nov. 1830, CO 123/41.
33. Minutes of Legislative Meeting, 4 and 5 July 1831, CO 123/42.
34. *The Honduras Almanack for 1830* (Belize, 1830), p. 8.
35. Ibid., p. 6.
36. Codd to R. Wilmot, 23 Feb. 1823, CO 123/34.
37. Ibid.
38. Melville J. Herskovits, *The Myth of the Negro Past* (New York, 1941), chaps. 3 and 7.
39. Orlando Patterson, *The Sociology of Slavery* (London, 1967), p. 192.
40. Burdon, *Archives of British Honduras* 1:195–96.
41. Arthur to Major Fraser, 19 Nov. 1816, CO 123/27. An account of 1850 reported that sometimes the slaves' "masters and mistresses were ... drawn into the crimes of Obeahism"; it referred to one "Miss Clarissa Parslow, a proprietress of land, houses, and slaves, who died about 1841" and was believe to have practiced obeah; Frederick Crowe, *The Gospel in Central America ...* (London, 1850), p. 324.
42. *The Honduras Almanack for 1830*, pp. 17–18.
43. Crowe, *Gospel in Central America*, pp. 324–25.
44. *The Honduras Almanack for 1830*, pp. 6–7.
45. "Journal of my Visitation of part of the District granted by His Catholic Majesty for the occupation of British Settlers ... ," by Thomas Graham, 27 Oct. 1790, CO 123/9.
46. William Usher's affidavit, in "A Narrative of the Publick Transactions in the Bay of Honduras from 1784 to 1790," Edward Marcus Despard, 8 March 1791, CO 123/10.
47. Supt. Hamilton to Gov. Coote, 26 Nov. 1807, CO 123/17.
48. Thomas Potts, Andrew Cunningham, Robert Douglas, and James Hyde to Hamilton, 3 May 1806, CO 123/17.
49. Magistrates to Dyer, 25 Jan. 1809, CO 123/18.
50. *The Honduras Almanack for 1830*, p. 18.
51. Supt. Pye to Bathurst, 25 July 1822, CO 123/31.
52. Capt. G. Henderson, *An Account of the British Settlement of Honduras ...* (London, 1809), pp. 76–77.
53. *The Honduras Almanack for 1830*, p. 17.
54. Archibald Robertson Gibbs, *British Honduras: An Historical and Descriptive Account of the Colony from Its Settlement, 1670* (London, 1883), pp. 75–76.
55. Quoted in Patterson, *Sociology of Slavery*, p. 152.
56. Gibbs, *British Honduras*, p. 52.
57. Codd to Bathurst, 27 Oct. 1826, AB, R.4.
58. Gibbs, *British Honduras*, p. 79.
59. *The Honduras Almanack for 1829* (Belize, 1829).
60. Crowe, *Gospel in Central America*, p. 33.
61. *The Honduras Almanack for 1830*, pp. 6–7.
62. Crowe, *Gospel in Central America*, p. 50.
63. Act. Supt. J. G. Anderson to Sec. of State, 28 April 1836, AB, R.6.
64. P. C. Codd's "Return of Slaves Imported and Exported," 15 Dec. 1823, CO 123/34, and 31 Dec. 1825, CO 123/37.
65. Anderson to Lord Glenelg, 10 Aug. and 20 Dec. 1836, CO 123/48.
66. Arthur to Pye, 3 April 1822, AB, R.2, and CO 123/31; see also Rev. John Armstrong to Bathurst, 25 Feb. 1822, CO 123/32.
67. Return of burials by Armstrong, 16 Dec. 1823, CO 123/34, and return from the church register by Rev. Mathew Newport, 19 Oct. 1829, AB, R.2.
68. Return of marriages by Armstrong, 16 Dec. 1823, CO 123/34.

69. Return of marriages by Newport, 31 Dec. 1825, CO 123/37.
70. Codd to William Huskisson, 10 July 1828, AB, R.6.
71. Philip D. Curtin, *Two Jamaicas: The Role of Ideas in a Tropical Colony, 1830–1865* (1955; rpt. ed., New York, 1970), p. 41.

CHAPTER 7

1. Cockburn, Bennett, Dickinson, and Young to Commissioners of the Compensation Fund, 17 March 1834, CO 123/45.
2. A "mulatto" was the child of a black and a white; a "sambo" was the child of a mulatto and a black; a "quadroon" was the child of a mulatto and a white; and a "mustee" was the child of a quadroon and a white.
3. Supt. Cockburn to Edward Stanley, 29 Oct. 1833, AB, R.6, and CO 123/44.
4. Act. Supt. J. G. Anderson to Sec. of State, 28 April 1836, AB, R.6.
5. Memorial to Cockburn, from minutes of Public Meeting, 26 Oct. 1833, CO 123/44. In a statement of the comparative cost of free and slave labor, the memorialists estimated that a slave cost £45.8.4 per year, compared to £69.11.8 for a free laborer.
6. Francis Young to J. E. Dickinson, 8 Aug. 1836, AB, R.2.
7. Minutes of Public Meeting, March 1833, CO 123/44.
8. Minutes of Public Meeting, 2 July 1819, CO 123/28.
9. Cockburn to Lord Goderich, 10 Jan. 1833, CO 123/44.
10. Ibid.
11. Report of Thomas Jefferies, 27 Feb. 1835, CO 123/46.
12. Report of Alex. Henderson, not dated but probably early 1835, CO 123/46.
13. Report of Mathew Newport, 28 Feb. 1835, CO 123/46.
14. Anderson to Sec. of State, 25 June 1836, CO 123/48.
15. Lord Glenelg to Cockburn, 25 Nov. 1835, CO 123/48.
16. Minutes of Public Meeting, 4 July 1836, CO 123/48.
17. Cockburn to John Lefevre, 13 Aug. 1834, CO 123/45.
18. Minutes of Public Meeting, 21 Oct. 1833, CO 123/44.
19. Minutes of Public Meeting, 25 Jan. 1834, CO 123/45.
20. Cockburn to Stanley, 15 March 1834, CO 123/45.
21. Cockburn to Lefevre, 25 July 1834, CO 123/45.
22. Williamson to Anderson, 1 Oct. 1836, CO 123/48.
23. L. M. McLenan to Supt. Macdonald, 1 Nov. 1837, CO 123/52.
24. William Gow to Macdonald, 30 April 1837, CO 123/50.
25. Returns of punishments from the Special Magistrates, CO 123/48.
26. Cockburn to Lefevre, 25 July 1834, CO 123/45.
27. Gow to Macdonald, 30 April 1837, CO 123/50.
28. Williamson to Anderson, 1 Oct. 1836, CO 123/48.
29. Capt. George Henderson, *An Account of the British Settlement of Honduras* ... (London, 1809), p. 60.
30. Cockburn to Goderich, 25 April 1831, CO 123/42.
31. "Sales negros Est. of P. C. Wall," 29 Aug. 1820, CO 123/40.
32. 7 July 1835, CO 318/117.
33. See Narda Dobson, *A History of Belize* (London, 1973), p. 175.
34. Williamson to Anderson, 1 Oct. 1836, CO 123/48.
35. McLenan's report, 1 April 1837, CO 123/50.
36. Williamson to Anderson, 1 Oct. 1836, CO 123/48.
37. McLenan to Macdonald, 1 Sept. 1837, CO 123/50.
38. McLenan to Macdonald, 1 Feb. 1838, CO 123/53.
39. Eric Williams, *Capitalism and Slavery* (1944; rpt. ed, London, 1964), p. 204.
40. Minutes of Public Meeting, 1 March 1830, CO 123/41.
41. Minutes of Public Meeting, 6 Nov. 1837, CO 123/50.
42. James Walker to Macdonald, 12 Feb. 1838, CO 123/52.
43. Macdonald to Glenelg, 29 March 1838, CO 123/52.
44. Macdonald to Glenelg, 20 June 1838, CO 123/53.

45. Minutes of Public Meeting, 9 July 1838, enclosed in Macdonald to Glenelg, 28 Aug. 1838, CO 123/53.
46. Ibid.
47. Macdonald to Glenelg, 10 Aug. 1838, CO 123/53.
48. Quoted in Dobson, *History of Belize*, p. 172.
49. Macdonald's report enclosing return of prisoners confined in jail, 8 April 1839, CO 123/55.
50. Sidney Mintz, "The Question of Caribbean Peasantries: A Comment," *Caribbean Studies* 1 (1961):31–34.
51. Proclamation, 28 Oct. 1817, enclosed with "Report of the Commissioners appointed to investigate the claims by which all Land and Works are held in the Settlement of Honduras, 27 July 1820," enclosed in Supt. Arthur to Lord Bathurst, 13 Sept. 1820, CO 123/29.
52. Circular from Glenelg, 15 Sept. 1838, AB, R.15.
53. Quoted in Macdonald to Sec. of State, 9 Feb. 1839, AB, R.14.
54. Ibid.
55. Lord Normanby to Macdonald, 22 April 1839, AB, R.15, emphasis added.
56. Supt. Stevenson to Gov. Barkly, 30 July 1855, AB, R.48.
57. Lt. Gov. Longden to Gov. Grant, 6 March 1868, AB, R.98.
58. Archibald Robertson Gibbs, *British Honduras: An Historical and Descriptive Account of the Colony from Its Settlement, 1670* (London, 1883), pp. 85, 93, 106–7.
59. Cockburn to Sec. of State, 21 Jan. 1835, AB, R.6.
60. Anderson to Glenelg, 10 Aug. 1836, AB, R.6 and CO 123/48.
61. Anderson to Sec. of State, 20 Dec. 1836, CO 123/48.
62. Gow to Macdonald, 1 Feb. 1838, CO 123/53.
63. Gow to Macdonald, 1 March 1838, CO 123/53.
64. Philip D. Curtin, *Two Jamaicas: The Role of Ideas in a Tropical Colony, 1830–1865* (1955; rpt. ed., New York, 1970), p. 116.
65. F. R. Augier et al., *The Making of the West Indies* (London, 1960), p. 186.
66. Minutes of Public Meeting, 20 Jan. to 7 Feb. 1852, AB, R.20.
67. "An Act to amend the Law relating to Contracts for Hire and Service," 18 Vic. Cap. 12, *Laws of the Settlement of British Honduras* (Belize, 1857).
68. Douglas Hall, *Free Jamaica, 1838–1865: An Economic History* (1959; rpt. ed., London, 1969), p. 162.
69. Augier, *Making of the West Indies*, p. 187.
70. Ibid., p. 186.
71. Gibbs, *British Honduras*, p. 175.
72. Supt. Fancourt to Gov. Grey, 19 June 1847, AB, R.25.

CHAPTER 8

1. *Honduras Observer and Belize Gazette*, vol. 4, no. 30, 12 June 1847.
2. Ibid., vol. 5 no. 51, 30 Oct. 1847.
3. Letter to G. Berkley, 17 March 1848; see also W. W. Coffin to Supt. Fancourt, 18 March 1848, AB, R.28.
4. See Nelson Reed, *The Caste War of Yucatan* (Stanford, 1964).
5. Statement of Encalada's commissioners, Feb. 1867, AB, R.89.
6. Alfonso Villa Rojas, *The Maya of East Central Quintana Roo* (Washington, D.C., 1945), p.17.
7. George Hyde to Marshall Bennett, 12 Feb. 1826, CO 123/37.
8. Reed, *Caste War of Yucatan*, p. 141.
9. Supt. Stevenson to Gov. Bell, 9 Sept. 1856 and 16 Oct. 1856, AB, R.55.
10. Supt. Seymour to Gov. Eyre, 12 Nov. 1862, AB, R.81.
11. AB, R.52.
12. Ibid.
13. Ibid.
14. Seymour to Bell, 17 June 1857, AB, R.52.
15. Edward Rhys to Seymour, 3 Nov. 1862, AB, R.78.
16. J. Eric S. Thompson, *Maya History and Religion* (Norman, Okla., 1970), p. 71.

17. "Departamento de Verapaz, Año de 1832," CO 123/47.
18. Rhys to Seymour, 3 Nov. 1862, AB, R.78.
19. See AB, R.93, passim.
20. Capt. Delamere to Gov. Austin, 4 Oct. 1866; Pablo Encalada to Austin, 8 Nov. 1866, AB, R.89.
21. Asuncion Ek to Austin, 9 Nov. 1866, AB, R.89.
22. J. Swasey to Young Toledo & Co., 5 Dec. 1866, AB, R.89.
23. Gen. Canul and Com. Chan to Austin, 9 Dec. 1866, AB, R.89.
24. Major McKay to Austin, 24 Dec. 1866, AB, R.95; R. Williamson to Austin, 26 Dec. 1866, AB, R.89.
25. A later account stated that "the inhabitants, Governor Austin's family, at least included, if not himself, were all packed up and ready to take to the shipping"; Archibald Robertson Gibbs, *British Honduras: An Historical and Descriptive Account of the Colony from Its Settlement, 1670* (London, 1883), p. 138.
26. Lt. Col. Harley to Austin, 9 Feb. 1867, AB, R.95.
27. Harley to Austin, 15 Feb. 1867, AB, R.95.
28. Capt. Carmichael to Thomas Graham, 30 March 1867, and Harley to Austin, 7 Sept. 1867, AB, R.95.
29. Major Johnston to Gov. Cairns, 11 Sept. 1872; Serapio Ramos to Johnston, 15 Sept. 1872, AB, R.111.
30. For example, one J. C. McRae, an ex-Confederate general, purchased a large tract of land on the Belize River in 1868; see Wayne M. Clegern, *British Honduras: Colonial Dead End, 1859–1900* (Baton Rouge, 1967), p. 43.
31. *Laws of British Honduras* (1881?), pp. 31–33.
32. 28 Feb. 1867, AB, R.96.
33. Lt. Gov. Longden to Gov. Grant, 6 March 1868, AB, R.98. Emphasis in original.
34. Gibbs, *British Honduras,* pp. 162 and 176. Gibbs had been the commissariat officer in the field force that destroyed the Maya villages in the Yalbac Hills region in 1867.
35. See William Young, *An Account of the Black Charaibs in the Island of St. Vincent* (1795; rpt. London, 1971); Douglas MacRae Taylor, *The Black Carib of British Honduras* (New York, 1951); Joseph Palacio, "Black Carib History up to 1795," *Journal of Belizean Affairs,* no. 1 (June 1973), pp. 31–41.
36. Sir John Alder Burdon, *Archives of British Honduras,* 3 vols. (London, 1935), 2:57, 60.
37. Ibid., 2:146.
38. Thomas Miller to Under Sec. Gladstone, 13 Feb. 1835; AB, R.11 and CO 123/47.
39. Act. Supt. Anderson to Sec. of State, 28 April 1836, AB, R.6.
40. Minutes of Public Meeting, March 1833, CO 123/44.
41. Capt. Bird Allen, "Sketch of the Eastern Coast of Central America...," *Journal of the Royal Geographical Society of London* 2 (1841):86–87.
42. John L. Stephens, *Incidents of Travel in Central America, Chiapas and Yucatan,* 2 vols. (1842; rpt. New York, 1969), 1:28.
43. "An Act to declare the Laws in Force in this Settlement," 18 Vic. Cap. 22, *Laws of British Honduras in force on 31 Dec. 1881* (1882).
44. 16 Oct. 1857, AB, R.58.
45. J. H. Faber to Seymour, 21 Oct. 1857, AB, R.58.
46. Seymour to Gov. Darling, March 1858, AB, R.55.
47. Great Britain, Colonial Office, *Report of the British Guiana and British Honduras Settlement Commission,* Cmd. 7367 (London, 1948), p. 223.
48. D. Morris, *The Colony of British Honduras: Its Resources and Prospects* (London, 1883), p. 31.
49. Longden to Grant, 6 March 1868, AB, R.98.

CHAPTER 9

1. Supt. Macdonald to Chairman, Public Meeting, 4 March 1839, AB, R.16, and *The Honduras Almanack* (Belize, 1839).

2. Lord Normanby to Macdonald, 29 June 1839, AB, R.15.
3. Petition to the House of Commons, 2 March 1841, AB, R.20.
4. Supt. Fancourt to Gov. Grey, 19 June 1847, AB, R.25.
5. 504,635 in 1841 to 256,381 in 1854: Supt. Seymour to Gov. Darling, March 1858, AB, R.55.
6. Supt. Stevenson to Lt. Gov. Bell, 2 March 1857, AB, R.55.
7. Seymour to Darling, 16 Nov. 1857, AB, R.55.
8. Edmund Burke to Seymour, 2 Nov. 1857, AB, R.58.
9. Seymour to Darling, March 1858, AB, R.55.
10. *West Indian Census 1946, Part E, Census of British Honduras, 9th April, 1946* (Belize, 1948) p. viii.
11. Supt. to Chairman, Public Meeting, 20 Jan. 1852, AB, R.20.
12. *Votes of the Honourable House of Assembly, Sessions 1854–1859,* 22 Jan. 1856.
13. Seymour to Darling, 22 June 1859, AB, R.65.
14. Ibid.
15. There was an element of truth in these distinctions, though the basis was in culture, not in genetics. On the one hand, the Africans had acquired the particular skills of mahogany cutting and, at the same time, had come to associate cultivation with "inferior" strength and skills. On the other hand, the Maya, who had not been subjected to such a change in their culture of cultivation, were still devoted to their *milpas,* and would have resisted forced labor in the forests.
16. In 1870, in a memorial claiming compensation for losses suffered as a result of Canul's raid on the town of Corozal, John Carmichael claimed "depreciation of real property of 14 sugar estates $28,250; and in the remaining 23,500 acres of freehold, 8,625 of which are occupied by annual tenants, at an annual rental of $5,000, the most of whom have fled the country, $16,666; and in the value of 350 lots in the Town of Corosal, yielding an annual rental of $3,500, another $11,666" (J. Carmichael et al. to Act. Supt. Mitchell, n.d., AB, R.106). Carmichael was therefore letting arable land to annual tenants, mostly Maya subsistence farmers, at a rate of about 60 cents per acre per annum, and town lots at an annual rental of $10.
17. Macdonald to Sec. of State, 9 Feb. 1839, AB, R.14.
18. *Votes of the Honourable House . . . ,* 22 Jan. 1856.
19. Ibid.
20. Stevenson to Gov. Barkly, 5 April 1856, AB, R.55.
21. Stevenson to Gov. of Jamaica, 2 March 1857, AB, R.55.
22. Seymour to Darling, August 1857, AB, R.55.
23. Treasurer to Act. Supt. Price, 4 April 1860, AB, R.66.
24. Lt. Gov. Longden to Gov. Grant, 19 June 1868, AB, R.98.
25. Longden to Grant, 17 May 1869, AB, R.98. The report makes clear, however, that timber products continued to predominate in the colony's exports, despite this rapid rise in sugar exports. Of the total export earnings of over £68,000, about £57,000 were gained from timber products, while sugar accounted for less than £10,000.
26. See Grant D. Jones, *The Politics of Agricultural Development in Northern British Honduras* (Winston-Salem, N.C., 1971).
27. Thomas Miller to Under Sec. Gladstone, 13 Feb. 1835, CO 123/47.
28. Sir John Alder Burdon, *Archives of British Honduras,* 3 vols. (London, 1935), 3:228, 233, 241–42.
29. Longden to Grant, 27 May 1868, AB, R.98.
30. Quoted in Wayne M. Clegern, *British Honduras: Colonial Dead End, 1859–1900* (Baton Rouge, 1967), p. 36.
31. Burdon, *Archives of British Honduras* 3:257, 262, 264, 265, 266–67.
32. Ibid., 3:310, 313, 315.
33. Longden to Grant, 17 May 1869, AB, R.98.
34. Census of 1946, p. xxix.
35. *British Honduras Colonist and Belize Advertiser,* 11 March 1865.
36. Longden to Grant, 27 May 1868, AB, R.98.
37. Longden to Grant, 17 May 1869, AB, R.98.
38. Ibid.
39. Clegern, *British Honduras: Colonial Dead End,* p. 37.

40. Lt. Gov. Austin (to Sec. of State?), 9 July 1867, AB, R.98.
41. Austin to Grant, 13 March 1867, AB, R.92.
42. Clegern, *British Honduras: Colonial Dead End,* p. 44.
43. Narda Dobson, *A History of Belize* (London, 1973), pp. 247–49; Archibald Robertson Gibbs, *British Honduras: An Historical and Descriptive Account of the Colony from Its Settlement, 1670* (London, 1883), pp. 151–52.
44. Gibbs, *British Honduras,* pp. 119–23.
45. Census of the Population of British Honduras, 8 April 1861, AB, R.74.
46. Austin to Gov. Eyre, 26 May 1864, AB, R.81.
47. Ibid.
48. Edwin Adolphus to Longden, 15 Jan. 1870, AB, R.105.
49. Ibid.
50. R. Downer to Longden, 27 Jan. 1870, AB, R.105.
51. Ibid.
52. Mag. Hamilton to Longden, 17 Feb. 1870, AB, R.106.
53. Ibid.
54. Police Magistrate Cockburn to Longden, 24 Feb. 1870, AB, R.106.
55. Ibid.
56. "Returns shewing the number of laborers hired under 18 Vic Cap 12, the names of the employers and the rates of wages . . . ," for 1868 and 1869, enclosed in Cockburn to Longden, 24 Feb. 1870, AB, R.106.
57. Hamilton to Longden, 17 Feb. 1870, AB, R.106.
58. "Returns of cases between Master and Servant brought before the Police Court Belize . . . " in 1868 and 1869, enclosed in Cockburn to Longden, 24 Feb. 1870, AB, R.106.
59. Hamilton to Longden, 17 Feb. 1870, AB, R.106.
60. Adolphus to Longden, 15 Jan. 1870, AB, R.105.
61. Gibbs, *British Honduras,* pp. 176–78.
62. Lindsay W. Bristowe and Philip B. Wright, *The Handbook of British Honduras for 1888–89* (London, 1888), p. 199.

CHAPTER 10

1. See O. Nigel Bolland and Assad Shoman, *Land in Belize, 1765–1871: The Origins of Land Tenure, Use and Distribution in a Dependent Economy* (Kingston, 1975).
2. Arghiri Emmanuel, "White-Settler Colonialism and the Myth of Investment Imperialism,' *New Left Review* 73 (1972):36.
3. Ibid., p. 40.
4. Ibid., p. 43. Emphasis in original.
5. "Report of the Commissioners appointed to investigate the claims by which all Land and Works are held in the Settlement of Honduras, 27 July 1820," enclosed in Supt. Arthur to Earl Bathurst, 13 Sept. 1820, CO 123/29.
6. "The Memorial of His Majestys Subjects driven from the Bay of Honduras in September 1779 . . . ," from Robert White to Thomas Townshend, 10 Feb. 1783, CO 123/2.
7. Archibald Robertson Gibbs, *British Honduras: An Historical and Descriptive Account of the Colony from Its Settlement, 1670* (London, 1883), p. 117.
8. Ibid., p. 93.
9. Letter from Supt. Despard, 4 March 1788, CO 123/6.
10. "Laws of Honduras 1806–1810," GRB.
11. Letter from Despard, 4 March 1788, CO 123/6.
12. Lord Sydney to Despard, 26 June 1787, enclosed in Arthur to Bathurst, 13 Sept. 1820, CO 123/29.
13. Despard to Sydney, 17 Aug. 1787, CO 123/5.
14. Letter from Despard, 31 Oct. 1787, CO 123/6.
15. "A Narrative of the Publick Transactions in the Bay of Honduras from 1784 to 1790" Edward Marcus Despard Esq, 8 March 1791, CO 123/10.

16. Arthur to Bathurst, 17 Oct. 1816, CO 123/25.
17. Ibid.
18. Ibid.
19. Bathurst to Arthur, 12 March 1817, AB, R.1.
20. "Laws of Honduras 1806–1810," GRB.
21. Enclosed with "Report of the Commissioners... 1820" CO 123/29.
22. Ibid.
23. Ibid.
24. Arthur to Bathurst, 13 Sept. 1820, CO 123/29.
25. "Laws of Honduras 1806–1810," GRB.
26. Arthur to Bathurst, 13 Sept. 1820, CO 123/29.
27. "Report on the Land Question," Lt. Gov. Longden to Gov. Grant, 6 March 1869, AB, R.98.
28. Arthur to Bathurst, 13 Sept. 1820, CO 123/29.
29. Arthur to Maj. Gen. Pye, 3 April 1822, AB, R.2.
30. Supt. Cockburn to Lord Goderich, 10 April 1831, AB, R.6.
31. "An Act to declare the Laws in Force in this Settlement," 18 Vic Cap 22, Clauses 2 and 3, *Laws of British Honduras in force on 31 Dec. 1881*, 1882.
32. The effects of this situation are apparent to this day, when the vast majority of Crown land lies south of the Sibun River.
33. "Report of the Commissioners... 1820," CO 123/29.
34. "List of the Inhabitants of Honduras... " 1790, CO 123/11.
35. Census of 1816, GRB.
36. Census of the slave population, 31 Dec. 1820, GRB.
37. "Census of the Population of the British Settlement of Honduras," 31 Dec. 1835, GRB.
38. In 1829 Supt. Macdonald said of Bennett that, though he was a member of a commission appointed "for administering the Government... he has not been near the Colony for three years," Macdonald to Sec. of State, 28 Sept. 1829, AB, R.6.
39. William J. Griffith, *Empires in the Wilderness: Foreign Colonization and Development in Guatemala, 1834–1844* (Chapel Hill, 1965), pp. 28–30.
40. "Laws of Honduras 1806–1810," GRB.
41. "A Sketch of the British Settlement of Honduras... ," by H. C. Du Vernay, 9 March 1814, CO 123/23.
42. Sir John Alder Burdon, *Archives of British Honduras*, 3 vols. (London, 1935), 2:321.
43. Ibid., 2:337.
44. George Hyde to Bathurst, 3 Feb. 1827, CO 123/38.
45. Cockburn to Sir George Murray, 27 Jan. 1830, AB, R.6 and CO 123/41.
46. Ibid.
47. "A Narrative of the Publick Transactions... ," CO 123/10.
48. Letter from Despard, 11 Jan. 1788, CO 123/6.
49. Petition from Robert English et al. to Despard, 20 Aug. 1787, CO 123/5.
50. Despard to Sydney, 24 Aug. 1787, CO 123/5.
51. See R. A. Naylor, "British Commercial Relations with Central America 1821–51" (Ph.D. diss., Tulane University, 1958).
52. C. Dashwood to J. Backhouse, 28 Jan. 1830, FO 15/10, cited in Narda Dobson, *A History of Belize* (London, 1973), p. 139.
53. James Stephen to Lord Glenelg, 4 Oct. 1838, CO 123/54.
54. Dobson, *History of Belize,* p. 98.
55. Lord Liverpool to Col. Smyth, 15 June 1810, CO 124/3, cited in Dobson, *History of Belize,* p. 99.
56. Supt. Codd to Murray, 1 Jan. 1829, CO 123/40.
57. See CO 123/33.
58. Supt. Hamilton to Gov. Coote, 26 Nov. 1807, CO 123/17.
59. George Dyer to Robert Peel, 10 May 1811, CO 123/20.
60. Smyth to Bathurst, 12 Nov. 1813, CO 123/22.
61. Law Officers to Liverpool, Feb. 1812, CO 123/21.
62. Dobson, *History of Belize,* p. 121.

63. Arthur to Bathurst, 11 Jan. 1817, CO 123/26.
64. Quoted in Dobson, *History of Belize,* p. 122.
65. Report of the "Commissioners of Inquiry into the Administration of Criminal and Civil Justice... on the Settlement of Honduras," 24 Feb. 1829, CO 318/77.
66. Bathurst to Arthur, 30 Nov. 1819, CO 124/3, cited in Dobson, *History of Belize,* p. 109.
67. Ibid., p. 106.
68. Minutes of Public Meeting, 28 Feb. 1809, in Burdon, *Archives of British Honduras* 2:127.
69. Arthur to Bathurst, 2 Dec. 1814, CO 123/23.
70. Quoted in Dobson, *History of Belize,* p. 107.
71. Minutes of Quarterly Court, 6 and 7 Dec. 1793; meetings of Magistrates, MM A1, GRB.
72. Arthur to Bathurst, 2 Dec. 1814, CO 123/23.
73. Dobson, *History of Belize,* p. 107.
74. Magistrates to Sec. Luson, 4 Sept. 1801, CO 123/15.
75. Minutes of Public Meeting, 29 Oct. 1808, in Burdon, *Archives of British Honduras* 2:123.
76. Arthur to Bathurst, 2 Dec. 1814, CO 123/23.
77. Minutes of Public Meeting, 24 July 1820, in Burdon, *Archives of British Honduras* 2:232. However, it is not certain whether, or for how long, these restrictions were operative, as in 1827 it was stated that the property qualifications were £250 for whites and £500 for colored (letter from Stephen Lushington, 28 Oct. 1827, CO 123/38).
78. Letter from Lushington, 28 Oct. 1827, CO 123/38.
79. Minutes of Public Meetings, 7 July 1823, CO 123/34; 6 July 1829, CO 123/40; 1 March and 5 July 1830, CO 123/41.
80. Cockburn to Murray, 27 Jan. 1830, CO 123/41 and AB, R.6.

CHAPTER 11

1. Supt. Cockburn to Horace Twiss, 7 Feb. 1830, CO 123/41.
2. Archibald Robertson Gibbs, *British Honduras: An Historical and Descriptive Account of the Colony from Its Settlement, 1670* (London, 1883), p. 93.
3. CO 123/43–45.
4. Gibbs, *British Honduras,* p. 102.
5. Information on mahogany prices is sketchy and unreliable. In 1784 a Public Meeting resolved that, in Belize, "the established price of Mahogany shall be Fifteen Pounds pr thousand feet" (Sir John Alder Burdon, *Archives of British Honduras,* 3 vols. [London, 1935] 1:145), or about 3½d. per foot. A century later it was stated that "the price was originally 2s. 6d. per foot, fell gradually to 1s., and eventually to quotations of 4½d. to 7½. In 1847 the quotations in the Liverpool prices current are 5d. to 1s. 4d. It is now [1882] quoted at 5d. to 9½d" (Gibbs, *British Honduras,* p. 118). Certainly the prices fluctuated rapidly, for example, from 4½d. per foot in 1866 to 2¼d. per foot in 1868 (Lt. Gov. Longdon to Gov. Grant, 17 May 1869, AB, R.98).
6. Gibbs, *British Honduras,* pp. 113–14.
7. Longden to Grant, 19 June 1868, AB, R.98.
8. Hooper's report, 1887, cited in C. Hummel, *Report on the Forests of British Honduras* (London, 1921), p. 12.
9. Longden to Grant, 17 May 1869, AB, R.98.
10. Gibbs, *British Honduras,* p. 114.
11. Cockburn to Twiss, 7 Feb. 1830, AB, R.6 and CO 123/41.
12. Treasurer to Act. Supt. Price, 4 April 1860, AB, R.66.
13. Supt. Codd to R. Hay, 12 July 1828, CO 123/39.
14. Minutes of the Public Meeting, 6 July 1829, CO 123/40.
15. Cockburn to Twiss, 9 Aug. 1830, AB, R.6 and CO 123/41.
16. Cockburn to Twiss, 8 Nov. 1830, AB, R.6 and CO 123/41.
17. Minutes of Meetings in CO 123/41.
18. Minutes of Meeting, CO 123/42.
19. Sir George Murray to Cockburn, 28 Oct. 1829, CO 124/3, quoted in Narda Dobson, *A History of Belize* (London, 1973), p. 103.

20. Minutes of Legislative Meeting, 4 and 5 July 1831, CO 123/42.
21. Cockburn to Lord Goderich, 20 Nov. 1832, CO 123/43.
22. Goderich to Cockburn, 18 Oct. 1832, CO 123/43.
23. Henry Taylor to Hope, 15 Oct. 1841, CO 123/59, quoted in Dobson, *History of Belize*, p. 114.
24. Goderich to Cockburn, 18 Oct. 1832, CO 123/43.
25. Cockburn to Goderich, 4 Jan. 1833, CO 123/44.
26. Earl Bathurst to Supt. Arthur, 30 Nov. 1819, CO 124/3, quoted in Dobson, *History of Belize*, p. 109.
27. Goderich to Cockburn, 21 March 1833, CO 123/3, quoted in Dobson, *History of Belize*, p. 109.
28. Minutes of Public Meeting, 29 July 1848, AB, R.20.
29. John Young to Sir F. Rogers, 2 Aug. 1860, AB, R.70.
30. Treasurer to Price, 4 April 1860, AB, R.66.
31. F. R. Augier et al., *The Making of the West Indies* (London, 1960), p. 132.
32. L. C. B. Gower, *The Principles of Modern Company Law*, 2d. ed. (London, 1957), p. 49.
33. Petition to the House of Commons, 2 March 1841, AB, R.20.
34. "An Act to amend the system of Government of British Honduras," 16 Vic Cap 4, *Minutes of British Honduras Public Meeting and House of Assembly, 1853–1855*.
35. 18 Vic Cap 22.
36. 22 Vic Cap 11 and 18 Vic Cap 19.
37. Lord Newcastle to Gov. Darling, 24 June 1859, AB, R.64.
38. Rogers to H. Merivale, 26 June 1858, enclosed in E. B. Lytton to Darling, 30 July 1858, AB, R.64.
39. Henry John Ball's report, 12 April 1858, AB, R.66.
40. Newcastle to Darling, 24 June 1859, AB, R.64.
41. 24 Vic Cap 18.
42. GRB.
43. Claims book, 1859–1862, GRB.
44. *The Honduras Almanack* (Belize, 1839).
45. Land titles register, folios 470 and 549–56, GRB.
46. Lindsay W. Bristowe and Philip B. Wright, *The Handbook of British Honduras for 1888–89* (London, 1888), p. 81.
47. In the twentieth century, the Belize Estate and Produce Company, Ltd, has relinquished some of its poorer land but still remains by far the biggest single landowner. In 1971 the company owned 994,626 acres in Belize, or 42 percent of all the freehold land (see O. Nigel Bolland and Assad Shoman, *Land in Belize, 1765–1871: The Origins of Land Tenure, Use, and Distribution in a Dependent Economy.* ([Kingston, 1975], p. 105).
48. Carmichael had been "formerly a Liverpool merchant, became a planter at Corozal, and was the first to persist in the attempt in sugar-planting on a large scale" (Gibbs, *British Honduras*, p. 127).
49. See R. A. Humphreys, *The Diplomatic History of British Honduras, 1638–1901* (London, 1961), pp. 101, 103–4, and Wayne M. Clegern, *British Honduras: Colonial Dead End, 1859–1900* (Baton Rouge, 1967), pp. 53–54.
50. E. B. Squier, *The States of Central America . . .* (New York, 1858), p. 588.
51. Gibbs, *British Honduras*, p. 158.
52. Ibid., p. 174.
53. James Walker to Supt. Macdonald, 12 Feb. 1838, CO 123/52.
54. See, for example, Supt. Fancourt to Lord Stanley, 15 April 1844, CO 123/68, and Fancourt to Earl Grey, 10 Aug. 1848, CO 123/74.
55. Fancourt to Grey, 10 Aug. 1848, CO 123/74, quoted in Dobson, *History of Belize*, p. 118.
56. The act was passed by the Public Meeting on 14 Jan. 1853 and is included in *Votes of the Public Meeting At Its Special Sitting in January 1853* (Belize, 1853).
57. Ibid. It was assumed that the term "person" excluded all women, despite the fact that the head of state was female.
58. D. A. G. Waddell, *British Honduras: A Historical and Contemporary Survey* (London, 1961), p. 53.

59. Burdon, *Archives of British Honduras,* 3:235–36.
60. See Philip D. Curtin, *Two Jamaicas: The Role of Ideas in a Tropical Colony, 1830–1865* (1955; rpt. ed., New York, 1970), pp. 178–203.
61. Gibbs, *British Honduras,* p. 155.
62. Longden to Grant, 4 Dec. 1867, AB, R.98.
63. Gibbs, *British Honduras,* p. 152.
64. Despite frequent agitation, the elective principle was not reintroduced until 1936; it was not until 1954 that with universal adult suffrage, the Legislative Assembly included a majority of elected members, and not until 1960 that the Executive Council featured a majority of elected members.
65. Friedrich Engels to Joseph Bloch, 21–22 Sept. 1890, in *The Marx-Engels Reader,* ed. Robert C. Tucker (New York, 1972), p. 641.
66. Clegern, *British Honduras,* p. 53.
67. Assad Shoman, "The Birth of the Nationalist Movement in Belize, 1950–1954," *Journal of Belizean Affairs,* no. 2 (1973), p. 7.
68. Clegern, *British Honduras,* pp. 53–54.
69. W. R. Robertson to R. W. Herbert, 9 June 1874, quoted in Clegern, *British Honduras,* p. 54.

CHAPTER 12

1. John Rex, *Race Relations in Sociological Theory* (London, 1970), p. 43.
2. Gordon Lewis, "The Social Legacy of British Colonialism in the Caribbean," *New World Quarterly* 3, no. 3 (1967): p. 15.
3. Ibid., p. 17.
4. Douglas Hall, "Slaves and Slavery in the British West Indies," *Social and Economic Studies* 11 (1962):309.
5. Police Magistrate Cockburn to Lt. Gov. Longden, 24 Feb. 1870, AB, R.106.

Bibliography

Two useful bibliographies are:
Comitas, Lambros. *Caribbeana 1900–1965: A Topical Bibliography*. Seattle, 1968.
Minkel, Clarence W., and Alderman, Ralph H. *A Bibliography of British Honduras, 1900–1970*. East Lansing, Mich. 1970.

MANUSCRIPT SOURCES

1. Colonial Office records, Public Records Office, London.

CO 137/59–81: Original correspondence and Jamaica correspondence from 1749 to 1781, which includes some of the earliest materials on the Bay of Honduras.

CO 123/1–56: Original correspondence from the Bay of Honduras from 1744 to 1839, including special volumes CO 123/10–12, on the events of 1784 to 1790 by Superintendent Despard and the Magistrates; CO 123/14, "Honduras Bay: Promiscuous Papers"; and CO 123/33, "Proclamations 1814–1822."

The Colonial Office records contain official dispatches, many enclosures sent from Belize, and various memoranda by Colonial Office officials. These manuscripts were invaluable for the earlier periods for which there are few records in Belize.

2. Archives of Belize, Belmopan.

AB, R.1–120: various records and manuscripts from 1805 to 1884.

These archives are of little value for the early years of the settlement (all that remains from 1805 to 1820 is included in the first volume, R.1), but they contain increasing quantities of manuscripts from 1820 onward. They are organized primarily in volumes of official "Despatches Inwards" and "Despatches Outwards," many of which are duplicated in the Colonial Office records in London. Of special interest and value are the volumes such as R.20, "Proceedings Public Meeting" 1841 and 1848–53, and the reports of local correspondents from the districts to Belize, military correspondence and other material concerning the struggles with the Maya (see especially R.33, "Indian Correspondence" 1849–50; R.88, R.91, and R.95, "Military Letters Inwards" 1864–68; R.93, "Correspondence Indian Raids," 1866–68; and R.119 and R.120, "Orange Walk Letters Inwards," 1872–84).

The archives also contain the invaluable slave register of 1834.
3. General Registry, Belize City.
Contains court records, "Meetings of Magistrates," from 1793, which include useful information on the composition of the Magistrates and jurors, on crimes and punishments, civil suits, wills and settlements of estates, manumissions, etc. Also contains the invaluable early censuses (1816, 1820, 1823, 1826, 1829, 1832, 1835, and 1839), the earliest collection of the "Laws of Honduras 1806–1810," and information on land holdings in the claims book (1859–62) and the land titles register, begun in 1863. Some of these records are being moved into the archives in Belmopan.

PRINTED SOURCES

1. Colonial Office records CO 318/77. "Third Report of the Commissioners of Inquiry into the Administration of Criminal and Civil Justice in the West Indies and South American Colonies: Honduras and the Bahama Islands. Dated 24 February 1829."
2. Newspapers. Until the late nineteenth century, newspapers were few and short-lived, for example, the *Honduras Gazette and Commercial Advertiser,* published between July 1826 and June 1827, or the *New Era and British Honduras Chronicle,* which lasted from February 1871 to May 1872. Of special interest are the *Honduras Observer* (1844–45) which became the *Honduras Observer and Belize Gazette* on 5 April 1845 and published reports on the conflicts in Yucatán and Belize in 1846 and 1847, and the *British Honduras Colonist and Belize Advertiser* (1864–68).
3. Burdon, Sir John Alder. *Archives of British Honduras.* 3 vols. London, 1935. This is a useful but unreliable collection of printed source material. The first volume (1670–1800) includes material from local archives and Colonial Office records, while the second and third volumes (1801–40, 1840–84) contain only records in the Archives of Belize. Unfortunately, the work of selection, editing, and summarizing was carried out by amateurs and is frequently haphazard and inaccurate. However, for some of the local records which were subsequently lost, this collection is the only source.
4. Contemporary books and articles.

Allen, Capt. Bird. "Sketch of the Eastern Coast of Central America, compiled from Notes of Captain Richard Owen...." *Journal of the Royal Geographical Society of London* 11 (1841):76–89.

Allen, Capt. D. M. *Report of Indian Soldiery.* Belize, 1887.

Armstrong, John. *A Candid Examination of "The Defence of the Settlers of Honduras."* ... London, 1824.

Atkins, John. *A Voyage to Guinea, Brasil, and the West Indies....* London, 1735.

Bancroft, H. H. *History of Central America.* 3 vols. San Francisco, 1883–87.

Bannantine, James. *Memoirs of Edward Marcus Despard.* London, 1799.

Bridges, G. W. *The Annals of Jamaica.* 2 vols. London, 1828.

Bristowe, Lindsay W., and Wright, Philip B. *The Handbook of British Honduras for 1888–89.* London, 1888.

Crowe, Frederick. *The Gospel in Central America, containing... a History of the Baptist Mission in British Honduras....* London, 1850.

Dampier, William. *Voyages and Descriptions.* 2 vols. London, 1699.

Defence of the Settlers of Honduras Against the Unjust and Unfounded Representations of Colonel George Arthur. Jamaica, 1824.

Fancourt, Charles St. John. *The History of Yucatán from Its Discovery to the Close of the Seventeenth Century.* London, 1854.

Fowler, Henry. *A Narrative of a Journey across the Unexplored Portion of British Honduras.* Belize, 1879.

Gibbs, Archibald Robertson, *British Honduras: An Historical and Descriptive Account of the Colony from Its Settlement, 1670.* London, 1883.

Henderson, Capt. G. *An Account of the British Settlement of Honduras.* . . . London, 1809.

Honduras Almanacks. Vols. for 1826, 1828, 1829, 1830, and 1839.

Laws of the Settlement of British Honduras. Belize, 1857.

Morris, D. *The Colony of British Honduras: Its Resources and Prospects.* London, 1883.

Rogers, Lt. Col. E. "British Honduras: Its Resources and Development." Paper delivered before the members of the society at the Manchester Athenaeum, 14 Oct. 1885, in the library of the Royal Commonwealth Society, London.

Squier, E. G. *The States of Central America.* . . . New York, 1858.

Stephens, John L. *Incidents of Travel in Central America, Chiapas and Yucatan.* 2 vols. 1842. Reprint. New York, 1969.

Swett, Charles. *A Trip to British Honduras and to San Pedro, Republic of Honduras.* New Orleans, 1868.

Thompson, G. A. *Narrative of an Official Visit to Guatemala from Mexico.* London, 1829.

Uring, Capt. Nathaniel. *A History of the Voyages and Travels.* . . . 2d ed. London, 1727.

Votes of the Public Meeting At Its Special Sitting in January 1853. Belize, 1853.

Young, Thomas. *Narrative of a Residence on the Mosquito Shore, During the Years 1839, 1840, and 1841.* . . . London, 1842.

Young, William. *An Account of the Black Charaibs in the Island of St. Vincent.* 1795. Reprint. London, 1971.

5. Modern secondary works.

i Books:

Anderson, A. H. *Brief Sketch of British Honduras.* 8th ed. Belize, 1963.

Ashcraft, Norman. *Colonialism and Underdevelopment: Processes of Political Economic Change in British Honduras.* New York, 1973.

Augier, F. R., et al. *The Making of the West Indies.* London, 1960.

Augier, F. R., and Gordon, S. C. *Sources of West Indian History.* London, 1962.

Banton, Michael. *Race Relations.* London, 1967.

Bastide, Roger. *African Civilisations in the New World.* New York, 1971.

Beckford, George L. *Persistent Poverty: Underdevelopment in Plantation Economics of the Third World.* New York, 1972.

Belizean Independence Secretariat. *Belize: New Nation in Central America.* Belize City, 1972.

Bolland, O. Nigel, and Shoman, Assad. *Land in Belize, 1765–1871: The Origins of Land Tenure, Use, and Distribution in a Dependent Economy.* Kingston, 1975.

Boxer, C. R. *The Golden Age of Brazil, 1695–1750: Growing Pains of a Colonial Society.* Berkeley, 1964.

Brathwaite, Edward. *The Development of Creole Society in Jamaica, 1770–1820.* London, 1971.

Browne, Major G. St. J. Orde. *Labour Conditions in the West Indies.* London, 1939.
Buhler, Richard, ed. *Recent Archaeology in Belize.* Belize City, 1976.
Burn, W. L. *Emancipation and Apprenticeship in the British West Indies.* London, 1937.
———. *The British West Indies.* London, 1951.
Burns, A. *History of the British West Indies.* London, 1954.
Caiger, Stephen L. *British Honduras, Past and Present.* London, 1951.
Census of British Honduras, 9th April, 1946. Belize, 1948.
Census of British Honduras, 1960. Kingston, n.d.
Chamberlain, Robert S. *The Conquest and Colonization of Yucatan 1517–1550.* Washington, D.C., 1948.
Chevalier, François. *Land and Society in Colonial Mexico: The Great Hacienda.* Berkeley, Calif., 1970.
Clegern, Wayne M. *British Honduras: Colonial Dead End, 1859–1900.* Baton Rouge, 1967.
Coe, Michael D. *The Maya.* 1966. Reprint Harmondsworth, 1971.
Cohen, David W., and Greene, Jack P. *Neither Slave nor Free: The Freedman of African Descent in the Slave Societies of the New World.* Baltimore, 1972.
Comitas, Lambros, and Lowenthal, David. *Slaves, Free Men, Citizens: West Indian Perspectives.* New York, 1973.
Craton, Michael. *Sinews of Empire: A Short History of British Slavery.* New York, 1973.
Cumper, George, ed. *The Economy of the West Indies.* Jamaica, 1960.
Curtin, Philip D. *Two Jamaicas: The Role of Ideas in a Tropical Colony, 1830–1865.* 1955. Reprint. New York, 1970.
———. *The Atlantic Slave Trade: A Census.* Madison, Wisc., 1969.
Davis, David Brion. *The Problem of Slavery in Western Culture.* Ithaca, 1966.
Degler, Carl N. *Neither Black nor White: Slavery and Race Relations in Brazil and the United States.* New York, 1971.
Dobson, Narda. *A History of Belize.* London, 1973.
Donohoe, William Arlington. *A History of British Honduras.* Montreal, 1946.
Downie, Jack. *An Economic Policy for British Honduras.* Belize, 1959.
Elkins, Stanley M. *Slavery: A Problem in American Institutional and Intellectual Life.* 2d ed. Chicago, 1968.
Floyd, Barry. *Focus on British Honduras (Belize).* Jamaica, 1970.
Fogel, Robert William, and Engerman, Stanley, L. *Time on the Cross: The Economics of American Negro Slavery.* Boston, 1974
Foner, Laura, and Genovese, Eugene D., eds. *Slavery in the New World.* Englewood Cliffs, N.J., 1969.
Frank, Andre Gunder. *Capitalism and Underdevelopment in Latin America.* Harmondsworth, 1971.
Franklin, John Hope, ed. *Color and Race.* Boston, 1968.
Freyre, Gilberto. *The Masters and the Slaves.* New York, 1946.
Frucht, Richard, ed. *Black Society in the New World.* New York, 1971.
Gann, T. W. F. *The Maya Indians of Southern Yucatan and Northern British Honduras.* Washington, 1918.
———. *Mystery Cities: Exploration and Adventure in Lubaantun.* London, 1925.
———. *Ancient Cities and Modern Tribes.* London, 1926.

———. *Maya Cities: A Record of Exploration and Adventure in Middle America*. London, 1927.

Genovese, Eugene D. *The Political Economy of Slavery*. New York, 1965.

———. *The World the Slaveholders Made*. New York, 1969.

Gordon, David L. *The Economic Development Program of British Honduras*. Washington, 1954.

Goveia, E. *A Study on the Historiography of the British West Indies*. Mexico City, 1956.

———. *Slave Society in the British Leeward Islands at the End of the Eighteenth Century*. New Haven, 1965.

Government of Belize. *Belize: New Nation in Central America*. Belmopan, 1976.

Gower, L. C. B. *The Principles of Modern Company Law*. 2d ed. London, 1957.

Great Britain Colonial Office. *Report of the British Guiana and British Honduras Settlement Commission, Cmd. 7533*. London, 1948.

Gregg, Algar Robert. *British Honduras*. London, 1968.

Griffith, William J. *Empires in the Wilderness: Foreign Colonization and Development in Guatemala, 1834–1844*. Chapel Hill, 1965.

Guerra y Sanchez, Ramiro. *Sugar and Society in the Caribbean: An Economic History of Cuban Agriculture*. New Haven, 1964.

Hall, Douglas. *Free Jamaica, 1838–1865: An Economic History*. 1959. Reprint. London, 1969.

———. *Five of the Leewards, 1834–1870*. Barbados, 1971.

Hammond, Norman. *Lubaantún 1926–70: The British Museum in British Honduras*. London, 1972.

Harris, Marvin. *Patterns of Race in the Americas*. New York, 1964.

Herskovits, Melville J. *The Myth of the Negro Past*. New York, 1941.

Hoetink, H. *The Two Variants in Caribbean Race Relations*. London, 1967.

Horowitz, Irving Louis. *Three Worlds of Development: The Theory and Practice of International Stratification*. New York, 1966.

Horowitz, Michael M., ed. *Peoples and Cultures of the Caribbean*. New York, 1971.

Hummel, C. *Report on the Forests of British Honduras*. London, 1921.

Humphreys, R. A. *The Diplomatic History of British Honduras, 1638–1901*. London, 1961.

Hunter, A. A. *Rural Land Utilization Tax . . . A Beneficial Just and Equitable Piece of Legislation*. Belize, n.d.

Hurwitz, Samuel J., and Hurwitz, Edith F. *Jamaica: A Historical Portrait*. New York, 1971.

Hyde, Evan X *Knocking Our Own Ting*. Belize, n.d.

James, C. L. R. *The Black Jacobins: Toussaint L'Ouverture and the San Domingo Revolution*. 1938. Reprint. New York, 1963.

Jones, Grant D. *The Politics of Agricultural Development in Northern British Honduras*. Winston-Salem, N.C., 1971.

———. *Anthropology and History in Yucatán*. Austin, 1976.

Jones, N. S. Carey. *The Pattern of a Dependent Economy: The National Income of British Honduras*. Cambridge, 1953.

Klein, Herbert S. *Slavery in the Americas: A Comparative Study of Virginia and Cuba*. Chicago, 1967.

Knight, Franklin W. *Slave Society in Cuba During the Nineteenth Century*. Madison, Wisc., 1970.

Lewis, Gordon K. *The Growth of the Modern West Indies*. London, 1968.

Lowenthal, David. *West Indian Societies*. New York, 1972.

Metzgen, M. S., and Cain, H. E. C., eds. *The Handbook of British Honduras*. London, 1925.

Metzgen, Monrad Sigfrid, ed., *Shoulder to Shoulder, or the Battle of St. George's Caye 1798*. Belize City, 1928.

Morley, Sylvanus Griswold. *The Inscriptions of Petén*. 5 vols. Washington, D.C., 1937–38.

———. *The Ancient Maya* 3d ed. Stanford, Calif, 1956.

Mörner, Magnus. *Race Mixture in the History of Latin America*. Boston, 1967.

———, ed. *Race and Class in Latin America*. New York, 1970

Oman, Sir Charles. *The Unfortunate Colonel Despard and Other Studies*. London, 1922.

Ortiz, Fernando. *Cuban Counterpoint: Tobacco and Sugar*. New York, 1947.

Parry, J. H., and Sherlock, P. M. *Short History of the West Indies*. 3d ed. London, 1971.

Patterson, Orlando. *The Sociology of Slavery*. London, 1967.

Pendergast, David M., ed. *Palenque: The Walker-Caddy Expedition . . . 1839–40*. Norman, Okla., 1967.

———. *Altun Ha*. Belize, 1969.

Pitman, F. *The Development of the British West Indies 1700–1763*. 1917. Reprint. Hamden, Conn. 1967.

Prado, Caio. *The Colonial Background of Modern Brazil*. Berkeley, Calif. 1967.

Price, Richard, ed. *Maroon Societies: Rebel Slave Communities in the Americas*. New York, 1973.

Quijano, J. A. Calderon. *Belice 1663(?)–1821: Historia de los establecimientos britanicos del Rio Valis hasta la independencia de hispanoamerica*. Seville, 1944.

Ragatz, L. J. *The Fall of the Planter Class in the British Caribbean, 1763–1833*. 1928. Reprint. New York, 1963.

Redfield, Robert. *The Folk Culture of Yucatan*. Chicago, 1941.

Reed, Nelson. *The Caste War of Yucatan*. Stanford, Calif., 1964.

Rex, John. *Race Relations in Sociological Theory*. London, 1970.

Richardson, Patrick. *Empire and Slavery*. London, 1968.

Roberts, G. M. *The Population of Jamaica*. Cambridge, 1957.

Rodriguez, Mario. *Central America*. Englewood Cliffs, N.J., 1965.

Roys, Ralph L. *The Indian Background of Colonial Yucatan*. Washington, D.C., 1943.

Rubin, Vera, ed. *Caribbean Studies: A Symposium*. Jamaica, 1957.

Sampson, H. C. *Report on Development of Agriculture in British Honduras*. London, 1929.

Sheridan, Richard B. *Sugar and Slavery: An Economic History of the West Indies, 1623–1775*. Baltimore, 1974.

Smith, M. G. *The Plural Society in the British West Indies*. Berkeley, Calif., 1965.

Stone, Doris Zemurray. *Some Spanish Entradas 1524–1695*. Middle American Papers No. 4. New Orleans, 1932.

Bibliography

Tannenbaum, Frank. *Slave and Citizen: The Negro in the Americas*. New York, 1947.

Taylor, Douglas MacRae. *The Black Carib of British Honduras*. New York, 1951.

Thompson, E. P. *The Making of the English Working Class*. New York, 1963.

Thompson, J. Eric S. *Ethnology of the Mayas of Southern and Central British Honduras*. Chicago, 1930.

———. *Archaeological Investigations in the Southern Cayo District, British Honduras*. Chicago, 1931.

———. *Excavations at San Jose, British Honduras*. Washington, D.C., 1939.

———. *The Rise and Fall of Maya Civilization*. 2d ed. Norman, Okla., 1966.

———. *Maya History and Religion*. Norman, Okla., 1970.

Van Den Berghe, Pierre L. *Race and Racism: A Comparative Perspective*. New York, 1967.

Veliz, Claudio, ed. *Latin America and the Caribbean: A Handbook*. London, 1968.

Vickers, T. D. *The Legislature of British Honduras*. Belize, 1953.

Villagutierre y Soto-Mayor, Juan De. *Historia de la Conquista de la Provincia de el Itza*. Madrid, 1701. Reprint. Guatemala, 1933.

Villa Rojas, Alfonso. *The Maya of East Central Quintana Roo*. Washington, D.C., 1945.

Waddell, D. A. G. *British Honduras: A Historical and Contemporary Survey*. London, 1961.

———. *The West Indies and the Guianas*. Englewood Cliffs, N.J., 1967.

Whitten, Norman E., Jr., and Szwed, John F., eds. *Afro-American Anthropology: Contemporary Perspectives*. New York, 1970.

Willey, Gordon R., et al. *Prehistoric Maya Settlements in the Belize River Valley*. Papers of the Peabody Museum of Archaeology and Ethnology No. 54. Cambridge, Mass., 1965.

Williams, Eric. *Capitalism and Slavery*. 1944. Reprint. London, 1964.

Winzerling, E. O. *The Beginning of British Honduras 1506–1765*. New York, 1946.

Wolf, Eric R. *Sons of the Shaking Earth*. Chicago, 1959.

Wood, Donald. *Trinidad in Transition: The Years After Slavery*. London, 1968.

Worsley, Peter. *The Third World*. 2d ed. London, 1967.

Wright. A. C. S., et al. *Land in British Honduras: A Report of the British Honduras Land Use Survey Team*. London, 1959.

ii Articles:

Allsop, S. R. R. "British Honduras: The Linguistic Dilemma." *Caribbean Quarterly* 11 (1965):54–61.

Ashcraft, Norman. "The Domestic Group in Mahogany, British Honduras." *Social and Economic Studies* 15 (1966):266–74.

Ashcraft, Norman, and Jones, Grant, "Linguistic Problems in British Honduras." *Caribbean Quarterly* 12 (1966):55–57.

———, and Grant, Cedric. "The Development and Organization of Education in British Honduras." *Comparative Education Review* 12 (1968):171–79.

Beckford, George. "B. H. and Regional Economic Integration." *New World Quarterly* 3 (1967):51–53.

Bolland, O. Nigel. "The Roots of Black Power in the West Indies." *Afrasian* 3 (1969).

――――. "The Social Structure and Social Relations of the Settlement in the Bay of Honduras (Belize) in the 18th Century." *Journal of Caribbean History* 6 (1973):1–42.

――――. "Maya Settlements in the Upper Belize River Valley and Yalbac Hills: An Ethnohistorical View." *Journal of Belizean Affairs* 3 (1974):3–23.

――――. Review of Norman Ashcraft, *Colonialism and Underdevelopment: Processes of Political Economic Change in British Honduras,* in *Social and Economic Studies* 23 (1974):643–46.

Borah, Woodrow. "New Spain's Century of Depression." *Ibero-Americana,* no. 35 (1951).

Braithwaite, Lloyd. "Social Stratification in Trinidad: A Preliminary Analysis." *Social and Economic Studies* 2 (1953):5–175.

Bullard, William R., Jr. "Stratigraphic Excavations at San Estevan, Northern British Honduras." Art and Archaeology Occasional Papers No. 9. Royal Ontario Museum, Toronto, 1965.

Cacho, C. P. "British Honduras: A Case of Deviation in Commonwealth Caribbean Decolonization." *New World Quarterly* 3, no. 3 (1967):33–44.

Clegern, Wayne M. "British Honduras and the Pacification of Yucatán." *The Americas* 18 (1962):243–55.

Conzemius, Eduard. "Enthnographical Notes on the Black Carib." *American Anthropologist* 30 (1928):183–205.

Craig, Alan K. "Logwood as a Factor in the Settlement of British Honduras." *Caribbean Studies* 9, (1969):53–62.

Curry, Herbert F., Jr. "British Honduras: From Public Meeting to Crown Colony." *The Americas* 13 (1956):31–42.

Dodge, Peter. "Comparative Racial Systems in the Greater Caribbean." *Social and Economic Studies* 16 (1967):249–61.

Emmanuel, Arghiri. "White-Settler Colonialism and the Myth of Investment Imperialism." *New Left Review* 73 (1972):35–57.

Fox. David J. "Recent Work on British Honduras." *Geographical Review* 52 (1962):112–7.

Grant, C. H. "The Civil Service Strike in British Honduras: A Case Study of Politics' and the Civil Service." *Caribbean Quarterly* 12 (1966):37–49.

――――. "Rural Local Government in Guyana and British Honduras." *Social and Economic Studies* 16 (1967):57–76.

Grant, Cedric. "The Cultural Factor in B. H. Politics." *New World Quarterly* 3 (1967):53–55.

Gregory, James R. "Image of Limited Good, or Expectation of Reciprocity?" *Current Anthropology* 16 (1975):73–92.

Hall, Douglas. "Slaves and Slavery in the British West Indies." *Social and Economic Studies* 11 (1962):305–18.

Handler, J. S. "The History of Arrowroot and the Origin of Peasantries in the British West Indies." *Journal of Caribbean History* 2 (1971):46–93.

Holridge, Desmond. "Toledo: A Tropical Refugee Settlement in British Honduras." *Geographical Review* 30 (1940):376–93.

Jones, Grant D. "Maya Intergroup Relations in Nineteenth Century Belize and Southern Yucatan." *Journal of Belizean Affairs* 1 (1973):3–13.

――――. "Revolution and Continuity in Santa Cruz Maya Society." *American Ethnologist* 1 (1974):659–83.

Jones, Rhett S. "Race Relations in the Colonial Americas: An Overview." *Humboldt Journal of Social Relations* 1 (1974):73–82.

Lewis, Gordon. "The Social Legacy of British Colonialism in the Caribbean." *New World Quarterly* 3, no. 3 (1967):13–33.

Mackie, Euan W. "New Light on the End of Classic Maya Culture at Benque Viejo, British Honduras." *American Antiquity* 27 (1961):216–24.

Marshall, Ione. "The National Accounts of British Honduras." *Social and Economic Studies* 11 (1962):99–127.

Marshall, Woodville K. "Notes on Peasant Development in the West Indies Since 1838." *Social and Economic Studies* 17 (1968):252–63.

Mazzarelli, M. "Intercommunity Relations in British Honduras." *Human Organization* 26 (1967):222–29.

Mintz, Sidney. "The Question of Caribbean Peasantries: A Comment." *Caribbean Studies* 1 (1961):31–34.

Mintz, Sidney W. "The Caribbean as a Socio-Cultural Area." *Journal of World History* 9, no. 4 (1966):912–37.

———. "The Caribbean Region." *Daedalus* 103 (1974):45–72.

Muntsh, Albert. "Xaibe, A Mayan Enclave in Northern British Honduras." *Anthropological Quarterly* 34 (1961):121–26.

Naylor, Robert A. "The British Role in Central America Prior to the Clayton-Bulwer Treaty of 1850." *Hispanic American Historical Review* 40 (1960):361–82.

Palacio. Joseph. "Black Carib History up to 1795." *Journal of Belizean Affairs* 1 (1973):31–41.

Patterson, Orlando. "Slavery and Slave Revolts: A Socio-Historical Analysis of the First Maroon War, 1655–1740." *Social and Economic Studies* 19 (1970):289–325.

Shoman, Assad. "The Birth of the Nationalist Movement in Belize, 1950–1954." *Journal of Belizean Affairs* 2 (1973):3–40.

Sio, Arnold A. "Interpretations of Slavery: The Slave Status in the Americas." *Comparative Studies in Society and History* 7 (1965):289–308.

———. "Society, Slavery and the Slave." *Social and Economic Studies* 16 (1967):330–44.

Smith, M. G. "Some Aspects of Social Structure in the British Caribbean About 1820." *Social and Economic Studies* 1 (1953):55–79.

Solien, Nancie L. "West Indian Characteristics of the Black Carib." *Southwestern Journal of Anthropology* 15 (1959):300–307.

Strumpel, Burkhard. "Preparedness for Change in a Peasant Society." *Economic Development and Cultural Change* 13 (1965):203–16

———. "Consumption Aspirations: Incentives for Economic Change." *Social and Economic Studies* 14 (1965):183–93.

Thompson. J. Eric S. "Sixteenth and Seventeenth Century Reports on the Chol Mayas." *American Anthropologist* 40, no. 4 (1938):584–604.

Van Aken, Mark J. "British Policy Considerations in Central America Before 1850." *Hispanic American Historical Review* 42 (1960):54–59.

Willey, Gordon R., and Shimkin, Demitri B. "The Collapse of Classic Maya Civilization in the Southern Lowlands: A Symposium Summary Statement." *Southwestern Journal of Anthropology* 27, no. 1 (1971):1–18.

Wolf, Eric R., and Mintz, Sidney. "Haciendas and Plantations in Middle America and the Antilles." *Social and Economic Studies* 6 (1957):380–412.

iii Unpublished works:

Ashcraft, Norman. "Land-Use and Trade: The Processes of Economic Change in British Honduras." Ph.D. dissertation, Brandeis University, 1968.

Bolland, O. Nigel. "The Formation of a Colonial Society: Belize, From Conquest to Crown Colony." Ph.D. dissertation, Hull University, 1975.

Jones, Grant D. "Los Cañeros: Sociopolitical Aspects of the History of Agriculture in the Corozal Region of British Honduras." Ph.D. dissertation, Brandeis University, 1968.

Leon, Narda D. "Social and Administrative Developments in British Honduras, 1798–1843." B. litt., Oxford University, 1958.

McLeish, J. "British Activities in Yucatan and the Moskito Shore in the Eighteenth Century." M.A., University of London, 1926.

Naylor, R. A. "British Commercial Relations with Central America 1821–51." Ph.D. dissertation, Tulane University, 1958.

Index

Adolphus, Edwin, 149–151, 154, 155
Advance system, 122–123, 124, 149–151, 153, 154, 195, 196
Africans, 4, 49–50, 61, 77, 82, 83, 95–105, 110, 111, 114, 121, 134–135, 138–139, 144, 146, 194
African tribalism, 98–102, 103
Agriculture: development of, 2, 6–9, 14–15, 130, 136–137, 139–142, 146, 196; peasant or subsistence, 7–8, 30, 58–61, 90, 109, 118–124, 132–133, 135, 136, 138, 140, 141–142; plantation or estate, 4, 6–9, 53, 60, 119, 136, 139–142, 195; swidden, 14, 24, 127, 135, 141
Alcalde, 128, 131
Altun Ha, 15, 16
Angola, 50, 95
Apprenticeship, 53, 80, 106, 112–117, 121, 123
Armstrong, John, 65, 71, 83
Arthur, Superintendent George, 40, 62, 66, 70–71, 76, 89–92, 103–104, 111, 118, 160–163, 168, 171, 173
Austin, Lieutenant Governor, 131, 144–145
Axmen, 55, 56, 147

Bacalar, 19, 21, 75, 77, 78, 125, 137, 139, 149
Bananas, 6, 132, 135
Barbados, 49, 53, 105, 114, 116, 143
Barrow, Superintendent, 40, 170
Barton Ramie, 15–17
Bathurst, Lord, 62, 91–92, 160–161, 168–170, 182

Bay Islands, 189
Belize (Town or City), 4, 5–6, 42, 57, 60, 100, 134, 137, 148, 160, 176
Belize Estate and Produce Company. *See* Companies, Belize Estate and Produce (British Honduras)
Belmopan, 6
Benin, Bight of, 50, 95
Bennett, Marshall, 64, 123, 164, 166, 171
Bermuda, 49
Brazil, 53, 81, 100
British or Commonwealth Caribbean. *See* West Indies
British Honduras Company. *See* Companies, Belize Estate and Produce (British Honduras)
Burdon, Sir John Alder, 23
Burnaby's Code, 27, 29, 35, 36–37, 73, 157, 170

Caiger, Stephen, 23
Campbell, Duncanette, 83
Campeche, 25, 26, 126
Canada, 7, 8
Canul, Marcos, 128–130, 191, 193
Caribs, 4, 5, 18, 90, 105, 110, 111, 115, 120, 132–135, 136, 137, 142, 144, 146, 148, 150, 152, 195
Carmichael, John, 187
Carrera, Rafael, 177
Carty, Michael, 66, 82
Cattlemen, 55, 109
Central America, 80, 164, 166–167, 169, 173, 176–178, 183, 184, 188

235

Chan, Rafael, 129
Chetumal, 18, 20
Chinese, 4, 5, 143, 152
Christmas holiday, 70, 79, 98–100, 103, 122, 149, 154–155
Citrus, 7, 8, 132
Cockburn, Superintendent, 80, 111–113, 163, 172–173, 178–182, 192
Cockscombe Coast, 25
Codd, Superintendent, 71, 78–79, 93, 167, 172–173
Colonial Office, 10, 12, 40, 93, 105, 116, 119–120, 168, 169, 180–181, 188, 190, 192
Columbus, Christopher, 17
Companies: Belize Estate and Produce (British Honduras), 7–8, 9, 131, 141, 142, 143, 153, 184, 186, 187–188, 190, 193; Carmichael Vidal, 183, 187; James Hyde (Hodge & Hyde), 183, 184, 186, 187; Sheldon Byass, 183, 187; Young Toldeo, 127, 131, 145, 152, 153, 183, 186, 187
Compensation for emancipation, 106, 110, 112, 114
Congo, 50, 95, 157
Consolidated slave laws of Jamaica, 62, 63, 70
Constitution, 1854, 10, 40, 171, 184, 189, 190
Constitutional amendments, 11–12
Convention of London. *See* Treaty, Convention of London, 1786
Convention Town, 34, 42
Corozal, 4, 6, 129, 137, 149, 187
Cortéz, Hernán, 17, 20
Coxen, Captain, 26
Creoles, 50, 95, 97, 101, 111, 134–135, 137, 148, 150–152, 197
Crown Colony, 10, 132, 191, 192–193, 197
Crown Lands Ordinance, 1872, 131, 134

Davey, Captain, 74–75
Dávila, Alonso, 18, 20, 21
Delamere, Captain, 129

Demographic rates: birth, 5; death, 5, 51, 52; infant mortality, 5; population growth, 3–5, 8, 16–17, 50–51; reproduction, 51–52
Despard, Superintendent Edward Marcus, 32–36, 37, 38–39, 41, 42, 58, 158–159, 167
Districts: Belize, 135; Northern, 4, 137–142, 144, 148, 197; Southern, 137, 144, 148, 152; Stann Creek, 7; Toledo, 18; Western, 130, 137
Domestics, 53, 57–58, 59, 61, 70, 82–83, 109, 114, 115
Downer, Magistrate, 151
Duck Run, 23, 128

Education, 104, 105, 111–112
Ek, Asunsion, 127–128, 129, 130
Emancipation, 4, 116–117, 118–124, 192, 195–196
Emigration, 4–5, 79
Emmanuel, Arghiri, 156–157
Encalada, Pablo, 126
Executive Council, 9, 11–12
Exports, 6–7, 8, 27–28, 119, 120, 136, 138, 140–141, 144, 158, 166, 173, 174–177

Faber, J. H., 133–134
Fancourt, Superintendent, 124, 126, 189
Fife, Andrew, 96
Fishing, fishermen, 8, 41, 46, 90, 132
Franchise, 11, 37–38, 93, 172, 178–181, 189, 190, 193
Free blacks and free colored, 4, 32, 39, 42, 45–46, 52, 60, 64, 82–83, 86–89, 109–111, 123, 143; and civil rights, 10, 47, 89–94, 172–173, 178, 180–181, 195; and conflict with white settlers, 34–36, 38, 46–47, 158, 165, 178, 181, 188–189, 192; culture of, 95–105
French Guiana, 81
Fuensalida, Bartolomé de, 19

Gentle, William, 93
Gibbs, Archibald Robertson, 29, 61, 146–148, 154–155, 158, 174–175
Glenelg, Lord, 112, 119
Goderich, Lord, 181–182
Government: British (Imperial), 10–12, 31, 90, 92, 133, 157, 163–164, 167–170, 180–182, 184, 188–189, 191–193; executive, 10–12, 36–40, 44, 74, 160, 167–168, 169, 171, 192; judicial, 10, 36, 44, 92, 168–171, 173, 190; legislative, 12, 44, 92–93, 168, 171–172, 178–181; local, 131, 190
Governor, 11–12
Great Britain, 7, 8, 9–10, 13, 31, 36, 144, 166–167, 177, 181, 184, 188–189, 194
Guatemala, 4–5, 13, 17–18, 23, 127, 145, 164, 166, 176–177, 189
Guerra de las Castas, 3–4, 126, 130, 137, 139, 146, 177, 190
Guyana (British Guiana), 5, 8, 114, 120, 122, 123, 143

Hall, Douglas, 196
Hamilton, Magistrate, 154
Hamilton, Superintendent, 40, 97, 167, 168
Hariza, Francisco de, 19
Harley, Lieutenant Colonel, 129
Havana Mixed Commission, 121, 142
Henderson, George, 22, 54, 56, 59, 68–69, 70
Hodge, John, 143, 183, 186
Hogstye Bank, 21
Honduras, 4, 17, 132, 145, 152, 177
Honduras Land Titles Act, 1861, 185, 193
Housekeepers, 57–58, 82–83
Howel, Lucas, 154
Hunter, Superintendent, 40, 46, 77
Huntsmen, 56–57, 109, 147
Hurricanes, 1–2, 11
Hyde, George, 79, 84, 92, 93, 164, 165
Hyde, James, 164, 165, 183, 186
Hyde, James Bartlett, 183, 186

Ibo, 50, 100, 101
Immigration, 3–5, 16, 31–32, 89, 121, 127–128, 130, 132, 137–138, 142–146, 156, 187, 188, 190, 197
Imports, 8, 44, 135, 139, 177
Indian (East), 4, 122, 143
Industry, 8
Itzá, 17, 19–20

Jamaica, Jamaicans, 2–3, 4, 8, 25, 42, 49–50, 52, 53, 81, 82, 93, 100, 103, 105, 114, 116, 120, 122–124, 191–192, 197
Jefferies, Thomas, 122, 133
Joint Stock Companies Act, 1856, 184, 186
Jones, Joshua, 34–35, 46
Judd, Captain W., 75

Labor: conditions, 110–111, 114, 146–155; division of, 15, 53–61, 109; laws, 115–116, 122, 149, 153–154; supply and demand of, 49, 53, 120–121, 130–131, 133–134, 138–139, 142–146, 148, 152–153, 194–195
Land: Crown, 118–120, 123–124, 131, 134, 144–145, 160–161, 163; laws, 29–30, 119, 131, 133–134, 157, 161–163, 184–187; and structure of ownership, 7–8, 32–33, 43–45, 124, 156, 158–163, 182–188; taxes, 9, 188, 191; use, 6–9, 14, 135, 136–142, 146, 156, 166, 188
Lawrie, James Pitt, 42, 45
Laws in Force Act, 1855, 133, 163, 184–185
Leas, Charles, 143
Legal Commissioners' Report, 1829, 62–63, 64, 66–67, 169
Legislative Assembly, 10–12, 143, 155, 171, 184, 185, 190, 191, 192
Legislative Council, 11, 155, 179, 192–193
Lewis, Gordon, 196
Liverpool, Lord, 167, 168

Locations or works, 29–30, 33–34, 54, 57, 90, 133, 157, 158, 162–163, 184–185, 187
Logwood: cutters, 2, 4, 21–23, 26, 28, 49, 72, 151; extraction, 10, 21, 28–30, 31, 43, 49, 54, 56, 138–139; trade, 2, 25–28, 29, 31, 43–44, 73–74, 157–158, 175–176, 194
London agent, 26, 39, 79, 169
Longden, Lieutenant Governor, 131, 135, 162
Lubaantún, 15
Lushington, Stephen, 92, 93
Lynch, Governor, 25–26

Macdonald, Superintendent, 116–117, 119–120, 139
McKay, Major, 129
McLean, Captain, 71
McLenan, L. M., 113, 115
Macleod, Ian, 13
Magistrates, 10, 33–35, 36–38, 40, 43–45, 64, 67, 76, 90, 93, 132, 165, 167–172, 179, 181–182, 192; District, 148–154, 190, 196; Special, 112–115, 117, 181, 188
Mahogany: cutters, 2, 21–22, 33, 69, 76, 107, 109–111, 120–121, 123, 124, 128, 137, 149, 153, 160, 162, 174, 176, 182–183, 186; extraction, 2, 31, 33, 43, 54–57, 59, 61, 77, 112, 114, 120, 124, 128, 134, 136, 146–148, 158–159, 174–175, 183, 186, 194; trade, 6, 21, 27–28, 120–121, 134, 152, 158, 174–176, 177–178, 183, 192, 194, 196–197
Maize (Indian corn), 14–16, 58, 60, 124, 131, 132, 138, 139, 141, 146
Manatee Lagoon, 30, 89, 162
Manumission, 42, 52–53, 63–64, 87–89
Markets: international (metropolitan, export), 2, 6–8, 137, 139, 156, 174, 176, 183–184, 194–195; national (local, domestic), 8, 59–60, 116, 123–124, 135, 137, 140, 166
Maroons, 81, 134

Maya, 3–5, 10, 18, 20–24, 41, 76, 125–126, 130–143, 137–139, 141–142, 144, 146, 148–151, 173, 175, 190–192, 195–197; ancient, 14–17; Chichanha, 126–127, 129; Chol, 18; Icaiché, 127, 128–130, 191; Ixcanha, 126; Kekchi, 18; Lochha, 126, 129; San Pedro, 127–129, 130; Santa Cruz, 126–127, 129, 130, 143; Tipu, 18–20, 22, 23, 128
Meighan, Priscilla, 63–64
Mennonites, 5
Merchants: Belize, 44, 46–47, 69, 123–124, 126, 137, 153, 157, 165, 166–167, 177–178, 191; London, 26, 44, 74, 157, 167, 176–177, 182–184, 186, 192
Mérida, 19, 21, 30, 126
Mestizos, 3–5, 137–139, 141, 142, 144, 146, 148–149, 190, 196
Mexico, 4–5, 17, 20, 23, 79, 183
Militia, 45, 46, 62, 74, 79, 82, 87, 90, 92, 94, 100
Miller, Thomas, 142
Modyford, Governor, 25
Montejo, Francisco de, 18
Morant Bay rebellion, 1865, 191, 192
Morris, Daniel, 135
Mosquito Indians, 22, 49, 91, 95, 168
Mosquito Shore evacuees, 31–32, 32–34, 38, 40–46, 50, 87, 158–160, 162, 165, 195

Ná, Cristobal, 19
National Assembly, 12
New Limits, 31, 32–34
New River Lagoon, 21, 125, 127, 128
Nigeria, 97, 100

Oligarchy, settler, 10, 12, 37–40, 43–45, 47, 164–173, 178–182, 188, 192–193, 194, 197
Omoa, 78, 80, 176
Orange Walk, 6, 130, 137, 151
Orbita, Juan de, 19

Index 239

Parry, Admiral, 36–37
Paslow, Thomas, 78, 164
Peasants (small farmers), 7–8, 15, 46, 60, 118–124, 134, 135, 138, 140, 141–142, 146, 195, 196
People's United Party, 11, 12
Peten, 16–17, 20, 22, 78–81, 127–128, 142
Plaintains, 58–60, 70–71, 124, 132, 135, 150
Population: density of, 3, 5, 118; foreign-born, 4, 50, 95; racial/ethnic composition of, 5, 41, 42, 46, 50–51, 130, 134, 188, 194, 197; sex ratio of, 42, 52, 86, 107; size of, 2–5, 16, 30, 32, 41, 50–51, 137
Price, George, 11, 12
Proclamations, 62, 70, 76, 118, 161, 168, 172
Public Meeting, 10, 36–38, 40, 43, 57, 90, 93, 105, 111–112, 116, 121, 123, 132, 160–161, 167, 170, 171–172, 178–181, 189–190
Public Treasurer, 170, 179
Punta Gorda, 6, 132, 134

Qualm Hill, 128

Regalia, 152, 154
Religion: African, 95–97, 103, 105; Anglican, 103–105, 112; Baptist, 103–105, 111–112; Catholic, 5, 18–19, 50, 77, 137; Maya, 14–17, 18, 19, 131; and missionaries, 18, 19, 103–105, 111–112; and obeah, 95–96; Protestant, 5; Wesleyan, 103–105, 111–112, 133
Rex, John, 196
Rhys, Edward, 129
Rivers: Belize, 1, 15–17, 19–20, 22, 41–42, 125, 130, 159; Booth's, 127, 128; Bravo, 125, 128; Deep, 31, 132; Grande, 31; Hondo, 1, 21, 75, 81, 118, 126, 148–149; Labouring Creek, 128; Moho, 31, 163; New, 1, 19, 21, 31, 58, 143, 148; Sarstoon, 31, 118; Sibun, 1, 21, 31, 59, 81, 89
Roaring Creek, 21, 30, 128
Roberts, George, 52
Rodney, Admiral, 37, 74–75
Ruatan, 4, 30, 31, 132
Rum, 28, 137, 140, 141
Rural Land Utilization Ordinance, 1966, 9

Saint Domingue, 39, 75–76, 96
St. George's Cay, 21, 27, 30, 42, 160; Battle of, 1798, 10, 48, 72, 75, 77, 78, 173
St. Lucia, 93
St. Vincent, 4, 132
Salvador, El, 2–3
San Antonio, 18
San Estevan, 137
Seymour, Superintendent, 127, 128, 130
Slaves, slavery, 22, 30, 32, 37, 39, 46–47, 62–64, 68–72, 86, 91, 118–120, 169, 173, 194–196; and abolition, 10, 53, 88, 106, 114, 117, 155, 188, 196; and culture, 95–105; and demographic characteristics, 50–52, 107–109, 121; and desertion and runaways, 50, 53, 61, 72–73, 76–82, 84–85, 100, 111, 195; and families, 102–103; and occupations, 53–61, 107–110, 123–124, 136; and punishment, 64–66, 71, 82–83, 84, 113–114, 116; and recreation, music and dance, 95, 96, 97–100, 103; register of, 60–61, 102–103, 106–107; and revolts, 22, 39, 65, 70, 72–76, 80–82, 85, 96, 100, 173, 194; rights of, 66–67; and structure of ownership, 41–43, 45–46, 106, 164–165; trade and importation of, 4, 49–53, 79, 83, 97, 103, 107, 170; value of, 56, 83, 114
Slusher, Johann Jacob, 89
Smyth, Superintendent, 40, 167
Social structure, 32, 41–47, 137, 141, 156, 188, 192, 194, 196–197

Sovereign, Louis, 75
Sovereignty, Spanish, 10, 27, 29, 31, 157, 160, 163, 188, 194
Spain, 9–10, 26–27, 58, 169, 188, 194
Spanish incursions, 9, 18–20, 21, 23, 26–27, 30, 32, 49, 50
Stann Creek (Dangriga), 5, 31, 105, 111–112, 132–134, 137
Stephen, James, 36, 79, 167
Stephens, John L., 132
Stevenson, Superintendent, 138–140
Sugar, 6–8, 49, 53, 60, 120, 134, 135, 137–142, 143–144, 146, 148, 176
Superintendent, 10, 32, 35, 37, 38, 40, 46, 47, 112, 132, 139, 159–163, 167–173, 179, 180, 184, 188, 189, 190
Supreme Court, 10, 62, 63, 92, 164, 165, 169, 171, 172
Surinam, 81
Sydney, Lord, 32, 37, 39–40, 158, 160

Taxation, 44, 191–193
Tayasal, 17, 19, 23
Thompson, Sir J. Eric S., 18, 20, 22, 128
Tipu. *See* Maya, Tipu
Toledo Settlement, 145
Treaty: Clayton-Bulwer, 1850, 184, 189; Convention of London, 1786, 10, 27, 31, 32–34, 37, 58, 159, 160; Madrid, 1667, 25; Madrid, 1670, 26; Paris, 1763, 9–10, 27, 29, 30, 36, 157; Versailles, 1783, 10, 31
Trinidad, 93, 99, 114, 120, 122, 143
Truck system, 122, 124, 149–155, 195, 196
Truxillo, 78, 142, 176

United States, Americans, 4, 7–8, 31, 50, 53, 68, 130, 143, 144, 145, 189
Uring, Nathaniel, 28
Usher, William, 90–91

Villagutierre Soto-Mayor, Juan de, 20–21

Waddell, D. A. G., 23
Wages, 123, 150, 151–153, 154–155, 177
West India Regiments, 4, 75, 79, 82, 89, 100–101, 121, 152, 162
West Indies (British or Commonwealth Caribbean), 5, 90, 92–93, 120, 123–124, 143, 168, 191, 196
White, Robert, 26–28
Willey, Gordon R., 16–17
Williams, Eric, 115
Wodehouse, Superintendent, 126

Xunantunich, 15, 16, 19

Yalbac, 128
Yalbac Hills, 127–130, 144
Young, Aaron, 34–35
Young Toledo and Company. *See* Companies, Young Toledo
Yucatán, 3–4, 17–18, 20, 22, 50, 77, 125–127, 137–138, 144, 148–150, 177, 197

Zuc, Luciano, 127